FOREIGN RELATIONS

FOREIGN RELATIONS

Analysis of Its Anatomy

Elmer Plischke

Contributions in Political Science, Number 213

GREENWOOD PRESS
New York • Westport, Connecticut • London

Library of Congress Cataloging-in-Publication Data

Plischke, Elmer, 1914-
   Foreign relations : analysis of its anatomy / Elmer Plischke.
      p.   cm. — (Contributions in political science, ISSN 0147-1066 ;
   no. 213)
   Bibliography: p.
   Includes index.
   ISBN 0-313-25245-9 (lib. bdg. : alk. paper)
   1. United States—Foreign relations—1945- 2. United States—
Foreign relations administration. I. Title. II. Series.
JX1417.P55 1988
327.73—dc19   88-3121

British Library Cataloguing in Publication Data is available.

Library of Congress Catalog Card Number: 88-3121
ISBN: 0-313-25245-9
ISSN: 0147-1066

First published in 1988

Greenwood Press, Inc.
88 Post Road West, Westport, Connecticut 06881

Printed in the United States of America

The paper used in this book complies with the
Permanent Paper Standard issued by the National
Information Standards Organization (Z39.48-1984).

10 9 8 7 6 5 4 3 2 1

TO STATESMEN AND SCHOLARS
WHO SEARCH FOR MEANING

CONTENTS

TABLES AND FIGURES

FOREWORD

For almost half a century, Elmer Plischke has quietly and consistently contributed to our understanding of international relations. No one has dedicated his scholarly life more faithfully to the clarification of basic issues. Not only has his own work been a valued source of knowledge but Professor Plischke has had a unique ability to bring together scholars and observers of diverse viewpoints in seminars and colloquia. It would be difficult to think of anyone who over a long and respected career has done more to further rational thought on his subject.

The present volume is no exception as Plischke continues his mission of analysis and definition. His Table of Contents is in effect an enumeration of the central questions in the discipline: national interest, vital interests, national power, national purposes, national goals and policy objectives and national planning and strategies. His discussion provides reading material alike for an introduction to such subjects and for advanced graduate seminars. Students require guidance as they look for historical background on evolving theories and logical distinctions needed in applying the concepts, instruments and tools of international studies. In sum, Plischke supplies intellectual resources that have been absent before the publication of his work.

Thus a senior scholar has added to the literature of international relations another important work. In a sense he has done what earlier scholars such as Quincy Wright and Hans J. Morgenthau did in the later stages of their careers. The work is a capstone of his earlier theoretical work. Professor Plischke continues to add in many important ways to the corpus of the literature of foreign relations. We shall all remain in his debt for years to come.

Kenneth W. Thompson
Director, The White Burke Miller Center
of Public Affairs
University of Virginia

ACKNOWLEDGMENTS

The production of this study was made possible by a fellowship research grant from the Earhart Foundation, which is acknowledged with gratitude.

I would also like to thank A. Bruce Boenau (Professor of Political Science, Gettysburg College), Wayne S. Cole (Professor of Diplomatic History, University of Maryland), Cecil V. Crabb, Jr. (Professor of Political Science, Louisiana State University), Ambassador Hermann F. Eilts (Director, Center for International Relations, Boston University), Norman A. Graebner (Professor Emeritus, University of Virginia), and Donald E. Nuechterlein (Professor of International Relations, Federal Executive Institute, Charlottesville, Virginia)--who kindly read portions of this volume, and whose comments and suggestions are appreciated.

Gettysburg, Pennsylvania   Elmer Plischke
1988

1

INTRODUCTION

> To question all things...above all, to insist upon
> having the meaning of a word clearly understood be-
> fore using it, and the meaning of a proposition be-
> fore assenting to it--these are the lessons we
> learn from ancient dialecticians.
> > John Stuart Mill, Inaugural Address as Rector,
> > University of St. Andrews, February 1, 1867.

> "When *I* use a word," Humpty Dumpty said, in a rath-
> er scornful tone, "it means just what I choose it
> to mean--neither more nor less." "The question is,"
> said Alice, "whether you *can* make words mean so
> many different things." "The question is," said
> Humpty Dumpty, "which is the master--that's all."
> > Lewis Carroll, *Alice Through the Looking Glass*
> > (1872)

Analysis and experience, in all areas of human learning and
activity, are presumed to produce comprehensible concepts to
facilitate understanding. As in science, statecraft should
be expected to possess its share of common and intelligible
discernment of basic components, factors, and principles--and
their conceptualization--that permeate its cosmography.

The conduct of foreign relations, theories of international politics, and particular perspectives of linking the
foreign policies and actions of individual nations--including
those that focus on ideology, realism, the political process,
the framing of policy, the balance of power, interdependence
and international integration, and other matters--are subjects of widespread inquiry and burgeoning literature. The
chronicles of diplomatic historians, and the commentaries of
descriptive and systematic analysts explore not only the
"who," the "when," and the "what," of foreign affairs, but
also the "why" and the "how." Yet, unlike the exponents of
natural and physical science in their fields, behavioral and
social scientists, as well as political practitioners, fail
to dispel the confusion and misunderstanding that permeate
the nature and functioning of the fundamental ingredients of
the foreign policy-making process.

Areas of general consensus, though minimal, are important. Few would contest, for example, that foreign policy
making, both in practice and theory, is inordinately complex
and difficult. Also, most studies acknowledge the integral
pertinence of all of the principal components of the foreign
relations system. Third, this process as a whole is universally directed toward the production of rational and viable
policies and national strategies as its end products. These,
in turn, are deemed to constitute the means for the application, fulfillment, or preservation of the nation's interests
and the achievement of its purposes, goals, and concrete
objectives.

Finally, there is common agreement that the modifier
"national," ascribed explicitly to these foreign relations
factors signifies the overall national community served by
them. This is distinguished, on the one hand, from more restricted geographic, parochial, minority, vested, partisan,
and other subnational and specialized interest groups or
factions and, on the other hand, it is also differentiated
from global, universal, regional, or functional societies.

On most matters of conceptualization, definition, and
interlinkage, however, statesmen, historians, and other commentators differ substantially. Such disagreement results
in perplexity respecting not only critical distinctions between singular and plural usages of a number of concepts
(such as apposing "foreign policy" as an amalgam or aggregate
versus sets of "foreign policies," or "*the* national interest"
versus an assortment of major and minor concerns of the nation), but also the ingredients of the ends-means relationship (illustrated by equating national interests with national purposes or basic goals with more specific policy objectives, and by viewing national power or capability as both a
means and an end of national action). There are also disa-
greements as to whether certain foreign affairs components
are essential or merely desirable (such as a motivating national purpose), whether in their operationalizable form they
are universally applicable to all countries or they vary a-
mong individual nations, and whether they are compatible with
or extraneous to other ingredients in hierarchical relationships.

As the scientist distinguishes the element from its mol-
ecules and the cell from its nucleus and its components, so
the public policy maker and scholar ought to be conscientious
if not unequivocal in differentiating among the major constituent parts of the foreign relations anatomy. This analysis, conceptualistic rather than pragmatic--that is, concerned with the essence and functioning of these factors as
conceptualized rather than with their implementation in actual national practice--examines the variety of meanings attributed to them. It also suggests ways of refining them to reduce ambiguity and misunderstanding, it interrelates them in
terms of logic and practical application, and it seeks to
render them more comprehensible, precise, and useful to decision makers and more intelligible in scholarly research and
commentary.

The need for clarity in understanding the meaning of

fundamental concepts and the terminology employed to characterize them is essential in all fields of human knowledge.
Some of those pertaining to internetional relations were developed and have been used for centuries by philosophers,
political leaders, and historians. A few, including the expressions "foreign policy," "balance of power," and "international equilibrium" were introduced by diplomats and international lawyers, or in the case of the term "collective security," by visionaries and exponents of international integration. By and large, these have long been incorporated
into the mainstream of political thought and action. Nevertheless, the principal components of foreign affairs, whether
dealt with by theorists, empirical analysts, or other commentators are employed in many, often misleading ways, leading
to what Winston Churchill called "terminological inexacti-
tude,"[1] to misapprehension, and sometimes to critical miscalculation in policy-making and review.

To illustrate this problem, discussing national interests and national security, Arnold Wolfers cautioned that, as
these expressions gain popularity, "they need to be scrutinized with particular care." They may not mean the same thing
to different nations or persons, and he suggests that they
may not be given "any precise meaning at all." He warns,
therefore, "while appearing to offer guidance and a basis for
broad consensus they may be permitting everyone to label
whatever policy he favors with an attractive and possibly de-
ceptive name."[2]

In one of the earlier post-World War II explorations of
foreign policy analysis, while acknowledging the dynamic
character of essential concepts, Feliks Gross declares: "A
precise use of terms is relevant in any systematic study and
application of scientific method in research." However, he
admits, "for centuries the field of foreign policy was an
area of human activity in which words were used to conceal,
rather than to express actions." Language, he observes, is
an important tool of scientific method, which "requires a
careful selection and use of terms, a proper agreement on
content of various word-symbols." And he contends that no
structured manner of inquiry "can be advanced without proper
terminology and definitions."[3] The dilemma, it appears, is
to be precise enough to facilitate clear thinking and enlightened cognition, while permitting sufficient flexibility
to accommodate imagination, experimentation, and change.

Political writing, Walter Lippmann complained in 1915,
"is asphyxiated by the staleness of its language." He condemned reducing political commentary to "a kind of algebra,"
and added, "if we deal only with colorless and vacant symbols, the world we see and the world we describe soon becomes
a colorless and vacant place."[4]

In recent years serious attempts have been made not only
to study the nature and functioning of the basic foreign affairs components and to refine their conceptualization in order to eliminate or at least to reduce philological, semantic, theoretical, and practical confusion respecting their
role and meaning,[5] but also to examine them systematically
and therefore to search for reliable means for determining

their connotations.[6]   One such method is to distill meaning
from articulated sentence contexts and other   forms of actual
usage.   This tends to focus attention on research techniques
from a limited perspective--often mutating normative and subjective into   objectifiable   perceptions,   qualitative   into
quantitative treatment, and pragmatic application into fabricating hypotheses and theoretical or technical variables.
Alternatively, in view of the lack of a single, universally
acceptable process of diagnostic scrutiny, their purport may
be ascertained by critical and logical reflection on the effects and   implications of degrees of consensuality on their
meaning.

     The need for clarity and precision in dealing with con-
cepts is both self-evident and   complex. Care needs to be
exercised not only to avoid having them and their linguistic
characterization serve as labels that produce automatic mental reactions, or to reduce them to symbols that are expres-
sible and   used as integrants of mathematical formulas but,
perhaps expecially important, also to overcome convenient if
not slippery oversimplifications for intricate, mutating, and
multifarious perceptions, situations, and relationships. As
Charles Burton Marshall notes, in international affairs the
need is pressing to "refresh comprehension . . . to restore
the edges of words dulled by ill usage."[7]

     To accommodate this need, the approach employed in this
study is to provide an in-depth survey of ideas, literature,
and national practice with extensive and intensive, but selective and at times illustrative and comparative, treatment
of the major foreign relations constituents--emphasizing distinctions between ends and means--and interrelating them in
decision-making and the determination of national interests
and aims and the devising of policies and strategies. Nine
key components are given greatest credence in state practice
and depth of scholarly concern. These embrace national interests, vital interests, national purposes, goals, and concrete
policy objectives, foreign policies, national power and capability, national planning and strategies, and the integrative
process of decision-making. Of these, interestingly, despite
their importance, the least amount of scholarly attention is
paid to vital interests and national planning.

     Some of these nine primary ingredients are supplemented
by sub-components, including power politics, balance of power, international equilibrium, contingency planning, the
overall policy complex, grand strategies, and bureaucratic
politics and options analysis in arriving at decisions. Additional matters also are touched on, such as national ideals
and ideology, national morality, and political realism. In
summary, this study focuses on the major elements of the foreign affairs anatomy, analysis of their conceptualization
and interpretation, and the totality of the framework of foreign relations rather than merely on the essence of foreign
policy, which constitutes the practical application of only
one of these factors.

     Over the years, much has been said and written about
these nine basic components, or specialized aspects of them.
But little has been done to define and explain their concept-

ualized meanings in a single volume, with a view to coalescing them into a synthesized, viable aggregate.

It should be noted that all of them are pertinent to the
examination and understanding of both international politics
and foreign affairs. The principal distinction between these
fields devolves upon perspective. Whereas traditionally international relations is contemplated from a supernatural
level--looking down, in effect, upon the interrelations of
nations from above--foreign relations is perceived rather by
looking outward from the perspective of the nation-state.
Though useful for certain purposes of content consideration
and treatment, and functional analysis, this differentiation
has little impact upon the matter of comprehending and explaining the essence and qualities of these basic factors--
and they are incorporated into the corpus and literature of
both fields--except that the process of national decision-
making is normally viewed strictly from the perspective of
the nation-state.

Since World War II, particularly in the 1950s and 1960s,
both of these fields experienced what Charles Lerche and
Abdul Said call an explosive "conceptual revolution." This
produced an enormous quantity of studies--monographs, treatises, essays, journal articles, and textbooks--produced by
statesmen, theorists, historians, political scientists, other
scholars, and journalists--"using a broad variety of techniques of analysis and synthesis," according to Lerche and
Said, which has resulted in "a massive and many-sided effort"
to probe, scrutinize, assess, and operationalize these concepts.[8]

This undertaking is based largely on a broad-scale survey of such English-language literature and the development
of American ideas, interpretations, and commentary. Treatment
is historical, explanatory, and systematic, with the objective of relating and progressing from perceptions to ideas,
to conceptualizations, and thence to usable terminology, and
of distilling meanings that may be compared, refined and,
where possible, universalized--to render them, as concepts,
generally applicable to all nations at all times. Emphasis
is on defining them and interpreting their essence and form
of articulation rather than on describing or evaluating their
practical application by an individual nation at a particular
time.   Hence, the focus is broader than contemporary United
States or comparative policy and practice.

Attention is devoted to examining not only the meaning
of each concept, but also to the major alternative perceptions and delineations ascribed to them, and how they have
mutated from time to time, as well as to various aspects of
their essence, such as the substance, characteristics, categories, formal definitions, the qualities of each component,
and commentary upon them and upon the development of literary
interest in and analysis of them. It presents judgments with
the hope of clarifying and recommending usage oriented toward
reducing ambiguity and misunderstanding and to improve official and scholarly comprehension and communication. To facilitate this it suggests general working definitions for each
concept. Where useful, it compares basic interpretations and

correlates the fundamental segments of the foreign affairs anatomy in the coalescing process of policy formulation, strategy designing, and decision-making.

Treatment is tailored to provide a compromise between the theoretical and the empirical, between the abstract and the idiosyncratic--to bridge the hypothetical and speculative with the concrete. To be helpful to the generalist and the practitioner, it seeks to examine the foreign relations cosmography in a comprehensible and rational but non-technical manner, minimizing specialized or esoteric terminology. It reveals critical disparities between the singular and plural usages of certain expressions--including national interest(s), purpose(s), policy(ies), and strategy(ies). It acknowledges substantial consensus on the connotation of several terms, such as foreign policies which, technically, are widely characterized as courses of action to promote national interests and achieve national goals and concrete objectives. But it also recognizes five perceptions of the concept "national interest," four interpretations of "national purpose," differentiation between but also confusion respecting the terms "goals and objectives" and "power and capability," and multiple singular and plural applications of the expressions "foreign policy" and "national strategy."

On the other hand, this volume is not intended to provide a description of or commentary on United States substantive foreign policy--whether historical or contemporary--or the mechanism or political system for the conduct of foreign relations. Nor does it present a disquisition on the diplomatic process, a glossary of terminology,[9] or an anthology of basic precepts, maxims, or rules for guidance in the management of international affairs.[10] Nor does it aspire to produce, assess, or support any particular theory of foreign relations or international politics, to propose or endorse any unique approach to their study or analysis, to argue the validity or invalidity of any component as a reliable or consensualized analytical tool, to devise or judge any specific model or paradigm for structuring theoretical depiction, to suggest a formula for purposes of prediction, or to "scientize" the foreign affairs process.

NOTES

1. Winston Churchill, Speech, House of Commons, February 22, 1906.

2. Arnold Wolfers, "'National' Security as an Ambiguous Symbol," *Political Science Quarterly* 47 (December 1952): 481.

3. Feliks Gross, *Foreign Policy Analysis* (New York: Philosophical Library, 1954), pp. 39, 40, 44. But he also recognizes the difficulty of providing adequate definitions and precise symbols in foreign policy research and analysis.

4. Walter Lippmann, "Books and Things," *The New Republic* 4 (August 7, 1915): 24.

5. By way of illustration, attention to meaning is provided in such general sources as the *Encyclopedia of American Foreign Policy*, edited by

Alexander de Conde, 3 vols. (New York: Scribner, 1978), *The Encyclopedia of the Social Sciences*, edited by Edwin R. A. Seligman, 15 vols. (New York: Macmillan, 1930), the *International Encyclopedia of the Social Sciences*, edited by David L. Sills, 16 vols. (New York: Macmillan, 1968), and *The International Relations Dictionary*, 3rd ed., edited by Jack C. Plano and Roy Olton (Santa Barbara, Calif.: ABC-CLIO, 1982).

6. For example, see Giovanni Sartori, ed., *Social Science Concepts: A Systematic Analysis* (Beverly Hills, Calif.: Sage, 1984) which, on the basis of a prescribed formula, treats seven general social science concepts, only one of which--namely, power--pertains to the foreign affairs process. For Sartori's systematizing guidelines for concept development and analysis, see Chapter 1, and for discussion of power, see Chapter 7. Another illustration is provided in the *Key Concepts of International Relations* series, edited by Paul Wilkinson, including volumes by Clive Archer on *International Organizations* and by Alan James on *Sovereign Statehood: The Basis of International Society* (London: Allen and Unwin, 1986).

7. Charles Burton Marshall, *The Exercise of Sovereignty: Papers on Foreign Policy* (Baltimore: Johns Hopkins Press, 1965), p. 94.

8. Charles O. Lerche, Jr., and Abdul A. Said, *Concepts of International Politics*, 1st ed. (Englewood Cliffs, N.J.: Prentice-Hall, 1963), p. iii. This volume provides a comprehensive expository treatment of selected basic concepts of international politics, ranging from values, interests, goals, objectives, policy, and capability to decision making, techniques to implement decisions, and certain aspects of global politics including conflict adjustment and war. See *Concepts of International Politics in Global Perspective*, 3rd ed. (Englewood Cliffs: Prentice-Hall, 1979). For a brief essay on international relations concepts, see also William Reitzel, Morton A. Kaplan, and Constance G. Coblenz, *United States Foreign Policy, 1945-1955* (Washington: Brookings Institution, 1956), Appendix A, pp. 471-74.

9. For illustrations of glossaries of relevant terms in diplomacy see Thomas A. Bailey, *A Diplomatic History of the American People*, 7th ed. (New York: Appleton-Century-Crofts, 1964), pp. 901-5; Robert B. Harmon, *The Art and Practice of Diplomacy: A Selected and Annotated Guide* (Metuchen, N.J.: Scarecrow Press, 1971), pp. 160-74; William Macomber, *The Angels' Game: A Handbook of Modern Diplomacy* (New York: Stein and Day, 1975), pp. 205-18; Melquiades J. Gamboa, *Elements of Diplomatic and Consular Practice: A Glossary* (Quezon City, Philippines: Central Law Book Publishing Company, 1966); and Elmer Plischke, *Conduct of American Diplomacy*, 3rd ed. (Princeton: Van Nostrand, 1967), pp. 643-51.

10. For brief commentaries on some 265 such fundamental precepts and maxims for the conduct of United States foreign relations, see Thomas A. Bailey, *The Art of Diplomacy: The American Experience* (New York: Appleton-Century-Crofts, 1968). The bibliographical notes provided in the following chapters present selective and illustrative citations and are not intended to be definitive.

2

NATIONAL INTERESTS

But it is a maxim, founded on the universal experience of mankind, that no nation is to be trusted
farther than it is bound by its interest; and no
prudent statesman or politician will venture to de-
part from it.

George Washington, Letter to the Congress,
November 14, 1778

We have taken it for granted that we must discover
the true American national interest. We must bear
in mind always that there is at stake the life or
death of multitudes, victory or defeat in war, the
well-being and indeed the survival of the nation.
Therefore we must consider first and last the
American national interest.

Walter Lippmann, *U.S. Foreign Policy:*
Shield of the Republic (1943)

National interest is one of the most basic factors in the
conduct of foreign affairs. It has been invoked by statesmen
since the birth of the nation/state system and pervades the
burgeoning literature on foreign affairs. Practitioners and
commentators variously refer to it as the key concept or the
bedrock upon which foreign policy is founded, the polestar of
diplomacy, the focus of statecraft, the yardstick of choice,
and the only generally employed criterion for the valuation
of foreign policy.

In the eighteenth century French political philosopher
Montesquieu declared: "nations ought in time of peace to do
to one another all the good they can, and in time of war as
little harm as possible, without prejudicing their real interests."[1] In 1848 British Prime Minister Lord Palmerston
told the House of Commons: "We have no eternal allies and we
have no perpetual enemies. Our interests are eternal and
perpetual and these interests it is our duty to follow."[2]
Thirty years later Benjamin Disraeli informed the House of
Lords: "We have a substantial interest in the [Middle] East;
it is a commanding interest, and its behest must be obeyed."[3]
In his memorable broadcast of October 1, 1939, Winston
Churchill described Soviet foreign relations as "a riddle

wrapped in a mystery inside an enigma." It is less well remembered that he also added that "perhaps there is a key"--
namely, "the Russian national interest," and that Russia pursues "a cold policy of self-interests."[4]   More recently
Charles de Gaulle confessed that nations have no friends--
"only interests."[5]

   In the United States, from the very outset national interest was given unmistakable credence by the Founding Fathers, who set a precedent and fixed the tone of American
foreign relations.   In a letter written in 1795 President
Washington professed: "In every act of my administration, I
have sought the happiness of my fellow citizens. My system
for the attainment of this object has uniformly been to over-
look all personal, local, and partial considerations . . .
and to consult only the substantial and permanent interests
of our country."[6]   He also observed: "A small knowledge of
human nature will convince us that, with far the greatest
part of mankind, interest is the governing principle; and
that almost every man is more or less, under its influence."[7]
Relating interest and duty, in 1805 Thomas Jefferson asserted: "We are firmly convinced . . . that with nations as with
individuals our interests soundly calculated will ever be
found inseparable from our moral duties."[8]   In *The Federalist*
papers Alexander Hamilton defended the Constitution as the
embodiment of national interests, regarded it as absurd not
to ascribe to the government "the direction of the most
essential interests" and called it the "depository of the
NATIONAL INTERESTS" of the new nation.[9]

   Writing on the influence of sea power upon history, Alfred T. Mahan, the late-nineteenth-century historian, publi-
cist, and avid exponent of national interest, contended that
"self-interest is not only a legitimate, but a fundamental
cause for national policy" which, in his judgment, requires
neither rationalization nor justification. He believed that
"it is vain to expect governments to act continuously on any
other ground than national interest."[10]   Commenting on its
importance to policy-making, in 1923 Secretary of State
Charles Evans Hughes insisted: "Foreign policies are not
built upon abstractions. They are the result of practical
conceptions of national interest arising from some immediate
exigency or standing out vividly in historical perspective."[11] Analyzing United States foreign affairs in the
post-World War I era, the following year Paul Scott Mowrer,
Pulitzer prize winning journalist, relating national interest
and the new diplomacy, wrote: "Policies whose foundations are
sunk, not in the firm rock of national interest, but in such
ideologies as prejudice, unjustified fear, sentimental affec-
tions or hatreds, the spirit of reform and crusade, the sense
of moral superiority, are built upon quicksand."[12]

   Although he acknowledges having difficulty with the concept, in his comprehensive, more recent disquisition on the
subject, Joseph Frankel, of the University of Southampton,
agrees that national interest constitutes a fundamental element in the making of foreign policy to which "statesmen pro-
fess to attach great importance."[13]   Anthologizing guiding
precepts for the conduct of foreign affairs, American diplomatic historian Thomas A. Bailey stipulates: "Self-interest

is the mainspring of foreign policy . . . . Sentiment changes
but self-interest persists" and, reminiscent of Lord Palmerston, "There are no enduring international friendships, only
enduring interests."[14] In sum, while policy analysts may
differ in their perspectives and judgments, they can scarcely
ignore or reject the attitude of the political practitioner
and the historian concerning the significance of national interests.

Hans J. Morgenthau, acknowledged as the post-World War
II authority on the role of national interest in the realm of
international affairs--who wrote widely not only on its value
but also its relationship to power politics, balance of power, national morality, and international relations theory--
concludes his classic *In Defense of the National Interest*:[15]

> And, above all, remember always that it is not only
> a political necessity but also a moral duty of a
> nation to follow in its dealings with other nations
> but one guiding star, one standard of thought, one
> rule for action:

THE NATIONAL INTEREST

AMERICAN USAGE

Awareness of national interest as a paramount consideration in the foreign relations of the United States paralleled
the founding of the Republic. George Washington--who addressed himself to "this great assemblage of communities and
interests" in his first inaugural address and referred frequently to the interests of the nation in his public pronoun-
cements--summarized his philosophy in his Farewell Address.
Diplomatic historian Norman A. Graebner recounts that in this
famous valedictory to his countrymen, the first President advocated flexibility to enable the young country to preserve
its national interests whenever and wherever challenged and
cautioned against universalizing interests under the blanket
of abstract ideals. Characterizing national interests as the
cement of the Union, Washington predicted: "If we remain one
people . . . the period is not far off . . . when we may
choose peace or war, as our interest, guided by justice,
shall counsel."[16]

Historian Charles A. Beard reports that the Founding
Fathers, rejecting monarchy and church-related institutions--
with their circumscribed dynastic, elitist, and clerical con-
cerns--deliberately created a republican and secular system.
As political realists, he says, they chose national interest
as the keystone for the conduct of the new nation's foreign
affairs. Although the framers of the Constitution avoided
the word "national," Beard notes, they made it unmistakable
that their new instrument of governance was designed to protect, realize, and promote "certain great common interests"
that were neglected by the Articles of Confederation. He
maintains that the authors of *The Federalist* emphasized the
promotion of six classes of national interests, especially
the nation's security and international commerce. He also
claims that "the authors of that remarkable series of state

papers do not shrink from calling them 'national' interests
or from summing up their philosophy of foreign relations
under the heading of 'national interest'."[17]

   Evidencing the frequent reliance on the concept in American history, Presidents have repeatedly alluded to the nation's interests. Surveying presidential inaugural addresses, for example--which uniformly provide a newly elected
President's attitude and operational principles--it is significant that from 1789 through World War II every President
except Theodore Roosevelt and Warren G. Harding referred to
such "interests" or "concerns." In recent decades, beginning
with Presidents William McKinley and Woodrow Wilson, however,
greater emphasis has been given to "national purposes," as
indicated in Chapter 4.

   Overall, of the thirty-four Presidents who delivered
fifty inaugural addresses since 1789, twenty-eight used these
expressions some fifty-five times.[18] The first seven Presi-
dents--Washington to Andrew Jackson--accounted for more than
twenty such references, with James Monroe the most liberal in
his usage. Only Presidents Polk and Taft actually referred
specifically to "national" interests, although many used such
comparable expressions as the interests of the nation, the
country, the Union, the United States, or the people, and
President Pierce preferred "the great objects of our pursuit." Presidents Jefferson and Monroe clearly distinguished
between foreign and domestic concerns. Other usages combined
interests with aspirations, rights, or duties. Some Presidents colored the concept with descriptive adjectives--in-
cluding "great," "highest," "patriotic," or "important" interests.[19] Reflecting the pluralistic nature of the American
Republic, occasionally early Presidents also manifested their
awareness of the subnational interests of economic and functional as well as sectional groups or the states within the
Union. In these addresses most Presidents spoke of interests
in the plural or, using the term in the singular, referred
either to a particular interest or to the common interest.
None seemed to regard American interests as something more
than a collection of individual interests, and none employed
the expression "in the national interest."

   In addition to American Presidents, other early states-
men--such as Benjamin Franklin, Alexander Hamilton, and
Thomas Paine--also evoked the concept, and it has been employed widely in presidential messages to Congress, public
addresses, and diplomatic communications.[20] To illustrate,
President Wilson observed, on the one hand, that in the real
world "The economic relations of two great nations are not
based upon sentiment; they are based upon interest" but, sub-
scribing to the global perspective, he also philosophized:
"The interests of all nations are our own also . . . What affects mankind is inevitably our affair," and "No nation
stands wholly apart . . . when the life and interests of all
nations are thrown into confusion and peril."[21]

   More recently, addressing the American Legion in 1948,
President Truman proclaimed: "No nation can afford to disregard self-interest . . . We have taken it as a first principle that our interest is bound up with the peace and eco-

nomic recovery of the rest of the world. Accordingly, we
have worked for all three together--world peace, world economic recovery, and the welfare of our own nation."[22]   During
the Cold War, in his widely heralded address in June 1963
President Kennedy, recognizing the "quarrels and conflicting
interests" plaguing Soviet-American relations, counseled that
Washington and Moscow should give "direct attention to our
common interests and to the means by which those differences
are resolved."[23]   In his memoirs, President Johnson reported
that when meeting with Soviet Deputy Premier Anastas Mikoyan,
who came to Washington to attend President Kennedy's funeral
in 1963: "I considered it essential to let Mikoyan understand
that while the United States wanted peace more than anything
else in the world, it would not allow its interests, or its
friends' and allies' interests, to be trampled by aggression
or subversion."[24]

During the first year of his administration, addressing
the United Nations General Assembly on launching the "era of
negotiations," President Nixon informed the world: "I believe
that our relations with the Soviet Union can be conducted in
a spirit of mutual respect, recognizing our differences and
also our right to differ, recognizing our divergent interests
and also our common interests, recognizing the interests of
our respective allies as well as our own." In his annual
foreign policy report for 1971, he wrote: "In our relations
with all countries we proceeded to give effect to our new
policy of insisting that the United States has neither the
prescriptions nor the resources for the solution of problems
in which ours is not the prime national interest."[25] Addressing the nation by radio in 1983, also referring to Soviet-
American relations, President Reagan declared: "We do not
insist that the Soviet Union abandon its standing as a superpower or its legitimate national interests," and in a later radio address he professed: "The most important duty of a
President is to defend the Nation and its vital interests."[26]

Recent Secretaries of State have also spoken freely
about American national interests. For example, in his historic speech on the Far East in 1950, Dean Acheson informed
the National Press Club: "We must take the position we have
always taken--that anyone who violates the integrity of China
is the enemy of China and is acting contrary to our own interests. That . . . is the first and the greatest rule in regard to the formulation of American policy toward Asia."[27]
Prior to outlining a series of specific American national interests, in an address in 1964, Secretary Dean Rusk generalized: "But the foreign policy of a government chosen by the
people obviously should be designed to serve their interests,
and these become the national interest. And as a rule, our
Presidents, beginning with Washington, have sought to justify
their foreign policies primarily in terms of national interest."[28]   In his memoirs, Henry Kissinger pronounced: "The
philosophical thrust of the foreign policy of the Nixon Presidency was to develop such a prescription of the national interest and to educate our own people to its complexities
. . . The statesman's duty is to bridge the gap between his
nation's experience and his vision. If he gets too far ahead
of his people he will lose his mandate; if he confines himself to the conventional he will lose control over events."[29]

Paralleling such official usage, substantial American literature was produced to analyze and to justify or criticize the use of the concept. The two most influential on policy-making and thinking for several decades are Mahan and Morgenthau. Alfred T. Mahan considered national interest as the prime consideration in foreign affairs and argued that self-preservation accompanied by self-defense tower above all other interests, that national power is essential to preserve the nation's interests, and that it is vain to expect a nation to act consistently from any other motive than that of its interest.[30]

After World War I, by which time the United States was catapulated into a position of international opportunity and responsibility, the American people and some of their leaders were unprepared for power wielding. Their impact had not begun to be felt until the late 1940s. Morgenthau, generally espousing Mahan's precepts, went further in developing a theory of political realism in the 1950s--holding that political relationships are governed by objective rules deeply rooted in human nature. Policy founded on interest, he maintains, is superior to both that based on universal moral principles--because the latter derives from the former--and that based on utopian, legalistic, and ideological criteria. He also contends that politics is the struggle for power, and national interest is equated with the pursuit of such power but that interest and power cannot and need not be quantified, that the primary national interest is survival, and that, to be realistic, interest should be proportionate to capability.[31]

Career diplomat George F. Kennan, providing the professional diplomat's perspective, also endorses some of these views. Considering national interest as that which is good for the nation, he condemns the legalistic-moralistic approach to national aspirations and contends that national interest is more justifiable than dogmatic support of abstract peace. He differs from Morgenthau in that he does not propound a particular version of national interest except that of keeping any single power from dominating the Eurasian land mass and, taking international morality in stride, he expects leaders to exercise moral responsibility without surrending to abstruse moralism.[32]

Other literature on the subject, constituting one of the most substantial and controverted segments of foreign relations analysis since World War II, represents a variety of approaches. These focus largely on descriptive application, the assessment of national interest as an analytical tool, the ordination of national interest as the epicenter of a theory of international politics, the appositional relationship of political realism and idealism (the interaction of national interests and national ideals), debates on the morality-immorality-unmorality of grounding foreign policy on national interests, and the attempt to reduce examination and application of the concept to a science. There are also those who, concentrating on pragmatizing consideration, seek to establish a concrete method systematically utilizing national interest for policy-making and review. All of these are touched on later and finally, it needs to be noted, since the 1940s scores of American textbooks and symposia have de-

voted some attention to general description and assessment
of the nature and role of national interest in international
politics and foreign affairs, but this has begun to decline.

As with presidential inaugural addresses, other public
pronouncements and American literature contain a broad spectrum of adjectival qualifications of the concept. Some emphasize substantial, great, best, highest, or essential interests, or true and genuine interests. Others denote them
as fundamental, basic, permanent, or minimum interests. A
few refer to enlightened self-interest, while others label
them selfish, self-seeking, self-serving, or calculating
interests. In a more critical vein, still others call them
materialistic or venal. Occasionally reference is made to
patriotic interests, and some discuss mutual or common interests or appose national to international or global interests, or the overarching interests of mankind, as noted
later. In certain cases adjectival expressions are helpful in
delimiting concrete understanding, while in others they appear to be designed to invoke automatic favorable or unfavorable reaction.

DEVELOPMENT OF CONCEPT AND ANALYSIS

It is axiomatic that national states, like individuals
and other political institutions, do have their interests.
Nevertheless, views differ as to the meaning, role, and significance of the concept. As is the case with other factors
in the conduct of foreign affairs, two interlinked aspects
need to be distinguished--its functions in both actual state
practice and as an element of foreign relations inquiry--its
character and validity as "an instrument of political action"
and as "an analytical tool."

Beard, who calls national interest a modern conception,
describes its origins as consisting of the "will of the
prince" propounded by Niccolo Machiavelli, the "dynastic interests" of ruling monarchies, "*raison d'etat*" or "*Staats-
raison*," and "national honor."[33] Feliks Gross, who provides
one of the earlier comprehensive expositions on foreign relations as an organic process, claims that both national interests and *raison d'etat* are either vague expressions, inter-
mixed with social myths such as the "mission of a nation" and
political dogmas, or they are deemed to be absolutes not subject to question or discussion, which he calls "*imponde
rabilia*." In a democracy, he suggests, foreign policy should
be guided rather by "*raison de citoyens*"--or the interests
of the citizens.[34] In democratic countries, it is countered,
these may be mutually supportive if not identical, when the
interests of citizens are conceived not as those of vocal
parochial interest groups, or even a popular majority, but as
those of the citizenry or the society as a whole.

As a mutation of its predecessors, the notion of national interest had its origin in the birth and development of
the modern state and the republican system of governance.
Beard asserts that the concept was introduced into general
use by evolutionary process and eventually came to be employed almost universally in international relations. Indeed,

he suggests, its advancement and defense by various means and instrumentalities of power is the paramount consideration of diplomacy. He makes it clear that his primogenial inquiry is not one of exact science, nor is it intended as the study of philology via an excursion into etymology resulting merely in a dictionary definition. The essence of national interest, he concludes, can be identified only through descriptive and historical analysis by responsible statesmen and publicists and by discovering the matters and patterns of conduct encompassed within its scope.[35]

Beard's survey introduced two threads of discourse on the American experience. As a reaction to foreign policy developments following the Spanish-American War, at which time the United States joined the ranks of the major naval powers and, acquiring the Philippines, reversed its traditional posture by becoming engaged in Asian affairs. Many criticized this geopolitical change. In his widely read diplomatic history of the United States, first published in 1936, Samuel Flagg Bemis branded involvement in Asia as "The Great Aberration of 1898"--the most serious diplomatic blunder since the inception of the Republic.[36] Writing his short, critical analysis of American foreign policy in 1943, Walter Lippmann contends that the United States failed to readjust its foreign policy to these events after the turn of the century, and the American people, divided on the management of foreign affairs, were unable to agree on the specification of their "true interest."[37] The following decade George Kennan, in his prize winning survey of American diplomacy from 1900 to 1950, argues that the consequences of the war with Spain so altered the position of the United States in the Far East that substantial discongruity ensued between its policies and interests, and between its commitments and capabilities.[38] Simultaneously, Morgenthau declared that President McKinley led the United States "beyond the confines of the Western Hemisphere, ignorant of the bearing of this step upon the national interest, and guided by moral principles completely divorced from the national interest."[39] The decline in the equation of commitments to capability is also stressed by Graebner, which he illustrates with a good many documents.[40]

The second thread interjected by Beard suggested abandoning Wilsonian idealism and moralism following World War I and returning to the national interest as the basis for the conduct of American diplomacy. In his Mobile address on October 27, 1913, for example, President Wilson regarded it as "very perilous" for nations to formulate foreign policy in terms of what he decried as "material interest," and he declared that to formulate policy on the basis of national interest "not only is unfair to those with whom you are dealing, but it is degrading as regards your own actions . . . . We dare not turn from the principle that morality, and not expediency, is the thing that must guide us."[41] He viewed national interests, power politics, and the principle of the balance of power not only as failures in maintaining peace and progress but also as morally questionable and detrimental to the democratic reform of both nations and the international order. He and his followers held the genuine interest of the United States--as well as of other nations--to be the

creation of a rational, peaceful, and democratically governed
international system that possesses a consortium of power and
is founded on morality, legality, self-governance, humanitarianism, and collective security, with common or collective
interests superseding national interests. As an antidote to
United States isolationism and the pursuit of its national
interest--which Graebner characterizes as a "great crusade"
for utopian internationalism--Wilsonianism was supported by
an active school of American leaders and thinkers through
World War II.[42]

The central theme of the line of reasoning that rejected
such Wilsonian idealism argued that to be rational the policy
of the nation must be founded on the pursuance of its own interests. The writings of Morgenthau, epitomized by his general survey on international politics first published in
1948,[43] advanced the thesis that political leaders think and
act in terms of interests and that the national interest is
synonymous with the survival of the nation--with the protection of its physical, political, and cultural identity.[44]

In the late 1940s and early 1950s Morgenthau, together
with Kennan, and perhaps to a lesser extent Walter Lippmann,
Frederick L. Schuman, Robert Strausz-Hupé, Stefan T. Possony,
and others, became the progenitors of what came to be called
the post-World War II school of "realists."[45] The essence of
political realism in the international arena is that statesmen devise policies in keeping with national interests as
they conceive them and rely on national power and influence
to implement them. Members of this school decry reliance primarily on utopianism, legalism, moralism, and sentimentalism
--which Morgenthau calls abstract principles. The principle
they advocate is sometimes characterized as realpolitik,
which is rarely defined conceptualistically nor is it ascribed to political leaders except in a negative or critical
sense--implying the absence of ideals while extolling self-
serving power politics and the use of naked force. And yet,
most writers concede that the successful conduct of foreign
relations must be realistic, and few would deny that moral
force often constitutes a critical element of political
power.

To a large degree this movement constituted a mid-twen-
tieth century reaction to the "idealist" approach to international affairs. A national ideal, according to Robert E. Osgood, "is a standard of conduct or a state of affairs worthy
of achievement by virtue of its moral value. The motive of
national idealism is the disposition to concern oneself with
moral values that transcend the nation's selfish interests."[46] In the 1930s and early 1940s Secretary of State
Cordell Hull epitomized such idealism, eschewing the national
interest while regarding peace as the ultimate good. Specifically, he laid down a series of "pillars of peace," advocating international self-restraint, abstinence from the use of
force in the pursuit of policy, respect for the rights of
other nations, revitilizing and strengthening international
law, non-intervention in the internal affairs of other nations, peaceful change, faithful observance of international
agreements, upholding the sanctity of treaties and modifying
them by orderly process, protection of the economic security

of all   nations, lowering   economic barriers to international
trade, equality of commercial opportunity,   and   the limita-
tion/reduction   of   armaments. Meritorious and appealing
though they are in principle, Julius W. Pratt, in his biog-
raphy of Hull, views these pillars of peace as visionary at
the time, which he contends "had little relation to the way
in which the world was being run."[47]

     Idealists and moralists focus on peace and stability
rather than on interests and on individuals not as members of
a nation-state but of mankind as a whole, emphasizing such
factors as   freedom, justice,   and the   right of self-governance, the   absence of   violence, common welfare, and collective security.[48] Supporters of this view, promoting global
interests and the elimination of power politics include,
aside from Hull, such leaders as Franklin D. Roosevelt and
academicians Dexter Perkins, Thomas I. Cook, Malcolm Moos,
and Frank Tannenbaum. Although united in principle, in their
opposition to political realism and in their search for a
credible alternative, they can   scarcely be regarded as constituting a concordant philosophical school.

     Despite the necessity of resorting to realistic prac-
tices in coping with certain strategic problems of World War
II, President Roosevelt was essentially motivated by idealistic goals. Among his well known major policy developments
are his espousal of the Four Freedoms, the Atlantic Charter,
the United Nations Declaration, the Lend-Lease program, international cooperation in drafting the United Nations Charter and the treaties establishing the United Nations Relief
and Rehabilitation Administration, the Food and Agriculture
Organization, the Internationai Bank, the International Mone-
tary Fund, and the International Civil Aviation Organization,
as well as regional cooperation with Canada and the inter-
American system. He sought by diplomatic and legal means to
promote peace, stability, collective security for all provided by global institutions, and liberty for Americans and
liberation of others from the scourge of Axis domination.
But he opposed power politics, the balance of power, and
spheres of influence, and he spoke of America's "larger purposes" rather than of its national interests.[49]

     Writing in 1948, diplomatic historian Dexter Perkins
insisted: "No one can study the history of American foreign
policy without observing the force of general principles" and
"deviations from a reasonable standard of public ethics have
again and again been condemned by the United States," so that
"there is, as there ought to be, a corrective in American
opinion against the immoderate or unscrupulous use of national power." Other than discussing the Monroe Doctrine, the
Open Door policy, democracy, and collective cooperation in
such international institutions as the United Nations, he
fails to define those principles or standards.[50]

     A number of more comprehensive responses to the realists
were published in the 1950s. Thomas I. Cook and Malcolm Moos,
seeking to relate idealism and realism, present an eclectic
proposition, acknowledging that states do pursue their own
interests while rejecting the concept of the sacrosanct national interest in the struggle for national achievement

through power politics. They argue, rather, that the historic principles on which the American nation rests--presumably
its ideals, heritages, values, and traditions--are universally applicable and that it is "our international interest" to
pursue and further those principles throughout the world. In
effect, they broadly identify America's national interests as
the interests of mankind, as determined by the United States.
One of the consequences produced by this alloying of national
and international interests is the difficulty of determining
the beneficiary which, if it is primarily other nations, is
bound to be altruistic.[51] A second, more significant paradox
relating to such conjunction flows from the incongruity of
equating "national" with "international" interests, which
appears in principle to be inherently fallacious. In addition, as a practical matter, if it is not universally and
equally applicable, such a confluence may destabilize relations among states and impede if not contravene their own
progress and welfare.

Frank Tannenbaum, on the other hand, writing on "the
American tradition" in foreign affairs, rejects outright the
idea of national interest. He maintains that the United
States always has and should continue to base its foreign
policy on the concept of what he calls the "coordinate state"
rather than on the adversarial relationship implied in the
mutual pursuance of national interests. The question arises
as to whether this position and that of the realists are inherently and necessarily incompatible. It may also be questioned whether counsel regarding the true posture of one nation correctly connotes uniformity on the part of others or
ignores the issue of universal applicability and, therefore,
whether it is reasonable to impose a more restrictive and
disadvantageous standard on a particular country than that
applied by other, especially adversary, nations.[52]

These developments not only produced a substantial body
of literature, but this "great debate" on realism versus
idealism also evoked secondary controversies over issues of
international morality versus power politics. They also generated attempts to define the nature of national interest by
empirical research, to quantify national power as the measurable concomitant of national interest, to design models
of government action and policy analysis on the basis of
decision-making formulae involving national interest as a key
factor, to suggest methods of policy prediction, and to devise an overall theory of international and foreign relations
centered upon the pursuance of national interests.

PROBLEMS OF DEFINITION

The concept national interest is generally regarded as
abstract, ambiguous, and elusive. Charles Lerche and Abdul
Said, in *Concepts of International Politics,* describe it as
"notoriously vague and difficult to define."[53] It is held to
be unconsensualized if not unconsensualizable, easier to interpret pragmatically than conceptualistically, lacking in
inherent meaning, and uncertain as to specific content. Vernon Van Dyke finds much of the problem to be definitional
rather than epistomological and, presumably alluding to its

practical substance, Feliks Gross claims that the concept is
man made. Charles Burton Marshall goes so far as to say that
it "is inadequate and misleading even as a broad concept on
which to found a policy," and Raymond Aron--French philosopher who wrote extensively on peace, war, and diplomacy--
concludes that in view of the plurality of concrete and ultimate objectives of a nation the rational prescription of its
national interest is impossible.[54]

On the other hand, it cannot be denied that in practice
attempts are made to define the concept and states do have
their national interests, that they formulate their policy in
keeping with them, and that they seek to consciously act in
accordance with them. In international politics, according
to Vincent Davis, the most powerful "ism" is nationalism--or
national interests as nationally defined.[55] Despite all the
doubts and qualifiers applied to it, the concept ought to be
intellectually comprehensible and, therefore, definable.
Nevertheless, in addition to differences in usage of the concept in the singular and the plural, a series of difficulties
impede the quest for comprehension.

Meaning of "Interests"

At the outset there is the question of genus. Are national interests ends or goals, or are they something else?
The preponderant majority of analysts regard them as that
which is sought or pursued, and they generally call them
aims, ends, goals, or objectives, or they call them values,
which are generally viewed as transcendent ends. The pre-
sumption that as ends they are always fully attainable is
erroneous. Some writers therefore add qualifications, such
as the general and continuing ends for which a nation acts,
the sum total of national goals, and the ideal set of purposes which a nation seeks to realize in the conduct of its
foreign relations. "The core purpose of foreign policy,"
according to Martin C. Needler, who puts it more accurately,
"is the protection and promotion [not the fulfillment or
achievement] of national interests."[56] Other writers refer
to interests as motives or as wants, needs, or desires.[57] A
few even maintain that, as ends or needs, they exist independently of whether or not they are volitionally sought,
and Paul Seabury sees them rather as "end-products" of the
goal formulation process than as ends in themselves.[58]

A second group of analysts conceive national interests
as lying outside the hierarchical ends-means spectrum of foreign affairs, and refer to them as criteria, guides, standards, or determinants. For example, national interest is
designated as a rough guide to, and a constraint on, policy
and action, a framework for the definition of objectives and
the management of foreign relations, or the utlimate determinant that governs decision-makers in devising foreign policy. Morgenthau denominates it the "ultimate standard,"[59]
Alexander George and Robert Keohane refer to it as a "super-
ordinate criterion,"[60] and Robert C. Good designates it "a
negative restraint on decision and action" which circum-
scribes "the outermost limits of choice."[61] Charles Lerche
summarizes this version when he says: "National interest is

the prime criterion (or criteria) in terms of which a state
judges situational factors, determines the relative priorities to be given to different goals, establishes and evalu-
ates courses of action, and makes decisions."[62] However described, in this usage national interests are held to be primordial, fundamental, and ongoing--canons of conduct--and
not necessarily entirely consummatable.

The third interpretation of national interests simply
equates them with national concerns. American Founding
Fathers and other leaders have used these terms interchangeably. While national interest is occasionally described as "a
generalized concern" in the best interests of the country as
a whole, most statesmen and publicists who synonymize interests and concerns use the terms in the plural. This connotation, as noted later, introduces an entirely different and
much more comprehensive perspective, encompassing all of the
country's concerns as falling within the purview of its national interests.

Meaning of "National"

The second problem involves the meaning of the modifier
"national." As a matter of rudimentary logic, semantically
it differentiates the interests of the nation (the biological
collectivity, or the people) from the country (the geographic
territory populated by those people) and the state (the legal
entity that encompasses those people as a component of the
community of nations), although most writers assume that it
applies to both the nation as a social group and the state as
its political institutionalization. But the word national also denotes a level of applicability, distinguishing the interests of the overall national community from both narrower
and broader interests. Some writers recognize two basic
kinds of interests--those of the society as a whole and those
of particular segments within it, and they claim that the
latter become national interests if the society espouses them
as its own. Ernest W. LeFever cautions, however, that what
is good for some subnational group is not ipso facto also
good for the people as a whole.[63]

Arnold Wolfers identifies four levels of interests--
those of individuals, subnational groups, the nation, and
mankind as a whole.[64] In specifying that the interests of
individuals and subnational groups are not necessarily compatible and, as an aggregate, they "do not constitute a general interest," Aron appears to equate the latter with the
national interest.[65] Morgenthau distinguishes national interests (pertaining explicitly to the nation-state) from subnational interests (of regional, functional, parochial, or
factional groups), other national interests (those of foreign
nation-states promoted under the guise of the nation's interests, such as those of the German-American Bund or the
China and Zionist Lobbies in the United States), and supranational interests (those of geographic or economic segments
of the world, of mankind as a whole, or of international
movements and agencies like the United Nations).[66]

A related aspect of this problem is confusion as to

whether the concepts "national interests" and "public interests" are identical, and whether these constitute the
"general interest," and whether the concepts public interests
and general interests are more elastic and encompass both
foreign and domestic interests. In other words, is there a
valid distinction between "national," "public," and "general"
interests? There are some who synonymize these in apposition
to the concerns of individuals and subnational groups, on the
one hand, and of supranational systems and institutions, on
the other hand. Thus, in his discourse on public philosophy,
Walter Lippmann conjoins domestic and foreign policy in analyzing the public interest.[67] In his theoretical essay on the
meaning of the public or common interest, Charles W. Cassinelli, neither differentiating between domestic and foreign
interests nor referring to "national" interests, defines the
public interest as "the standard by which governmental action
. . . is to be judged," and equates it with the "well-being
of the community" and "the highest political good." He also
discriminates between what the public is "interested in" and
the "interests possessed by" the public.[68]

Others hold that "public interests" pertain solely to
domestic affairs while "national interests" relate specifically to foreign relations. This perception is shared by
Glendon A. Schubert who discusses the historical and philosophical derivations of the two concepts as well as the rationalist, idealist, and realist theories respecting them,
and the connotation of "the public" and its role in determining interests.[69] Lippmann also probes the meaning of the
"public" which, in the practical work of governance, he
regards as pertaining to the "invisible community" over a
long span of time--that is, to the "corporate nation" or the
"historic national community" in the past, present, and
future. Defining the public in this manner--as distinguishable from the contemporary people, or the voters, or the
numerical majority--he contends that private persons cannot
readily surmount their particular circumstances and interests
and are likely to suppose that whatever is good for them
"must be good for the country, and good in the sight of God."
He adds that, as noted more fully later, the views of the
public do not necessarily represent the public interest, nor
does "the statistical sum of their opinions" automatically
define true public or national interest.[70]

Another school of analysis insists that, because of
changes in the community of nations and their increased interdependence, the cogency of the concept national interest
declined in the thinking of those that perceive the politics
of nations from the global rather than the national perspective and they have transmuted "international" into "world" or
"transnational" politics. John Herz and others argue that
traditional realism (invoking national interest, security,
and power) is obsolete and needs to be superseded by the notion of universalism.[71] Others, such as Richard K. Ashley
and Robert C. Johansen, propose to minimize national interests and substitute "human interests"--differentiating between practical and technical realism.[72]

More moderate in his view, J. Martin Rochester compares
the international and world politics perceptions, admits that

it is easier for scholars than policy makers to accept this transition, and suggests that, while the latter may continue to rely on the national interest in their policy decisions, they should modify their thinking if they are "truly to serve" the "national interest."[73] In response, others question whether overt action to satisfy worldwide needs and resolve global problems does not actually comport with national interests and whether, if national leaders are to serve the interests of their own nations in this fashion, to then regard as "truly serving" the national/transnational interest does not constitute a non sequitur.

National Interests as Self-Interests

Another difficulty concerns the question: Are national interests identical with self-interests, and are self-interests necessarily selfish interests? It goes without saying that national interests are self-interests in the sense that nations frame their policy and conduct their foreign relations to promote their own well-being and provide themselves with some betterment or advantage, rather than for purely altruistic reasons. The concept self-interest is used by Bailey, Mahan, and President Truman, as noted earlier, and Joseph Frankel has written: "Self-interest is, then, the vague but generally accepted criterion by which the extent of the international environment relevant for an issue is determined."[74] Robert E. Osgood, who makes a special point of equating national interest with self-interest, maintains that it "is understood to mean a state of affairs valued solely for its benefit to the nation."[75] Secretary of State Acheson told the House Foreign Affairs Committee in 1951 that "enlightened self-interest" is the only valid justification for any foreign policy or program.[76] Put another way, every nation conceives its national interest as asserting a benefit for--or as contributing to the welfare of--the nation. No nation is likely to formulate policy contrary to such interests as it conceives them.

The issue is not whether nations act in keeping with their own self-interests, but whether these are narrowminded selfish interests--what President Franklin Roosevelt, in his second inaugural address, called "heedless self-interest." Some characterize them as "self-seeking at the expense of others" or as "self-love transferred to the national group" that is motivated by "national egoism."[77] Whether or not they are deemed to be selfish depends largely on subjective interpretations. And yet, even the staunchest supporters of political realism, according to Aron, do not exalt "sacred selfishness" of states because "they fear that such selfishness will become even worse, more brutal, less reasonable if it hides behind words of a vague and grandiose kind."[78]

National interests are sometimes misconstrued as being materialistic or venal--as nationalistic minded, self-serving interests, lacking in social consciousness and magnanimity. In practice, however, inasmuch as these are not inherently antithetical and at times may actually be correlative if not mutually supportive, national interests may embrace both nationally oriented advantages and high-minded beneficence and

humanitarianism. Gross contends that endorsement of national
interests does not necessarily preclude "the acceptance of
international obligations" which in some cases "may conceivably be the best guarantee of" the country's interests.[79]

Determinator of National Interests

The fourth problem centers on who determines the interests of the nation. It is taken for granted that no government can prescribe the national interests of other countries.
Each nation ordains this for itself, which is to say that
what it postulates as its national interests, by public pro-
fession or official action, may not be ignored or overruled
by other governments.

Furthermore, it is generally agreed that within the nation its interests are designated by the government or, more
precisely, by the decision makers within it. Putting it
bluntly, it has been said that "the national interest is what
the nation, i.e., the decision-maker, decides it is,"[80] and
that "The delimitation of the national interest and of the
ways to further it must be, and is, in the final analysis a
political judgment by those having the power of decision
making."[81] Another more cautious view is that, while national interests are normally decided by ruling groups, in actual
practice, true national interests will be manifested to the
extent that policy corresponds in its broad outlines to the
ideals of the community as a whole and to the specific desires of contesting groups in particular.[82] In any case, it
is the political leaders that make this decision.

Fred A. Sondermann recognizes weakness in this arrangement: "If one focuses on such official definitions, on the
rhetoric that surrounds the policy output, he must make al-
lowance for the fact that in such rhetoric the term national
interest can easily serve to justify actions, hide mistakes,
rationalize policies, disarm the opposition." He nevertheless concedes that "After much agonizing, analyzing and de-
bating, after bravely marching up the sides of hills only to
march down the other side, the end result is that most of us,
most of the time, accept the definition of the national interest provided by a nation's high officials and policymakers."[83] In democratic countries there is the subsidiary issue as to whether this function devolves solely upon the executive, or whether the legislature is also involved. Most
analysts consider national interest articulation as essentially an executive function, but there are those who reason
that because in the American system members of Congress are
closer to the people they are better able to define contemporary national interests.

This raises a final aspect of the problem of determina-
tion--what is the role of the people in a democratic system,
and to what extent must national interests be popularly consensualized? Some writers contend that although government
leaders are held responsible for decisions on national interests, it really is "the people" who ultimately prescribe
them. On the other hand, the Department of State has declared
that while foreign policies are courses of action taken by a

nation in the interests of the welfare of the people, "It is
the job of the Government, as the agent of the people, to
promote these national interests."[84]   The specific issue is
whether the people play an active or passive role--whether
they overtly decide, or rather whether the specification of
national interests must in the long run be acceptable to
them.

Mahan proclaimed the basic precept that governments must
act in accordance with the interests of "their own wards--
their own people."[85]   In the eighteenth century British
statesman Edmund Burke, frequently quoted on this matter,
stated his interpretation of this relationship when he informed his electors at the Guildhall in Bristol: "I did not
obey your instructions. No. I conformed to the instructions
of truth and Nature, and maintained your interest, against
your opinions, with a constancy that became me."   He also
generalized: "Your representative owes you, not his industry
only, but his judgment; and he betrays, instead of serving
you, if he sacrifices it to your opinion."[86] Gross points out
that differences of view may exist between the government and
public opinion, and he rationalizes that in democracies,
where the matter is politically most acute, precepts are popularly approved a posteriori, "in an indirect way, through
elections," which "indicate consent rather on general principle . . . than on a detailed, elaborated concept of national interests."[87] It may also be argued that in a representative democracy, as suggested by Burke, leaders are elected
to represent the people, to serve as trustees of the nation,
and therefore to assume leadership in defining its interests.
In other words, to paraphrase Lincoln, in this case governance and policy-making are primarily *of* and *for* the people,
and only indirectly *by* them.

Explicating his view on popular participation in his
commentary on public philosophy, Lippmann maintains that the
"opinions and interests" of voters "should be taken for what
they are and for no more," and that "they are not--as such--
propositions in the public interest." Beyond reflecting what
various groups of voters are thinking, he claims, "they have
no intrinsic authority." In other words, national interests
are not determinable simply by public opinion polls, although
such surveys may influence policy makers.[88] As a consequence,
in foreign relations governments normally listen and react to
other governments rather than to foreign peoples, or their
opinion polls, in assessing their national interests. Yet,
it is unlikely, especially in a democracy, that a government
would in the long run act in support of national interests
overwhelmingly rejected by the people. In other words, while
the people may not expressly and directly mandate national
interests, they may delineate the ultimate parameters within
which their leaders decide and propound them in their behalf.

Substance of National Interests

The fifth difficulty centers on differing interpretations of the substance of national interests.   Leaving aside
the allegations that as a concept national interest is devoid
of content--that "it is a glittering but nevertheless unil-

luminating ambiguity[69] and that it is difficult to secure
"general agreement upon the substantive meaning of the concept"[90]--three aspects need to be considered. The first is
the question whether essence is definable a priori--on the
basis of hypotheses, in advance of pragmatic ascertainment--
or only a posteriori--deduced inductively or empirically
from past experience. In other words, are governments and
analysts capable of defining the essentials of the national
interest in advance of policy decisions and actions, is it
foreordained and needs to be "discovered," or as Morgenthau
and others insist, is it only derivable ex post facto from
the study of the past? If its substance can be established a
priori, it may be flexible and change with shifts in leadership and developments, whereas if it is only definable a posteriori, the national interest may be permanent, unvarying,
and teleological.

Therefore, an integral aspect of this matter involves
the question of whether the content of national interests is
fixed or variable, and whether it is possible to differentiate long-term, intermediate, and short-range interests. Ambassador Ellis O. Briggs and others, for example, hold that
national interests "tend to be general rather than specific,
long-term rather than ephemeral."[91] Some refer to them as
constants in the conduct of foreign affairs which, as compared with objectives and policies, are durable, few in
number, and capable of providing a broad frame of reference
for policy-making. Charles Lerche calls them "the closest
approximation to a fixed factor" in the foreign relations
process.[92]

On the other hand, others acknowledge that national interests may have both permanent and variable substance. The
fixed is irreducible, permeative, and durable, which Morgenthau defines as "logically required and in that sense necessary."[93] But in practice immutable components are complemented by a myriad of additional possibilities, flowing from
specific contemporary events, the personality and disposition
of political leaders, the policies and actions of other nations, and the exigencies of the times. They may also vary
in importance. As noted later, Donald E. Nuechterlein distinguishes among four categories of interests on the basis
of intensity. Those who support this view of multiplicity
are inclined, deliberately or subconsciously, to regard national interests not only as criteria but also as national
concerns.

The third aspect raises the issue of whether the substance of national interests is identical for nations, is
unique to individual countries, or may be both. Some, like
President Wilson, speak of a community of interests of the
nations of the world, and he specifically refers to peace and
stability. Those who consider the essence of national interests as limited and uniform for all peoples usually generalize them as survival, promotion of national welfare, and the
preservation of national security, identity, integrity, values, or political doctrine. This perception normally posits
the interest of the nation in the singular and in amorphous
terms.

There are those, however, who argue that states may have a variety of particularized national interests and that these may have diverse relationships with those of other states. In some instances, declares Charles Burton Marshall, they are correlative and mutually supportive. Often the interests of different nations harmonize without coinciding. At times they differ, but not incompatibly, and sometimes they are mutually exclusive.[94] The principal disagreement on this element of content results from contradictary connotations of national interests as unitary or multiple and as immutable or changeable.

Appositional Conceptions

The next major problem is that national interests are perceived in varying appositional--sometimes irreconcilable-- ways, with little consensus among the exponents of such conceptualized interpretations, resulting in an array of confusing linkages. In addition to such comparisons as authentic versus spurious and immediate versus long-term interests,[95] it is fairly common to contrast conceptualistic and pragmatic perceptions. Thus, the generic perception of national interests as applicable to all nations at all times, on which there is much difference of opinion, is differentiated from explicit prescriptions articulated by the nation's leaders on the basis of which action is taken and policy is made. Frankel converts this into three disparate approaches: the aspirational (the vision of the good life), the operational (the sum total of interests and policies actually pursued), and the explanatory/polemical (used as an argument in real life to explain, evaluate, rationalize, or criticize international behavior in order to prove oneself right and opponents wrong).[96]

By way of comparison, in 1973 Senator J. William Fulbright differentiated the following conceptions (without defining them): the ideological (exemplified by the American anti-Communist crusade in East-West relations), the geopolitical (treating international relations as a struggle for power as an end in itself), and the legal-institutional (subjecting international affairs to the rule of law and stabilizing interrelations within socio-political institutions like the United Nations).[97] Vernon Van Dyke, perceiving interests as aims rather than criteria, compares independent interests (those that are self-justifying and desired for their own sake) and dependent interests (which are means to achieve prescribed ends).[98] Others, such as Paul Seabury, emphasize normative and descriptive delineations. The normative, he suggests, identifies the ideal interests besought by the nation, whereas the descriptive approach defines the actual state of affairs pursued consistently through time.[99]

Another difference of perception apposes objectivists and subjectivists. Objectivists assume that the national interest of a country exists per se--that it is what some call a "real," "true," or "genuine" national interest that can be objectified or at least be examined on the basis of objectively definable standards. These encompass such basic interests as the survival and welfare of the nation and are based

upon fixed precepts comparable to the "natural laws" of
eighteenth century philosophers.[100]   Subjectivists, on the
other hand, interpret national interests as a pluralistic set
of the nation's preferences, which mutate whenever its requirements and aspirations change.[101]   These Senator Fulbright has called "a subjective and even capricious potpour-
ri."[102]

Nevertheless, attempts are made to empirically define
national interests by "scientific" process--subjecting investigation to what Woodrow Wilson in his first inaugural
address referred to as the "cool process of mere science"--
and the results are couched in amorphous terms.   Such determinations are not likely to be useful if they are not
founded on the animus of nations and their leaders, but this
brings one full circle to subjectivity. In the final analysis, at any given time the national interest is what the
country says, or thinks, or proves it is, rather than what
any rationalistic or electronic process concludes that it
might or ought to be.

NATIONAL INTEREST, POLITICAL REALISM, AND IDEALISM

While some of these conflicting distinctions are important primarily as matters of intellectual comprehension, the
most heated debate concerning the meaning and application of
national interest in the foreign relations process apposes
"realists" against "idealists," as noted earlier. Led by
Morgenthau, the realists--sometimes called pragmatists--argue
that national interests can be ascertained objectively--that,
given a country's location, resources, relative status, history, and similar factors, its practical and genuine national
interests can be deductively ascertained without the influence of sentimental and moral considerations.[103]   Critics--
including Cook and Moos, Tannenbaum, and recent Wilsonians--
emphasize idealistic and philosophical foundations of national aspirations and action, and some accentuate the vari-
ability of the interests of individual countries and their
policy makers. Even though they may agree on general ideals
or simply on their opposition to linking interests and
power, they exhibit little consensus on pragmatic prescriptions of national interests, sometimes even for a given
country. Although they refuse to accept the interpretation
of the realists, they fail to produce a common, inductively
generated, and convincing alternative. This leaves the anom-
oly of widespread criticism of the realists' judgment
coupled with the failure of the idealists to provide a persuasive, realizable substitute.   In actual practice it is
claimed, however, that realists, who advocate what they call
"the realities," are not without ideals, and the professions
of idealists often reflect political reality.[104] Inis Claude
maintains that realism focuses on "what is" and idealism on
"what should be," and that the main difference between them
should be "what is possible"[105]--which is the essence of political pragmatism.

Idealists also reject the concepts of both national interest and power as operational precepts for action on moral
grounds--which produced a noteworthy secondary debate. Rely-

ing on earlier political philosophers, they question the morality of basing foreign policy on self-interest rather than on "superior values," implying that interest-oriented policy is immoral. Morgenthau, on the other hand, distinguishing between morality and moralism, argues that "a foreign policy guided by moral abstractions, without consideration of the national interest, is bound to fail; for it accepts a standard of action alien to the nature of the action itself." All successful statesmen of modern times "have made the national interest the ultimate standard of their policies, and none of the great moralists in international affairs has attained his goals." Hence, he claims, "the antithesis between moral principles and the national interest is not only intellectually mistaken but morally pernicious. A foreign policy derived from the national interest is in fact morally superior to a foreign policy inspired by universal moral principles."[106] In short, according to Morgenthau "Moral principles and the national interest have contended for dominance over the minds and actions of men throughout the history of the modern state system . . .. . Between these two conceptions of foreign policy . . . there can be no compromise." The statesman must choose one or the other "as the ultimate standard of decision."[107]

Allowing greater flexibility in relating moralism and idealism with national interest, Dean Acheson--ridiculing the expectation that it is possible to conceive "a one-page statement of the democratic faith with all the impact of the Gettysburg Address and the Lord's Prayer combined"--contends in his memoirs that "in foreign affairs nothing was more dangerous than to base action upon moral or ideal conceptions unconnected with hardheaded practicality."[108] More recently, on this issue of linking morality to foreign policy, also from the perspective of the practitioner, Henry Kissinger expressed his view of contemporary diplomacy:

> I refuse to accept the premise that our moral values and policy objectives are irreconcilable.... Our choice is not between morality and pragmatism. We cannot escape either, nor are they incompatible. This nation must be true to its beliefs or it will lose its bearings in the world. But at the same time it must survive in the world of sovereign nations with competing wills. We need moral strength to select among agonizing choices and a sense of purpose to navigate between the shoals of difficult decisions.[109]

GENERAL THEORY OF INTERNATIONAL AND FOREIGN RELATIONS

Another problem generating controversy grows out of the attempt to convert national interest into the cornerstone of a theory of international politics and foreign affairs. Whether or not originally intended by Mahan, Beard, Morgenthau, and their associates and followers, combinations of thinkers--including behavioralists, decision-making analysts, geopolitical determinists, and philosophers--have scrutinized and assessed the principle of aligning national interest with national power, the functioning of power politics and the

balance of power, and the process of foreign policy-making as
providing the foundation of a basic theory of international
relations.

Participants in this venture proceed from the nature and
validity of national interest as one of the factors in world
affairs to enshrining it as the dominating keystone of international relations. The product of their endeavors tends to
exaggerate, perhaps deify, national interest. They have been
joined by objectivists who seek to particularize and quantify
interest and power in terms of measurable qualities for purposes not only of rational comprehension and appraisal, but
also of predicting national behavior.

The quest for a pervasive international/foreign relations theory based on national interest, though it achieved
widespread attention, failed to gain universal acceptance.
Both the conception of the realists and the theory of international politics based on their interpretation have been
subjected to wholesale review and severe criticism. Defending his position, Morgenthau explained: "In order to refute a
theory which pretends to be scientific, it is first necessary
to understand what a scientific theory is. A scientific
theory is an attempt to bring order and meaning to a mass of
phenomena which without it would remain disconnected and
unintelligible." Those who dispute the scientific character
of such a theory "either must produce a theory superior in
these scientific functions to the one attacked or must, at
the very least, demonstrate that the facts as they actually
are do not lend themselves to the interpretation which the
theory has put upon them."[110] Although this debate remains
unresolved, and alternative theories of foreign relations
have fared no better, the use of the concept in both state
practice and policy studies nevertheless continues.

NATIONAL INTEREST AS ANALYTICAL TOOL

Disquisition on national interest as the foundation of
international relations theory suggests a final issue--
whether the denial of national interest as a viable "scientific" instrument for analysis justifies rejecting its importance if not its very existence as a factor in the conduct
and assessment of foreign affairs. In addition to the error
of confusing descriptive and analytical theory, and dispute
over deciding whether to pursue discovery by investigation or
by reflection, the argument is sometimes made that because
national interest is questionable as a reliable and systematic analytical tool it is equally questionable as an essential factor in practical policy-making, and therefore is unreliable for understanding and evaluating political action.

Raymond Aron regards national interest as vague to the
point of being meaningless[111] and Cecil V. Crabb doubts that
it can serve as "a useful guide to diplomatic conduct."[112]
Michael Brower, commenting on United States practice, holds
that its use for purposes of discourse and policy formulation
is at best misleading and at worst dangerous to the achievement of basic goals and values, and he believes that no clarity would be sacrificed by dropping the concept entirely and

relying instead on such phenomena as basic goals, specific
objectives, and policy strategies.[113] But such a conclusion
appears to flow from a conception of interests as achievable
ends rather than as standards or guides and from a presump-
tion of incompatibility between interests and aims.

Marshall agrees that, the concept's usefulness being
limited, it begs more questions than it answers. He claims
to know of no case in American experience in which the settlement of a foreign policy problem "would have been facilitated by injecting the question--'Shall we or shall we not
try to serve the national interest'?" The issue, he argues,
"is not whether, but how, to serve the national interest."
Although he admits the existence of national interests, he,
like Kennan and others, proposes to substitute "responsibility" as the "guiding principle" of policy-making.[114] But
this raises new questions--whose responsibility to whom, for
what, and when, and how?

Other writers stop short of dropping the concept from
consideration. James Rosenau insists that, as an analytical
tool employed to describe, explain, and evaluate the sources
of adequacy of a nation's foreign policy, the concept con-
founds political inquiry. He maintains that it failed to
fulfill its early promise as a basis for analysis and that
the emergence of increasing numbers of supranational participants in global affairs is bound to diminish reliance on the
concept. He concedes, however, that in its "action usage,"
despite its shortcomings, the concept "serves its users,
political actors, well," and he concludes that, while the
national interest has little future as an empirical instrument, its employment in practical politics will, nevertheless, continue.[115] This would seem to suggest that, even
though it may be deficient as a foundation for scientific
scrutiny, it remains a valid and important ingredient in the
making, implementing, and evaluating of foreign policy--to
both the practitioner and the scholar--and therefore cannot
be ignored as a factor in foreign relations analysis.

In the 1970s interest in the concept revived because interested people wanted to reassess its applicability. For example, Alexander George and Robert Keohane, writing an essay
for an official report on the organization of the American
government for the conduct of foreign policy, agree that it
"continues to be important for foreign policy-makers despite
its limitations as a theoretical and scientific concept."[116]
Similarly, Sondermann, maintains that "it clearly remains" a
part of foreign policy analysis, and that it does have meaning "to those who make and execute policies," and "to those
on whose behalf policies are being made and pursued."[117]

Unwilling to accept the judgment of others concerning
the unsuitability of national interest as an analytical tool,
Donald E. Nuechterlein not only continues to defend the ap-
propriateness of national interests as a foreign relations
component, but also presents a comprehensive system of analysis for its practical application. Posited on the precept
that national interests constitute a central feature of foreign policy-making, he establishes, elucidates, and applies
his design for analysis, based on what he calls a matrix of

factors.   It differentiates   among both   levels of intensity
and the   designation of   basic substantive   categories of in-
terests--applicable   to   all   states (which is discussed more
fully in the following chapter).   These he applies to a variety of   generic and concrete   relations and problems, which he
discusses both historically and   in relation   to contemporary
and future   developments.   Minimizing dispute over issues of
idealism, morality, theory development, and "scientizing," he
concerns himself principally with designing and applying systematic and rational policy making and analysis.[118]

BASIC INTERPRETATIONS OF NATIONAL INTERESTS

     To a large extent,   difficulty in   understanding the na-
ture and   use of   national interests in foreign relations results from   and   is   reflected   in   its   singular   and plural
usages.   To say   that a   nation has a number of national interests, or that a   particular matter   is an   interest of nations in   general or   of a   specific country, or that certain
interests are common to   all   nations   is   readily comprehensible.   On the other hand, employing the concept in ·the singular as "*the* national interest" to   denote   an integrated
aggregate or   a composite   of separable interests, or a fused
amalgam of interests, or a symbol   of all   that a   nation regards as   essential,   important,   or   beneficial to national
well-being, or a   universal   and   immutable   single interest,
such as survival, is less readily understood.

     Both the   singular and   the plural   are utilized in state
practice and intellectual inquiry.   If   used in   the singular
as applying   to a   precise, explicitly identified interest or
in the   plural to   denote a   group of   such interests, little
confusion arises.   When   Marshall says that in any practical
policy issue "there are   many   national   interests,   not just
one," his meaning is clear.[119]   However, statesmen and scholars often use the term in the singular   as meaning something
other than one among several prescribable interests, and some
attribute to it a quality   that   exceeds   either   concrete or
general interests.   Morgenthau   suggests that in certain respects the expression is similar to   the "great generalities"
of   the   American   Constitution--such   as due process and the
general welfare--and that it   embodies   a   "residual" meaning
which   is   "inherent   in   the   concept   itself."[120]   In other
words, to some,   in   the   singular,   it   represents something
greater than   the term   normally connotes, and it is presumed
to exceed the sum of its explicit constituents.

     One option is to use the expression "*the* national inter-
est" solely   to mean   the overall and continuing postulate on
which a state acts--admittedly   a generalized interpretation.
Because any   lower level of generalization tends to lose substantive meaning and the term,   in   the singular,   becomes increasingly ambiguous,   this   line   of reasoning suggests, at
all lower levels of   application it   is preferable   to employ
the expression   in the   plural as "national interests."[121]   A
good many commentaries   recognize   such   multiplicity of interests, as   developed more   fully in   the following chapter.
While the matter of the dichotomy of the   singular and plural
forms may appear to be intellectually simplistic and inconse-

quential, the distinction is central to understanding the
meaning and usage of the concept. On the basis of both practical usage and scholarly analysis, the concept is interpreted in five different ways.

THE NATIONAL INTEREST

The most pretentious interpretation--as THE NATIONAL IN-
TEREST--used and accentuated in the singular, conceives it as
the sole, permeative, regnant, and immutable factor that dom-
inates foreign relations. Thus employed by Morgenthau and
others it coalesces with national survival or self-preservation. Morgenthau, to recapitulate, defines this exalted version of national interest in terms of national power, proclaims survival as the overriding interest of all nations and
contends that, in turn, it can only be prescribed as national
security--or the preservation of the national entity and the
integrity of its territory, populace, and institutions. This
prescription enthrones survival as the irreducible and therefore elemental epicenter of foreign relations.[122] He also has
written: "Self-preservation . . . is not only a biological
and psychological necessity, but in the absence of an overwhelming obligation, a moral duty as well."[123] In a similar
vein, Kalevi J. Holsti declares that although there may be
some immutable national interests, such as self-preservation,
to which all will agree, "no one can claim with certainty
that any other specific goal or set of goals is in the national interest."[124]

This linkage of national interest with survival or self-
preservation, which Bailey characterizes as "paramount to all
law," in short, is usually conceived as maintaining independence and the integrity of the national domain, basic political and social system, and culture. Gross puts it briefly--
"it means always survival of a state, of a nation, of a system, of a ruling group, of certain values--always survival
either of ideas or of certain groups and their interests."[125]

In this extreme and elevated sense it may be regarded by
some as so sacrosanct that it transcends all else in the life
of the nation and therefore epitomizes the highest national
cause. If natural law recognizes the right of an individual
to life, this line of reasoning argues, the same principle
applies to the life of the nation-state within the community
of sovereign nations because it is inconceivable that a nation could not be most concerned about its very survival. In
the relations of nations, therefore, the exercise of this
right and obligation to preserve the nation-state is its
prime policy concern--the "iron law" or "elemental truth,"
according to Morgenthau--and is conceived as THE NATIONAL IN-
TEREST.

The National Interest

The second manifestation--as *The National Interest*--also
employed in the singular, is applied either to an undefined,
mythical, cohesive amalgam of foreign policy imperatives consisting of the nation's major needs and desires or to a su-

preme, synthesized, and sacrosanct symbol of such factors. In
both cases the concept represents an agglomerate and is used
only in the singular. Thus conceived, it tends to be generalized simply as that which is regarded as presumptive, and
beneficial, if not essential, not only for the survival but
also for the welfare of the nation. Little attempt is made to
articulate it concretely because--usually deemed self-evident
--this is unnecessary. In this sense, it constitutes a mysti-
cal and amorphous shield or screen behind which policy makers
and often publicists hide to rationalize their positions and
decisions without explanation or justification.   It is particularly attractive to political leaders because of its inherent appeal and aura of sanctity, and the ease with which
it may be invoked. Some who maintain that national interest
is undefinable--both conceptualistically and pragmatically--
tend to view it in this fashion. In response to such definition by default, there is merit to the claim of those who
suggest that alternatives should be employed.

"The National Interest"

This third interpretation--as "The National Interest"--
similarly expressed in the singular, on the other hand, comprises an aggregate of multiple interests, usually a combination of those that are considered to be important, comprehensive, and continuing. They represent the generalized interests of the nation in the sense of Lippmann's perception of
the public interest pertaining to "the invisible and transcendant community" in the long run.[126] Often policy makers
employ the concept in this collective way but, unless articulated in a practical context, or at least prescribed in
basic, preferably concrete terms, it tends to be indistinguishable from the first two interpretations--as a single,
predominant, and inalienable interest or as an agglomerate.

Those analysts who utilize it in this guise are usually
agreed that, in addition to survival, it encompasses such
elemental components as self-preservation, national security,
the conservation of national institutions, and the welfare of
the nation and its people. This interpretation, therefore,
differs little from those already discussed. However, some
commentaries broaden its scope to embrace economic and social
well-being, the preservation of the nation's political heritage and doctrine, its way of life and national character,
its standard of living, its national prestige, pride, honor,
and credibility, and its contribution to peace, world order,
and internal and international stability. To these, occasionally writers append such ancillary matters as national
elbowroom, self-sufficiency in the conduct of foreign relations, and freedom of diplomatic maneuver.[127] This list may
be extended, but these constituents tend to remain generalized, constant, and incontestable. The meaning of this aggregate usage should be definable--conceptualistically and prag-
matically--at least in fundamental terms. Yet, both policy
makers and scholars reveal the difficulties of drawing the
line of distinction between inclusion and exclusion--that is,
in the refining of priorities--and of differentiating interests from objectives and policies when applied to the realities of statecraft.

National Concerns

The fourth perception, as a national interest in the singular and as multiple interests in the plural, equates interests with public concerns. This interpretation postulates the plurality of interests and sanctions the potentiality of an inclusive as well as a preferential or selective application. Paraphrasing John Stuart Mill who, referring to individuals, declared simplistically, "A man's interest consists of whatever he takes an interest in,"[128] it may be employed to denote all those foreign relations matters with which the nation is concerned and which it regards as action or policy relevant--directly or indirectly, and manifestly or passively. In this sense, the very reality of a government's acknowledged concern, on behalf of the nation, raises it to the ranks of a national interest.

For example, representing this view, British authority on international relations F. S. Northedge bridges the relationship between national interest and interests with facility. He simply distinguishes the nation's concerns (plural) from the national interest (singular), both of which, in his judgment, are legitimate conceptions. He defines the concerns broadly as "that *melange* of wants, desires, needs and claims" that governments pursue abroad. He characterizes such lesser interests as "the totality of the country's stake in the prevailing international system, the entire congeries of rights and privileges it exercises beyond its borders, the amenities and assets it enjoys, and the commitments and obligations it shoulders."[129] Without discussing levels of concerns or interests--which is considered in the next chapter-- he merely acknowledges governmental usage of both the singular and plural versions of the concept.

Emphasizing the multiplicity of United States interests shortly after World War I, Paul Scott Mowrer declared: "The first thing to be understood is that the United States today has interests literally everywhere . . . . I think the complacent, home dwelling citizen would be astonished if he could be brought to realize the primary fact that there is probably today not a country, not a city in the world, in which the United States has not genuine interests of some description."[130] And he spends pages listing a sampling. If this view was tenable in the early 1920s, it is even more cogent since World War II. In this broad version of concerns, a nation's interests therefore may be applicable throughout the world and to a host of matters that affect its functioning and well-being, and respecting which it formulates its aims and policies.

To illustrate the possible multiplicity of a nation's interests, aside from self-preservation and the matters already mentioned, the following suggest a few of the more obvious contemporary concerns of many countries: to encourage self-determination of peoples, democratization of governance, and internal stability; to have reliable and strong allies; to prevent nuclear and restrain conventional arms proliferation and warfare; to preserve access to strategic waterways and important raw materials; to promote international trade and exports; to maintain international financial credibility,

currency stability, and a favorable balance of payments; to
enhance national prestige abroad; to constrain international
terrorism and aerial hijacking; to protect the property and
the lives of the country's diplomats and other nationals
abroad; to produce agreed arrangements for the economic development and modernization of newly independent countries;
and the like. Such a list can be extended by scores of additional more precise policy guidelines, and who can deny
that any one is not a country's national interest if its
government insists that it is.[131]

No claim is made that many of these interests are essential to the nation's security, survival, or self-preservation.   This becomes even more apparent when broader concerns
are extrapolated to narrower and even subsidiary supportive
subinterests or concerns, rendering the panoply more complex
and virtually endless. Often when the political practitioner
pronounces that some explicit matter constitutes a national
interest, he is applying the concept to denote his government's concern, and those who contest its validity do so because they miscalculate or conceive the meaning of the concept as something more comprehensive and fundamental.

While some analysts differentiate between this interpretation and the national interest as a sacrosanct symbol,
agglomerate, or aggregate of unquestionable, permeative interests, if such concerns are held to be among the motivating
"interests of the nation," logic would suggest that they must
be "national interests." If not, it would need to be presumed that "national interests" must be distinguished from
"the interests of the nation," which would accord extraordinary meanings to ordinary terms and augment confusion. However, such interests, as concerns, would still be differentiated from "*the* national interest" by those who prefer to
denominate the concept in this singular fashion.

Due to the pragmatic complexity--in some cases seeming
imponderability--of a nation's multifarious network of concerns, they are not likely to be concretely itemized in their
entirety, or even for a major functional or geographic segment of the policy spectrum, and they normally come to be
identified piecemeal only as suggested by specific public
pronouncements and actions. If they are conceived as ends
rather than criteria or standards, they tend to be confused
with national purposes, basic national goals, and more precise policy objectives. But, if they simply represent standards, in accordance with which such purposes, goals, and policies are designed regardless of their inherent generality
or import, they nevertheless serve as guides in the formulation of national policy.

Definition

Bridging these various interpretations of the concept
and to provide a working definition for practical and scholarly usage:

*National interests are those fundamental determi-
nants, intrinsic needs, operational criteria, or*

ultimate standards in accordance with which a na-
tion frames its national purposes and goals, pre-
scribes its concrete objectives, and formulates its
foreign policies, strategies, and diplomatic tac-
tics to preserve and enhance its status and welfare
in its relations with other nations. Such inter-
ests, or concerns, may vary in degrees of constan-
cy, importance, and intensity, are subjectively de-
termined by each nation for itself, and--whether
they are generalized or particularized, and whether
they are articulated clearly or are assumed to be
understood--serve as critical guideposts for deci-
sion makers throughout the foreign relations proc-
ess.

"IN THE NATIONAL INTEREST"

A final usage is denoted by the expression "in the national interest" or, occasionally, "for the national interest." This version is often employed interchangeably with
the national interest.[132] If differentiation is intended,
however, it signifies simple linguistic distinction between
the use of national interest as a grammatical subject (that
which is affirmed as a perceivable reality) and its use as a
grammatical object within a prepositional phrase (that which
conforms with the perceived reality as conditioned by the
verbal expression). Substantively applied, this means that
many concrete criteria, standards, and concerns may be in
pursuance of, or in conformity with, national interests without actually constituting either a national interest or *the*
national interest. Moreover, in practice, much the same aura
of sanctified imprecision accrues to such prepositional use
as by employing the agglomerate, aggregate, or symbol as a
consecrated watchword behind which its user seeks refuge to
render it incontestable without even assuming the candor of
professing it to constitute a tangible national interest.

Given five major interpretations of the concept, much of
the uncertainty and difficulty of comprehension and objection
to its application in the conduct of foreign affairs flows
from its careless and equivocal use by political leaders and
the biased and parochial interpretations of some of its analysts. But these are scarcely valid reasons for justifying
the invalidation of a concept as prevailing and important as
national interests in managing and understanding the foreign
relations process.

REFINING OPTIONS

It is manifest that foreign policy-making clearly involves considering the nation's interests, that existing
confusion in both defining and usage of the concept is de-
lusive to statesmen, scholars, the media, and the citizenry,
and that when employed it is desirable that its meaning be
understood. It would seem incumbent upon social scientists
and historians to be able to logically distinguish, prescribe, and employ its varying interpretations intelligibly,
and the process of refinement would be facilitated if certain

interpretations were avoided and others were consensualized.

A great deal of perplexity would be eliminated if interests ceased to be simply equated with amorphous national motives or values, which is unnecessary if not inappropriate,
and if aims were more accurately identified as purposes,
goals, and foreign policy objectives. Additional clarity
would be achieved if the semantic plurality of interests were
universally acknowledged and the concept were dissociated
from attempts to formulate foreign relations theory. This
would reduce the concept to three usages: (1) national concerns of various types, (2) "The National Interest" as an aggregate of fundamental and relatively stable but concrete interests, including those associated with survival, and (3)
considerations "in the national interest," applicable to either the singular aggregate or the pluralized concerns of the
nation. Conceding that in actual practice nations do have
multiple interests, it would even be preferable if the plural
were employed consistently except in reference to an individual or particularized national interest. Much confusion could
be overcome, according to Frankel, if it were acknowledged
that, "As national interest . . . is the filter through which
all international considerations have to pass before affecting national actions even a partial clarification of the concept should serve the important purpose of making foreign
policy more realistic, more in tune with the international
environment within which it operates."[133]

In short, misunderstanding could be reduced by characterizing national interests as no more than the interests of
the nation--as its concerns, great and small, vital or tan-
gential--subject to the understanding that they vary not only
substantively but also in degrees of criticality, importance,
and intensity. Thus, misleading use of the expression as a
sacrosanct symbol, a heralded though inexplicable shield, a
questionable abstraction, or a sanctified, ambiguous agglomerate would be eliminated. Then political leaders, historians, and other scholars could be held accountable for more
precise and comprehensible usage, and types of national concerns could be more clearly defined on the basis of logical
priorities.

Understanding would be furthered if both political practitioners and publicists would accept such interpretations,
and if they gave up avoiding concrete specification and their
debates over the incompatibility of idealism and realism and
of expediency and moralism, as well as over the extent to
which interests are scientifically determinable or value
laden, and the necessity to systematize predictability and
devise a universal foreign relations theory. In other words,
confusion could be minimized if they simply accepted national
interests, in both their conceptual and pragmatized versions,
as central to the nation's foreign policy process--which they
are--and candidly articulated them in the context in which
they are used. This would aid both the decision maker in the
formulation and explication of foreign policies and the foreign affairs analyst and historian in assessing them.

NOTES

1. Montesquieu, *The Spirit of Laws* translated by M. de Secondat (Baron de Montesquieu), (Glasgow: printed by David Niven, 1793), I, 6.

2. Address, March 1, 1848, in Alan and Veronica Palmer, *Quotations in History* (Hassocks, Sussex, England: Harvester Press, 1976), p. 175.

3. Quoted in Hans J. Morgenthau and Kenneth W. Thompson, eds., *Principles and Problems of International Politics: Selected Readings* (New York: Knopf, 1950), p. 55.

4. Broadcast address, October 1, 1939, quoted in Winston Churchill, *The Second World War: The Gathering Storm* (Boston: Houghton Mifflin, 1948), p. 449.

5. Quoted in *Morrow's International Dictionary of Contemporary Quotations* (New York: Morrow, 1982), p. 103.

6. Jared Sparks, ed., *Writings of George Washington* (Boston: Russell, Shattack, and Williams, 1836), XI, 42.

7. John C. Fitzpatrick, ed., *The Writings of George Washington* (Washington: Government Printing Office, 1931-1944), X, 363.

8. Second Inaugural Address, March 4, 1805.

9. *The Federalist*, No. 23. Hamilton makes dozens of references to interests in his contributions to *The Federalist* papers, using such expressions as "true" and "real" interests, "general" and "mutual" interests, and "aggregate interests of the Union." For comments on Hamilton's devotion to national interests, see Hans J. Morgenthau, *In Defense of the National Interest: A Critical Examination of American Foreign Policy* (New York: Knopf, 1952), pp. 14-18. Norman A. Graebner concludes that "Hamilton's brilliance in arguing for the national interest has hardly been exceeded anywhere in the modern world." See Graebner's *Ideas and Diplomacy: Readings in the Intellectual Tradition of American Foreign Policy* (New York: Oxford University Press, 1964), p.16.

10. Quoted in Charles A. Beard, *The Idea of National Interest: An Analytical Study in American Foreign Policy* (New York: Macmillan, 1934, republished Westport, Conn.: Greenwood, 1977), pp. 337-38, 382. Also see note 30 for Mahan's principal writings.

11. Opening statement of address delivered to American Academy of Politician and Social Science, Philadelphia, November 30, 1923 (celebrating centenary of the Monroe Doctrine) in Charles Evans Hughes, *The Pathway of Peace* (New York: Harper, 1925), p. 142.

12. Mowrer, *Our Foreign Affairs: A Study in the National Interest and the New Diplomacy* (New York: Dutton, 1924), p. 49.

13. Frankel, *National Interest* (New York: Praeger, 1970), p. 18. He also has said: "All statesmen are governed by their respective national interests, but this does not mean that they can never agree on anything. On the contrary, they often do, but only on the basis of their conceptions of these national interests." See p. 48.

14. Bailey, *The Art of Diplomacy: The American Experience* (New York: Appleton-Century-Crofts, 1968), pp. 82, 85.

15. Morgenthau, *In Defense of the National Interest*, p. 242.

16. Washington's Farewell Address, September 17, 1796, given in James D. Richardson, *A Compilation of the Messages and Papers of the Presidents, 1789-1908* (1909), I, 222. Graebner's comments appear in his *Ideas and Diplomacy*, p. 73.

17. Beard, *The Idea of National Interest*, pp. 34-37. For commentary on Beard's subsequent publications as they relate to national interest, see Robert E. Osgood, *Ideals and Self-Interest in America's Foreign Relations: The Great Transformation of the Twentieth Century* (Chicago: University of Chicago Press, 1953), pp. 372-74.

18. Counting Grover Cleveland only once, although his terms were not consecutive.

19. John Quincy Adams even stressed "this transcendently important interest."

20. For a sampling of such usage throughout American history, see Graebner, who documents dozens of major policy statements in his *Ideas and Diplomacy*, including the debate of Jefferson, Hamilton, and James Madison on the applicability of the Franco-American Alliance commitment of 1778 during the war following the French Revolution. See pp. 16-17, 54-73. Also see Morgenthau, *In Defense of the National Interest*, pp. 14-18.

21. Saul K. Padover, ed., *Wilson's Ideals* (Washington: American Council on Public Affairs, 1942), pp. 70, 72, 81.

22. October 18, 1948, in *Papers of the Presidents: Harry S. Truman, 1948*, p. 816.

23. June 10, 1963, in *Papers of the Presidents: John F. Kennedy, 1963*, pp. 461-62.

24. Lyndon B. Johnson, *The Vantage Point: Perspectives of the Presidency, 1963-1969* (New York: Holt, Rinehart, and Winston, 1971), p. 24.

25. September 18, 1969, in *Papers of the Presidents: Richard Nixon, 1969*, p. 727; and *U.S. Foreign Policy for the 1970's: The Emerging Structure for Peace--A Report to Congress by Richard Nixon, February 9, 1972* (Washington: Government Printing Office, 1972), p. 9.

26. January 8, 1983, in *Papers of the Presidents: Ronald Reagan, 1983*, p. 24.

27. Acheson, "Crisis in Asia: An Examination of U.S. Policy," *Department of State Bulletin* 22 (January 23, 1950): 111-18. His second rule is to keep national purposes perfectly straight, pure, and aboveboard. For commentary on this address, see Kenneth W. Thompson, ed., *Traditions and Values: American Diplomacy, 1945 to the Present* (New York: University Press of America, 1984), pp. 6-8.

28. Address, June 7, 1964, "The National Interest--1964," *Department of State Bulletin* 50 (June 22, 1964): 956.

29. Kissinger, *Years of Upheaval* (Boston: Little, Brown, 1982), p. 168.

30. Mahan published dozens of volumes and essays propounding his views. His principal writings include: *The Influence of Sea Power Upon History, 1660-1783* (Boston: Little, Brown, 1890); *The Interest of America in International Conditions* (Boston: Little, Brown, 1910); *The Interest of America in Sea Power--Present and Future* (Boston: Little, Brown, 1898); *The Problem of Asia and Its Effect Upon International Policies* (Boston: Little, Brown, 1900); and articles in the *Atlantic Monthly, Forum, Harper's, North American Review*, and other periodicals. For a brief survey of Mahan's ideas, see Beard, *The Idea of National Interest*, especially pp. 1-2, 331-32, 337, 382; Osgood, *Ideals and Self-Interest*, pp. 32-41; and William D. Puleston, *Mahan: The Life and Work of Captain Alfred Thayer Mahan* (New Haven, Conn.: Yale University Press, 1939).

31. Morgenthau's ideas are presented in detail in his *A New Foreign Policy for the United States* (New York: Praeger, 1969); *Dilemmas of Politics* (Chicago: University of Chicago Press, 1958), especially Chapter 4; *In Defense of the National Interest; Politics Among Nations: The Struggle for Power and Peace* (New York: Knopf, 1948, and later editions); and his essays cited separately later and included in the bibliography. For commentary on Morgenthau's views, also see "Symposium in Honor of Hans J. Morgenthau," *International Studies Quarterly* 25 (June 1981): 182-241; and Thomas W. Robinson, "A National Interest Analysis of Sino-Soviet Relations," *International Studies Quarterly* 11 (June 1967): 138-41.

32. Kennan's views are developed in his *American Diplomacy, 1900-1950* (Chicago: University of Chicago Press, 1951); *The Cloud of Danger: Current Realities of American Foreign Policy* (Boston: Little, Brown, 1977); *Realities of American Foreign Policy* (Princeton: Princeton University Press, 1954); *Memoirs, 1925-1950* and *Memoirs, 1950-1963* (Boston: Little, Brown, 1967 and 1972); and his volumes on Russia and Soviet-American relations. For a comparison of the ideas contained in Morgenthau's *In Defense of the National Interest* and Kennan's *American Diplomacy, 1900-1950*, see the review article by Grayson L. Kirk, "In Search of the National Interest," *World Politics* 5 (October 1952): 110-15; and Arthur M. Schlesinger, Jr., "Policy and National Interest," *Partisan Review* 18 (November-December, 1951): 706-9, for a comparative review of Kennan's *American Diplomacy, 1900-1950* and other works. See also Martin F. Herz, ed., *Decline of the West? George Kennan and His Critics* (Washington: Ethics and Public Policy Center, Georgetown University, 1978).

33. Beard, *The Idea of National Interest*, Chapter 1; also see commentary in Fred A. Sondermann, "The Concept of the National Interest," *ORBIS* 21 (Spring 1977): 122-23. For a general survey of "American Foreign Policy in the Light of National Interest," by George A. Lundberg, see Harry Elmer Barnes, ed., *Perpetual War for Perpetual Peace* (Caldwell, Idaho: Claxton, 1953), Chapter 9.

34. Gross, *Foreign Policy Analysis* (New York: Philosophical Library, 1954), p. 76.

35. Beard, *The Idea of National Interest*, p. 26. On the origins of political realism in the United States, see Kenneth W. Thompson, *Political Realism and the Crisis of World Politics: An American Approach to Foreign Policy* (Princeton: Princeton University Press, 1960; republished Lanham, Md.: University Press of America, 1982). Also see David W. Clinton, "The National Interest: Normative Foundations," *Review of Politics* 48 (Fall 1986): 495-519, which notes that from the normative perspective, criticism of national interest derives from confusion over the meaning of the concept. For additional commentary on national interest,

see David Clinton, ed., *The National Interest: Rhetoric, Leadership, and Policy* (Lanham, Md.: University Press of America, 1988).

36. Bemis, *A Diplomatic History of the United States* (New York: Holt, 1936), title of Chapter 26; also continued in his later editions.

37. Lippmann, *U.S. Foreign Policy: Shield of the Republic* (Boston: Little, Brown, 1943), Introduction and p. 3.

38. Kennan, *American Diplomacy: 1900-1950*, especially Chapters 1-3.

39. Morgenthau, *In Defense of the National Interest*, p. 23. Morgenthau categorizes the periods of United States diplomacy as the realistic, ideological, and utopian eras; see pp. 13-28. Also see his "The United States as a World Power: A Balance Sheet," *International Studies Quarterly* 11 (October 1969): 113-16, and note 44 below.

40. Graebner, *Ideas and Diplomacy*, especially pp. 334-78; for his views on Mahan and Theodore Roosevelt, see pp. 378-85.

41. Arthur S. Link, *The Papers of Woodrow Wilson* (Princeton: Princeton University Press, 1978), XXVIII, 450, 452. Also quoted with commentary in Ernest W. LeFever, *Ethics and United States Foreign Policy* (New York: Meridian, 1957), p. 13.

42. For Graebner's essay on President Wilson's idealistic views and actions, see *Ideas and Diplomacy*, pp. 406-17. See also Morgenthau, "The United States as a World Power: A Balance Sheet," p. 120, and Arthur S. Link, *The Higher Realism of Woodrow Wilson and Other Essays* (Nashville: Vanderbilt University Press, 1971). For Wilson's papers, see Ray Stannard Baker, *Woodrow Wilson, Life and Letters*, 7 vols. (New York: Doubleday, Doran and Doubleday, Page, 1927-1939), and Link, *The Papers of Woodrow Wilson*, 53 vols. (Princeton: Princeton University Press, 1966-1986).

43. Morgenthau, *Politics Among Nations* (1948 and later editions).

44. For Morgenthau's analysis of the development of American foreign affairs--discussing three historical periods: realist (thinking and acting in terms of national interest and power), ideological (acting in terms of power but thinking in terms of moral principles), and moralist (thinking and acting in terms of moral principles)--see his "The Mainsprings of American Foreign Policy: The National Interest vs. Moral Abstractions," *American Political Science Review* 44 (December 1950): 833-54; see also *In Defense of the National Interest*, pp. 13-28.

45. This should not be thought of as a revolutionary innovation of the 1950s because aspects of this perception of the relations of nations can be traced to such earlier writings as those of Niccolo Machiavelli, Francis Bacon, Thomas Hobbes, Johann Fichte, Georg Hegel, Heinrich von Treitschke, and Friedrich W. Nietzsche. For a survey on the essence and development of realism/realpolitik, see Cecil V. Crabb, Jr., *Policy Makers and Critics: Conflicting Theories of American Foreign Policy* (New York: Praeger, 1976), Chapter 5, and for his "synopsis of pragmatic thought," listing ten basic precepts, see his *The American Approach to Foreign Policy: A Pragmatic Perspective* (New York: University Press of America, 1985), pp. 9-11.

46. Osgood, *Ideals and Self-Interest*, p. 4.

47. For Hull's foundations of foreign policy, see *Foreign Relations of the United States, 1937* (Washington: Government Printing Office, 1954), I, 699-700; and Graebner, *Ideas and Diplomacy*, pp. 581-82, 591-96. For an assessment of Hull's views, see Julius W. Pratt, *Cordell Hull, 1933-1944*, I, 29-30, in *American Secretaries of State and Their Diplomacy*, edited by Robert E. Farrell (New York: Cooper Square Publishers, 1964), vols. XII and XIII. Pratt reports that Hull originally established four Pillars of Peace which he later expanded to more than a dozen. By way of comparison, for Richard Nixon's more realistic "eight indispensable pillars of peace" (in U.S.-Soviet relations), see his address "The Pillars of Peace," Los Angeles, March 6, 1986.

48. For a succinct statement on the relationship of the realist and idealist schools, see Arnold Wolfers, "The Pole of Power and the Pole of Indifference," *World Politics* 4 (October 1951): 39-63. Also see his "Statesmanship and Moral Choice," *World Politics* 1 (January 1949): 175-95.

49. For general commentary on Roosevelt's idealism, see Graebner, *Ideas and Diplomacy*, pp. 637, 648-60, and for documentation and analysis on his administration's policy for international cooperation during and after World War II, see Department of State, *Postwar Foreign Policy Preparation, 1939-1945* (Washington: Government Printing Office, 1949). For the interesting view of Senator J. William Fulbright, who declared: "I believe our own selfish interests--in fact our very survival as a great nation--is dependent upon an intelligent and practical system of collective security," see Eugene Brown, *J. William Fulbright: Advice and Consent* (Iowa City: University of Iowa Press, 1985), p. 16.

50. Perkins, *The Evolution of American Foreign Policy* (New York: Oxford University Press, 1948), especially Chapter 10. Others disagree with Perkins' interpretation, arguing, for example, that despite the ideals and precepts specified in its Charter, the United Nations was originally designed to provide collective security by establishing an overpowering anti-Axis coalition in keeping with the national interests of its founders.

51. Cook and Moos, *Power Through Purpose: The Realism of Idealism as a Basis for Foreign Policy* (Baltimore: Johns Hopkins Press, 1954); and "The American Idea of International Interest," *American Political Science Review* 47 (March 1953): 28-44.

52. Tannenbaum, *The American Tradition in Foreign Policy* (Norman: University Press of Oklahoma, 1955); "The American Tradition in Foreign Relations," *Foreign Affairs* 30 (October 1951): 31-50; and "The Balance of Power Versus the Coordinate State," *Political Science Quarterly* 67 (June 1952): 173-97. For a more recent view, emphasizing ideology, see Bayless Manning, "Goals, Ideology and Foreign Policy," *Foreign Affairs* 54 (January 1976): 271-84, and Bayless Manning, *The Conduct of United States Foreign Policy in the Nation's Third Century* (Claremont, Calif.: Claremont University Center, 1975), in which he discusses ideology and consensus, with analysis of five issues regarding American ideology for the future.

53. Lerche and Said, *Concepts of International Politics*, 3rd ed. (Englewood Cliffs, N.J.: Prentice-Hall, 1963), p. 27. Also see Frankel, *National Interest*, p. 15.

54. Vernon Van Dyke, "Values and Interests," *American Political Science Review* 56 (September 1962): 567; Feliks Gross, *Foreign Policy*

Analysis, p. 75; Charles Burton Marshall, *The Exercise of Sovereignty: Papers on Foreign Policy* (Baltimore: Johns Hopkins Press, 1965), pp. 29-33, 60-70; also Marshall "National Interest and National Responsibility," *Annals of the American Academy of Political and Social Sciences* 282 (July 1952): 84-90 in which he relates national interest, national power, and national responsibility, and "The National Interest and Current World Problems," *Department of State Bulletin* 26 (May 5, 1952): 699; and Raymond Aron, *Peace and War: A Theory of International Relations*, translated by Richard Howard and Annette Baker Fox (Garden City, N.Y.: Doubleday, 1966), p. 91.

55. *Christian Science Monitor*, July 24, 1981.

56. Needler, *Understanding Foreign Policy* (New York: Holt, Rinehart, and Winston, 1966), p. 4.

57. Edgar S. Furniss, Jr., and Richard C. Snyder, *An Introduction to American Foreign Policy* (New York: Rinehart, 1955), p. 16 and Alwyn H. King, "Flexible National Interests and U.S. Foreign Policy," *Military Review* 57 (April 1977): 80 refer to national interests as "wants or needs." Donald E. Nuechterlein defines them as "the perceived needs and desires of a sovereign state"; see his "The Concept of 'National Interest': A Time for New Approaches," *ORBIS* 23 (Spring 1979): 75; "National Interest and Foreign Policy," *Foreign Service Journal* 54 (July 1977): 6; and *America Over-committed: United States National Interests in the 1980s* (Lexington: University Press of Kentucky, 1985), p. 7. For additional commentary on the meaning and content of national interest, see Friedrich Kratochwil, "On the Notion of Interest in International Relations," *International Organization* 36 (Winter 1982): 1-30; and Alan Tonelson, "The Real National Interest," *Foreign Policy* 61 (Winter 1985-1986): 49-72.

58. Seabury, *Power, Freedom, and Diplomacy: The Foreign Policy of the United States of America* (New York: Random House, 1963), p. 82.

59. Morgenthau, *In Defense of the National Interest*, p. 34.

60. George and Keohane, "The Concept of National Interests: Uses and Limitations," *Report of the Commission on the Organization of the Government for the Conduct of Foreign Policy* (Washington: Government Printing Office, 1976), Appendixes, II, 65.

61. Good, "The National Interest and Political Realism: Niebuhr's 'Debate' with Morgenthau and Kennan," *Journal of Politics* 22 (November 1960): 597. For Niebuhr's views, see his *Christian Realism and Political Problems* (New York: Scribner, 1953), especially Chapters 1 and 2; *Christianity and Power Politics* (New York: Scribner, 1940), especially Chapters 4, 8, and 11; *The Irony of American History* (New York: Scribner, 1952); and *Moral Man and Immoral Society: A Study in Ethics and Politics* (New York: Scribner, 1934), especially Chapter 4, republished in 1960.

62. Lerche, *Foreign Policy of the American People*, 3rd ed. (Englewood Cliffs, N.J.: Prentice-Hall, 1967), p. 5.

63. "It depends," he says, "upon the effect of the particular interest on the general interest." Ernest W. LeFever, *Ethics and United States Foreign Policy*, p. 15.

64. Wolfers, "'National Security' as an Ambiguous Symbol," *Political Science Quarterly* 47 (December 1952): 481.

65. Aron, *Peace and War*, p. 92.

66. Morgenthau, "Another 'Great Debate': The National Interest of the United States," *American Political Science Review* 46 (December 1952): 973-78. In part, this responds to and amplifies a number of points made by Edward H. Carr in his *Nationalism and After* (New York: Macmillan, 1945); for commentary on Carr, also see Morgenthau, *Dilemmas of Politics*, Chapter 21. For additional commentary on this matter, regarding interests as ends, comparing the views of Osgood (see note 17) with those of Cook and Moos (see note 51), see Warner R. Schilling, "The Clarification of Ends: Or, Which Interest is the National," *World Politics* 8 (July 1956): 566-78.

67. Lippmann, *Essays in the Public Philosophy* (Boston: Little, Brown, 1955), Chapter 4.

68. Cassinelli, "Some Reflections on the Concept of the Public Interest," *Ethics* 69 (October 1958): 48-61; see also commentary of Frank J. Sorauf, "The Public Interest Reconsidered," *Journal of Politics* 19 (November 1957): 616-39, and Cassinelli's response, "Comments on Frank J. Sorauf's 'The Public Interest Reconsidered'," *Journal of Politics* 20 (August 1958): 553-56. Clarke E. Cochran, "Political Science and 'The Public Interest'," *Journal of Politics* 36 (March 1974): 327-55, also regards public interest as the common good.

69. Schubert, *The Public Interest: A Critique of the Theory of a Political Concept* (Glencoe, Ill.: Free Press, 1960); also his "'The Public Interest' in Administrative Decision-Making: Theorem, Theosophy, or Theory?" *American Political Science Review* 51 (June 1957): 346-68, in which he discusses how public interest is given credence by administrative officials and concludes that they have no unified theory on defining the concept and have produced no recognized theoretical model.

70. Lippmann, *Essays in the Public Philosophy*, pp. 31-42. Raymond Aron agrees that the interests of individuals and subnational groups do not constitute the general interest; see his *Peace and War*, pp. 91-92.

71. John Herz, "Political Realism Revisited" in the "Symposium in Honor of Hans J. Morgenthau," *International Studies Quarterly* 25 (June 1981): 182.

72. Richard K. Ashley, "Political Realism and Human Interests," in the "Symposium in Honor of Hans J. Morgenthau," pp. 204-36; and Robert C. Johansen, *The National Interest and the Human Interest: An Analysis of U.S. Foreign Policy* (Princeton: Princeton University Press, 1980), pp. 391-92.

73. Rochester, "The 'National Interest' and Contemporary World Politics," *Review of Politics* 40 (January 1978): 77-96, and "The Paradigm Debate in International Relations and Its Implications for Foreign Policy Making: Toward a Redefinition of the National Interest," *Western Political Quarterly* 31 (March 1978): 48-58; see also his paper "The 'National Interest' in the Conduct of Contemporary World Politics: Shifting Conceptions and Perceptions," prepared for the National Security Education Seminar, Colorado College (July 1975).

74. Joseph Frankel, *The Making of Foreign Policy: An Analysis of Decision Making* (New York: Oxford University Press, 1963), p. 55.

75. Osgood, *Ideals and Self-Interest*, p. 4.

76. "Defenses Against Menace of External and Internal Attack," address to House Foreign Affairs Committee, *Department of State Bulletin* 25 (July 9, 1951): 47.

77. See Gross, *Foreign Policy Analysis*, p. 53, and Osgood, *Ideals and Self-Interest*, p. 4.

78. Aron, *Peace and War*, p. 594.

79. Gross, *Foreign Policy Analysis*, pp. 53-54. In 1985 Ambassador Jeane Kirkpatrick observed: "Often people react as if the national interest were value free and amoral, as if it took no account of freedom, democracy, human rights and the civilization of which we are a part. In fact, all these good things...depend on the strength of our country." Francis Boyer Lecture, *The United States and the World: Setting Limits* (Washington: American Enterprise Institute, 1986), p. 2.

80. See Furniss and Snyder, *An Introduction to American Foreign Policy*, p. 17.

81. See Norman J. Padelford and George A. Lincoln, *The Dynamics of International Politics* (New York: Macmillan, 1962), p. 235. Also see George Modelski, *A Theory of Foreign Policy* (New York: Praeger, 1962), p. 71, who claims that national interests are never advocated by the "nation," but by "the policy-maker."

82. See Ernst B. Haas and Allen S. Whiting, *Dynamics of International Relations* (New York: McGraw-Hill, 1956), pp. 45-46.

83. Sondermann, "The Concept of the National Interest," pp. 131-32.

84. Department of State, *Our Foreign Policy*, 1952 (Washington: Government Printing Office, 1952), pp. 6-7.

85. Quoted in Gross, *Foreign Policy Analysis*, p. 78.

86. Quoted in Lester B. Pearson, *Democracy in World Politics* (Princeton: Princeton University Press, 1955), pp. 108-10.

87. Gross, *Foreign Policy Analysis*, pp. 78-79.

88. Lippmann, *Essays in the Public Philosophy*, pp. 41-42. This raises the issue of the will of the majority, how it is to be ascertained, and how valid and appropriate such determinations may be.

89. See Charles P. Schleicher, *International Behavior: Analysis and Operations* (Columbus: Merrill, 1973), p. 92.

90. See Modelski, *A Theory of Foreign Policy*, p. 70.

91. Briggs, *Anatomy of Diplomacy: The Origin and Execution of American Foreign Policy* (New York: McKay, 1968), p. 6.

92. Lerche, *Foreign Policy of the American People*, p. 4.

93. Morgenthau, "Another 'Great Debate': The National Interest of the United States," p. 972.

94. Marshall, "The National Interest and Current World Problems," p. 698.

95. Martin Needler differentiates "authentic" and "spurious" interests, see *Understanding Foreign Policy*, p. 12; and Dean Acheson distinguishes "immediate" and "long-term" interests, see "Defenses Against Menace of External and Internal Attack," p. 46.

96. Frankel, *National Interest*, Chapter 2.

97. Fulbright, Address to Congress, "Accomplishment of World Peace," October 9, 1973, in *Congressional Record*, 119, No. 150, p. 1.

98. Van Dyke, "Values and Interests," pp. 570-73.

99. Seabury, *Power, Freedom, and Diplomacy*, pp. 85-86. See also W. David Clinton, "The National Interest: Normative Foundations," *Review of Politics* 48 (Fall 1986): 495-519, in which he contends that much criticism of national interest on normative grounds results from confusion over the meaning of the concept which fails to distinguish between the common good of the national society and the concrete objects of value over which states bargain.

100. For example, according to Robert W. Tucker, Morgenthau arrives at certain "iron laws" or "elemental truths" that govern the behavior of states, whereas other analysts question whether the laws really govern or are merely presumed to apply. See Robert W. Tucker, "Morgenthau's Theory of Political 'Realism'," *American Political Science Review* 46 (March 1952): 216.

101. See Frankel, *National Interest*, pp. 16-17.

102. Address, "Accomplishment of World Peace," p. 1.

103. For example, see Morgenthau's summary analysis in "Another 'Great Debate': The National Interest of the United States," especially pp. 963-71, in which he defends his view of scientific theory. For commentary on supporters and critics of "Morgenthauism," see Robert O. Keohane, ed., *Neorealism and Its Critics* (New York: Columbia University Press, 1986).

104. On this issue also see John Herz, *Political Realism and Political Idealism* (Chicago: University of Chicago Press, 1951). One school of antirealism supports alternatives to power politics, as explained in the last section of Chapter 7. For example, see Louis René Beres, *Reason and Realpolitik: U.S. Foreign Policy and World Order* (Lexington, Mass.: Heath/Lexington, 1984); and Ray Maghroori and Bennett Ramberg, eds., *Globalism vs. Realism: International Relations Third Debate* (Boulder, Col.: Westview, 1982)--the first debate apposed realism vs. idealism, and the second involved traditionalism vs. behavioralism. For additional references on the matter of power politics vs. globalism, see note 254 of Chapter 7.

105. Inis L. Claude, commenting on John Herz in "Symposium in Honor of Hans J. Morgenthau," pp. 198-200. Claude also stresses the distinction between "soft" and "hard" idealists and realists.

106. Morgenthau, *In Defense of the National Interest*, pp. 33-34, 38-39. On his theory of international relations, also see his *Dilemmas of Politics*, Chapter 3.

107. Morgenthau, "The Primacy of the National Interest," *The American Scholar* 18 (Spring 1949): 208, 212.

108. Acheson, *Present at the Creation: My Years in the State Department* (New York: Norton, 1969), p. 461. Also see his essay on "Morality, Moralism, and Diplomacy," *Yale Review* 47 (June 1958): 481-93.

109. Quoted in Harry M. Joiner, *American Foreign Policy: The Kissinger Era* (Huntsville, Alabama: Strode Publishers, 1977), pp. 301-2. See also Kissinger's comments on the conflict between and confluence of morality and pragmatism in his *For the Record: Selected Statements, 1977-1980* (Boston: Little, Brown, 1981), pp. 78-80. For commentary on how Secretary of State Charles Evans Hughes' "tendancy to frame American interests in terms of general principles did have a positive aspect" of producing "a restrained and balanced statement of American interests," see Betty Glad, *Charles Evans Hughes and the Illusion of Innocence* (Urbana: University of Illinois Press, 1966), pp. 319-20.

110. Morgenthau, "Another 'Great Debate': The National Interest of the United States," p. 963.

111. Aron, *Peace and War*, pp. 89-92, 280, 285. For systematic policy-making, Aron prefers what he calls "the national constants," see pp. 285-91.

112. Crabb, *American Foreign Policy in the Nuclear Age* (Evanston, Ill.: Row, Peterson, 1960), p. 502. In Crabb's revised edition, he changed this to "the sole guide" (1965), p. 465. In both editions he admits, however, that it serves as an antidote or corrective against debilitating tendencies that interfere with successful foreign policy.

113. Brower, *The U.S. National Interest: Assertions and Definitions* (Cambridge: Center for International Studies, Massachusetts Institute of Technology, 1959).

114. Marshall, "The National Interest and Current World Problems," pp. 698-99; also see pp. 701-2. Also note Max Weber's comments on what he calls the "ethic of responsibility," in which he compares justification of means and ends, "Politics as a Vocation," *From Max Weber: Essays in Sociology*, translated by H. H. Gerth and C. Wright Mills (New York: Oxford University Press, 1946), especially pp. 120-28. See also note 54.

115. Rosenau, "National Interest," *International Encyclopedia of the Social Sciences* (1968), XI, especially pp. 34, 36, 39.

116. George and Keohane, "The Concept of National Interests," pp. 64-65.

117. Sondermann, "The Concept of the National Interest," Section IV, especially p. 135.

118. Nuechterlein, *America Overcommitted;* also see his *National Interests and Presidential Leadership: The Setting of Priorities* (Boulder, Colo.: Westview, 1978); *United States National Interests in a Changing World* (Lexington: University Press of Kentucky, 1973); "The Concept of 'National Interest': A Time for New Approaches," pp. 73-92; and "National Interest and Foreign Policy," pp. 6-8, 27.

119. Marshall, "The National Interest and Current World Problems," p. 699.

120. Morgenthau, "Another 'Great Debate': The National Interest of the United States," p. 972.

121. See the assessment of William Reitzell, Morton A. Kaplan, and Constance G. Coblenz, *United States Foreign Policy, 1945-1955* (Washington: Brookings Institution, 1956), pp. 471-72.

122. Morgenthau, *Politics Among Nations* (1948 ed.), p. 6.

123. Morgenthau, "The Mainsprings of American Foreign Policy," p. 854.

124. Holsti, *International Politics: A Framework for Analysis* (Englewood Cliffs, N.J.: Prentice-Hall, 1967), p. 126.

125. Gross, *Foreign Policy Analysis*, p. 77.

126. Lippmann, *Essays in the Public Philosophy*, p. 36.

127. See Briggs, *Anatomy of Diplomacy*, p. 6, and Fred Greene, *Dynamics of International Relations: Power, Security, and Order* (New York: Holt, Rinehart, and Winston, 1964), p. 37.

128. Mill, quoted in Eugene E. Brussell, ed., *Dictionary of Quotable Definitions* (Englewood Cliffs, N.J.: Prentice-Hall, 1970), p. 292.

129. Northedge, *The Foreign Policies of the Powers* (New York: Free Press, 1974), pp. 18-19.

130. Mowrer, *Our Foreign Affairs*, pp. 307, 309. He discusses this matter in Part IV, Chapter 1, which he entitles "Our Manifold Interests."

131. See also commentary on multiple national interests in the introductory section of Chapter 3.

132. See, for example, Holsti, *International Politics*, p. 126; Marshall, "The National Interest and Current World Problems," p. 699; and Padelford and Lincoln, *The Dynamics of International Politics*, p. 235.

133. For purposes of clarifying usage, Frankel also adds: "It should help us to reconcile and synthesize in contemporary terms the traditionally opposed idealist and realist, power political and irenical, approaches." See Frankel, "National Interest: A Vindication," *International Journal* 24 (Autumn 1969): 720.

3

VITAL INTERESTS

Politics is the science of the vital interests of
States in its widest meaning . . . The great axioms
of political science proceed from the knowledge of
the true political interests of all states; it is
upon these general interests that rests the guarantee of their existence.

Metternich, *Memoirs*

Any serious foreign policy must begin with the need
for survival. And survival has its practical neces-
sities. A nation does not willingly delegate control over its future. For a great power to remit
its security to the mercy of others is an abdication of foreign policy.

Henry A. Kissinger, Lecture 1977

Except for the use of the expression national interest in the
singular either as THE NATIONAL INTEREST (the transcendent
dictum equated with survival) or *The National Interest* (the
undefined agglomerate), as noted in the preceding chapter,
conceptual interpretations presume the plurality if not the
multiplicity of interests. Many political leaders and analysts refer to interests that are vital, implying that there
must be other types of interests, also knowledging an array
of interests. Lord Brougham, early nineteenth century
British parliamentarian, observed: "All particular interests, prejudices, or partialities must be sacrificed to the
higher interest . . . of uniting against oppression or a-
gainst the measures which appear to place the security of
all in jeopardy."[1] Others that pragmatize examples usually
list series of what they regard as national interests, ranging from self-preservation and other vital interests to additional important and lesser concrete interests.

To illustrate, F. S. Northedge prescribes the following
as basic categories of interests, in descending order of seriousness: (1) self-preservation ("the maintenance of physical integrity of the country and unity of its people," to
which, he says, all else including ideology must be subordi-
nated on the basis of the principle *salus populi suprema
lex*); (2) independence ("relative freedom" from interference

in internal affairs by other powers and "an independent
viewpoint on external affairs"); (3) role in the international community (such "attributes" as influence, authority,
status, or simply "pull"); (4) stake in the international
system (rights and privileges exercised beyond the nation's
borders and commitments and obligations the nation shoulders,
which must take into consideration the interests of other
countries in the international order); and (5) the "expectations and demands of the people" in relation to higher living
standards (which, in the last analysis, "will if necessary be
sacrificed for 'higher' national interests," as in wartime).[2]

On the other hand, simply exemplifying a random sampling, Charles Burton Marshall lists the following "as clearly in our national interest: To avoid war; to avoid infla-
tion; to have a prosperous civilian economy; to find common
grounds on which to stand with the various nations which have
newly come to responsibility; to preserve our access to strategic waterways and vital raw materials; and to protect property and safety of our nationals abroad."[3] Conceived as national concerns, such functional interests of nations can be
proliferated endlessly.

CATEGORIES OF NATIONAL INTERESTS

Although the range is extensive and complex, the degree
of concern with particular national interests varies from the
crucial (evidenced by those that are deemed to be absolute
and affect the nation's very existence) to the important
(which are consequential though not necessarily crucial) and
the subordinate (which, though desirable, are clearly neither
absolute nor critical). Under this broad interpretation,
national interests reflect varying degrees of significance
and may be situational and procedural as well as substantive,
contemporary as well as historic, malleable as well as in-
flexible, tangential as well as pivotal, and negotiable as
well as indispensable. Viewed in this manner, in practice if
not in theory, at times specific interests may be competitive
or even conflicting, so that choices must be made in fixing
priorities, based on the nation's imperatives and desires,
and sometimes on their practicality.

Given such a panoply of interests, and their differing
impact on the foreign relations process, it is clearly necessary for both policy making and analysis to weigh and
structure them in a rational way. The literature is replete
with volunteers. Even Hans J. Morgenthau, who wrote so liberally on THE NATIONAL INTEREST, recognized a distinction
between it, which he describes as "primary," and lesser interests.[4] Similarly Morton Kaplan, who argues that "there
are as many national interests as national needs," differentiates between "the national interest" and "other interests."[5]

While most policy makers and analysts recognize this
distinction between primary and secondary interests, other
obvious comparisons can be made between domestic and foreign,
long-term and short-term, inchoate (rudimentary or incipient)
and actual (genuine), permanent and variable, and global and

regional (to which might be added subregional and neighbor to
neighbor) interests, as well as among interests that reflect
past, present, and future applicability.[6] Addressing themselves to criteria for delineation, Thomas W. Robinson stresses three fundamental types--those based on the degree of
primacy, the degree of permanence, and the degree of generality of interests,[7] and Martin E. Goldstein defines nine specific criteria for assessing events and relations in deducing
a nation's security interests, ranging from proximity, importance of physical and population resources, and trade and
markets to military power.[8]

Several analysts seek to project more systematic, comprehensive, or theoretical distinctions. In addition to
Northedge's hierarchical delineation, for example, Joseph
Frankel compares aspirational, operational, and explanatory/
polemical interests. He proposes seven qualities of the
aspirational, which he regards as long-term interests, and
eight for operational or short-term interests. The aspirational apply to "the vision of the good life," the operational embody the totality of interests actually pursued, and
the explanatory/polemical encompass those employed in political argument--to explain, evaluate, rationalize, or criticize
foreign relations behavior. He also supports refinement
founded on what he calls inconsonant structural, behavioral,
and relational factors in identifying "significant and logically coherent" categories, and suggests discernment based
on "cognitive and volitional (or effective) and other variables."[9]

Morton Kaplan prefers a different approach, analyzing
the interests of five "system levels"--consisting of individuals and subnational, national, supranational, and international systems, which stand "on an equal footing" so that
there is "no natural order of priority" by which one system
level "ought to defer to another." While this categorizes
systems levels, further extrapolation is essential to identify subsidiary categories within them.[10] Vernon Van Dyke
devotes much of his attention to fundamental hierarchical
interrelations, distinguishing between "independent interests" (those that are assumed, postulated, and accepted on
faith--or what ought to be for its own sake) and "dependent
interests" (those that are instrumental and serve the independent interests).[11]

Contemplating inherent significance some writers and
practitioners emphasize what they designate "minimum interests" or an "irreducible core" of interests. Representing
this view, George Modelski declares: "In the process of coordinating the interests of their community, policy-makers
cannot ignore the rule that a certain minimum of interests
belong to all members of the community [i.e., the nation]"
which "must at all costs be safeguarded" and which "are so
important and so well grounded that they turn into 'principles' and gain unquestionable and unreasoned acceptance" so
that they "become part of the articles of faith and are up-
held with great vigor."[12] Put another way, Alexander George
and Robert Keohane simply distinguish between "irreducible
national interests" and such "other interests" that are not
elevated to the rank of national interests. In the case of

the United States, they maintain, the irreducible are only
threefold--physical survival, liberty, and economic subsis-
tence.[13]   Alwyn H. King also speaks of a nation's "irreducible core of interests," but he equates them all with vital
interests.[14]

Whatever the categorization, many statesmen and writers
utilize the term "vital interests" as a working concept, differentiating them from those that are less than vital. Commentary on these interests is more limited and less structured than that on the general concept of national interests
and such analysis engages in less debate on issues of morality and theory building, or objectivity versus subjectivity,
or their import in the foreign relations process. Nevertheless, in both practice and analysis the expression the vital
interests of the nation is the most commonly recognized category of national interests--a term employed universally in
the plural except when applied to some specific essential
interest.   Governments thereby acknowledge a hierarchical
ranking in that not all their national interests are vital,
and those that are override the non-vital in the conduct of
foreign affairs.

Some analysts, basing their assessments on importance,
as already noted, prefer to differentiate largely between
primary and secondary interests.   But because interests may
theoretically be primary without being vital, or they may be
non-vital and still be viewed as more important than those of
secondary significance, some writers prefer a more sophisticated delineation.   Assuming that survival may be regarded
either as superior to or within the purview of the vital and
that major non-vital interests are more important than lesser
concerns, it would seem logical that several distinct categories of national interests need to be prescribed.

However delineated, the most critical problems with categorization are the lack of agreement on the nature and application of explicit criteria to assess the degree of "vitalness" or intensity of national interests and the absence
of a universalized method of determination.   The problem
hinges on how and where the dividing line between categories
is drawn, and this is determinable, even so far as concrete
details affecting national self-preservation are concerned,
from the pronouncements and actions of national governments.
It would seem that vital is that which a nation deems to be
essential, which it will not willingly forsake, and for which
if necessary it will fight--diplomatically, politically, and
militarily.

To systematize thinking and usage, George and Keohane
developed a model of analysis consisting of two sets of primary factors--namely, "scope of interests principally affected" and the "seriousness of effects." The first of these
distinguishes the interests of the nation from those of the
international system collectively and those of other states
and their nationals.   The sub-categories of seriousness of
effects include those that are either major or minor. According to this framework, so far as the national interests
of a given country are concerned, analysis merely requires
differentiating between the major and the minor.[15]

The analytical system of Donald E. Nuechterlein--which he describes as his "national interest matrix"--is more sophisticated and useful. It establishes two essential sets of factors, designated "basic interest at stake" and "intensity of interest," and each of these consists of four components. The basic functional interests at stake embrace (1) "defense of the homeland" (protection of the people, territory, and institutions of the nation against foreign dangers--or the national defense interest); (2) "economic well-being" (promotion of trade and investment, including protection of private interests in foreign countries--or the national economic interest); (3) "favorable world order" (establishment and maintenance of a peaceful international environment in which disputes can be resolved peacefully and mutual defense and collective security operate to deter aggression--or the international security interest); and (4) "promotion of values" or "ideology" (the promulgation and support of ideals presumed to be universally good and worthy of emulation by other nations).

The intensity of interests, which Nuechterlein admits may vary from time to time, consist in descending order of four components: (1) "survival" (where the very existence of the nation is in peril); (2) "vital" (where probable serious harm to the security and well-being of the nation will result if strong measures, possibly including military action, are not taken rapidly; (3) "major" (where potential harm could result to the nation if no action is taken to counter unfavorable developments); and (4) "peripheral" or minor (where little if any harm will result if action is deferred). This gradation incorporates consideration of the time dimension, with survival interests demanding immediate attention, vital interests necessitating urgent planning, major interests requiring serious study, and peripheral interests suggesting "watchful waiting." To apply this matrix to policy making or re-analysis it is necessary, therefore, to make decisions on the substantive essence of the nation's concerns to identify those that are vital, degrees of intensity, and urgency--with sets of priorities inherent in all determinations.[16]

Vexatious problems of discernment and application arise, whatever the system of categorization. To note some of the most difficult and significant, at the outset it is essential to fabricate dependable and stable criteria for differentiating among categories, even if they are inherently hierarchical. Second, if distinction is founded on such factors as importance, short-term and long-term time relevance, or other major intrinsic relationships (independent/dependent, minimum or irreducible/comprehensive, global/regional) lines of delineation need to be established. In short, vital interests must be distinguishable from other categories of national interests. Third, if substantive interests are extrapolated comprehensively--projecting not only primary but also secondary and subsidiary interests--attention must be paid to actual and potential conflict among them, in which the successful pursuance of one interest may contravene or invalidate the quest of another. In addition, as with national interests in general, the same problems of subjective versus objective prescription, determination by government leaders and the role of popular approval, and pragmatic state practice as compared with theoretical analysis arise, which are discussed in the preceding chapter.

CONCEPTUAL INTERPRETATION OF VITAL INTERESTS

While considerable analysis concerning national interests in general is conceptualistic, seeking to elucidate fundamental meaning and relevance to the foreign relations process, commentary on vital interests tends instead to pragmatize the concept, which is reflected in attempts to designate concrete interests that are regarded as vital to a given nation at a particular time. Those few who address themselves to its conceptual meaning nevertheless vary substantially in their definitions.

Propounding his fourfold categorization, Nuechterlein focuses on interests that are subsidiary to survival but portend potential serious harm and require urgent though not necessarily immediate response. He contends that survival interests denote "an imminent, credible threat of massive destruction to the homeland" and that vital interests are those that may utimately be crucial to the nation, are potential rather than imminent, and are "so important to a nation's well-being that its leadership will refuse to compromise beyond the point that it considers to be tolerable."[17]

Others generally conjoin survival and other critical interests as vital interests but differ in their conceptualizations. For example, Walter Lippmann writes: "When we speak of the 'vital interests of the nation' we mean those interests which the people of the nation are agreed they must defend at the risk of their lives . . . for which they are prepared to die" because such interests "transcend their own lives." He introduces the concept of popular endorsement and recognizes the possibility of sacrificing life by means other than warfare.[18] K. J. Holsti supports this interpretation, describing it as a core of interests for which "most people are willing to make ultimate sacrifices."[19]

An alternative interpretation perceives vital interests as those over which a nation will go to war. Frederick H. Hartmann, writing in 1957, called vital interests "an irreducible core" of national interests "for which a state is normally willing to go to war immediately or ultimately." To test whether an interest is vital, he says, is simple--"will a nation, unless it feels hopelessly outclassed in terms of power, ultimately go to war to preserve it? If the answer is affirmative, it is considered a vital interest." Later he broadened his conception, substituting the idea of willingness to "fight for" vital interests rather than "going to war" over them, and added that, if interests are vital, alternatives will be rejected out of hand and that non-vital interests are not worth a war and may not even be achieved by violence.[20] This view is supported by others, such as Vernon Van Dyke, who qualifies his position by stating that the nation "is willing to wage war if necessary."[21] Some construe it as being willing "to fight for,"[22] which is not limited solely to warfare. Others go so far as to include fighting

even a doomed war,[23] while still others temporize by recognizing a gradation of possibilities running the gamut of
available means, with war as only the last resort.

A third, historically more flexible and useful interpretation stipulates:

> Vital interests are those national interests that
> are indispensable and intrinsically non-negotiable;
> they are those interests that the nation will not
> willingly or voluntarily bargain away, irrespective
> of the inducement, that it holds to be absolute on
> which it is unwilling to make detrimental or de-
> meaning concessions, and conversely, that it will
> preserve at any cost, including resort to force if
> necessary.

At least by implication, this prescription is supported by
Nuechterlein, which he describes as unwillingness to compromise beyond certain limits, and by Joseph Frankel who contends: "The traditional hallmark of an interest which is
deemed to be vital is that the state is unwilling to make
concessions on it and that it is prepared, if necessary, to
go to war over it."[24] This interpretation has the advantage
of broadening the options of action beyond simply either
giving in on the nation's most consequential interests or
turning to force. In times of crisis, when conflict over
vital interests is most crucial, it allows room for living
with the problem while continuing negotiation without either
backing down or going to war.

SUBSTANCE AND PRAGMATIZATION OF VITAL INTERESTS

At a minimum, as noted, vital interests are acknowledged
to include the preservation of independence, national identity, and territorial integrity--sometimes expressed as the
maintenance of national sovereignty--and they are also usually held to encompass freedom from foreign subversion or military invasion and the safeguarding of the national political, economic, and social order against foreign or internal
interference, the preservation of national well-being, and
the conservation of the nation's honor and prestige. Such
broadly conceived vital or irreducible national interests are
applicable to all nations and therefore may be taken for
granted. Thus generalized, as a package they differ little
from the conception of "The National Interest" as a symbol,
an agglomerate, or perhaps an aggregate, three of the versions of national interest referred to in Chapter 2.

However, if the panoply of vital interests are subjected
to specialized refinement--as when delineated in practical
international politics--they vary from country to country and
time to time. They may embrace, by way of illustration, the
protection of certain legal rights (self-determination, diplomatic inviolability, expatriation, and freedom of international transit), and particular international roles of the
nation (involvement in international decision-making, in diplomatic relations and the negotiation of treaties, and in
trade relations necessary to maintain economic existence).

They may also pertain to a number of established international practices--guaranteeing the personal security and respect-
ful treatment of political leaders visiting foreign lands,
the appointment of ambassadors and other diplomats, the
launching of space probes, the preservation of national territory from serving as a base of military operations by a
foreign power without its own consent, and many others. These
must then be applied to concrete sets of circumstances.

To systematize this consideration, Nuechterlein established a table of sixteen factors to ascertain whether particular national interests are vital. Eight of them he calls
"value factors," such as the proximity of the danger, the
nature of the threat, the economic stake involved, and the
effect on key allies and the balance of power. Among his
eight "cost/risk factors" he includes economic costs of hostilities, estimated casualties, risk of protracted and of
enlarged conflict, cost of defeat or stalemate, and risk of
public opposition. Each of these factors--applied in terms
of its significance to a specific foreign relations consideration, even if attempt is made to assess them on the basis
of a calibrated scale--is intended, he claims, to furnish a
basic guideline to systematize policy formulation, not necessarily to produce a precisely quantified or empirical
calibration.[25] In this, as in many other foreign relations
determinations, additional factors need to be considered and
judgments respecting both factor assessments and final decisions admittedly are bound to be subjective.

So far as pragmatization is concerned, government leaders normally restrain themselves to specifying only the most
important and constant, or in concrete sets of circumstances,
to particular vital interests. Aside from those more general
interests already mentioned, more finite vital interests differ from case to case, and in matters of policy planning it
may be necessary to extend consideration to the assessment
of alternative but explicit sets of possibilities, with attention paid to the management of events by diplomatic and
other political processes.

The problem of drawing the dividing line between the
vital and lesser categories of national interests is that the
obvious dictionary definition--as that which is essential to
survival or otherwise important--is inadequate because, as a
matter of foreign relations practice, judgment is subject to
human and political interpretation. Each nation decides for
itself those matters that it deems to be vital, and there are
no objectively prescribable or automatic precepts for producing this delineation. The result is considerable diversity
between minimal vital interests--the irreducible core--and a
potential maximal spectrum of concerns regarded as vital.
Some statesmen and analysts may even predicate degrees of
"vitalness" and regard the concept of vital interests as a
flexible catchall for those specific concerns that are held
to be of transcendent importance to the nation, which tends
to produce exaggeration, and may lead to serious miscalculation. Another problem flows from the difficulty of periodically re-assessing and overhauling the hierarchy of the nation's interests to accord with new realities in a rapidly
changing world.

CONFRONTATION OVER VITAL INTERESTS

History reveals that, as in the case of national interests in general, the vital interests of two or more nations are diversely interrelated. If they have little or no direct impingement upon one another, no serious international problem arises. When they parallel each other--in cases of concurrently standing up to an aggressor, aligning fiscal and trade policies to avert widespread economic or financial crisis, or combating the spread of a devastating plague--they are jointly supportive and are likely to lead to mutual cooperation. On the other hand, even where vital interests are identical they may be competitive--though not necessarily non-negotiable. Thus, two neighboring countries may desire a boundary settlement, neither being willing to concede the entire contested territory to the other, but if each can salvage the element that is most essential to it--perhaps a coastline, a river basin, a port, certain economic resources, or a national minority--a compromise may be achievable and the vital interests thereby accommodated.

Or equally intent upon maintaining their security--against each other--two countries may nevertheless find areas of negotiability, such as the renunciation of a particular type of weapon or disarmament of their mutual frontier, and thus reach understanding resulting in the reciprocal preservation of their individual interests. For example, in U.S.-Soviet strategic nuclear weapons negotiations, neither side is prepared to accept an arrangement that leaves it vulnerable or substantially inferior, though both may be willing to compromise on specific types of weaponry, facilities, or other concessions.

However, when nations, particularly those that possess relatively equal power or potential, confront one another on a matter that each regards as involving its non-negotiable vital interests, their relations reach a particularly critical stage, and, as emphasized by Nuechterlein, correctly assessing the intensity of an adversary's national interest is imperative in determining the nation's policy and action. In many such instances, as in the Berlin and Cuban missile crises, the alternatives of backing down on vital interests and going to war may be unacceptable options. If both sides are unwilling to risk the possible consequences of military confrontation, additional alternatives need to be sought, and frequently they are. President John Kennedy made this clear when, in his foreign policy address on June 10, 1963, he warned that "while defending our own vital interests," the United States and other nuclear powers "must avert those confrontations which bring an adversary to a choice of either a humiliating retreat or a nuclear war."[26]

In state practice--as distinct from theoretical considerations--when situations arise that pose a serious threat to the nation's vital interests, policy makers must make a series of difficult decisions. What is the nature of the threat, the magtitude of the possible damage to the nation's interests, the need for initiatory or responsive action, the optional courses of action that may be taken, and the feasibility, risks, costs, and likely consequences of implementing the alternatives?

     Most crisis situations in international politics arise,
and the most crucial choices must be made, when important
political stakes involving vital interests hinge upon the
possibility of resorting to military force. When nations
pursue antithetical vital interests to the point of irreducible non-negotiability--that is, to paraphrase Secretary of
State Dean Rusk's characterization, they stand eyeball to
eyeball waiting for the other side to blink--and the options
are reduced to either one of the disputants backing down or
resorting to war, if neither nation really wants war, they
may turn to a third option--namely, mutually backing off from
the confrontation, accompanied by negotiations concerning
peripheral aspects of the issue. Even though this alternative
does not resolve the primary issue, neither side is obliged
to surrender on its vital interest, and backing off may amel-
iorate the criticality of the negotiatory impasse and thus
avert the possibility of hostilities. The function of diplomacy then is to manage the retreat from the brink in such a
way as to be mutually accommodating, usually affording reciprocal face-saving for the participants.

     The longer-range task of policy-making, on the other
hand, is to devise tactical processes in such a way as to
avert escalation to a climax of frozen confrontation over
vital interests. In practice, negotiation on most issues is
restrained from reaching this crisis stage by deliberately
injecting policy flexibility and room for diplomatic maneu-
ver--by keeping options open. In other words, as the relations of nations advance to the point of impasse over vital
interests, particularly among relatively equal major powers,
governments often search for those aspects of the issue on
which negotiations may continue in order to avert the alternatives of abject backing down or open warfare.   If both
parties are willing, they generally find ways to return the
disputed issue to the *status quo ante* of negotiability, and
sometimes, as in the East-West conflict over the Berlin situation, they mutually accede to an arrangement that, although
not preferred by either nation, is condoned as "livable" in
the sense that more severe alternatives are unacceptable.

     In such time of crisis policy makers need to carefully
rationalize their options to avoid wishful thinking in broad
moral terms or miscalculation, as well as either risky pro-
crastination or peremptory and extreme reaction unconcerned
with risk, cost, or consequences. When possible and desirable, they must seek ways of minimizing deleterious effects
on vital interests while maximizing amelioration of conflict
although the central issues may not be resolved. Criticality
of confrontation is especially acute when a nation is subjected to an ultimatum. In such cases, reaction requires a
staged process--negotiating modification or removal of the
time limit, and then coping with the substantive issues.[27]

     Because the tolls of modern warfare are so great, es-
pecially among nuclear powers, international politics produce
not only a continuum of challenges, demands, probings, maneu-
verings, and counteractions, but also, significantly, determined demarches from the threshold of confrontation over

vital interests. Nations are most likely to go to war when
they miscalculate the "vitalness" of the interests of others
(to say nothing of misjudging their own), when they become
convinced that they can maintain their own interests and
secure their objectives with relative advantages by threating
violence, or even at the cost of resorting to hostilities
when they fail to discern any acceptable alternative, or when
they permit the situation to escalate to the height of such
unmanageability that forces set in motion cannot be con-
strained or reversed. Sometimes, however, crises may be
averted or moderated if vital interests are revealed clearly
and early enough, are propounded with sufficient cogency,
conviction, and credibility, and are sustained by tangible
and forceful persuasion.

It goes without saying, therefore, that nations and
their leaders are foolhardy to be extravagant or cavalier
about the nation's interests. Both understatement and over-
statement that may produce miscalculation by the adversary
are hazardous. If understated, the nation may be bluffed or
outmaneuvered to its disadvantage, but if overstated its
bluff may be called and it may face confrontation and need to
back down or risk war. It is imperative, therefore, that the
nation's goals, policies, and commitments do not exceed its
ability to sustain them, that it clearly defines for itself
and for others, including its adversaries, those interests on
which it will stand, and that it is prepared to negotiate on
matters that are not truly vital.

NOTES

1. Lord Brougham, quoted in Norman A. Graebner, ed., *Ideas and Diplomacy: Readings in the Intellectual Tradition of American Foreign Policy*
(New York: Oxford University Press, 1964), p. 5.

2. Northedge, *The Foreign Policies of the Powers* (New York: Free
Press, 1968), pp. 19-20. Some prefer a more modest list--reduced to survival, economic well-being, and national prestige; see Gene E. Rainey,
Patterns of American Foreign Policy (Boston: Allyn and Bacon, 1975), pp.
5-6.

3. Marshall,"The National Interest and Current World Problems," *De-
partment of State Bulletin* 26 (May 5, 1952): 699. See also commentary in
Richard A. Watson, *Promise and Performance of American Democracy* (New
York: Wiley, 1975), p. 568.

4. Morgenthau acknowledges that the United States "has one primary
national interest" and "a number of secondary interests"--which he denotes as his number one principle for guiding foreign policy; see *A New
Foreign Policy for the United States* (New York: Praeger, 1969), p. 241.

5. Kaplan, *Systems and Process in International Politics* (New York:
Wiley, 1957), p. 151 and title to Chapter 8.

6. For example, assessing United States national interests, Anthony
Lake identifies priorities among four regional interests and also among
four long-term interests, which he calls ideals or goals; see his "Defining the National Interest," *Proceedings of the American Academy of Political and Social Science* 34, No. 2 (1981): 202-3.

7. Robinson, "A National Interest Analysis of Sino-Soviet Relations," *International Studies Quarterly* 11 (June 1967): 135-75. His commentary is based largely on the writings of Morgenthau, in which he finds delineations not only of primary/secondary interests but also of general/specific and identical/complementary/conflicting categorizations; see pp. 138-41.

8. Goldstein, "The Role of National Interests in International Relations," *Intellect* 104 (November 1975): 157-61.

9. Frankel, *National Interest* (New York: Praeger, 1970) pp. 31-38, 52-54; see also his *Contemporary International Theory and the Behavior of States* (New York: Oxford University Press, 1973), pp. 78-79.

10. Kaplan, *Systems and Process in International Politics*, pp. 156-65.

11. Van Dyke, "Values and Interests," *American Political Science Review* 56 (September 1962): 568-73.

12. Modelski, *A Theory of Foreign Policy* (New York: Praeger, 1962), pp. 86-87.

13. George and Keohane, "The Concept of National Interest: Uses and Limitations," *Report of the Commission on the Organization of the Government for the Conduct of Foreign Policy* (Washington: Government Printing Office, 1976), Appendixes, II, 67-71.

14. King, "Flexible National Interests and U.S. Foreign Policy," *Military Review* 57 (April 1977): 80. See also Frederick Hartmann below and note 20.

15. For depiction, see Figure in George and Keohane, "The Concept of National Interest," p. 67.

16. Nuechterlein, *America Overcommitted: United States National Interests in the 1980s* (Lexington: University Press of Kentucky, 1985), Chapter 1, and *National Interests and Presidential Leadership: The Setting of Priorities* (Boulder, Colo.: Westview, 1978), Chapter 1. See also his "National Interest and Foreign Policy," *Foreign Service Journal* 54 (July 1977): 6-8, 27 and "The Concept of 'National Interest': A Time for New Approaches," *ORBIS* 23 (Spring 1979): 75-80. For his earlier version, see his *United States National Interests in a Changing World* (Lexington: University Press of Kentucky, 1973), Chapter 1.

17. Nuechterlein, *America Overcommitted*, pp. 10-11. He also distinguishes vital from major interests, a difference he deems "crucial"; see pp. 17-19. See also his *National Interests and Presidential Leadership*, pp. 4-12, and *United States National Interests in a Changing World*, pp. 9-15.

18. Lippmann, *U.S. Foreign Policy: Shield of the Republic* (Boston: Little, Brown, 1943), p. 86.

19. Holsti, *International Politics: A Framework for Analysis* (Englewood Cliffs, N.J.: Prentice-Hall, 1967), p. 132.

20. Hartmann, *The Relations of Nations* (New York: Macmillan, 1957), pp. 5, 73; for his later version, see *The Relations of Nations*, 5th ed. (New York: Macmillan, 1978), pp. 7, 76.

21. Van Dyke, *International Politics* (New York: Appleton-Century-Crofts, 1957), p. 200.

22. Such as Bernard Brodie, *War and Politics* (New York: Macmillan, 1973), p. 342, who describes vital interests as those for which nations "are ready to fight to preserve."

23. For example, see Charles O. Lerche, Jr., *Principles of International Politics* (New York: Oxford University Press, 1956), p. 121.

24. Frankel, *National Interest*, pp. 73-74. He also argues that vital interests apply mainly to the strategic/political sphere and are essential "for national survival and for the attainment of many national goals"; see p. 76.

25. Nuechterlein, *National Interests and Presidential Leadership*, Chapter 2, with table of factors on p. 26 accompanied by discussion on pp. 21-37. For an earlier version, see his *United States National Interests in a Changing World*, Chapter 2.

26. Kennedy, *Public Papers of the Presidents: John F. Kennedy, 1963* (Washington: Government Printing Office, 1964), p. 462.

27. For commentary on problems of "operationalizing" national interests in crisis situations, see George and Keohane, "The Concept of National Interest," pp. 72-74.

4

NATIONAL PURPOSES

Men want to be part of a common enterprise, a cause greater than themselves. And each of us must find a way to advance the purpose of the Nation, thus finding new purpose in ourselves.
> Lyndon B. Johnson, Inaugural Address,
> January 20, 1965

Until he has been part of a cause larger than himself, no man is truly whole.
> Richard M. Nixon, Inaugural Address,
> January 20, 1969

Among his basic precepts for the conduct of foreign relations, diplomatic historian Thomas A. Bailey declares: "Policies without purpose are pointless"--which has been documented throughout the ages.[1] In the seventeenth century French moralist Francois de La Rochefoucauld observed: "However brilliant an action may be, it should not be accounted great when it is not the result of a great purpose."[2] Emphasizing the need for motivating public purposes, Kingman Brewster, then President of Yale University and later Ambassador to Great Britain, maintains: "A nation, like a person, needs to believe that it has a mission greater than itself,"[3] and reiterating the relationship of citizens to national purpose, in 1970 President Richard Nixon told Congress: "The greatest privilege an individual can have is to serve in a cause bigger than himself."[4]

However, in 1959 columnist and political philosopher Walter Lippmann warned America: "the critical weakness of our society is that . . . our people do not have great purposes which they are united in wanting to achieve . . . . We talk of ourselves these days as if we were a completed society, one which has achieved its purposes, and has no further great business to transact." The United States, he added, is dominated by the attitude that it has "fulfilled and outlived most of what we used to regard as the program of our national purposes" and "they do not now mobilize our energies."[5]

Since the days of early statesmen like Washington and Jefferson, who propounded unity of the people for "the common

good," political leaders have been concerned with the viability of "the American experiment." Whereas earlier leaders
stressed the concept of national interests, every President
since World War II has raised--many times--the issue of the
fundamental aims of the nation. Reviewing the state of the
nation in his annual message to Congress in January 1980, for
example, President Jimmy Carter while lauding the traditional
willingness of Americans "to sacrifice for larger goals,"
nevertheless emphasized the urgent need of the people to
"rise above narrow interests" and forge "a new national consensus and sense of purpose."[6]

A year later, in his inaugural address President Ronald
Reagan appealed to Americans to "begin an era of national renewal," "dream heroic dreams," and focus on reviving faith in
the nation and its credibility and prestige at home and
abroad.[7] Putting it bluntly, Secretary of State Alexander
Haig, critical of what he termed "excessive American intro-
spection," proclaimed it necessary to overcome the uncertainty "of our purposes" and to achieve a national consensus, a
resurgence of the American spirit, and restoration of national self-respect, pride, and confidence in the American
dream.[8]

AMERICAN USAGE

As is the case with the concept of national interest,
throughout history leaders of the United States have been
concerned with the nation's aspirations and the objectives
being sought by public policy. Many references to purposes
and goals are recorded in *The Federalist* and other official
papers, presidential documents, and public addresses. To
illustrate, again reviewing the fundamental statements embodied in presidential inaugural addresses,[9] during the
early years of the Republic, President Washington alluded to
"discernment and pursuit of the public good," and asserted
that "the preservation of the sacred fire of liberty and the
destiny of the republican model of government are justly
considered, perhaps, as *deeply*, as *finally*, staked on the
experiment intrusted to the hands of the American people."
President Jefferson spoke of the people uniting "in common
efforts for the common good," and President Monroe, referring to the Constitution, advocated "infusing into the National Government sufficient power for national purposes."
Subsequently in the nineteenth century President Polk addressed himself to the "legitimate purposes" of the Union,
President Pierce to both "purposes in the conduct of foreign
affairs" and "the great objects of our pursuit as a people,"
and President McKinley to "the declaration of the purposes of
the Government."

Usage of the expression intensified with the administration of President Wilson who, rejecting the salience of promoting national interests, as noted in Chapter 2, referred
frequently to American purposes. Since 1912 twelve Presidents used some varient of the expression more than fifty
times in their inaugural addresses. In addition to the terms
purposes, goals, objectives, and motives, they employed such
expressions as aspirations, ideals, values, causes, needs,

and desires, and even the American heritage and birthright.
While most Presidents preferred the generic word purpose,
some recent Presidents have used more flamboyant expressions,
including the American spirit and the American dream. Adjec-
tivally some call them firm, honorable, supreme, or sacred
purposes, or they employ alternative language, referring to
"fixed principles," "rules of conduct," and the "great cathe-
dral of the spirit" of the nation. Beginning with the Eisenhower administration, Presidents have particularly stressed
renewed dedication to national purposes, and several of them,
reflecting times of political turnover in the White House,
have recommended change in national purpose, using expressions like making "a new beginning" and "the birth of a new
order."

Interpreting the essence of the concept, a number of
recent Presidents have projected the importance of elemental
and constant aims--as "deeply rooted in the principles of our
national life," "our dedication and devotion to the precepts
of our founding documents," or simply our "fundamental
goals." Increasingly Presidents emphasize the matter of
public sacrifice to achieve national purposes and the need
for supportive popular consensus. In 1917 President Wilson
declared: "But nothing will alter our thought or our purpose
. . . . They are too deeply rooted in the principles of our
national life . . . . We always professed unselfish purpose
and we covet the opportunity to prove our professions sincere
. . . . Upon this as a platform of purpose and of action we
can stand together."

At his first inaugural President Eisenhower proclaimed:
"We must . . . display stamina in purpose. We must be willing, individually and as a Nation, to accept whatever sacrifices may be required of us. A people that values privileges above its principles soon loses both." In 1965 President Johnson--associating national interest and purpose--
implored the people: "Let us now join reason to faith and
action to experience, to transform our unity of interest into
unity of purpose." Focusing on public dedication, President
John Kennedy ended his inaugural address with the memorable
exhortation: "And so, my fellow Americans, ask not what your
country can do for you; ask what you can do for your country."

Two centuries of these inaugural addresses also provide
an array of pragmatic prescriptions of national aims. Sometimes they may be conjoined in lists, but more frequently
they are specified individually. Not surprisingly, these
vary from particular historic aspirations and political precepts to concrete contemporary objectives. The general purposes of America most frequently mentioned in these addresses
include union and unity, liberty and personal freedoms, national security and stability, order and safety, peace and
amity, justice, prosperity, and human happiness.

Even more frequently American leaders expound similar
views in other types of public documents. In addition to
those already cited, for example, in 1971 President Nixon
reported: "America has always had a belief in a purpose larger than itself. Two centuries ago our mission was to be a

unique exemplar of free government. Two decades ago it was
to take up worldwide burdens of securing the common defense,
economic recovery, and political stability. Today we must
work with other nations to build an enduring structure of
peace."[10]   Commenting on purpose and policy, in an interview
published in 1978, former Secretary of State Henry Kissinger
stated: "What is expected of a President is to define clearly
what the national purpose is, what the policies are, and to
defend this against the inevitable criticisms that a pluralistic society tends to generate."[11]

RECENT AMERICAN CONCERN OVER NATIONAL PURPOSE

     During the formative years of the United States as an
independent nation, its experience was unique in two major
respects. Relating nationhood to statehood Henry Steele
Commager, noted historian, holds that this country, as the
first of the "new" nations in the late eighteenth century,
differed from other new states in that "in the Old World the
nation came before the state; in America the state came before the nation." The United States was born without a national past. "In the Old World," he explains, "nations grew
out of well-prepared soil, built upon a foundation of history
and traditions," whereas when the United States government
was established, the nation's "foundations were still to be
laid, the seeds to be planted, the traditions still to be
formed," which obliged the new country to fabricate its "historic past" ex post facto and focus largely on the future.[12]

     The United States is also unique in that its fundamental
purpose was devised before the nation, the state, and its
system of governance were created. On this matter, Hans J.
Morgenthau contends: "The rule that action precedes reflection in the discovery of the national purpose suffers but one
complete exception." The United States is the only nation
that "reversed the sequence by reflecting upon its purpose
before it had come into existence. The awareness of its purpose was not an afterthought. The United States was founded
as a nation with a particular purpose in mind."[13] Also commenting on the philosophical and historical origins of the
United States, Herbert von Borch has written: "Only in America has there ever been a society created--and maintained--on
the basis of a philosophy--the optimistic philosophy of progress." Founded on the notions of the perfectibility of man
and that man by nature possesses the capacity to be free, the
Founding Fathers espoused "the American dream, the Utopia
without which America believed . . . that it could not live."
Reaffirming its uniqueness, he maintains: "Before America was
a nation, it was an experiment, an idea, a plan, a Utopia, a
promise, a dream"--with a purpose.[14]

     "For 200 years," observed Winston Lord, Director of the
Department of State Policy Planning Staff, "America has been
confident of its purposes . . . and certain of its growing
prosperity." But as the United States approached its third
century it needed to redefine its "national purposes in an
ambiguous age."[15]   Although statesmen and analysts have
recognized the centrality of the ends-means relationship in
the foreign affairs process--discussed in the following sec-

tion--it was not until the 1950s, paralleling growing attention paid to the concept of national interests, that widespread concern over national purposes was aroused in the
United States. While some celebrated the advantages of national purposelessness, others magnified the continuing importance of traditional, official, and popular purposefulness of the country. Still others initiated a search for a
motivating national mission--to reassess American values, to
overcome the weaknesses produced by pluralism, factionalism,
and individualism in the United States, and to reinvigorate
its role in world affairs.[16]

     Reflecting this growing sense of malaise and the call
for national renewal, in his first inaugural address President Eisenhower spoke of strengthening dedication to America's founding principles, proclaiming anew our faith, rein-
vigorating our supreme aspiration, and the need for personal
and national sacrifice.[17] In a report to Congress his Secretary of State, William P. Rogers, affirmed the relationship of national purpose and public attitudes: "Under our
system of government, the only source of a strong, steady,
and durable national purpose lies within the people . . . .
My greatest hope is that the path we are taking can help
create among Americans a new national unity and purpose in
our foreign policy."[18]

     In both his State of the Union message and address of
1980, President Carter referred to our uneasy era, internal
tensions, important challenges, and our common vision of
America, but also to the need for the renewal of the nation's
faith and a new spirit of unity and resolve. After criticizing the pressures on government policy brought by single issue and special interest groups, and emphasizing the demands
of unity and personal sacrifice, in his Farewell Adress he
argued that this pluralistic milieu "tends to distort our
purposes," and counseled that "we must not forget that the
common good is our common interest and our individual responsibility."[19]

     Turning to the literary commentary on national purposes,
after surveying those propounded by the Founding Fathers,
historian Richard Morris concludes: "In sum, the creative
years of revolution and constitution-making, two hundred
years behind us, provide us the occasion to reexamine our
national purpose and priorities . . . to redefine and reshape
them to fit the national interest as we perceive it in a
changing world, and to ensure that generations yet unborn may
still enjoy the blessings of liberty under a government rest-
ing upon the consent of the governed."[20] On the other hand,
suggesting that America's purposes be new, transcendent, and
elevating, Brewster alleges: "We will not regain our self-
confident spirit until we believe once more that we do have
something special to contribute to the prospect of humanity
generally, both because of what we are as a society and because of what we might mean to the hopes of all peoples." In
the United States, he adds, "we yearn for some belief that
our nation has a significance for mankind generally which can
be measured by some scale larger than our own survival and
well-being."[21]

Examining the aims of American foreign policy in greater
detail, in 1954 Ambassador George F. Kennan--one of the initial post-World War II analysts of public purpose--stressed
the necessity of a nation to have "some overall purpose." He
acknowledged that nations have their own individualized purposes, which is "only natural" because a dominant "unifying
purpose" applicable to all nations leads to political unification, or "the trappings of national sovereignty . . . become meaningless." He also discussed the early development
of national purposes in the United States and the essence of
the "American dream," which he regards as marked by certain
innocence, ignorance, and utopianism, and he recognized the
growing lack in the United States of a motivating national
mission. In a later address, his indictment of purposelessness was more severe: "If you ask me . . . whether a country
in the state this country is in today . . . has, over the
long run, a good chance of competing with a purposeful, serious, and disciplined society such as that of the Soviet
Union, I must say the answer is 'no'."[22]

Another early exposition on national purpose--not of its
essence but rather of its application throughout the history
of the United States--produced by the political scientist
Edward McNall Burns, examines in considerable detail the
ideas and activities embodied in the American concepts of its
mission, its national purpose, and its destiny--terms he uses
interchangeably. On the assumption that America's "sense of
mission" has "run like a golden thread through most of its
history," he asserts that "no theme has ever dominated the
minds of the leaders of this nation to the same extent as the
idea that America occupies a unique place and has a special
destiny among the nations of the earth." Branding this "a
grandiose conception," he probes the significance of such
aspects as the national heritage, democracy, freedom and
equality, individualism, spiritual and moral foundations,
pacifism, imperialism, and world leadership. He also examines the views of those that forecast the inevitable "decline
and fall" of this mission, the causes responsible, and the
proposals made to reaffirm the precepts on which the United
States was founded.

In his final chapter Burns coalesces the principal components of the American mission and reviews the extent to
which they are realizable. He maintains that America's "myth
of purpose and destiny" consists of five elements: to proclaim liberty throughout the world, to set an example of
equality for all nations, to provide the truest democracy in
the world, to be the most peaceful and nonmilitaristic of the
leading nations, and to be the exemplar of the highest standard of living the world has ever known. Admitting that none
of these have been fully realized, he insists that, despite
its weaknesses, "the mission of America remains one of the
noblest expressions of idealism that any nation has em-
braced," but that what the nation needs most "is more wisdom
and tolerance in carrying it out."[23]

In the early 1960s the issue of national purpose gripped
American attention, resulting in the publication of a series
of monographic studies, symposia, and essays. Responding to
what he calls the "crisis in American politics," in 1960 Hans

Morgenthau published his commentary on American political purpose as a companion volume to his *In Defense of the National Interest*. In it he discusses the essence, validity, and practical viability of the concept of national purpose and the American experience. He declares that: "All great nations have blasphemously identified their mission with a divine purpose" and they derived them "from the superiority of race or the laws of history or economic necessity." But, he concedes, "a nation must pursue its interests for the sake of a transcendent purpose that gives meaning to the day-to-day operations of its foreign policy." Contemplating the reality of a country's political purpose, he claims that it "resides in the political and social history of the nation-- that is, in a continuum of actions that reveal a common and unique pattern pointing to a common and unique purpose. That purpose may well be implicit in the action, only to be discovered in retrospect."

Morgenthau contends that American purpose does not consist of a substantive ideal, but of procedures and ways of thinking. In all nations but the United States, he adds, the awareness of the national purpose in conscious thought followed upon its achievement in action. Discussing America's experience, he concludes that its threefold purpose is to build "a certain kind of society," to establish "equality in freedom" in the nation (which he calls "the fundamental and minimal purpose of America"), and to maintain such equality in freedom "as an example for other nations to emulate."[24]

Taking the matter to the general public, in 1960 the editors of *Life* magazine and *The New York Times* published a series of articles constituting what they called "an urgent debate" on the nature of, and the need for, national purposes. Initially John K. Jessup, *Life*'s chief editorial writer, and eight prominent Americans wrote essays presenting their views on the problem and their individual interpretations of American national purposes. Following the presidential nominating conventions, the two presidential candidates --John Kennedy and Richard Nixon--were also invited to contribute, increasing the anthology to eleven analyses. These deal with such aspects as growing concern and need, the distinction between self-conscious and other purposes, the relationship of ends and means in the foreign relations process, past American national causes, and the difficulty of establishing and delineating a national sense of mission. Substantively the contributors expounded on the traditional precepts of the American socio-political system, human freedom, spiritual revival, enduring peace, the pursuit of excellence, the need for effective leadership, and the process of choice based on reflection.[25]

This symposium was also republished in a separate volume. It does not include the contributions of presidential candidates Kennedy and Nixon, rearranges the sequence of the articles, and incorporates an added piece by columnist James Reston, which first appeared only in *The New York Times*.[26] Broadening the scope of this venture, a year later historian Oscar Handlin produced a more comprehensive anthology. It contains all of the *Life* and *New York Times* articles, supplemented with series of prepublished documents, essays,

poems, and commentaries. These aggregate more than one hundred additional selections, providing a broad spectrum of
thinking on matters related to American aims and principles.
Authored by dozens of former statesmen, historians, novel-
ists, journalists, and other writers--spanning more than
three centuries--their contributions provide a rich and varied disquisition on Americana.[27] However, aside from some
of the *Life* articles, it adds little to understanding the
meaning of national purpose as a concept in general or its
status in the armor of American policy considerations in the
1960s.

Walter Lippmann, one of the contributors to the *Life*
symposium, presented his views in two major editorials published in 1959 and 1960. In the first, as already noted,
contemplating the "critical weakness" of the United States,
he deplores the lack of an energizing American national
purpose and regards this as an incipient debility. In his
contribution to the *Life* series, he links national purpose
with political leadership, and discusses "three innovating
Presidents"--Theodore Roosevelt, Woodrow Wilson, and Franklin
Roosevelt--who led the country on its course for over half a
century. He reiterates his concern over the absence of a
potent national purpose and sense of direction following
World War II and warns that if the country is not galvanized
behind a national cause, it is bound to decline.[28]

In 1963 Leonard G. Benson published one of the most comprehensive treatises on the subject--from the sociological
perspective--interrelating the concepts of national purpose
and ideology. Treating them from the universal point of
view, he applies them specifically to the American experience. His thesis is that certain kinds of ideologies have a
vital function in the contemporary world, and his intent is
to make explicit "the uses of ideology for purposive action
in the modern nation." He considers the reasons for America's grave concern during the 1950s and 1960s and its widespread ambivalence about what he calls the national "social
purpose," and he deals in some detail with the distinction
between purpose and ideology, national purpose and the international environment, and contemporary American weakness. He
asseses the cases for and against the need for national purposes and extrapolates their differences from national interests, values, myths, mysticism, and the doctrines of ideo-
logues. And he relates purpose with national power and prestige and examines its role in national planning.[29]

Interest in the national purposes of the United States
also resulted in publications that sought to conjoin purpose
and national power. In response to Morgenthau's defense of
the importance of national interest, as related in Chapter 2,
Thomas I. Cook and Malcolm Moos wrote their volume on national power as evidenced through purpose, in which the concepts
of national interests and purposes are used interchangeably
and the latter is regarded as synonymous with goals, ideals,
and values. To counter Soviet ideology and action during the
Cold War, they claim that America's root need for the effective conduct of foreign affairs is a coherent theory of political ethics that conceives of human beings as endowed with
ultimate dignity and worth. As already noted, Cook and Moos

also seek to sublimate national into international purposes. Reflecting America's uniqueness, they say, its view of life "not only permits but positively necessitates the unifying of internal and international principles of policy."[30]

Another volume on power and purpose, edited by Gene M. Lyons, constitutes a collection of nine essays prepared by individual authors (largely historians and political scientists). Each concentrates on a specific contemporary functional subject. Again purposes are broadly conceived as national aims rather than as a special type of national goal.[31] Neither of these volumes copes with the conceptualized meaning of national purpose or national power and therefore contribute little to understanding the concepts. Nor do they deal with the need for revitalization or change in America's national purpose.

In connection with the American Bicentennial, a series of sessions were held at Columbia University in 1976 to reconsider American national purposes. This resulted in an anthology of essays, each prepared by a different author and focused on a distinct substantive policy problem. In his historical prologue, Richard Morris, concerned with extrapolating the guiding purposes of the Founding Fathers as a benchmark for contemporary analysis, observes "that a moral imperative has continuously motivated America and its people," and he speaks of "older prevailing American notions of mission" and "a reassertion of long-cherished first principles." In the concluding essay Dona Baron, editor of the volume, contends that "the American national purpose should be understood as the pursuit of certain ideals which, by their very nature, can never be attained once and for all, but must be continuously related to the evolving processes and conditions of a dynamic society."[32]

Also reflecting America's growing apprehension concerning its national purposes, substantial additional materials have been published since the beginning of the 1960s in a variety of public addresses, essays, monographs, textbooks, and other commentaries on international relations and foreign affairs, some of which are indicated elsewhere in this chapter and in the bibliography.[33] By way of illustration, aside from decrying the lack of or arguing the need for national purpose, some insist that it requires definition and specification, although they concede that it is not easy to prescribe. Some distinguish categories of aims, differentiate between single and multiple purposes, and caution against the risk of cross-purposes, or address themselves to ultimate, central, overall, or true purposes. Most, however, are inclined to pragmatize rather than conceptualize their interpretations and, as indicated in the following section, many take special note of the dichotomy of ends sought in foreign affairs and the means designed to achieve them.

While there are occasional analysts like Benjamin R. Barber who argue that "public purposelessness" is traditional in the United States and has been the case since its founding, others, represented by Benson, maintain that a convincing case against purposefulness cannot be made. Barber ridicules the "loss of public purpose" phenomenon, maintains that

America has never had enduring purposes, that for a long time
this was held to be one of the nation's major strengths, and
that the country was founded on the "political theory of
classical republicanism," in which the motives of its founders were complex and its aims were plural. He reasons,
therefore, that the "constitutional solutions" devised were
directly responsible "for the national purposelessness that
has characterized American public life ever since" and,
strangely, equating purposes and interests, that "private
interests *were* the only public interests America could afford
to pursue."[34] Benson, on the other hand, after commenting on
the views of certain critics, arrives at his judgment against
the case of such dissenters and declares that their position
is untenable and is not likely to guide the efforts of either
nations or their governments.[35]

In any case, most political leaders and publicists acknowledge the need for governments and peoples to possess a
compelling sense of purpose. In addition to the statements
quoted in the opening paragraphs of this chapter, for example, diplomatic historian Samuel Flagg Bemis goes so far as
to call the American national purpose its "original *raison
d'etre*."[36] In his introductory essay in the 1960 *Life*
series, Jessup asserts that "the United States has hitherto
been a country associated with great purpose" and that the
world needs a purposeful America,[37] and Clinton Rossiter
predicts that "America will not flourish unless it can develop an inspiring sense of mission,"[38] and in a lecture
presented in 1977 Henry Kissinger declared: "If our foreign
policy is well conceived, it must reflect fundamental national purposes."[39] Even a skeptic like Bayless Manning,
who minimizes the need for national consensus, admits that
"the surest way for the United States to influence for the
better the ideological future of mankind everywhere is by
being sure that we present an unwavering example of commitment to our principles at home. And that *is* an ideological
target that can be--has been--set for all Americans."[40]

ENDS AND MEANS IN FOREIGN RELATIONS

It is widely held that, at the heart of managing public
affairs, including the foreign policy process of every country lies the imperative of correlating the ends sought and
the means to achieve them. It may be debated whether as a
matter of ethical principles the frequently quoted sixteenth-century Machiavellian allegation that "the end justifies the means" is valid,[41] and it may be contested whether,
as the seventeenth-century British moralist Sir Thomas
Browne believed: "Every country hath its Machiavel."[42] In
the early eighteenth century, on the other hand, the British
diplomat Matthew Prior put it differently: "The end must
justify the means."[43] In any case, it is far from unreason-
able to assume that in public policy-making for national
actions or programs to be fruitful, there ought to be identifiable ends to justify them, and for a government to decide
on policy without seeking to comport with explicit aims to be
attained is foolhardy.[44]

Few would disagree with the view that ends do--or should

--logically determine means in the management of diplomatic
relations. But, according to Charles Lerche and Abdul Said,
in their comprehensive examination of concepts in international politics, there is some temptation to formulate foreign policy to permit the means to determine the ends--or to
accept the aims most easily attained as those that should be
sought. Even fewer would contest their notions that the
foreign affairs of a nation are apt to suffer from confusion
"in the ends-means relationship" and that "there is no substitute for a clearly rationalized and thoroughly understood
purpose in foreign policy."[45]   Nevertheless, in his study
specifically on the conduct of United States foreign relations, Lerche notes that "the translation of purpose into
concrete terms" necessitates a reversal of "the American
preference for the elaboration of means at the expense of
discussion of ends." Only by making the ends of policy paramount, he insists, "can rational choices be made among the
several means that are available."[46]

Individual components of this ends-means juxtaposition,
at least in theory, are readily understandable as either ends
or means, whereas in actual practice this is not always simple. Types of ends differ in importance, degree of motivity,
and permeability, and the same may be said of means, although
they are likely to be more flexible than ends. Significant
distinctions between substantive means and those that pertain
to method or procedure must also be recognized. As a consequence, both sets of factors--the ends and the means--consti-
tute variegated threads that must blend in the intricate
fabric of public policy-making.

Although it may be variously depicted, for purposes of
analysis this hierarchically structured segment of the foreign relations cosmography may be called the "national pur-
pose/national goals/concrete objectives/foreign policy" system. Both the ends sought by a nation and the policies and
strategies designed to achieve them may be conceptualized as
intrinsically apposed though pragmatically correlative and
interrelated. As diagnostic media, these standards help to
distinguish the primary from the secondary (in terms of importance), the general from the specific (in terms of scope),
the substantive from the procedural (in terms of content),
the strategic from the tactical (in terms of applicability),
and the long-range from the short-range (in terms of mutability).

Degrees of "endness"--or "intentionality"--are denoted
in various ways. Aside from such encompassing expressions as
aims, values, ideals, intentions, motives, or causes, logic
and usage tend to distinguish three basic types of ends in
the public policy arena. These include an intricate network
of national *purposes*, fundamental and other national *goals*,
and specific action-oriented policy *objectives*. Although
clear and precise delineation among them is far from universal, these three categories tend to be differentiated on the
basis of primacy, generality, permanence, and consensus. The
very essence of each of them implies the necessity of means
for their achievement. Used generically the words purposes,
goals, and objectives are identical, but in both practice and
rationalization the concept of national purpose has acquired

a unique and significant connotation in conducting foreign
affairs.

Nevertheless, considerable confusion arises in practical
public policy considerations. This occurs in part because
the national purpose of a country may be regarded as identical with an individual national goal or cluster of objectives.[47] More frequently ambiguity results from the fact
that the concepts goals and objectives--discussed in the
next chapter--are technically applicable to differing levels
of aims, whereas, as ordinary lexicographical expressions
they are not inherently distinguishable and therefore are
often used interchangeably.

Misunderstanding is compounded by the failure to differentiate the ends sought by the nation-state in the long run
from those pursued by a particular government or regime of
the country, and from those directly applicable to the formulation and implementation of current policy. Variations of
interpretation also result from contrasting idealist and
realist approaches.[48] Moreover, if conceived as both multiple and complex (consisting of more basic and important
components together with their supportive subsidiaries) when
they are projected pragmatically uncertainty may arise as to
whether a specific element is really an end, a means, or
both.

Even though peace and security are viewed as collateral,
unequivocal, and permanent aims of a nation, for example, as
the foreign relations spectrum is extrapolated peace may also
be held to constitute one of the means for maintaining security, whereas the security of each country in a given group
may be looked upon as a means of preserving peace among them.
In other words, in this case peace is perceived as a means of
achieving security, and vice versa, so that each is both an
end and a means, depending on the perspective and orientation
of the policy maker or analyst.

Commenting on this issue of mutations, Arnold Wolfers
professes that it is often impossible to draw a sharp line of
demarcation between ends and means. Grouping all ends as
goals, he reasons: "all means can be said to constitute intermediary or proximate goals, and few goals if any can be
considered ultimate, in the sense of being sought as ends in
themselves." He goes on to add: "what constitutes a means or
immediate goal in one context may be a remote if not ultimate
goal in another, with specific objectives changing places
from one instance to another."[49]

Put another way, Joseph Frankel explains this complexity
of ends and means on the basis of levels of sequence: "In an
endeavor to reach a high-ranking objective the decision-maker
must first determine some intermediate, lower ones, which
constitute means for its achievement. At the same time, these
lower objectives constitute ends in the processes leading to
them, assume validity of their own and sometimes, while pursued, serve also other ends." He defines means as "the instruments, methods, and subsidiary objectives employed to
obtain" the ends sought.[50] Cautioning his readers about the
interaction of ends and means, Kennan suggests "that the con-

duct of foreign relations ought not to be conceived as a purpose in itself . . . but rather as one of the means by which
some higher and more comprehensible purpose is pursued."[51]

This conception of ends and means postulates a continuum
of interrelationships. Thus, a nation may seek to promote
its national security by various methods, including bilateral
and/or multilateral alliances.   A given alliance, in turn,
may be consummated by a variety of means--treaty or agreement, automatic or conditional commitment, unified or joint
military forces in being, particular types, quantities, and
disposition of such forces, permanent or ad hoc policy-making
machinery, unilateral or unified command structure, and on
down to systematizing technical military nomenclature.   In
each step the means may become an end besought by subsidiary
means. As a result, while the ends/means relationship is
simplistic in theory, it may be intricate if not perplexing
in practice.

Finally, contemplating what he calls "primary truths or
first principles" of politics, and correlating ends, means,
and power to implement them, in *The Federalist* papers Alexander Hamilton has written "that there cannot be an effect
without a cause; that the means ought to be proportionate to
the end; that every power ought to be commensurate with its
object; that there ought to be no limitation of a power des-
tined to effect a purpose, which is itself incapable of limitation."[52] Lippmann synthesizes the task of the statesman
as bringing "his ends and means into balance"--otherwise "he
will follow a course that leads to disaster."[53]

Also prescribing a series of precepts concerning the interaction of ends and means, Charles Burton Marshall contends
that "the goal aspect of foreign policy is essential," that
the foreign policy process requires "not the mere conceiving
of ends but the establishment of purposes of action and the
allocation of means," that "the capacity of the mind to conceive ends is limitless" whereas "the means at hand are invariably limited," and that it is essential "to maintain balance between those portions of ends chosen as purposes for
action and the means available." He also cautions that the
balance between ends and means "is not solely a quantitative
matter" in that not only must the means be "sufficient to the
purpose" but they must also be "qualitatively appropriate to
the purpose." The crux of this relationship, he declares, is
volition--or will--which consists of three levels: motives
(the impulses that emanate "from some inner need or desire"),
ends ("the satisfaction of the need or desire identified as
the source of motivation"), and intentions ("the projection
of action in pursuit of them").[54]

Despite many differences of interpretation and conflicting perceptions of the nature and interaction of ends and
means in the public policy process, it must be concluded that
policy makers need to be conscious--both in theory and prac-
tice--of the distinction between that which is sought and
the means to achieve it. Simple logic prescribes a hierarchical relationship of ends and means, which is crucial to
the effective formulation and implementation of a nation's
foreign policy.

INTERPRETATIONS OF NATIONAL PURPOSES

In view of the importance of national purpose in the
conduct of foreign relations, it is surprising that in official usage and political commentary little attention is
devoted to propounding its conceptual meaning or to systematically analyzing its inherent essence, ramifications, and
significance. Nevertheless, it is generally agreed that, however conceived, national purpose crowns the hierarchy of ends
sought by peoples and their governments, and it has been
called "the top part of the means-principles-ends hierarchy."[55] It is central to both political action and policy
consideration. In terms of applicability this "magic phrase"
is broad in scope, ranging from the permeative and elemental
causes of human society in general, of an individual nation-
state or people, or of a particular governmental administration, to a country's specific public affairs at a given moment in history.

In considerations of policy analysis--as in the case of
the concept of national interest--the qualifiers "national"
and "public" are often held to be interchangeable if not
identical.[56] This creates little difficulty respecting the
matter of whose purpose it is but may produce uncertainty
concerning its beneficiary. Definitions of the term "purpose," however, differ considerably. Some publicists use it
generically, as encompassing all ends, equating it vaguely
with national goals and objectives. This leads to confusion
if general goals and concrete policy objectives are distinguished from national purposes as specific categories of ends
sought. National purpose is also broadly construed as the
national image or national effort--or as the national aspiration, vision, or outlook. Others prefer to depict it as the
"national mission," or to concentrate attention on a "sense
of purpose" or "sense of destiny." Even though a case may be
made for each of these interpretations, explicitly or implic-
itly they all denote that which is sought or pursued by the
nation.

As with other factors in the foreign affairs process,
significant variations of delineation hinge on differences in
singular and plural usage. Some hold that national purpose
is unitary, others that it may be multiplex or, occasionally,
that it must integrate all purposes into an ultimate purpose,
or that lesser or mini-purposes serve to support greater or
maxi-purposes. Sometimes usage reflects disparate perceptions of the ultimate purposes not only of the particular
nation in its current environment but also of mankind, or
civilization, or life itself.[57]

Basic Interpretations

A survey of modern literature and practice reveals that
the concept is defined and used in several different ways.
In addition to its generic usage, "a national purpose" (finite end of the scale) may be employed in the singular,
which presumes that there may be more than one purpose;
therefore it is also applied in the plural, "national purposes." Albert Wohlstetter, who utilizes this expression

interchangeably with goals, has pointed out: "While we may talk about national purpose in the singular, the first thing to observe about our aims is that we have many of them."[58] A number of other publicists and political leaders either recognize or prefer such plural usage. Acting Secretary of State Chester Bowles alludes to "America's true purposes," but he, like a good many others, equates purposes with such phenomena as "universal values" or aims, thus failing to distinguish it from other types of ends sought.[59] Although he employed the expression in both the singular and plural, Secretary of State Dean Rusk specified a series of purposes "which are compelling when great public . . . policy decisions are being made."[60] Such equivocal usage neither explicates nor denies the uniqueness of the concept.

The second interpretation, "The National Purpose", used solely in the singular denotes a synthesized aggregate of purposes. Sometimes this consists of the elemental, long-range causes of the country or, alternatively, of its more precisely circumscribed but fundamental aims.[61] In the United States this application often encompasses sets of historical principles, including those ordained in the Declaration of Independence, the preamble to the Constitution, and the Bill of Rights. To these a few would add other examples of compelling public doctrine: self-determination, popular sovereignty, the rule of law, government as the servant of the people, and similar precepts.

According to Reston, who contributed to the symposium sponsored by *Life* magazine and the *New York Times*, in the United States "it would be an impertinence to try to improve on the second paragraph of the Declaration of Independence" as a guide to prescribing America's national purpose.[62] In the same anthology Archibald MacLeish calls it "the most precisely articulated national purpose in recorded history,"[63] and Archer Blood insists that each generation is called upon "to reapply the Declaration of Independence or . . . to redefine the national purpose."[64] Embracing such hallowed "self-evident truths" as "that all men are created equal, that they are endowed by the Creator with certain unalienable rights, that among these are life, liberty, and the pursuit of happiness," the impact of such traditional precepts on American thinking and practice for more than two centuries--and for the future--are undeniable.

Similarly, writing positively and enthusiastically on the subject, Richard Nixon, then Vice President, professed "that it is America's national purpose to extend the goals of the preamble of our Constitution to our relations with all men," and he reiterated these well-known principles: to form a more perfect union, establish justice, insure domestic tranquility, provide for the common defense, promote the general welfare, and secure the blessings of liberty to ourselves and our posterity. "I believe," he concluded, "that the inseparability of these propositions from human destiny is the American purpose and that it will prevail."[65] To these general principles others append the personal freedoms and other guarantees sanctified by the Bill of Rights; and Jessup, chief editor of *Life* magazine, includes, among others, Lincoln's characterization of the American system as a gov-

ernment "of the people, by the people, and for the people."[66]
Such aggregates of lofty causes are also epitomized as
"Americanism," "the American way," and "the American Utopia."

    Referring to "the principles that are vital to our
national greatness, that underlie our national purpose, that
foster our 'American dream'," in 1960 presidential candidate
John Kennedy broadened the conception of national purpose
considerably. It embraces not only the precepts embodied in
the Declaration of Independence, the Constitution, and the
Bill of Rights, he declared. They are also contained in the
writings of Jefferson, Madison, and Hamilton, the words of
Jackson and Lincoln, the works of Emerson and Whitman, the
judicial opinions of Marshall and Holmes, and Wilson's New
Freedom and Roosevelt's Four Freedoms. In addition to survival, peace, and prosperity, he proposed a series of ten
ideals which, he said, "can never be fully attained, but the
eternal quest for which embodies the American National Purpose." These ideals--although basic but in some cases also
specific--vary from the perfection of the democratic process,
the achievement of a constantly expanding economy, and the
attainment of world peace and disarmament based on world law
and order, to the elimination of slums, the conquest of
dreaded diseases, and the enrichment of American culture.[67]
His conception of American national purpose, therefore, appears to encompass a host of long-range and short-term goals.

    To these and similar characterizations of the national
purpose, Fisher Howe, of the Department of State, and others
add the preamble of the United Nations Charter. It contains
such global aspirations as eliminating the scourge of war,
affirming faith in fundamental human rights, respecting the
sanctity of treaties, tolerating other peoples and their
governments, maintaining international peace and security,
and promoting the economic and social advancement of
peoples.[68] Brewster goes so far as to say that what the
United States needs "is a resounding Declaration of International Independence" to launch "global arrangements and institutions to safeguard the common defense and the general
welfare of humanity everywhere," and thereby rediscover our
sense of purpose.[69] But Wolfers warns against the supersession of national by international purposes, suggesting that
this produces critical conceptual incongruity.[70] Thus,
those who regard national purpose as an aggregate differ in
their perceptions and are unable to produce universal consensus on its components.

    The third form of the concept, *The National Purpose*, is
used only in the singular as a sacrosanct, generally immutable, and often abstract agglomerate--or grand purpose. At
times it is employed in an amorphous if not undefinable way,
or to symbolize (not constitute) an aggregate. Though popularly stimulating, this interpretation tends to obviate or
ignore the necessity of practical delineation. Its meaning
may be viewed as elemental as the quest of the nation to per-
severe or survive.[71] Or it may be perceived as the preservation of a particular culture or civilization--or "a way of
life."

    According to Cook and Moos, in response to the real-

politik of Morgenthau: "It is America's special mission, as
it is our one hope for sustained enjoyment of our way of
life, to champion in the world the lasting ethical insights
of Western tradition."[72] By comparison, at Gettysburg President Lincoln extolled America as a nation "conceived in
liberty and dedicated to the proposition that all men are
created equal," and diplomatic historian Bemis distills
American national purpose into "the blessings of liberty,"
one of six tenets listed in the preamble to the Constitution,
which he calls "the values America evokes today and applies
to other free peoples of the world."[73] Or it is said to be
imbedded in the founding doctrine of a nation's heritage
which, in the case of the United States, brings it full circle to the precepts specified in the Declaration of Independence, the Constitution, and similar historic documents.

Despite its significance, heading the ends-means complex
of public affairs, most statesmen and publicists are less
concerned with national purpose as a concept than with its
practical application. Perhaps this is due to the difficulty
in both defining it conceptualistically and determining inductively or deductively its explicit applications, or because it is confused with fundamental goals, policy objectives, and other more finite motivations. Occasionally the
problem is that national purposes are mistakenly equated
with national interests.[74]

The difficulty may also flow from the perception of THE
NATIONAL PURPOSE as an intangible myth. It has been described as "those mass-shared values in foreign policy whose maximization by government is demanded by a broad consensus,"
or a nation's "more or less well-formulated image of its
national mission."[75] Much as in the case of national interests, in this guise the concept may be predicated and supported without defining it. Unless concretely defined, national purpose may be viewed as ranging in meaning from comprehensive national goals, whether articulated or not, to an
equivocal amorphism under the aegis of which the polity expects policy objectives and action to lie.

Coping with the dialogue on contemporary need, some analysts consider the role of myth or ideology, referred to
earlier, which Benson describes as "an overreaching cause
which synthesizes and integrates all other efforts." He goes
on to characterize national purpose as presupposing "the
existence of some inner conviction on the part of each responsible citizen about what social qualities, above all
else, the nation is trying to establish, both at home and in
the international environment." Conceding the existence of a
nation's many public missions, he says, "underlying them and
infusing the processes of their fulfillment is the possibility of a National Purpose--a popular awareness of the interrelationships and priorities among various goals and an intense concern for their realization."[76]

One version of overarching purpose is represented by
Walter Lippmann's "public philosophy"--to funnel popular
beliefs into political action.[77] In a broader vein, Joseph
Campbell philosophises that, apposing religion and humanism,
peoples need to fabricate canons and symbols comparable to

the grand myths of old, which in contemporary international
society might be regarded as a call for national purpose.[78]
In the realm of foreign relations, as already noted, others
discuss the nature, value, and limitations of ideology,[79] and
occasionally an attempt is made to clear the slate of major
"illusions," "fallacies," and "prejudices," in order to encourage more realistic consideration of national purposes.[80]

Sense of National Purpose

Some analyses stress the motivational aspect of national
purpose. For example, Benson maintains: "The need for some
sense of purpose to give direction to national efforts, one
transcending immediate issues, has become a standard assumption in America."[81] Speaking more generally, Andrew M. Scott
argues: "Purpose may be said to exist in a system only when
key decision makers . . . share a common purpose or set of
purposes."[82]

Relating ideology and purpose in a study prepared for
the Senate Committee on Foreign Relations in 1960, the Center
for International Affairs at Harvard University raised issues
of popular motivation as well as expectations and the willingness to bear the necessary burden. Referring to certain
conditions as "fertile soil for political movements" that depend on "large-scale political support," this study insists
that to mobilize popular incentive and action, "leaders must
be able to translate vague aspirations into political goals
which can infuse in the masses a sense of purpose, a conviction of success, and a readiness to sacrifice."[83]

Emphasis on the motivational aspect of national purpose,
consequently, suggests a fourth interpretation--"a sense of
national purpose" or "national mission." This usage focuses
more on the attitudinal aspects of national purpose than on
its essence, however national purpose is functionally perceived and however historic or immediate it may be. This
aspect has caused the greatest concern and generated the most
intensive inquiry on the subject in the United States.

Some publicists--like Benson, Nixon, and Reston--who
employ the expression as either an aggregate of traditional
values and doctrine or an inalienable agglomerate, contravening the view of Barber, believe that this country has always
been purposeful and that the great causes of the past, although they may become dormant, remain unimpaired. Others--
including Bemis, Howe, and especially Lippmann and several
recent Presidents--however, contend that to be authentic,
national purposes must really stimulate the body politic in a
positive way, must be popularly consensualized, and must be
sufficiently compelling to warrant sacrifice for its fulfillment. Relating motivation and sacrifice, Brewster declares:
"History does seem to suggest that it takes the discipline of
great sacrifice or the threat of imminent disaster to lift a
people from their day to day habit of life and mind to a
higher level of concern and a broader scope of loyalty."[84]

Despite their desirability or historicity, residual or
inchoate aims that fail to inspire the people to overcome

personal and parochial aspirations, interests, and pressures, though they may be real, are no more than residual and inchoate aims. Some commentators, like Lippmann and Reston, suggest that genuine national purpose can be generated if effective leadership is forthcoming. The crux of the matter is whether the political system produces leaders with the requisite vision and ability, and if so, whether the people are prepared to follow those leaders in elevating the needs and welfare of the nation above their own special aspirations and desires.

Infusing "The National Purpose" as an aggregate or *The National Purpose* as an agglomerate with a driving sense of immediacy and urgency, although possible at certain stages of a nation's development, is usually more difficult on a continuing basis in pluralistic, democratic polities--what some refer to as zero-sum societies--especially those characterized by adversary politics and beset by conflict over power distribution. In times of adversity, it might be possible to concentrate on a more circumscribed purpose, or set of concrete purposes, provided conditions enable leaders to articulate them intelligibly and convert them into a moving national cause that is supported by popular consensus.

The task is to sublimate substantive and psychological perspective and value to the benefit of the country at large --that is, to orient thinking and action to integrate the aims, interests, and welfare of individuals, their interest groups, and partisan factions within the national community with the aims, interests, and welfare of that community composed of those same individuals and groups. Resolving this quandary is a true test of statecraft. Linking purpose and statesmanship, Henry M. Wriston, Chairman of President Eisenhower's Commission on National Goals, declares: "The politician makes compromises essential to keep the daily business of government operative; the statesman sets a goal beyond the range of immediate fulfillment."[85] To be viable, therefore, the emergent prescription of national purpose must be more than pro forma or nebulous doctrine. It must be more credible than strident rhetoric or mere symbolism--a guiding beacon rather than an obsolete shibboleth. It must be accepted as addressing an overriding need, possess intrinsic merit, and enjoy reasonable promise of fulfillment. If it satisfies these requisites, popular support is likely to follow.

Individual Interpretations

Applying the concept of national purpose to the United States and emphasizing popular consensus and dedication, in 1960 presidential candidate Nixon defined it: "Fundamentally, purpose must be examined in terms of what an entire people can regard as the ends of human existence and their relation to the external universe and to God . . . when I speak of national purpose I will mean both the purpose that should unite us and the dedication of mind and spirit necessary to achieve it."[86] At the same time John Kennedy interpreted it in a more ambiguous fashion: "Our national purpose consists of the combined purposefulness of each of us *when we are at our moral best*: striving, risking, choosing, making decisions, engaging

in a pursuit of happiness that is strenuous, heroic, exciting
and exalted."[87]

Emphasizing qualities of motivation, consensualization,
and possible nebulousness, according to Fisher Howe:[88]

> "National Purpose" is a set of principles or values
> which are differently held by individuals yet col-
> lectively shared in sufficient measure to give to
> the American people a common, compelling force,
> real even if defiantly elusive. To define such a
> set of purposes in a manner acceptable to all is
> quite impossible. Failure to try however leaves
> altogether unsaid something fundamental in the
> logic of planning in foreign affairs.

Delineating it in a more universal manner, Ambassador
Kennan, endorsing the theoretical verifiability but not
necessarily the explicit, practical essence of national
purpose, maintains:[89]

> If we look closely at other sovereign entities, in
> history as in our own time, I think we will see
> that each of them has had some overall purpose, go-
> ing beyond just the routine chores of government--
> some purpose to which the total of its political
> life was supposed to be dedicated and by which its
> existence as a separate political entity was sup-
> posed to be justified. This purpose may often have
> been crude and not too clearly formulated. It may
> in some instances have been more felt than ex-
> pressed. It may at times have been repressed and
> temporarily forgotten under the stress of some
> great external danger.

Addressing himself to the orthodoxy of national purpose
and what he calls the reality of politics, in a more critical
vein Morgenthau proclaims:[90]

> The history of the formulation of the national pur-
> pose, in America as elsewhere, is the story of bad
> theology and absurd metaphysics, of phony theories
> and fraudulent science, of crude rationalizations
> and vulgar delusions of grandeur."

Bridging the interpretations of Kennan and Morgenthau,
and acknowledging popular consensus and elusiveness, James
MacGregor Burns also provides one of the more provocative
definitions:[91]

> A nation may be said to exist only when most of its
> people share some common set of beliefs, expecta-
> tions, symbols, and ultimate values that together
> make up a national purpose. This purpose may be
> plain and positive; it may be obscure and unset-
> tled. It may be defined and trumpeted forth from
> the temple of God or government; or it may lie in
> "the hearts of the people." It may grow out of the
> conditions of a society; or it may be imported and
> imposed on it. And it may be badly formulated.

Then, after quoting the Morgenthau statement, he concludes:
"But it is there."

Is it? If so, the national purpose of the country ought
to be identifiable, preferably precise, and, hopefully, explicit. At least it ought to be knowable if not known, and
consensualizable if not consensualized. In some cases it is;
frequently it is not.

Definition of National Purpose

Several qualities of the concept emerge from these and
similar commentaries. National purpose is generally regarded
as substantively fundamental and important, popularly stimulating, applicable to the nation as a whole, crucial enough
to warrant public sacrifice, and preferably tangible but often amorphous. In essence, therefore:

> *The national purpose is the basic, pervading, and
> motivating mission of a nation, which ought to be
> identifiable to and comprehended by the body poli-
> tic, which imbues the government and people with a
> willingness to sacrifice for its fulfillment, and
> which is regarded as feasible even if not fully
> achievable.*

PRAGMATIZATION

National purposes of individual countries differ, and
they may change for a given people from generation to generation.   Kennan claims that there is no inherent uniformity
or "generally accepted universal pattern" of purposes among
nations.   "Had the objects of society not been in each case,
unique and specific ones," he says, "there would have been no
rationale for the maintenance of a separate state at all."[92]
On the other hand, as with national interests, two or more
states may have identical, similar, or parallel national
purposes, simultaneously or sequentially.

The achievement of independence and individual national
identity in the community of nations generally constitute the
initial national purposes of a people. Once secured and assured, they are likely to be superseded, although they remain
residual and dormant, revivable when that independence or
identity is endangered. Generalizing on this point, reminiscent of Dean Acheson and Dean Rusk, Paul Seabury notes that
the aim of foreign relations of a sovereign nation is in part
to protect and advance "the secure survival of its land and
people in a world of many other sovereign states."[93]

In the United States, political leaders and publicists--
emphasizing the principles embodied in the Declaration of
Independence, the preamble and precepts of the Constitution,
and the Bill of Rights--acknowledge that the national purposes of the Founding Fathers include life, liberty, and the
pursuit of happiness, the republican form of popular government, unity and the common good, pluralism and democracy,
human rights, and the sanctity of private property.[94]   Many

contemporary assessments   support some of these as continuing
American national causes. Even more liberal in his opinion,
referring to all the pragmatic purposes specified in the *Life*
magazine symposium,   John Kennedy considered all of them as
valid.[95]

Modern   history   provides   other   examples of primordial
drives of peoples. They may be patrimonial--such as the expansion of territory, securing a frontier, gaining access to
the sea and utilizing airspace and outer space, beating back
the jungle or tidal waters, controlling an isthmus or gulf,
or, in the case of divided countries, effecting territorial
reunification. Certain geopoliticians would include continental expansion, hegemony over the Afro-Eurasian "heartland,"
or maritime paramountcy. Others may be social and psychologi-
cal--enhancing the national image and prestige, advancing national credibility, or providing personal liberty, human
equality, religious freedom, and social justice--amalgamated
often as "universal human rights." Or they may be political
or economic--achieving self-determination and sovereign
equality, winning a war, fostering democracy, establishing
the rule of law, basing governance on popular sovereignty
and the consent of the governed, promoting "open" diplomacy,
organizing a system of collective security, gaining economic
independence or self-sufficiency, ending starvation, indus-
trializing the economy, expanding trade relations, ending a
major depression, or establishing a new international economic order.

Usually the national purpose of a nation is most clearly
perceived and forcefully motivating as a national mission
when it centers on surmounting some major or cataclysmic internal or international crisis, resolving a pressing, continuing public problem, or embarking on some pioneering venture of widespread concern.   In the absence of these conditions, it may be less evident or, in some cases, it may eva-
nesce.

Analysts differ as to whether national purpose must be
consciously designed and volitionally endorsed--or constitute
what is called "self-conscious purpose"--or whether it may be
latent or unconsciously motivational. Joseph Frankel holds
that "It does not really matter whether we postulate unconscious purpose based on impulse or conscious purpose based
upon rational processes."[96] Kennan, Morgenthau, MacGregor
Burns, and others imply this view in their interpretations.
Ernest W. LeFever also straddles the issues when he suggests
that a nation's central purpose is imbedded in the key values
"held by a majority of the people."[97] Writing on public
awareness and the blessings of liberty, Bemis maintains: "We
have not lacked a clear purpose as a nation. What we seem to
have been lacking is a continued consciousness of that purpose . . . . What we seem to have been losing is the hardened
will to make them prevail at all costs in the historically
shifted strategy of American defense and diplomacy."[98] On
the other hand, those who decry America's malaise and lack of
national purpose and stress its indispensability for a healthy society--such as Benson, Brewster, and especially Lippmann and recent Presidents--contend that to be genuine and
credible, national purpose must be actively and popularly

motivating.

To recapitulate, the concept of national purposes is unique and distinguishable from generic aims, goals, and objectives, as well as myths, ideals, and ideology. National purposes not only lead the complex of ends sought, but also must be energizing. To be realistic and effective in the foreign relations process, they must be endorsed by the public, or at least be popularly acceptable, and often they need to be supported by willingness to sacrifice. The crucial questions for a nation are not only what is its meaning and how does national purpose differ from national interests and from other types of national aims, but also whether the nation needs such motivating public purposes in order to prosper and, if so, whether they do exist in reality, what assurance the nation has that they are viable, and, most fundamentally, what is hoped to be accomplished by preserving the political society distinct from other nations? Concerned with national drift, frustration, disunity, and non-fulfillment of expectations, it is not uncommon for nations to return to historic or traditional aspirations, or to search for new causes that unify their governments and garner widespread popular support. This requires statesmanship of the highest order.

If the national purpose is to inspire the polity as a driving mission it must be more than a visionary aspiration or cliche. It should be realizable or at least believed to be experienceable.[99] It must be material and permeative, though not necessarily immutable. It may be unitary or multifaceted. It may reflect satisfaction with the national and international status quo, or it may seek change--in other words, it may be passively conserving (not necessarily conservative) or actively revisionist.[100] Some believe that national purposes may lie dormant, awaiting stimulation by leaders or events. A few allege that it does not really need to be discovered because it is inherently known; others say that to be genuine, it must be rationally framed and earnestly pursued. Still others claim that its explicit volitional formulation, unlike ideology and public policy, is visionary, that it resides rather in the political and social history of the nation, and is therefore only discoverable ex post facto.

Despite all these differences in perception, definition, and theory, there is general consensus that it is the most fundamental and impelling drive of the nation. Some would add that the health, strength, and progress of the national community--or at least the foreign impression of a nation's vitality and unity--are directly related to the vigor and soundness of its national purposes.

NOTES

1. Thomas A. Bailey, *The Art of Diplomacy: The American Experience* (New York: Appleton-Century-Crofts, 1968), p. 89.

2. *Maximes*, No. 160, quoted in *The Macmillan Book of Proverbs, Maxims, and Famous Phrases*, edited by Burton Stevenson (New York: Macmillan, 1948), p. 1920.

3. Kingman Brewster, Jr., "Reflections on Our National Purpose," *Foreign Affairs* 50 (April 1972): 399.

4. State of the Union Address, January 22, 1970, in *Papers of the Presidents: Richard Nixon, 1970*, p. 15.

5. Walter Lippmann, "Today and Tomorrow," *Washington Post*, September 17, 1959, and "The Country Is Waiting for Another Innovator," *Life* 48 (June 20, 1960): 114, 116.

6. State of the Union Message, January 21, 1980, in *Papers of the Presidents: Jimmy Carter, 1980*, I, 180.

7. Inaugural Address, January 20, 1981, in *Papers of the Presidents: Ronald Reagan, 1981*, pp. 1-4.

8. Commencement Address, Syracuse University, March 9, 1981.

9. Archer Blood, career diplomat, points out that a newly elected President "is in a good position to restate the national purpose or give a new dimension to its meaning." See his "In Search of the National Purpose," *Parameters* 7, No. 1 (1977): 61. For brief commentary on presidential inaugural addresses, see Dante Germino, *Inaugural Addresses of American Presidents: The Public Philosophy of Rhetoric* (Lanham, Md.: University Press of America, 1984).

10. Richard Nixon, *U.S. Foreign Policy for the 1970's--Building for Peace: A Report to Congress by Richard Nixon, February 25, 1971* (Washington: Government Printing Office, 1971), p. 6.

11. Henry Kissinger, *Selected Statements, 1977-1980* (Boston: Little, Brown, 1981), p. 131.

12. Henry Steele Commager, *In Search of a Usable Past and Other Essays in Historiography* (New York: Knopf, 1967), pp. 3-7.

13. Hans J. Morgenthau, *The Purpose of American Politics* (New York: Knopf, 1960), p. 11.

14. Herbert von Borch, "Farewell to Utopia," *The Unfinished Society* (New York: Hawthorn Books, 1962).

15. Winston Lord, *America's Purposes in an Ambiguous Age* (Washington: Government Printing Office, 1974), p. 1.

16. The decline of purpose has been attributed to, or characterized by, such factors as Cold War frustrations, challenges to American national power and leadership, declining unity and patriotism accompanied by intensified individualism and adversarial pluralism, mushrooming of new and different value systems, and difficulties in wearing the inherited mantle of caretaker of an old order. For an extreme criticism, see Gary Allen, "We Could Be Losing the American Dream," *American Opinion* 20 (June 1977): 1-6, 71-88, in which, although he claims that it still glows in the heads and hearts of many Americans, it is being clouded by growing cynicism and may be destroyed.
On the matter of motivating and re-energizing the country, see American Enterprise Institute, *Revitalizing America: What Are the Possibilities?* (Washington: American Enterprise Institute, 1981), which is concerned largely with domestic policy and the role of Congress. Moderator of the panel, John Charles Daly, posed the theme of discussion when he

said: "The times call for a new day, for a national will to take up arms against a sea of troubles and, by opposing those troubles, to end them."

17. Dwight D. Eisenhower, *Papers of the Presidents: Dwight D. Eisenhower, 1953*, pp. 1-8.

18. William P. Rogers, Department of State, *United States Foreign Policy, 1969-1970: A Report of the Secretary of State* (Washington: Government Printing Office, 1971), p. III. A few years later, in his memoirs, President Nixon observed: "As people got more material goods they became less 'hungry,' lost their drive, and became almost totally obsessed with self, selfishness, and every kind of abstract idea." See *The Memoirs of Richard Nixon* (New York: Grosset and Dunlap, 1978), p. 1033.

19. Jimmy Carter, State of the Union Message, January 21, 1980; State of the Union Address, January 23, 1980; and "Farewell Address," January 14, 1981, in *Papers of the Presidents: Jimmy Carter, 1980-1981*, I, pp. 114, 200, and III, pp. 2889, 2890, 2892. In an address to the nation on July 15, 1979, President Carter dwelt at length on the American malaise, in which he spoke of "a fundamental threat to American democracy," "a crisis of confidence" that "threatened to destroy the social and the political fabric of America," and national "paralysis and stagnation and drift;" see volume for 1979, pp. 1236-38.

20. Richard B. Morris, "Historical Prologue" in *The National Purpose Reconsidered*, edited by Dona Baron (New York: Columbia University Press, 1978), p. 9.

21. Brewster, "Reflections on Our National Purpose," pp. 399, 404.

22. George F. Kennan, *Realities of American Foreign Policy* (Princeton: Princeton University Press, 1954), pp. 4-23. Others support Kennan's view that national purpose must be unique, distinguishing one nation from another; see Charles Burton Marshall, *The Exercise of Sovereignty: Papers on Foreign Policy* (Baltimore: Johns Hopkins Press, 1965), pp. 24-29, and Blood, "In Search of the National Purpose," pp. 53-54. On the other hand, referring to his personal experiences, in his memoirs Kennan confessed: "Objectives were normally vainglorious, unreal, extravagant, even pathetic--little likely to be realized, scarcely to be taken seriously. People had to have them, or to believe they had them . . . . But methods are another matter. These were real. It was out of their immediate effects that the quality of life was really molded." See his *Memoirs, 1925-1950* (Boston: Little, Brown, 1967), I, p. 199.

23. Edward McNall Burns, *The American Idea of Mission: Concepts of National Purpose and Destiny* (New Brunswick, N.J.: Rutgers University Press, 1957), quotations from pp. vii, 5, 358-59. Others that equate purpose with mission include Arthur A. Ekirch, Jr., *Ideas, Ideals, and American Diplomacy: A History of Their Growth and Interaction* (New York: Appleton-Century-Crofts, 1966), Chapter 2 on "The Idea of Mission," and Brian Klunk, *Consensus and the American Mission* (Lanham, Md.: University Press of America, 1985). For other volumes dealing with particular aspects of the subject from differing perspectives, produced during this period, see Charles A. and Mary R. Beard, *The American Spirit: A Study of the Idea of Civilization in the United States* (New York: Macmillan, 1942); Henry S. Commager, *The American Mind: An Interpretation of American Thought and Character Since the 1880's* (New Haven, Conn.: Yale University Press, 1950); Eric F. Goldman, *Rendezvous With Destiny: A History of Modern American Reform* (New York: Knopf, 1952); Ernest L. Klein,

Our Appointment With Destiny: America's Role on the World Stage (New York: Farrar, Straus, and Young, 1952); Shepard B. Clough, *The American Way: The Economic Basis of Our Civilization* (New York: Crowell, 1953); Leland D. Baldwin, *The Meaning of America: Essays Toward an Understanding of the American Spirit* (Pittsburgh: University of Pittsburgh Press, 1955); Max Lerner, *America as a Civilization* (New York: Simon and Schuster, 1957); Dexter Perkins, *The American Way* (Ithaca, N.Y.: Cornell University Press, 1957), especially the last chapter, and *Foreign Policy and the American Spirit* (Ithaca, N.Y.: Cornell University Press, 1957), especially Chapters 1 and 8; Stow Persons, *American Minds: A History of Ideas* (New York: Holt, 1958); Emily S. Rosenberg, *Spreading the American Dream* (New York: Hill and Wang, 1982); and Daniel Yankelovich and Bernard Lefkowitz, "The New American Dream: The U.S. in the 1980s," *Futurist* 14 (August 1980): 3-15, on the possibility of a new American consensus.

24. Morgenthau, *The Purpose of American Politics*, especially pp. 7-10, 33-34. See also his "The United States as a World Power: A Balance Sheet," *International Studies Quarterly* 11 (October 1969): 111-48, in which he deals with national purpose as well as national power. See also Paul Seabury, *Power, Freedom, and Diplomacy: The Foreign Policy of the United States of America* (New York: Random House, 1963), Chapter 11 on "The Search for a National Purpose."

25. This symposium, edited by John K. Jessup, contains essays by Archibald MacLeish (Librarian of Congress and Pulitzer Prize poet and playright) and Adlai Stevenson (governor of Illinois and twice presidential candidate), Billy Graham (evangelist) and David Sarnoff (general manager and president of RCA), John Gardner (president of Carnegie Corporation) and Albert Wohlstetter (national defense specialist for the Rand Corporation), and Clinton Rossiter (professor of government) and Walter Lippmann (political commentator). These articles were published in issues of *Life*, vol. 48, nos. 20-24 (May 23-June 20, 1960). The contributions of presidential candidates Kennedy and Nixon were added in vol. 49, no. 8 (August 22 and 29, 1960). Several of these articles are cited separately in this Chapter.

26. Each essay is given a distinct title. See John K. Jessup, ed., *The National Purpose* (New York: Holt, Rinehart, and Winston, 1960).

27. *American Principles and Issues: The National Purpose*, edited by Oscar Handlin (New York: Holt, Rinehart, and Winston, 1961). It deals with Americanism, triumphant democracy, and American ideals, principles, and greatness, as well as such topics as aspirations and challenges, republicanism, freedoms, property rights, individualism, capitalism, industry, education, immigration, and orthodoxy versus change.

28. Walter Lippmann, "Today and Tomorrow," *Washington Post*, September 17, 1959. He also revealed in his personal correspondence his concern about America's purposelessness in competition with the Soviet Union during the Cold War; see *Public Philosopher: Selected Letters of Walter Lippmann*, edited by John Morton Blum (New York: Ticknor and Fields, 1985), p. 594. For his second article, see "The Country Is Waiting for Another Innovator," pp. 114, 116, 122, 125-26; this was also published as "A Nation on Dead Center Needs a Tow," *Washington Post* (June 19, 1960).

29. Leonard G. Benson, *National Purpose: Ideology and Ambivalence in America* (Washington: Public Affairs Press, 1963). For another sociological interpretation, see Kenneth Thompson, *Beliefs and Ideology* (London-Chichester: Tavistock, 1986), which analyzes conservative and

radical political philosophies and distinguishes ideologies from beliefs.

30. Thomas I. Cook and Malcolm Moos, *Power Through Purpose: The
Realism of Idealism as a Basis for Foreign Policy* (Baltimore: Johns
Hopkins Press, 1954). For commentary on the concept of international
purposes, see also Arnold Wolfer's statement in note 70.

31. *America: Purpose and Power*, edited by Gene Martin Lyons (Chicago: Quadrangle Books, 1965).

32. Richard Morris in *The National Purpose Reconsidered*, edited by
Dona Baron, pp. 1, 7-8, 120.

33. For purposes of this analysis, aside from those articles and
short essays published in *Life* magazine, see especially Samuel Flagg
Bemis, "American Foreign Policy and the Blessings of Liberty," *American
Historical Review* 67 (January 1962): 291-305; Blood, "In Search of the
National Purpose," pp. 53-62; Brewster, "Reflections on Our National
Purpose," pp. 399-415; Chester B. Bowles, "It Is Time to Reaffirm Our
National Purpose," *Department of State Bulletin* 45 (November 27, 1961):
875-80; Fisher Howe, "The Concept of National Purpose," paper presented
at the U.S. Army War College (processed, 1968); Bayless Manning, "Goals,
Ideology and Foreign Policy," *Foreign Affairs* 54 (January 1976): 271-84;
Elmer Plischke, "Above Narrow Interests: Our National Purpose," *Gettys-
burg Alumni Magazine* (August 1982): 5-7; and Dean Rusk, "American Purposes and the Pursuit of Human Dignity," *Department of State Bulletin* 57
(September 18, 1967): 343-49 and "The Central Purpose of United States
Foreign Policy," *Department of State Bulletin* 57 (August 28, 1967): 251-
55.

34. Benjamin R. Barber, "The Compromised Republic: Public Purposelessness in America," in *The Moral Foundations of American Public Life*,
edited by Robert H. Horwitz, 2nd ed. (Charlottesville: University Press
of Virginia, 1979), pp. 19-38, especially pp. 19-20, 24.

35. Benson comments on such critics as Hans Morgenthau, Daniel
Boorstin, and Reinhold Niebuhr; see his *National Purpose*, pp. 56-58.
The criticisms of Morgenthau, Boorstin, and Niebuhr are also mentioned
by Blood, "In Search of the National Purpose," p. 53.

36. Bemis, "American Foreign Policy and the Blessings of Liberty,"
p. 292.

37. John K. Jessup, "A Noble Framework for a Great Debate," *Life* 48
(May 23, 1960): 24.

38. Clinton Rossiter, "We Must Show the Way to Enduring Peace,"
Life 48 (June 13, 1960): 99.

39. Kissinger, *Selected Statements*, 1977-1980, p. 77. Relating national purpose to ideals, Kissinger also wrote: "Clearly we must maintain our values and our principles; but we risk disaster unless we relate them to concepts of the national interest and international order
that are based not on impulse but on a sense of steady purpose that can
be maintained by the American people for the long term." See his "Moral
Promise and Practical Deeds," *Department of State Bulletin* 75 (November
15, 1976), p. 600.

40. Manning, "Goals, Ideology and Foreign Policy," p. 284. On con-

sensus--though addressing himself to ideology rather than specifically to
national purpose--commenting on the need for public motivation in the
United States, Manning claims that in the 1960s "we too long retained a
consensus as to our perception of reality into a new era in which the
reality itself had radically changed," and that "even a high degree of
ideological content in our foreign policy will not produce consensus,
eliminate debate, or provide answers to foreign policy problems." See
pp. 272, 276.

41. Machiavelli wrote: "A prince . . . should seem to be all mercy,
faith, integrity, humanity, and religion" and he added: "in the actions
of men, and especially of princes, from which there is no appeal, the end
justifies the means." See *The Prince* (New York: Mentor Classic, New
American Library, 1952), p. 94. Machiavelli's expression was reiterated
verbatim by Hermann Busenbaum the following century in his *Medulla Theo-
logiae Moralis* (1650). For commentary on Machiavelli, see Harvey C.
Mansfield, Jr., "Machiavelli's Political Science," *American Political
Science Review* 75 (June 1981): 293-305.

42. Sir Thomas Browne, *Religio Medici*, section 20 (1642, and many
subsequent editions).

43. Matthew Prior in *Hans Carrel*, quoted in *Magill's Quotations in
Context*, edited by Frank M. Magill (Englewood Cliffs, N.J.: Salem Press,
1965), I, p. 205; also quoted in *Dictionary of English Quotations*, edited
by Philip Hugh Dalbiac (London: Swan Sonnerschein, 1896), p. 250.

44. In this context it may be difficult to accept Gandhi's allegation that "If one takes care of the means, the end will take care of itself." See *The Book of Unusual Quotations*, edited by Rudolf Flesch (New
York: Harper, 1957), p. 167. As early as the fifteenth century Sadi, a
Persian poet, had written: "Purpose without power is weakness; power
without purpose is fatuity," in *Gullistan*, Chapter 8, Maxim 59, quoted in
The Macmillan Book of Proverbs, Maxims, and Famous Phrases, p. 1920.

45. Charles O. Lerche and Abdul A. Said, *Concepts of International
Politics in Global Perspective*, 3d ed. (Englewood Cliffs, N.J.: Pren-
tice-Hall, 1979), p. 28. "To make fundamental choices," observes Albert
Wohlstetter, it is necessary to distinguish "specific means" from "gen-
eral ends." See his "A Purpose Hammered Out of Reflection and Choice,"
Life 48 (June 20, 1960): 126.

46. Charles O. Lerche, Jr., *Foreign Policy of the American People*,
3d ed. (Englewood Cliffs, N.J.: Prentice-Hall, 1967), p. 341.

47. Aside from "ideals," discussed elsewhere in this chapter, many
commentaries prefer to conjoin all ends by a single encompassing designation, such as "aims"--see *The Foreign Policies of the Powers*, edited
by F. S. Northedge (New York: Free Press, 1968), pp. 17-22; "goals"--
see Arnold Wolfers, "The Goals of Foreign Policy," in his *Discord and
Collaboration: Essays on International Politics* (Baltimore: Johns Hopkins
Press, 1962), pp. 67-80; and Cecil V. Crabb, Jr., *American Foreign Policy
in the Nuclear Age* (Evanston, Ill.: Row, Peterson, 1960), pp. 1-5, which
he later changed to "goals and objectives," see his 4th ed. (1983), pp.
15-20; "objectives"--see Joseph Frankel, *The Making of Foreign Policy:
An Analysis of Decision-Making* (New York: Oxford University Press, 1963),
Chapters 8-10, especially pp. 136-39; or "fundamental values"--see symposium *The National Purpose Reconsidered*, edited by Dona Baron, p. 120.

48. See James R. Cobbledick, *Choice in American Foreign Policy:*

Options for the Future (New York: Crowell, 1973), pp. 2-9.

49. Wolfers, *Discord and Collaboration*, pp. 68-69.

50. Frankel, *The Making of Foreign Policy*, p. 141.

51. Kennan, *Realities of American Foreign Policy*, p. 4.

52. Hamilton, *The Federalist*, No. 31.

53. Walter Lippmann, *U.S. Foreign Policy: Shield of the Republic* (Boston: Little, Brown, 1943), p. 10.

54. Charles Burton Marshall, *The "Limits" of Foreign Policy* (New York: Holt, 1954), pp. 29-32. Speaking of the proliferation of ends, Marshall also observes: "A government proclaims aims in excess of its means" so that becoming anxious over the difference between what it can do and what it desires, "it seeks to redress the disparity by even wider assertions of aims still more stridently proclaimed."

55. See Paul H. Nitze, "Necessary and Sufficient Elements of a General Theory of International Relations," in *Theoretical Aspects of International Relations*, edited by William T. R. Fox (Notre Dame, Ind.: Notre Dame University Press, 1959), p. 7.

56. See comments in Chapter 2.

57. Dealing with purpose at the highest level, for example, Joseph L. Blau philosophizes: "Ultimate purpose" must be the "one final known," and "all finite purposes, our purposes, must be justified as possession of a unique part of this unitary purpose." See his *Men and Movements in American Philosophy* (Englewood Cliffs, N.J.: Prentice-Hall, 1952), p. 215. Marshall, discussing "The Two Views of National Purpose," differentiates between the universal purpose of mankind, which remains "inherently a unity," and the purposes of individual nations pursued by their respective governments; see *The Exercise of Sovereignty*, pp. 24-26. On this matter of common versus varying purposes of nations, see also the views of George Kennan quoted earlier.

58. Wohlstetter, "A Purpose Hammered Out of Reflection and Choice," p. 115.

59. Bowles, "It Is Time to Reaffirm Our National Purpose," p. 880. But Bowles also uses the expression in the singular as "America's national purpose," denoting a combination of individual but related purposes.

60. Rusk, "American Purposes and the Pursuit of Human Dignity," p. 348.

61. For example, see the commentary of diplomatic historian William L. Langer, "The United States Role in the World," in The President's Commission on National Goals, *Goals for Americans* (Englewood Cliffs, N.J.: Prentice-Hall, 1960), pp. 327-29.

62. James Reston, "National Purpose: Reston Analysis," *New York Times* (June 20, 1960): 28.

63. Archibald MacLeish, "We Have Purpose: We All Know It," *Life* 48 (May 30, 1960): 86.

64. Blood, "In Search of the National Purpose," p. 58.

65. Richard Nixon, "Our Resolve is Running Strong," *Life* 49 (August 29, 1960): 94; also see Adlai Stevenson, "Extend Our Vision . . . to All Mankind," *Life* 48 (May 30, 1960): 87.

66. Jessup, "A Noble Framework for a Great Debate," p 34.

67. John F. Kennedy, "We Must Climb to the Hilltop," *Life* 49 (August 22, 1960): 70, 75, 76.

68. See Fisher Howe, "The Concept of National Purpose." See also Rusk, "The Central Purpose of United States Foreign Policy," p. 252.

69. Brewster, "Reflections on Our National Purpose," p. 415.

70. Relating goals and interests, Wolfers contends that there is "a danger in using the word international here because it might suggest either that these goals are not in the national interest or that governments can and should pursue goals other than those concerning the national interest." See his "The Goals of Foreign Policy" in *Discord and Collaboration*, p. 75. Also see comments on globalizing national interests in Chapter 2.

71. According to Dean Acheson, the national purpose of the United States "is to survive, and, if possible, to prosper." Archer Blood rejects this formulation as simplistic and because it is not unique to the United States; see his "In Search of the National Purpose," p. 53.

72. Cook and Moos, *Power Through Purpose*, p. 126. Also see their comments on national interest given in Chapter 2.

73. Bemis, "American Foreign Policy and the Blessings of Liberty." Others--including President Nixon, Dean Rusk, and Richard Morris--also refer to this expression in defining the national purpose of the United States. Similarly, Robert A. Taft has written: "Fundamentally . . . the ultimate purpose of our foreign policy must be to protect the liberty of the people of the United States . . . To achieve that liberty we have gone to war, and to protect it we would go to war again;" see *A Foreign Policy for Americans* (Garden City, N.Y.: Doubleday, 1951), p. 11. However later he changed this to "the peace and security of the people of the United States," p. 20. See also Lippmann, "The Country Is Waiting for Another Innovator," in which he epitomizes American national purpose as "the blessings of freedom." Dean Acheson, prescribing his views on lines of action to be pursued by the United States, heads his list with the principle of demonstrating that "our own faith in freedom is a burning and a fighting faith"--"the most dynamic and revolutionary concept in human history" and he contends that the value of freedom must be communicated to the four corners of the earth; see Department of State, *Strengthening the Forces of Freedom: Selected Speeches and Statements of Secretary of State Acheson* (Washington: Government Printing Office, 1950), pp. 1-7. On the "blessings of liberty," also see John C. Whitehead, "Securing the Blessings of Liberty," *Presidential Studies Quarterly* 17 (Summer 1987): 445-51, which deals with human rights and democracy; also see Zbigniew Pelczynski and John Gray, eds., *Conceptions of Liberty in Political Philosophy* (New York: St. Martin's Press, 1984).

74. These terms are frequently used interchangeably. For example, Feliks Gross states: "National interests may be defined as the general and continuing ends for which a nation acts." See his *Foreign Policy*

Analysis (New York: Philosophical Library, 1954), p. 53. See also commentary in Chapter 2.

On the other hand, Richard Nixon clearly differentiates between interests and purposes and points out that some articles in the *Life* series are concerned with purposes whereas others mistakenly deal with interests. Critical of the divisive consequences of competing pluralistic interests in the American policy process, he asked: "Would it not be more in keeping with our best tradition if we sought a larger purpose within which our separate interests could be united in a more elevated conception of our destiny?" See "Our Resolve is Running Strong," p. 87.

75. Lerche, *Foreign Policy of the American People*, 3d ed., pp. 5-6, 9.

76. Benson, *National Purpose*, pp. 58-59.

77. Walter Lippmann, *Essays in the Public Philosophy* (Boston: Little, Brown, 1955).

78. Joseph Campbell, *The Masks of God*, especially Vol. II *Creative Mythology* (New York: Viking, 1968).

79. Both Benson and Manning discuss ideology in some depth, and Baron and others relate purpose to ideals. But in his survey of precepts, Bailey claims that "Idealism can be fatal in foreign affairs;" see *The Art of Diplomacy*, pp. 86-88. On ideology see also note 83 below and Willard A. Mullins, "On the Concept Ideology in Political Science," *American Political Science Review* 66 (June 1972): 498-510.

80. See, for example, Ansell Mowrer, *The Nightmare of American Foreign Policy* (New York: Knopf, 1948), pp. 24-40; he discusses seven "illusions and fallacies," such as Machiavellianism, international law (legalism), moralism, sentimentalism, and "economania." Similarly, Lippmann decries "prejudices and illusions," which he brands as "mirages" that vitiate the capacty to think effectively about foreign relations. Among them he lists peace (noting that survival of the nation takes priority), disarmament, "no entangling alliances," and "collective security." See his *U.S. Foreign Policy*, Chapter 5.

81. Benson, *National Purpose*, p. 1.

82. Andrew M. Scott, *The Functioning of the International Political System* (New York: Macmillan, 1967), p. 30.

83. Center for International Affairs, Harvard University, "Ideology and Foreign Affairs," prepared for the United States Senate Committee on Foreign Relations (Washington: Government Printing Office, 1960), quoted in Harold and Margaret Sprout, *Foundations of International Politics* (Princeton: Princeton University Press, 1962), p. 525.

84. Brewster, "Reflections on Our National Purpose," p. 414.

85. Henry M. Wriston, "The Individual," in *Goals for Americans*, p. 39.

86. Nixon, "Our Resolve is Running Strong," p. 87.

87. Kennedy, "We Must Climb to the Hilltop," p. 70B.

88. Howe, "The Concept of National Purpose," p. 5.

89. Kennan, *Realities of American Foreign Policy*, p. 5. In a broader sense, one analysis of Kennan's thinking characterizes his unifying theme as "the quality of a civilization is the only true measure of its purposes, its methods, and its prospects in world affairs;" see Barton Gellman, *Contending with Kennan: Toward a Philosophy of American Power* (New York: Praeger, 1984), p. 140.

90. Morgenthau, *The Purpose of American Politics*, p. 7.

91. James MacGregor Burns, *Presidential Government: The Crucible of Leadership* (Boston: Houghton Mifflin, 1966), p. 239.

92. Kennan, *Realities of American Foreign Policy*, p. 6.

93. Paul Seabury, *The United States in World Affairs* (New York: McGraw-Hill, 1973), p. 22. See also note 71.

94. These items were regarded as national purposes by such early leaders as Hamilton, Jefferson, and Madison, by Presidents Kennedy and Nixon, and by many later analysts including Bemis, Blood, Jessup, MacLeish, Reston, and Rossiter. Dean Rusk broadens the list to embrace national security, international peace, and world order, but also includes the blessings of liberty; see his "American Purposes and the Pursuit of Human Dignity," and "The Central Purpose of United States Foreign Policy."

95. Kennedy, "We Must Climb to the Hilltop," p. 70B.

96. Joseph Frankel, *National Interest* (New York: Praeger, 1970), p. 24.

97. Ernest W. LeFever, *Ethics and United States Foreign Policy* (New York: Meridian, 1957), p. 12.

98. Bemis, "American Foreign Policy and the Blessings of Liberty," pp. 292-93.

99. Joseph L. Blau contends: "However we regard purpose, we must recognize that to say a purpose is achievable is to say that it is experienceable and therefore natural." See his *Men and Movements in American Philosophy*, p. 321.

100. It has been said that the nation "may be basically satisfied with its place in the world and seek no major changes in the international structure," or it "may decide that its place in the world is unacceptable." See Lerche and Said, *Concepts of International Politics*, 3d ed., p. 36; for discussion, see pp. 37-39.

5

NATIONAL GOALS
AND POLICY
OBJECTIVES

If we could first know *where* we are, and *whither* we
are tending, we could better judge *what* we do, and
how to do it.

Abraham Lincoln, "A House Divided,"
Address, June 16, 1858

Ideals are like stars; you will not succeed in
touching them with your hands...you choose them as
your guides, and following them you will reach your
destiny.

Carl Schurz, Address, Faneuil Hall,
Boston, April 18, 1859

It should be obvious that goals and objectives are essential
in the foreign relations process. Constituting the ends
sought to be achieved by foreign policies, in their study of
international relations concepts Charles Lerche and Abdul
Said observe that "foreign policy is purposeful" and "state
action in foreign policy is always in pursuit of an objective."[1] In his general study of contemporary foreign policy,
Cecil V. Crabb, Jr., writes equally succinctly that all members of the international community have certain goals and
objectives to which they are devoted--that they are purposeful.[2]

Putting it normatively in his anthology of diplomatic
precepts as noted, Thomas A. Bailey contends that without
purpose policies are pointless, and he warns that foreign
policies are not and should not be ends in themselves, presuming thereby that they are designed to attain such ends.[3]
Similarly, in his general text on American foreign affairs,
Charles Lerche argues that state action "must be purposive"
and, implying differentiation between goals and objectives,
that each state organizes its aspirations "into a set of
objectives that represent the goals it seeks to reach by
deliberate action."[4]

Goals and objectives designate the kinds of conditions,
developments, or adjustments desired by the state and therefore relate integrally to the nation's interests, motivating

purposes, foreign policies, capabilities, and strategies. Discussing the behavior of nations, K. J. Holsti character- izes their aims as "essentially an 'image' of a future state of affairs and future set of conditions which governments . . . aspire to bring about by wielding influence abroad and by changing or sustaining the behavior of other states."[5] A. F. K. Organski, in his study of world politics, calls them "a future state of affairs that someone considers desirable and worth spending some effort to achieve" which, he adds, "do not exist in the abstract" but rather "in someone's mind."[6]

Reflecting the universal perception that, in the foreign relations cosmography, goals and policy objectives embody the aims of the nation, they represent one of the primary factors in the ends-means relationship, discussed in Chapter 4. Views differ, however, as to whether greater consideration is paid to ends or to means, and which appear to be more important in both state practice and policy analysis. Some maintain that with the proliferation of goals and objectives insufficient attention is devoted by political leaders in public policy statements to the means for their successful implementation, and others contend that aspirations are often exaggerated and therefore are unlikely to be realized, so that the crucial test is the means decided upon to effectuate them.[7] But there are also those who claim that governments often act without defining their aims. Still others argue that, in practice as well as in theory, ends and means are clearly correlative and mutually supporting in the ends-means contin- uum of the nation and need to be coalesced in policy-making.

At the outset, it should be noted, according to certain diplomatic officials, the abstract formulation of national goals is the easiest and least demanding step in the conduct of foreign affairs, whereas defining concrete policy objec- tives (and deciding among foreign policy alternatives) is far more difficult. Often, as a result, these objectives remain ill-defined by political leaders, even with hindsight. Taken as a whole, or even for a particular functional, geographic, or time segment of a nation's foreign relations spectrum, the resulting network of goals and objectives is multiple and diverse, and at times it is unstructured if not inherently inconsistent. Most practitioners and social scientists en- dorse this pluralistic or multicausal approach, postulating multiple causation. But there are some theorists who espouse a monocausal or monistic perception which propounds a priori the overriding dictum of a single determinant, from an eco- nomic, geographic, or national security perspective.[8]

In practice most countries pursue their multiple aims concurrently, and often a single goal or objective may lead to several policy actions, and vice versa, several objectives may produce a single integrated policy development. Moreover, in moving from the realm of national goals to decisions on concrete objectives and the formulation of implemental for- eign policies, governments and peoples must realize that state action--or the pragmatization of policy--entails the probability of sacrifice, the commitment of resources, and other costs.

In both theoretical and practical usage, analysts are

generally united in distinguishing goals and objectives from
such conceptions as national interests (defined in Chapter
2); values and ideology (discussed in Chapters 2 and 4); intention and motivation (which Joseph Frankel construes as
psychological, often subconscious); aspirations (which Arnold
Wolfers perceives as aims that are not converted into actualized objectives); national purposes (the unique type of aim
defined in Chapter 4); principles (which Feliks Gross views
as standards of conduct or rules of action, rather than
ends); foreign policies (dealt with in the next chapter);
means (processes for implementing actualized goals); methods
(which Ambassador George Kennan regards as more crucial to
the conduct of foreign affairs than are objectives) or canons
of behavior (which Frankel calls international procedures);
planning (which involves the identification, objective analysis, and solution of discrete and concrete issues and which,
according to Frankel, facilitates the making of decisions in
advance); and strategy (defined in Chapter 8).⁹

CONCERN WITH GOALS AND OBJECTIVES

Dealing with foreign affairs, statesmen and commentators
are constantly concerned with defining and operationalizing
national aims. Hundreds of public documents are issued to
prescribe them, commissions and other agencies are established to interpret and refine them, political leaders pro-
mulgate them, parliaments embody them in resolutions and
enactments, and dozens of analysts assess their salience and
validity.

In the United States, for example, nearly every presidential inaugural address and state of the union message, a
host of foreign policy statements not only of the President
but also of the Secretary of State and other high officials,
and many congressional reports provide lists of, and discussion on, America's goals and policy objectives. Among the
best remembered twentieth-century statements are the Fourteen
Points enunciated by President Wilson during World War I, the
eight "principles" of the Atlantic Charter signed by President Roosevelt in 1941, and President Truman's twelve "Fundamentals of American Foreign Policy" proclaimed in his Navy
Day address in 1945.

To these, merely to cite a few illustrations, may be
added such contributions as the goals prescribed in George
Washington's Farewell Address, those laid down by President
Jefferson in his first inaugural address (including "peace,
commerce, and honest friendship with all nations, entangling
alliances with none"), and President Roosevelt's Four Freedoms. Other examples embrace Secretary of State Cordell
Hull's address on seven foreign relations fundamentals in
1938; Secretary of State Dean Acheson's emphasis on "freedom
and security" in an address of 1950, in which he suggested
six "lines of action;" President Eisenhower's inaugural address of 1953 in which he advocates ten "fixed principles"
or "basic precepts" on which to found foreign policy; Secretary of State Dean Rusk's address entitled "Five Goals of
U.S. Foreign Policy," delivered in 1962; President Carter's
inaugural address in which he lists six "hopes"; and Secre-

tary of State Cyrus Vance's statement on "U.S. Foreign Policy
Objectives" presented to the Senate Foreign Relations Committee in 1980 in which he identifies two "central points" and
seven basic "interests."[10]

Additional statements of goals may be found in presidential addresses at the sessions of the United Nations General
Assembly, in many international treaties and agreements (including the United Nations Charter, the North Atlantic Treaty, and the Charter of Punta del Este), in international policy declarations subscribed to by the United States (such as
the "Declaration of Peace and Progress in Asia and the Pacific" and the four "Goals of Freedom" signed by President Lyndon B. Johnson in 1966 during the Vietnam War), and in "presidential doctrines" bearing the names of Presidents Monroe,
Truman, Eisenhower, Johnson, Nixon, Carter, and Reagan.[11]
These may be supplemented with additional statements of goals
and objectives to be found in numerous presidential papers,
Department of State memoranda and publications, National Security Council documents, congressional reports, and many
other official sources.

CHARACTERISTICS OF GOALS AND OBJECTIVES

National goals and policy objectives are derived from a
variety of sources. Values, ideologies, cultures, national
characters, historical traditions and precedents, existing
political and social systems, and other general and abstract
factors are said to constitute or reflect the general sources
of national aspirations. These may vary from monistic religious, geographic, or economic determinism to various
pluralistic cultural and political considerations.

In most cases an almost endless array of specific internal and international needs and demands affect the prescription of ends sought. These include such broad categories
as crises and threats to national security, political stability, economic development, and human welfare; common international needs and problems; opportunities to take advantage of
situations created by foreign events and conditions; reaction
to the objectives and actions of other states; internal interests, desires, and pressures; shifts in public opinion;
and even the nature and functioning of a nation's institutional process by which decisions concerning foreign relations are considered and made, as well as the persuasions of
those leaders who are central to the framing of policy.[12]

So far as goal determination is concerned, it is arguable that for nations--as social organizations distinct from
those individuals who act in its behalf--such sources, especially those that are general or abstract, ordain the parameters within which goals and objectives may be defined.[13]
More pragmatic are those who regard goal formulation as a
political function that balances desires, interests, resources, capabilities, feasibilities, and costs.[14] Presumably this implies all those forces that influence the political process, including national leaders, political parties
and factions, ruling elites, interest groups, and public attitudes. Others ascribe this function more narrowly to de-

cision makers.[15]   Whether the end sought is construed as a
national purpose, goal, or objective, it is likely to be viable for the state considered as a political organism only
insofar as the nation's policy makers share in supporting and
are motivated to pursue it.[16]

Similarly, it is contended that national purposiveness
may be viewed differently by asking if, in foreign affairs,
"it is not merely an intellectual construct that man imputes
to himself" and then projects to "the social organizations of
which he is a member."   This boils down to the question
whether nations "pursue goals and objectives of their own
choosing or are moved toward those imposed upon them by
forces which lie primarily beyond their control."[17] In short,
whereas the more abstract and general goals may be volitionally determined, often a priori, some of the more precise and
concrete objectives may be evoked by international conditions
or events so that, in their totality, goals and objectives
encompass both those that are initiatory and others that are
essentially reactive.

Those who hold that nations have multiple goals and objectives use these concepts in both the singular and plural.
It is also agreed that while the more fundamental national
goals are constant, in their more finite supporting versions
they are mutable. By way of illustration, it has been said
that the modern state possesses "an endless proliferation of
diplomatic objectives" and that "the potential number of objectives is infinite."[18]   In his analysis of goals, Donald
J. Puchala maintains that most states "continually mix--si-
multaneously--multiple motivations to pursue multiple ends by
multiple means."[19] Referring to the practical functioning
of the policy process, Fisher Howe goes one step further by
suggesting that in national policy-making some explicit specification of goals would be useful if it constituted "a pervasive set of 'imperatives' for the conduct of foreign affairs" and if it provided "a statement formulated just before
the point where global principles must be broken down into
practicalities of action."[20]

Endorsing the multicausal approach to foreign relations,
Arnold Wolfers categorically states: "Appearances to the contrary, there is no division of opinion among analysts of international politics about the fact that the policy of nations aims at a multitude of goals." In his probing study he
writes: "there would be no need to concern oneself with the
problem of goals if nation-states were single-purpose organizations," and "even if foreign policy were directed predom-
inantly toward a single goal, such a goal would not monopo-
lize the entire activity of states, except in the emergency
of a war."[21]

The multiplicity of goals and objectives presupposes
that at least in their more finite extrapolation they are
mutable. Considering this point, Frankel acknowledges: "the
relevance of objectives can completely change during their
pursuit" and their ranking and permutation "lies at the very
core of the making of foreign policy."   Such adjustment, for
both subsidiary (short-range) and strategic (long-range)
goals and objectives, he stresses, is intricate and compli-

cates the foreign affairs process.[22]

   "Realizing that any formulation of interest is subject
to modification and that many situational factors themselves
are inherently unstable," observes Lerche, "we are led to
conclude that objectives . . . are themselves constantly liable to change . . . . It is no wonder that states are continuously overhauling their patterns of objectives." Some
of them decrease in significance, while others require adaptation to accord with current developments.[23]

   Many analysts warn of the potential risk of divergent
and conflicting goals and objectives--or the danger of "cross
purposes." They use such expressions as inconsistent, contradictary, incompatible, and not mutually exclusive, or, if
inconstant, in the language of policy studies, they call them
variables. Bailey declares that "cross-purposes are poor
purposes," which, although understandable within the government bureaucracy and at more finite levels, may be costly to
the nation, and they are inexcusable "at the highest levels."[24] On this matter, in his text on international relations Frederick H. Hartmann notes that incompatibility is
more common with the nation's concrete objectives than with
its general and abstract goals and, as a country's purposiveness is applied to specific sets of circumstances, the inconsistency becomes more visible.[25] The task of the policy
maker, therefore, is not only to decide upon interrelations
and priorities among the nation's goals and objectives, but
also to minimize incompatibility, although in the management
of multicausal foreign relations this is often difficult.

CATEGORIES OF GOALS AND OBJECTIVES

   National goals and objectives are classified in many
ways. In the broadest terms they may be categorized substantively as ideological, political, economic, and military,
or they may focus on human rights, national prestige, and
other factors. On the other hand, they may be characterized
as geographically oriented--as neighbor to neighbor, or as
areal--continental (i.e., European) or either broader (i.e.,
Western Hemisphere) or narrower (i.e., Baltic or Caribbean).
More useful, however, is a scheme of classification founded
on such criteria as their value, scope, generality, applicability, time relevance, beneficiaries, or the kinds of demands they impose on other states.[26]

   Analysis suggests a broad spectrum of categorization.
Reviewing the literature on the subject, it is possible to
design various contrasting types of goals and objectives. In
addition to idealistic versus pragmatic, explicit versus implicit, feasible versus infeasible,[27] positive (or affirmative) versus negative,[28] the more obvious include fundamental, intermediate, and lesser--or primary, secondary, and
subsidiary (based on importance);[29] general versus specific,
abstract versus concrete, or strategic versus tactical (based
on scope);[30] domestic versus foreign or internal versus external (based on applicability);[31] and long-range versus
short-range or remote versus immediate (based on duration
and mutability).[32] As indicated in the preceding chapter,

authorities disagree on whether purposeful action needs to be conscious (derived by rational processes) or may be unconscious (attributed to intuition or impulse).[33]

A number of writers differentiate between goals and objectives that are universal or particularized (that is, those that are common to all nations versus those that motivate individual countries), and those that are correlative or competing (those that are pursued by more than one nation to their mutual advantage versus those that bring nations into competition or adversarial relationships). In recent literature authors also distinguish among national goals and objectives as independent variables--as well as "crucial" variables--in foreign affairs.

In a policy study, Charles M. Fergusson also recognizes the difference between goals and objectives that relate to events and those pertaining to conditions, and he concludes that the latter are more significant.[34] Reviewing their role in world politics Organski adds distinctions between goals and objectives that are merely stated versus those that are actual;[35] those that are absolute versus those that are relative;[36] those that are unified versus those that are divergent;[37] and those that support the status quo versus those that seek change.[38]

Addressing the matter of the intended beneficiaries, Organski compares "national" and "humanitarian" goals, differentiating between those that are advantageous solely to that nation and those that are altruistic and also benefit others.[39] Dealing with another aspect of this issue, Wolfers distinguishes between what he calls direct and indirect goals and objectives --that is, those that are "meant primarily to serve the nation" and those that are "of prime interest to individual citizens or groups of citizens in their private capacity." If the latter should also promote the welfare of the nation as a whole, he explains, "this can only be in an indirect fashion."[40]

Also concerned with beneficiaries, Wolfers differentiates between possession and milieu goals. In devising policy to attain possession goals, a nation "is aiming at the enhancement or the preservation of one or more things to which it attaches value" and for which it is the direct, perhaps the primary if not the sole beneficiary. Milieu goals, on the other hand, "aim instead at shaping conditions beyond their national boundaries," such as peace or global stability, which may be altruistic. But, he warns, they "may turn out to be nothing but a means for or a way station toward some possession goal," providing an exceptional benefit to the nation.[41]

In addition, Wolfers discusses the differences among goals and objectives that promote either self-extension, self-preservation, or self-abnegation. Self-extension objectives, he claims, express "a demand for values not already enjoyed, and thus a demand for a change of the status quo." Self-preservation objectives denote "all demands pointing toward the maintenance, protection, or defense of the existing distribution of values, usually called the status quo"--

or "a whole catalogue of 'vital interests'." Self-abnegation
objectives are quite different; they transcend if not sacrifice the "national interest" in "any meaningful sense of the
term," thereby, placing a higher value on other national
aims.[42]

By comparison, in his study of policy analysis, Howard
H. Lentner, coalescing discussion of goals and policies from
the perspective of involvement, draws distinctions between
those that seek insulation, expansion, or engagement. Nations
may choose to insulate themselves from international situations (such as opting for a neutral stance), to become involved in them if the nation cannot reach its goals alone,
or to dominate by extending its control beyond the domain
that it previously controlled. He also differentiates between maximum and minimum goals, which may be perceived both
quantitatively and qualitatively. The quantitative interpretation apposes focus on a single goal or sub-goal versus
the simultaneous pursuit of multiple goals. The qualitative
aspect, which he emphasizes, raises the difficulty of a nation not only in determining its own priorities but also
those of other nations with which it must deal, cautioning
that either maximization or minimization may lead to miscalculation.[43]

PRIORITIES

Given so many types and specific applications of foreign
relations goals and objectives--and their differences in significance, longevity, and concreteness--nations are confronted with the task of determining preferences among them. Because no nation can reasonably expect to accomplish everything it wishes in its interaction with other nations, according to Lerche and Said, "every state must possess a system of priorities that governs its policy choices." Some
goals and objectives are absolute and brook no compromise and
among the many others there are those that are regarded as
most essential, basic, or desirable, and a few of these are
elevated to the special status of driving national purposes.

Whereas such goals and objectives may stand on their own
merits, others are essentially supportive, producing an intricate hierarchy. Ranking among them is critical, not only
with respect to the pertinence of the individual goal or objective, but also in the light of the demands it imposes on
the commitment of human energy, national resources, and the
very processes of policy-making.

Naturally, high priority goals and objectives take pre-
cedence over others, but conflict may arise between criteria
of fundamentality, importance, permanence, and urgency. In
dealing with this problem, lesser or supporting goals and
objectives may, in fact, need to be refined, altered, post-
poned, or abandoned. Much policy-making effort of the nation's leaders, therefore, must be devoted to determining
both the essence of aims and their logical interrelationships, and often this is done not only in an unsystematic
manner or in isolation from other considerations, but more
frequently decisions are made largely in terms of develop-

ments at a particular time.   However, the nation that fails
to establish and act on its priorities may find that they are
imposed upon it by other nations or by the force of circumstances.[44]   For this   reason such decisions become the keystone of the nation's foreign affairs planning and strategy,
which are discussed in Chapter 8.

DIFFERENTIATING GOALS AND OBJECTIVES

Many statesmen and analysts confusingly use the terms
"purposes," "goals," and "objectives" interchangeably. Although some prefer one or another of these expressions, and
a growing number regard national purposes as a unique type of
national aim, few draw intelligible conceptual distinctions
between goals and objectives.[45] Those who try, however, generally distinguish between "goals" as more generic, abstract,
or general ends[46] and "objectives" as those that are more
concrete and realizable which, in practice, are actualized in
policy formulation.

Defining national goals as ends that are postulated a
priori and objectives as deriving from specific requirements
or situations and relating them to national concerns, Lerche
and Said explain that, in their view, a national interest is
a long-range if not a permanent factor involving an ultimate
value judgment. A goal, they say, is considered to be "operational for as far into the future as can be anticipated
analytically," but which may change and which requires an intermediate value judgment. An objective, on the other hand,
is "immediate or short range in its time component" and is
the state of affairs "considered attainable in terms of
forces operative at the moment of decision."[47]

In the opinion of diplomatic historian William L.
Langer, national goals "contain a large measure of idealism,
for they represent what a nation considers ultimately desirable not only in its own interest but in that of the whole
international community. As such, they are for the most part
not immediately attainable. Indeed, they may remain forever
in the realm of aspiration." He also contends that "they give
meaning to national and international life and set for a
people an end toward which it may strive and toward which
specific plans and policies may be directed."[48] Regarding
national interests as ends, Gross avoids discussing national
goals and restricts himself solely to the concept of objectives.   He holds that when a national interest "becomes sufficiently compelling for a state to seek to establish it
with finality by the exercise of power or influence, it is
delimited and particularized for a given context" and therefore "becomes an objective."[49]

Perhaps the simplest and most useful distinction is that
objectives are identical with goals, or more likely with
action-oriented aspects of goals that are volitionally converted into concrete aims on the basis of which foreign policies actually are formulated and implemented.[50]   In other
words, a nation's aims remain goals and fall short of becoming policy objectives unless they are concretely refined
for which actions are projected and taken to realize their

fulfillment.   On the spectrum of generality and specificity,
therefore, goals are more general and basic, while objectives
are more precise and pragmatic.   Consequently, goals are
guides to where the nation wants to go, and objectives, although also concerned with direction, come to grips with how
the nation chooses to get there.[51]

FUNDAMENTAL NATIONAL GOALS

      Contemporary analysis makes little effort to prescribe
the conceptual interpretation of "fundamental goals," possibly because the meaning seems obvious. Briefly stated:

> Fundamental national goals are those basic aims of
> the nation in its internal affairs and external
> relations that are deemed to be most essential to
> preserving and enhancing its ideals, values, char-
> acter, traditions, and status, and to promoting its
> interests as a national entity within the interna-
> tional relationship, and which, in the aggregate,
> are desirable if not crucial to maintaining the
> national integrity of the individual state and to
> advancing its status and welfare within the com-
> munity of nations.

      Many commentators prefer the more generic definition
that a national goal simply connotes a future state of affairs that is pursued by the nation and is worth some effort
to achieve. Ignoring the qualification of fundamentality and
differentiating it from concrete policy objectives, some
conceive it as a quasi-utopian formulation in that--as an
aspiration, or hope, or desire--it exceeds what a nation can
realistically attain, or which, not fully realizable, is un-
ending. A number of writers deem such goals to be intangible
if not purposely vague, and find them broader in scope and
longer-lived than policy objectives. Or they are regarded as
"rock-bottom requirements" or "premises rather than objectives."[52] Imbedded in the culture of the nation, or in its
values and traditions, articulated by its government, and influenced by the past though directed toward the future, fundamental goals are often obscure and are expressed in qualitative rather than quantitative terms.

      Whereas it is impossible to devise a comprehensive cata-
logue of precise aims pursued by all states, the fundamental
and general goals clearly embrace the achievement of national
independence and identity (referred to as freedom and self-
preservation); the maintenance of national security and territorial integrity; the promotion of human welfare (including
economic well-being); the enhancement of national honor and
prestige; and the preservation of peace, order, and tranquil-
lity.[53] Some analysts add the development of national power
(the ability to influence, persuade, or coerce) and capability (the ability to perform) in their catalogue of national
goals. Although these are usually viewed not as ends, but as
means for implementing the nation's goals, some regard them
as ends in themselves, as noted in Chapter 7.

      In varying degrees, such permeating goals are presumed

to serve as the common pursuits of all peoples, but interpretations, emphases, priorities, and implemental policies
and actions differ from time to time and country to country.
As national phenomena their impact upon one another in the
international environment often renders them intrinsically
competitive though not necessarily incompatible. At times,
however, while not inconsistent in essence, as in the case of
the interrelation of self-preservation and the maintenance of
peace, they may be contradictory if not irreconcilable in
practice. Two adversaries, for example, may both seek to
preserve peace and their own security, and the precipitation
of forceful action by one country to enhance peace by improving its security posture vis-à-vis the other may be considered by the latter as a threat to its security--and therefore may prove to be destabilizing.

Of these universally acknowledged national goals, the
first--national independence--differs from the others in that
it is attainable and usually constitutes the country's highest priority during its formative period. Later it declines
or may even disappear from public consciousness unless its
loss is believed to be imminent. It therefore ranks first
among equals. The other fundamental goals are largely coordinate but, when necessary, the nation is likely to sacrifice internal betterment, prestige, and even peace in the
face of a serious challenge to its security or its territorial integrity. Should peace or individual human interests or
welfare be widely considered as more important, pressing, or
desirable than the nation's territorial integrity and the
preservation of its social order and political system against
outside threat, then independence and identity may be sacrificed. It is axiomatic that independence and self-preservation are primordial because the nation-state, like other organisms, cannot evolve and prosper unless it first survives.

Aside from these common basic goals, or in most cases of
prescribing supportive sub-goals, it is possible to discern a
broad spectrum of additional national aims. The literature on
the subject includes such matters as promoting a reasonable
standard of living, prosperity (or wealth maximization), the
flow of international trade, and cultural integrity; preserving the state's belief system, the existing political process, and either social homogeneity or diversity; strengthening the role of international law; and maintaining or enhancing the global and regional order.

While these are usually stated positively, in some
cases, as already noted, a national goal may be intended to
produce change rather than to maintain the status quo. Historically, among the most obvious are the seeking of spheres
of influence, domination, or hegemony; the retrieval of lost
territory; the expansion of maritime jurisdiction; the engaging in imperialism, expansionism, or aggrandizement; and
counteracting interventionism and aggression.

Those who address themselves specifically to the United
States also list such general goals as peacefully resolving
international disputes, creating a more durable sense of
international or global community, encouraging the development of democracy abroad, limiting or reducing national arm-

aments, assisting the economic advancement of less developed
countries, and many others.[54] Sometimes these will be epitomized as national missions--characterized as no entangling
alliances, the right of expatriation, open door trade relations, making the world safe for democracy, the self-determination of peoples, free trade, serving as the arsenal of
democracy, "good neighborism," containment of Communism,
Atlantic partnership, and "no more Munichs."

Whatever they may be called and however they may be delineated, these aims, as goals, are rarely prescribed pragmatically except in the broadest terms. Attempts to delineate them with precision tend to confound them with, or convert them into, more specific policy missions, and both public statements and foreign relations literature is replete
with this confusion. Moreover, because secondary and lesser
goals mutate with varying circumstances, it is difficult to
conceive a structured, consistent, durable, and inclusive
presentation of a nation's goals. Nevertheless, attempts are
sometimes made to specify and assess the cumulation of national goals at a particular moment in time, ostensibly to
establish priorities and plan policy strategy.

To illustrate, such an attempt was made in the United
States toward the end of the Eisenhower administration. In
his state of the union message of January 1959, the President
proposed a comprehensive projection of America's goals for
the 1960s which, he said, "must be goals that stand high, and
so inspire every citizen to climb always toward mounting levels of moral, intellectual, and material strength." Outlining the scope of the study, he suggested a series of public
concerns of individuals rather than limiting himself to those
of the nation at large. The task was undertaken by the President's Commission on National Goals, chaired by Henry M.
Wriston, President of the American Assembly and former President of Brown University. The commission consisted of ten
other well-known dignitaries drawn largely from the private
sector. Its report, entitled *Goals for Americans*, published
in November 1960, consists of fifteen segments; these are
based on sixteen individual substantive studies prepared by
groups of experts under the guidance of William P. Bundy,
staff director of the commission.[55]

Aside from its introductory chapters, three-fourths of
the report discusses "Goals at Home" and the remainder deals
with "The World We Seek." On foreign relations, it specifies
such goals as preserving independence and free institutions,
building an open and peaceful world, aiding less developed
nations, defending the free world, arms reduction and control, and strengthening the United Nations.

Despite the wave of independent thinking and analysis
the report generated, for purposes of refining America's
fundamental goals the results of the enterprise left much to
be desired. The focus was too far-reaching. The term goals
is interpreted broadly as ends of all kinds and degrees, and
therefore includes dozens of relatively finite policy and
procedural objectives and programs, resulting in a perplexing
array of details. These range from furthering the dignity of
the individual to improving national, state, and local public

service systems and the repeal of the Connally Amendment (which limits the jurisdiction of the International Court of Justice), from eliminating discrimination and enhancing education at all levels as well as tax reform to safeguarding the economy against market interruption, from preserving American independence and national traditions to endorsing technological change, increasing the compensation of senior public servants, and encouraging more qualified Americans to live and work abroad.

Some overrefinement of aims may have been inescapable in the formal report because the project and its end product encompass the gamut of possibilities--perhaps to produce a consensus of the disparate pluralistic interests represented in the deliberation. As its title specifies, the report constitutes an interpretation of aims and causes "for Americans"-- a smorgasbord to satisfy the tastes and concerns of many segments of the nation. This may be understandable and politically defensible, but the result must not be regarded as necessarily manifesting and clarifying the fundamental goals of the entire national community. Furthermore, the commission missed the opportunity to effectively deal with national priorities--to distinguish the vital from the desirable, or goals from either amorphous aspirations or operational policy objectives. As a practical guide to public policy-making for the 1960s--its avowed intent--the report failed to forge the alluring beacon for rallying America to great causes, and less than a decade later, in February 1970, in his syndicated column Chalmers M. Roberts cannily questioned "who can remember what it reported?"[56]

Another comprehensive example of American goals reassessment was undertaken by the President's Commission for a National Agenda for the Eighties, established by President Carter in October 1979. Its mission was to review major social, economic, and demographic trends that were likely to shape public choices for the coming decade. It consisted of forty-five representatives of academic, banking, business, labor, media, and public service organizations, chaired by William J. McGill, President Emeritus of Columbia University.

Its overall report, entitled *A National Agenda for the Eighties*, produced in January 1981, is supplemented by nine functional studies prepared by individual panels. These deal with such substantive subjects as the environment, the economy, social justice, government regulation, and the quality of life. One of these, entitled "The United States and the World Community in the Eighties," treats a number of important foreign relations issues--resolving conflicts, the world economy, national security requirements, human rights, and the institutional framework of foreign policy decision-making.[57]

Whereas it asserts that the United States has certain fundamental goals that are beyond compromise (called vital interests), this report fails to enumerate them. Instead, it contains approximately 130 italicized perceptions, guiding principles (some in the nature of truisms), and recommendations of varying generality, applicability, and impulsion. Included are such delimited recommendations as the develop-

ment of renewable energy resources, the strengthening of
regional peace-keeping organizations to resolve border disputes, the streamlining of the foreign relations bureaucracy,
and the annual delivery of a state of the world address by
the President. As in the case of earlier reports of this
type, it is more concerned with producing a comprehensive
synthesis of specific suggestions than with building a national consensus by defining basic goals, to say nothing of
determining interrelationships and preferences, national
policy strategy, and a genuinely motivating sense of national
direction.

Even though intentions may be laudable and certain segments of such studies provide useful contributions,[55] these
broad scale undertakings are disappointing.[59] Some of the
more limited surveys are more comprehensive and useful. In
1938, Secretary of State Hull outlined seven goals to maintain "satisfactory international order," including peace,
constructive negotiation, the sanctity of treaties, economic
security, and arms reduction.[60] Focusing primarily on the
free world, Secretary Acheson's six "lines of action," specified in 1950, embrace demonstrating a fighting faith in
freedom, communicating this to the four corners of the globe,
organizing our defenses wisely and prudently, helping create
a better material life for others, and integrating the nations of the free world, but also engaging in negotiations,
where feasible, with adversaries.[61]

Exemplifying the contemporary interpretation of American
foreign relations goals, in 1962 Secretary of State Dean Rusk
discussed five international propositions: security through
strength, progress through partnership, revolution of freedom, community under law, and peace through perseverance.[62]
In his statement to the Senate Foreign Relations Committee in
1980, in addition to listing the physical security of the nation, bringing peace to the troubled areas of the world, and
advancing the cause of human rights, Secretary Cyrus Vance
espoused improving East-West relations, controlling the
spread of nuclear and other weapons, strengthening the international economy, broadening ties with other nations, and
addressing environmental and other longer-term trends that
can imperil America's future.[63] Such goals at least are
amenable to concretization as viable policy objectives.

In the sphere of pragmatization, most useful would be a
systematic presentation and analysis of a nation's full range
of fundamental and secondary goals that would structure them
systematically, interrelate primary and supporting components, prescribe priorities, identify inconsistencies, and
raise issues of costs, feasibilities, commitments, and likely
foreign reactions. This is a difficult task, but the effort
should be made in order to provide practical guidance for
delineating more precise foreign relations objectives. The
deeper the gradation of goals penetrates to the level of precise aims, however, the more it impinges upon--or is transmuted into--the realm of actionable policy objectives--which
is even more complex and less likely to be comprehensively
extrapolated, either by statesmen or analysts.

CONCRETE POLICY OBJECTIVES

In dealing with the conduct of foreign affairs, as already noted, it is essential in theory and practice to clearly differentiate between not only national purposes and national goals, but also between them and concrete policy objectives. The latter--the operational layer of ends pursued
by nations--which are action oriented and therefore relate
the nation's aims to practical reality, are usually the most
immediate and often the most crucial to policy-making. They
differ in that they exceed the more general and abstract aspirations and desires, they affirm some fundamental goal or
sub-goal, and they engender the formulation of policy and the
taking of action to achieve them. In short:

> Foreign policy objectives are the concrete and ac-
> tionable aims of the nation, decided upon by gov-
> ernments, in the pursuance of national interests
> and in support of national purposes and basic na-
> tional goals, for the attainment of which foreign
> policies, both substantive and procedural, are
> formulated and implemented.[64]

In practice determinations concerning them are frequently bypassed by political practitioners, as they respond
piecemeal to existing situations, and they are often overlooked by historians and other commentators in their surveys
of the nation's foreign policies. Strangely, this belies the
logical validity of the foreign relations process, resulting
in the framing or assessment of policy before deciding upon
the objectives sought. In fact, even much of the literature
on policy analysis either pays less attention to them than it
does to other major components in the conduct of foreign affairs, or fails to distinguish them from more fundamental and
nebulous goals.

Policy objectives need to be precisely prescribed in the
context of the interests and aims of both the nation and
other countries, and decisions must be framed in terms of
what is possible as well as desirable. Feliks Gross notes
that because of the interplay of such factors policy objectives come to designate the immediate adjustments sought and
hence the palpable ends of foreign policy.[65]

As the targets of state action, policy objectives may be
distinguished from fundamental goals on the basis of several
criteria, especially duration, timing, specificity, optional-
ity, and achievability. They differ from goals in that policy
objectives usually are short-range objectives that reflect
currency rather than immutability.[66] They also may apply to
phases in a step-by-step longer-range venture, such as devising aims to be accomplished by a particular type of arrangement with other nations, beginning with the most friendly and
then proceeding to other groups of states on a scheduled basis. Unlike basic goals, policy objectives are also usually
precise and explicit. This is necessary because the state
must function in the real world.

Such broad-scale national goals as peace, security, human rights, or national honor cannot really be pursued unless

they are translated into more concrete components.[67] For
example, national security may be promoted either by non-involvement (isolationism or neutralism) or by the creation of
alliances, and each of these alternatives may be supported by
a variety of actionable objectives. If the nation opts for a
system of alliances, determinations will need to be made respecting the process whereby and when each alliance is to be
consummated, which states are to be included, what commitments are to be made, at whom the alliance is to be directed,
what mechanism is to administer it, how long it is to endure,
and the like. As each of these issues is decided, policies
must be devised to operationalize it.

Put another way, it is arguable that peace may be simultaneously perceived as an aspiration, an ideal, a national
interest, and a fundamental goal. But when it is to be reduced to practical effectuation through policies and actions,
it needs to be converted into specific objectives that implement such sub-goals as the creation of a balance of power
or an imbalance in one's own favor; the establishment of me-
diatory, arbitral, and adjudicatory commitments and processes; the employment of diplomatic techniques to acquire the
cooperation of other countries; the management and resolution
of crises; the disarming of nations; the application of the
rule of law; and/or the outlawry of war.

Similarly, the broader goal of promoting the nation's
economic welfare may be fulfilled by means of a series of
more finite possibilities--ranging from programs on tariffs,
currency exchange, credit, shipping, and taxation to technological research, resource management, and industrial modernization. By choosing among such alternatives, a nation
refines its priorities so as to project discrete objectives
and frame the policies it needs to attain them.

The most important difference between goals and policy
objectives, however, is whether they are practicable and
realizable. Admittedly, foreign policy is rational only if it
is feasible, and the specific objectives for which it is designed must be reasonably attainable. In other words, whereas the national goal may be said to represent the best conceivable state of affairs, the policy objective is the closest approximation to that which policy makers consider not
only preferable but also expedient. Thus, the broader goal
epitomizes the most desirable--the ideal--and the objective
represents the best among alternatives that is pragmatically
achievable under existing circumstances.

Even though governments may expound their foreign policies and explain their international actions, they rarely
reveal their concrete aims in any systematic and comprehensive way. As a consequence, rationalized and detailed de-
pictions of a nation's precise objectives are virtually non-
existent, even for a particular component of foreign policy.
Frequently intent is only articulated ex post facto to politically justify a policy or action. Moreover, adducing de-
terminate foreign policy objectives in advance is one of the
most neglected aspects of commentaries on foreign affairs.
It has been claimed that such an overall specification for a
major, highly involved country like the United States is too

difficult and complex, if not impossible, even for the expert. But this is scarcely an excuse for not trying to systematize the nation's objectives and actions in advance to
minimize policy inconsistency.

The final observation to be made is that, important as
it may be to particularize objectives, all too often decision
makers, reacting to conditions created by others, appear to
frame their policies to cope with developments as they occur
rather than predetermining the aims to be accomplished. Ret-
roactive acknowledgment of objectives merely to justify policy made previously impugns the rationality of the policy
maker. Furthermore, because important international problems
usually evoke alternative potential responses, choices among
them must be made, and these determinations must take into
account a variety of related factors, including the capabilities needed, the cost entailed, the risk involved, the time
available and necessary, the likely success of implementation, and the probable consequences, to say nothing of the
degree of motivation required to fulfill the objectives.

As indicated in Chapter 4, Charles Burton Marshall
stresses the necessity of maintaining balance between those
types of ends that are chosen as "purposes of action" and the
means available.[68] Putting it more comprehensively--and juxtaposing objectives, policies, capabilities, and feasibili-
ties--columnist Walter Lippmann has written: "Without the
controlling principle that the nation must maintain its objectives and its power in equilibrium, its purposes within
its means and its means equal to its purposes, its commitments related to its resources and its resources adequate to
its commitments, it is impossible to think at all about foreign affairs."[69]

NOTES

1. Charles O. Lerche, Jr., and Abdul A. Said, *Concepts of International Politics: In Global Perspective*, 3d ed. (Englewood Cliffs, N.J.:
Prentice-Hall, 1979), pp. 27, 28.

2. Cecil V. Crabb, Jr., *American Foreign Policy in the Nuclear
Age*, 4th ed. (New York: Harper and Row, 1983), p. 16.

3. Thomas A. Bailey, *The Art of Diplomacy: The American Experience*
(New York: Appleton-Century-Crofts, 1968), pp. 89-90.

4. Charles O. Lerche, Jr., *Foreign Policy of the American People*,
3d ed. (Englewood Cliffs, N.J.: Prentice-Hall, 1967), p. 20.

5. K. J. Holsti, *International Politics: A Framework for Analysis*
(Englewood Cliffs, N.J.: Prentice-Hall, 1967), p. 126.

6. A. F. K. Organski, *World Politics*, 2d ed. (New York: Knopf,
1968), p. 62. He refers specifically to goals and avoids referring to
objectives.

7. For this view, see comment of George F. Kennan in Chapter 4,
note 22.

8. On this dichotomy of monocausal and pluralistic approaches, see Feliks Gross, *Foreign Policy Analysis* (New York: Philosophical Library, 1954), pp. 31-34.

9. For commentary, see especially Joseph Frankel, *The Making of Foreign Policy: An Analysis of Decision Making* (New York: Oxford University Press, 1963), pp. 114, 122; Gross, *Foreign Policy Analysis*, p. 55; Lerche and Said, *Concepts of International Politics*, pp. 21-27, 156-57, 175-76, 200-202; and Arnold Wolfers, *Discord and Collaboration: Essays on International Politics* (Baltimore: Johns Hopkins Press, 1962), p. 71. For commentary distinguishing national interests, policies, commitments, and principles from objectives, see William Reitzel, Morton A. Kaplan, and Constance G. Coblenz, *United States Foreign Policy, 1945-1955* (Washington: Brookings Institution, 1956), p. 9 and Appendix A.

10. For texts, see Eisenhower, January 20, 1953, in *Papers of the Presidents: Dwight D. Eisenhower, 1953*, pp. 1-8; Carter, January 22, 1977, in *Papers of the Presidents: Jimmy Carter, 1977*, pp. 1-4; and for Secretaries of State Hull, Acheson, Rusk, and Vance, see notes 60-63 below.

11. See Cecil V. Crabb, Jr., *The Doctrines of American Foreign Policy: Their Meaning, Role, and Future* (Baton Rouge: Louisiana State University Press, 1982).

12. For commentary, see Robert L. Wendzel, *International Relations: A Policymaker Focus* (New York: Wiley, 1977), pp. 48-52.

13. For example, in *Goals, Priorities, and Dollars: The Next Decade* (New York: Free Press, 1966), p. 2, Leonard A. Lecht asks: "Are not national attitudes toward national goals very largely determined by the values and traditions embedded in our culture?" For his discussion of phases in the evolution of national goals consciousness, see pp. 2-5. See also his *The Dollar Cost of Our National Goals* (Washington, D.C.: National Planning Association, 1965).

14. This is intimated by Joseph Frankel, *National Interest* (New York: Praeger, 1970), p. 55, and others.

15. For example, see Charles M. Fergusson, Jr., "What Does It Mean to 'Win'?" (Carlisle Barracks, Pa.: U.S. Army War College, processed, 1965), p. 36. Organski points out that while states are said to have goals and objectives, in reality only human beings can act and only they, therefore, can have goals, but because the latter are common to the nation for which governments act, it is possible to speak of "national goals;" see *World Politics*, p. 62. Addressing himself in Chapter 5 of this volume to determinants of national goals, he discusses the ruling classes and the character of individual leaders, in addition to national character.

16. See Frankel, *National Interest*, p. 25.

17. See J. David Singer, "The Level of Analysis Problem in International Relations," in *International Politics and Foreign Policy: A Reader in Research and Theory*, 2d ed., edited by James N. Rosenau (New York: Free Press, 1969), p. 25.

18. See Frankel, *The Making of Foreign Policy*, p. 137.

19. As a consequence, Puchala says, "men in action seldom pause to unravel their mixed motivations and jumbled ends," so that "it is nearly impossible to identify acts taken in pursuit of only one goal." See Donald J. Puchala, *International Politics Today* (New York: Harper and Row, 1971), p. 92. See Chapters 4-7 of this volume for his analysis of goals in foreign affairs.

20. Fisher Howe, "The Concept of National Purpose," paper presented at the U.S. Army War College (Carlisle Barracks, Pa.: processed, 1968), p. 2.

21. Wolfers proceeds to show that, even in such extreme circumstances, the nation still would be concerned with many domestic goals. See *Discord and Collaboration*, pp. 71-72.

22. Frankel, *The Making of Foreign Policy*, pp. 137-38.

23. Lerche, *Foreign Policy of the American People*, p. 20.

24. Bailey, *The Art of Diplomacy*, pp. 96-97.

25. Frederick H. Hartmann, *The Relations of Nations*, 5th ed. (New York: Macmillan, 1978), pp. 74-75.

26. See Holsti, *International Politics*, p. 131.

27. Testing feasibility requires calculating and assessing the requirements, sacrifices, costs, and likely consequences of attaining the goal or objective and then deciding on the probability and benefit of its achievement. See comments in Fergusson, "What Does It Mean to 'Win'?" p. 33.

28. These obviously represent what the nation is for and what it is against; see Fergusson, "What Does It Mean to 'Win'?" p. 35.

29. Wendzel distinguishes between a nucleus of "fundamental objectives" necessary for the survival of the nation and its socio-political system, intermediate or "middle-range objectives" that are essentially conserving (that defend and protect), and "specific immediate objectives" (that support the fundamental); see *International Relations*, pp. 44-48.

30. See comments of William L. Langer, "The United States Role in the World," in The President's Commission on National Goals, *Goals for Americans: Programs for Action in the Sixties* (Englewood Cliffs, N.J.: Prentice-Hall, 1960), pp. 298-329. Organski concedes that the dividing line between these categories is extremely thin, and often it is difficult to make a clear distinction between them; see *World Politics*, p. 62. For Wolfer's comments on the difference between national and international, see Chapter 4, note 70.

31. Differing in his analysis, distinguishing among goals on the basis of importance, urgency, and generality, Crabb prescribes three categories: national security as the paramount goal, a hierarchy of secondary goals (which are pursued provided there is no impairment of national security), and "at the bottom of the list" those for which the nation's resources are not committed, which he calls wishes and hopes rather than goals. See *American Foreign Policy in the Nuclear Age*, pp. 16-18.

32. Fergusson prefers to delineate three time-related categories--immediate, intermediate, and ultimate; see "What Does It Mean to 'Win'?" p. 35.

33. See comments in Chapter 4 and notes 96-98.

34. Fergusson, "What Does It Mean to 'Win'?" pp. 33-34.

35. Organski compares those goals that are simply proclaimed publicly against those that are positively acted upon; see *World Politics*, pp. 82-84. On the other hand, Puchala emphasizes the distinction between actual and attributed goals, noting that because information concerning them often remains imprecise in practice, they are sometimes taken for granted on the basis of assumed traditional values, ideology, and similar factors; see *International Politics Today*, pp. 92-94.

36. By absolute, Organski means those that are "desirable in themselves, quite apart from what other nations do," whereas the competitive have meaning "only in relation to other nations;" see *World Politics*, pp. 63-65.

37. By this distinction, Organski refers to unity versus divergence of endorsement or support by the people and the interest groups within the nation; see *World Politics*, pp. 73-76.

38. For example, Organski points out that although goals and objectives are future-oriented, their achievement sometimes "merely means perpetuating the status quo" and that it is important for leaders to know whether this is the case or whether realization of such goals and objectives "requires change;" see *World Politics*, pp. 84-85.

39. Organski, *World Politics*, pp. 76-81. This perception needs to be distinguished from both the appositional national and international interests and purposes discussed in Chapters 2 and 4.

40. Wolfers, *Discord and Collaboration*, pp. 77-79.

41. Wolfers, *Discord and Collaboration*, pp. 73-77. It is at this point that Wolfers rejects the concept of international goals that do not serve the national interest, preferring to compare milieu goals with common national goals. Nevertheless, sometimes nations pursue mutual or parallel goals and objectives.

42. Wolfers, *Discord and Collaboration*, pp. 91-97.

43. Howard H. Lentner, *Foreign Policy Analysis: A Comparative and Conceptual Approach* (Columbus, Ohio: Merrill, 1974), especially pp. 6, 152-53, 248-64.

44. For commentary, see Lerche and Said, *Concepts of International Politics*, pp. 32-34.

45. See comments in Chapter 4, note 47.

46. They also have been called abiding, amorphous, nebulous, utopian, and vague ends.

47. Lerche and Said, *Concepts of International Politics*, pp. 29, 47.

48. Langer, "The United States Role in the World," in *Goals for Americans*, pp. 298-329.

49. Gross, *Foreign Policy Analysis*, p. 54.

50. Charles Burton Marshall, discussing ends and means, as noted in Chapter 4, refers to "purposes of action," whereas Dean Acheson prefers to call them "lines of action." See Charles Burton Marshall, *The "Limits" of Foreign Policy* (New York: Holt, 1954), p. 31; and Dean Acheson, *Strengthening the Forces of Freedom: Selected Speeches and Statements of Secretary of State Acheson* (Washington: Government Printing Office, 1950), pp. 1-9.

51. To quote Charles Burton Marshall on the task of policy-making, "The real work comes not in deciding where you want to go--that is the easiest part of it--but in figuring out how to get there." See *The Exercise of Sovereignty: Papers on Foreign Policy* (Baltimore: Johns Hopkins Press, 1965), p. 41.

52. See Kurt London, *How Foreign Policy Is Made* (New York: Van Nostrand, 1949), p. 13.

53. Lists, with discussion, of the principal national goals common to all states are to be found in a great many international relations and foreign policy monographs and textbooks, and usually number from four to six. Whereas there is consistency on some terms---independence, international security, and peace--such concepts as national prestige and welfare are variously interpreted. Some writers add the more amorphous promulgation and application of the nation's values and ideology to such lists.

54. To these may be added the stipulations of the classic goal-oriented American documents discussed in Chapter 4. For a summary historical statement of United States foreign relations goals and objectives, see Reitzel, Kaplan, and Coblenz, *United States Foreign Policy*, Chapter 1, and for post-World War II American "stated aims," see Chapter 2.

55. President's Commission on National Goals, *Goals for Americans*. The commission report, which contains the fifteen segments, comprises the first 23 of 372 pages and the remainder embraces sixteen topical chapters prepared by individual authors. Only four segments of the report and three of the supporting studies--aggregating 80 pages--concern foreign affairs.

56. Chalmers M. Roberts, *Washington Post*, February 1, 1970. On that day Roberts published two editorials on pending proposals for the study of, and reports on, United States foreign policy goals, referring to earlier official ventures and considering proposals for an annual presidential report to Congress on foreign affairs and for the establishment of a joint congressional committee on foreign policy.

57. President's Commission for a National Agenda for the Eighties, *A National Agenda for the Eighties*, and nine supplemental substantive studies, each with its own title (Washington: Government Printing Office, 1981).

58. Such as Wriston's introductory essay on "Fundamentals," and Langer's segment on "National Goals and National Purpose," in *Goals for Americans*, pp. 35-37, 327-29.

59. Some studies, such as periodic agenda reports and occasional volumes, represented by Lecht, *Goals, Priorities, and Dollars* and Stuart Chase, *Goals for America: A Budget of Our Needs and Resources* (New York: Twentieth Century Fund, 1942), are of only tangential relevance to comprehending the basic national goals of the United States.

60. Hull, address, March 17, 1938, in Department of State, *Peace and War: United States Foreign Policy, 1931-1941* (Washington, Government Printing Office, 1943), pp. 407-19.

61. Address, April 22, 1950, in Acheson, *Strengthening the Forces of Freedom*, pp. 1-9.

62. Dean Rusk, "Five Goals of U.S. Foreign Policy," *Department of State Bulletin* 47 (October 15, 1962): 547-58.

63. Cyrus Vance, "United States Foreign Policy Objectives," Department of State, *American Foreign Policy: Current Documents, 1977-1980* (Washington: Government Printing Office, 1983), pp. 60-62.

64. *The International Relations Dictionary*, edited by Jack C. Plano and Roy Olton, defines foreign policy objectives as the "concrete formulations derived by relating the national interest to the prevailing international situation and to the power available to the state. The objectives are selected by the decision makers seeking to change (revisionist policy) or to preserve (status quo policy) a particular state of affairs in the international environment." See 3d ed. (Santa Barbara, Calif.: ABC-Clio Press, 1982), p. 8.

65. Gross also stresses that they are made "precise in the light of a current pattern of international relations"; see *Foreign Policy Analysis*, pp. 54-55.

66. On the other hand, confusing the terms goals and objectives, it has been said that if a given country's foreign policy is observed over a long period, one can usually discern "some fairly stable and consistent basic policy goals pursued by that country." See John C. Harsanyi, "Game Theory and the Analysis of International Conflict," in Rosenau, *International Politics and Foreign Policy*, p. 370.

67. See commentary of Lerche and Said, *Concepts of International Politics*, p. 27.

68. Marshall, *The "Limits" of Foreign Policy*, p. 31. Compare with Dean Acheson's "lines of action" referred to in note 50.

69. Walter Lippmann, *U.S. Foreign Policy: Shield of the Republic* (Boston: Little, Brown, 1943), p. 3.

6

FOREIGN POLICIES

Nobody, in fact, who has had occasion actually to witness history in the making, and to observe how infrequent and adventitious is the part played in great affairs by "policy" or planned intention, can believe thereafter that history is ever quite so simple, or quite so deliberate, as it seems in retrospect; or that the apparent relation between cause and effect was the relation which at the time, and in the circumstances, actually determined the course of affairs.

Harold Nicolson, *The Congress of Vienna*

The policymaker must be concerned with the best that can be achieved, not just the best that can be imagined. He has to act in the fog of incomplete knowledge without the information that will be available later to the analyst. He knows--or should know--that he is responsible for the consequences of disaster as well as for the benefits of success. He may have to qualify some goals, not because they would be undesirable if reached but because the risks of failure outweigh potential gains. He must often settle for the gradual, much as he might prefer the immediate. He must compromise with others, and this means to some extent compromising with himself.

Henry Kissinger, *Years of Upheaval*

The fifth layer in the foreign affairs hierarchy--most crucial in the conduct of international relations--encompasses the gamut of foreign policies in accordance with national interests and in pursuance of national purposes, goals, and concrete objectives. Although it is presumed that the concept of foreign policy is widely understood, considerable confusion reigns, both in official usage and in descriptive and analytical studies.

At the outset it must be realized that foreign policy needs to be distinguished from such broader expressions as foreign affairs, international politics, and the foreign policy process. The latter consists of three elements--the mak-

ing of foreign policy, the policy made, and the execution of
the policy. Two of these components--the formulation and implementation of policy are often combined as the conduct of
foreign relations--or diplomacy[1]--which need to be differentiated conceptualistically from the essence of policy. As a
consequence, in this sense foreign policy, though produced by
a process, is not properly definable as that process.

Foreign policy is closely related to other primary factors in foreign relations--values, national interests, goals,
and objectives--and to be effective, it also bears relationship to the nation's capability and commitments, and to the
manner of executing policy. Jeane Kirkpatrick, former Ambassador to the United Nations, observes: "American foreign policy should reflect our own values and goals at the same time
that it seeks to protect our interests."[2] Career diplomat
Hugh Gibson has written: "The best possible policy is life-
less without a competent diplomacy to make it work. Diplomacy, on the other hand, is aimless without a recognized policy to guide it."[3] And, in his volume on American foreign
policy, columnist Walter Lippmann develops the thesis that
"in foreign relations, as in all other relations, a policy
has been formed only when commitments and power have been
brought into balance."[4]

Often the question is posed: "Does the nation have a
foreign policy?" Asking the question usually implies that
the nation does not. Those who raise the question or contend
that it does not fall into six groups. Among the most obvious critics are those who base their denunciation on an untenable assumption or interpretation of what foreign policy
is.[5] Then there are those who are uninformed of the policy,
either because they have not made the effort to become informed or because, at the time, policy is held in confidence
(such as detailed policy concerning certain defense and national security policy, or contingency plans that would be
disaffected by public knowledge). A third group is prema-
turely critical of the absence of policy while it is in the
formulation stage, which focuses more on the policy-making
process than the policy itself.

Another group of critics, who interpret foreign policy
in the singular as a coherent complex of major, secondary,
and tertiary policies, fails to understand the relation of
policies to varying objectives and circumstances. Such
critics concentrate on inconsistencies, actual or apparent,
within the policy network, which they regard as evidencing
the lack of policy. Or they contend that the nation should
have a particular policy as part of the complex.

Others are critical because they are unhappy or disagree
with the policy. This group includes not only super-nation-
alists and supra-nationalists, but also alienated and often
vocal policy minorities, vested interest groups, and extrem-
ists of various socio-political coloring. There are also
those that are politically motivated, directing their criticism, for partisan reasons, against a particular government,
regime, or political party.[6] This group includes those who
are unhappy with policy that has not yet successfully influenced other nations, or with policy that they regard as not

meeting their expectations or as not achieving the results they desire. Sometimes this group also includes those who, with hindsight, view the policy as faulty or harmful.

Finally there are many who, claiming the nation has no foreign policy, fail to distinguish between long-range, relatively constant, strategic policies and short-range, tactical policies, or between substantive and procedural policies. They usually emphasize the tactical and procedural but ignore the more fundamental, strategic, and substantive policies.

Certainly overanticipation, ignorance, disinterest, misinterpretation, confusion, overexpectation, vested interest or partisan antipathy, or dissatisfaction do not belie the existence of policy. They reflect the inadequacy or personal partiality of the critic rather than the reality or the quality of the policy. Nevertheless, in asking whether the nation has a foreign policy in the sense that it possesses an explicit, exhaustive "master list of dos and don'ts to guide the nation's conduct abroad," the answer must be "no."[7]

There are those who, interpreting the concept in some peculiar way, argue the lack of foreign policy. To illustrate, George Harvey, former American Ambassador to Great Britain, claimed that "The national American policy is to have no foreign policy."[8] During World War II Ambassador Gibson, no doubt having integrated strategy in mind, maintained that the United States had no definite or "real" foreign policy because, as he defined it, the nation possessed no "well rounded, comprehensive plan, based on knowledge and experience, for conducting the business of government with the rest of the world," and because, in his judgment, the United States understood neither its national interests nor its capabilities. "Anything less than this," he concluded, "falls short of being a national foreign policy."[9]

Similarly, in his volume on power and diplomacy, former Secretary of State Dean Acheson regards foreign policy essentially as "the grand strategy with which the United States proposes to deal with the main facts--the thrusts and problems they present--of the outside world."[10] Most observers and critics of a nation's foreign policy, however, are more modest, and some are more realistic. They address themselves, usually with hindsight, to specific former and contemporary policies, or to assessments of aspects of their nature or their implementation, rather then to the question of whether or not the nation has any foreign policies.[11]

In the case of the United States, the preponderant majority of commentators take the position that the nation does have many foreign policies. Among contemporaries of Gibson, for example, John W. Davis, appointed Ambassador to Great Britain,[12] and Loy W. Henderson, who served as both Deputy Under Secretary of State and ambassador to four countries,[13] have proclaimed the obvious--that the United States possesses a network of many policies. Furthermore, analysts who address themselves to the general issue contend that all independent nations have their own foreign policies. To illustrate, Norman Hill observes: "Using 'foreign policy' in the sense in which it is almost universally employed, the conclusion be-

comes inevitable that every nation has foreign policies,"[14]
and putting it differently, in his analysis of foreign policy, Feliks Gross insists that "every government has some
kind of relations with other governments."[15]

INTERPRETATIONS OF THE CONCEPT

Although often mistakenly used in official statements
and historical and analytical literature as synonyms of such
concepts as foreign affairs, international politics, diplomacy, and the foreign relations process,[16] as already noted,
and sometimes perceived as an idea,[17] a goal or objective,[18]
a national plan,[19] or a national strategy,[20] conceptualistically foreign policy differs from each of these. Such confusion over multiple meanings appears to be more a matter of
literary usage than explicit definition. Practitioners appear to be less prone to make this mistake, while some writers clearly employ the expression to embrace both ends and
means. Or they generalize it even more as the totality of
the conduct of foreign relations, including not only the
substance of policy, but also the methods of devising and
executing it, the diplomatic process, and other aspects of
the management of foreign affairs. Many volumes in the fields
of diplomacy and national or comparative foreign relations
that bear the title "foreign policy" deal with a variety of
matters that exceed the simple description, or discussion,
of foreign policies.[21]

Other analysts prefer to call foreign policies "measures,"[22] "programs,"[23] or "courses or lines of action." Or,
relating them to the ends-means continuum, they are designated as "means[24] or methods[25] of achieving national goals
and policy objectives."

General Interpretations

Some contemporary perceptions portray the concept broadly. Emphasizing applicability to the people, in an address
delivered in 1963, Secretary of State Dean Rusk declared:
"Foreign policy is about you.   It is about your home, your
community, your safety, your well-being, your chance to live
a decent life and to prepare a better world for your children
. . . . It is as close to you as the member of your family
. . . . Even more personal, foreign policy is as close as
your highest hopes."[26] Addressing the policy officers of the
Department of State, he also said, "Foreign policy is the
total involvement of the American people with the peoples and
governments abroad" and "we must think in terms of the total
context of our situation."[27]

Stressing content, according to diplomatic historian
William G. Carleton, foreign policy is thought of "as functional in the widest sense, a subject as broad as history
and life itself, including materials not only from political
science and history as conventionally conceived, but also
from economics, sociology, anthropology, social psychology,
practical and party politics, public opinion and propaganda,
public relations, and so forth."[28] It has also been said

that "Foreign policy is the sum of all the attitudes reflected in myriads of relationships and numberless points of
contact that one nation has with others, large and small."[29]

Some general surveys equate foreign policy with the totality of international relations and world affairs. In his
examination of the subject, K. J. Holsti contends that these
are "studies of foreign policy, where policy is defined as
the decisions that define goals, set precedents, or lay down
courses of action, and the actions taken to implement those
decisions."[30] Similarly, Harold and Margaret Sprout suggest
that from the interrelations of nations emerge "the patterns
which in the aggregate constitute the *foreign policy* of a
state," which can therefore be defined "as the scheme or pattern of ends and means explicit or implicit in that state's
actions and reactions vis-à-vis other states."[31]

Restricting himself to the United States, moderating his
perception, and considering it from the perspective of the
nation, Charles Beard has written: "A foreign policy . . . is
a broad program of action to be followed by the Government in
conducting relations with other powers and their nationals."
As for content and unity, "It consists of maxims, axioms, or
principles to be accepted as official and applied in practice
to concrete cases as they arise from day to day or circumstance to circumstance. Taken collectively these general
rules are supposed to form a consistent whole, logical in its
parts, devoid of mutually destructive contradictions."[32]

Relating policy and process, according to Paul Seabury
foreign policy is "often taken to mean some settled course of
action adopted and followed by a government. It usually means
concerted, purposive action arising out of rational deliberation among rational men." But he also recognizes that policy
may be the product of random, haphazard, or even irrational
forces and events, or that it is the result of deadlocked
judgments, indecision, and unwillingness or inability to act.
"Finally policy may be due to a statesman's abdication of
choice and rational judgment in the face of ruthless and
strong external pressures."[33]

Since World War II many commentaries have defined the
concept as courses of action in foreign affairs. In 1949
Kurt London observed: "A nation's foreign policy determines
its course of action vis-à-vis other nations . . . it expres-
ses the sum total of those principles under which a nation's
relations with other nations are to be conducted."[34] Three
years later Charles Burton Marshall construed policies "as
the courses of action undertaken by the United States in pursuit of national objectives beyond the span of jurisdiction
of the United States" through which the nation seeks to "influence forces and situations abroad."[35] Since the early
1950s the essence of these conceptualizations have been repeated by many others--statesmen, observers, and analysts.[36]

Emphasizing the importance of differentiating between
singular and plural usage of the term, Gross maintains that
foreign policy, in the singular, is a phenomenon, ideology,
or complex of "dynamic systems of actions" whereas foreign
policies are actualized "courses of action," and an individ-

ual foreign policy is a "single course of action, the latter
being only an element, or part of the concept used in the
plural."[37]

Usage

    Turning from interpretation of the concept to usage, the
predominant majority of statesmen, historians, and social
scientists employ it in three fundamental ways. The most
general and abstract--as THE FOREIGN POLICY--employed only in
the singular, represents the nation's idealized foreign policy. Some writers regard it as something more than the sum
of the country's policies and therefore attribute to it an
aura of sanctity denoting a synthesized amorphous entity.
This interpretation has been phrased by Wallace Irwin as "the
sum of everything the United States government does or says
that affects the nation's foreign relations,"[38] by Kurt London as the "sum total of those principles which have grown
out of the nation's history, beliefs or ideologies, power potential, and its cultural predilections"[39] and, quite differently, by Martin Needler as "the sum total of many decisions,
on both short-range and long-range questions."[40]

    Although perhaps useful for limited aspects of theoreti-
cal discourse, in practice such sweeping application, inti-
mating that the concept exceeds its components,[41] and sym-
bolizes a kind of image or spirit of foreign policy, is misleading even if it is meant to connote merely those basic,
permanent precepts by which a nation guides its policy relations with other governments. To use it even more broadly as
equatable with the totality of foreign affairs or international relations is bound to produce confusion.

    The second perception--"The Foreign Policy"--also uti-
lized solely in the singular, which is more defensible theoretically and more useful pragmatically, encompasses the aggregate of the nation's complex of policies, discussed later.
In this version the concept signifies the corpus or totality
of policies--both major and subsidiary as well as long-range
and short-range, and substantive and procedural policies. Or,
minimally, in the words of Dean Rusk, it embraces "the central themes" of policy that "are more or less constant."[42]

    The final manifestation--"a foreign policy" or two or
more "foreign policies"--relates them to specific needs or
sets of circumstances. In this fashion the expression is
usable both in the singular and plural, but in the singular
it denotes something quite different from either the sanctified abstraction or an aggregate network of policies. This is
the form in which the term is most frequently employed and
most readily comprehended.

    Understanding would be facilitated if usage were re-
stricted to the last two interpretations. Synonymizing foreign policy with the overall foreign relations process is
unnecessarily confounding, and conceiving it as an abstraction, or as meaning fundamental goals and concrete objectives, or as something greater than, or substantially different from, the totality of the nation's implemental foreign

policies, serves little intellectual or practical purpose.
Only the synthesized corpus, expressed as "The Foreign Policy" of the nation, and the designation of individual concrete policies, in either the singular or the plural as the
case may require, are needed by the practitioner or essential
to the analyst.

Definition

Based on this brief survey, a number of ideas and expressions emerge as salient features of interpretation. These
include policies are action oriented; they are interrelated
but not identical with national interests, purposes, goals,
or concrete objectives; they are the product, not the essence, of the policy process; they are not substantively
delimited to political affairs; nations have multiple policies; as an aggregate they provide a program of action; and
they apply to affairs external to the jurisdiction of the
nation.

Reducing these qualities to the most critical and material, and regarding foreign policies as means rather than
ends, and as methods rather than aims, the concept may be
defined as:

> *Foreign policies are courses of action in dealing
> with other nations, decided upon by the nation's
> policy makers exercising choice among alternative
> possibilities, designed in keeping with the na-
> tion's interests and in pursuit of its purposes,
> fundamental goals, and concrete objectives.*

Concerned with applicability, Edgar Furniss and Richard
Snyder maintain that foreign policies consist of two forms:
courses of action decided upon to be applied in particular
circumstances as they occur, and rules of action prescribed
in advance to be applied to future problems, conditions,
events, or demands, and to ways that nations perceive situations in which they may need to decide to act.[43] Also
from the perspective of application, Beard conceives foreign
policy as reflecting three essentials: "things deemed necessary, things deemed possible, and things deemed desirable." He stresses that "There is no sense in formulating
and asserting policy which necessity makes futile . . . .
Where possibilities arise and choice is permissible, then
the element of desirability . . . enters into the reckoning,
and hopes for the future are added to the image of the past
and present."[44]

Somewhat more complex, Charles Lerche views foreign policy in two different ways. In the singular, as an on-going
"social and political process," it embraces the totality of
what he calls "the chain of policy"--or the conduct of foreign affairs, including the courses of action decided upon.
On the other hand, he also perceives it in a narrower way,
simply calling policy a method for attaining an objective
which, in turn, has two connotations: "either the actions
actually taken" to accomplish such objectives or "the principles that govern such action."[45]

CHARACTERISTICS OF FOREIGN POLICIES

      Reminiscent of earlier discussion on national interests
and purposes, a number of commentaries compare realistic,
ideological, and analytical approaches to understanding foreign policy. Kenneth Thompson and Roy Macridis, who appose
ideological and analytical perspectives, contend that the
former pertains to the policies of states vis-à-vis the rest
of the world that "are merely expressions of prevailing political, social, and religious beliefs," whereas the analytical treatment is founded on "the proposition that policy
rests on multiple determinants, including the state's historic tradition, geographical location, national interest,
and purposes and security needs."[46]

      Speaking of policy-making, in another comparison it is
claimed that there are two lines of analysis--rationality and
ideology.   The first of these pertains to the organization
and structure of policy formation which usually "reflects a
belief that certain policy-making relationships or arrangements can be found that are for one reason or another more
'rational' than others."   Ideology, by comparison, concerns
policy-making that "reflects a belief that foreign policy
decisions should be made by politically responsive and responsible individuals or groups" and that the policy made
"can be wise and strong only to the extent that it commands
the understanding and support of the public."[47]

      Gibson conjoins realism and idealism, suggesting that
"to have a sound foreign policy it must be realistic" while
at the same time it may also be idealistic.   If realism is
meant "to describe a policy that can be brought into operation to achieve desired results, there is nothing in realism
that excludes idealism."   On the contrary, he says, "to be
genuinely realistic a policy must be lighted by idealism."[48]

      A related consideration evokes the question of whether
foreign policy (or the policy-making process) is an art or a
science. "The poets," according to Dean Acheson, "say things
are not what they seem.   The trouble is sometimes they are
what they seem. And the question is are they or aren't they
what they seem. That is what makes government, and particularly foreign affairs, an art and not a science."[49]

      Others regard it as both an art and a science.   Felix
Morley holds that foreign policy is an art in that it "is always affected by emotional, sometimes even by wholly irrational, considerations."   But it is also a science "in the
sense that predictable results follow from predisposing
causes."[50] In addition to juxtaposing intuitive and rationalized policy, Seabury considers foreign policy as reflecting
"the art of fashioning order, congruence, and purpose" out of
the interrelations of nations and the science of discerning
"the broad impulses" of nations that express themselves in
their external relations, "the broad historical trends" in
international behavior that produce consistency, and the
long-term "patterns of relationships" established over the
course of time.[51] A separate body of literature has emerged
that seeks to systematize if not standardize the study of
hypotheses concerning the use of foreign policy as an analy-

tical tool, the variables in both policy and policymaking, and the decision-making process, seeking to produce explicit precepts of foreign policy theory.

Another characteristic of foreign policies is that they are dynamic and incremental, and that they constitute components of a continuum. Because flexibility is essential for the nation to accommodate its relations to changing circumstances, even though certain basic policies remain constant--or in some cases even bear the aura of permanence--others, including most of the supportive and more finite policies mutate from time to time.[52] In view of such changes, some critics conclude that the nation only devises "scraps of policy" rather than a cohesive set of policies.[53]

Considering incrementalism, Roger Hilsman notes that in state practice there is a tendency to decide as little as possible--or rather, only that which needs to be decided at the time. This is due, in part, to the difficulty of envisioning the totality of the policy complex applicable to all functional subjects, all nations, and all circumstances. As a consequence, he concludes, individual segments of policy are devised by a series of incremental steps. "All of this-- the bouncing from crisis to crisis, the overselling, the incrementalism--leads to what might be called discontinuity of policy development."[54] But this argument may be overstated. Primary policies may be supplemented by implemental policies on a gradual basis, and each of these may be extrapolated incrementally into lesser and even lesser supportive policies as they are needed. Otherwise much of the totality of policy formulated in advance would be contingency policy which, because of changing circumstances, might never be implemented or would need to be modified.

There is little question that policy-making is a continuous process and the policy made is subject to constant development, refinement, and alteration. According to James Rosenau, who has written widely on the subject, foreign policy is sequential and does not have "a beginning, an existence, and an end." Rather, it is "constantly unfolding," so that "at any given moment" it is "partly a function of what it was previously and what it may become in the future."[55] In short, the evolving policy as well as the process constitutes a continuum.

Discussing sequential foreign policy stages, Rosenau lists three that apply to the interrelations of nations. The first, or initiatory, is that which stimulates nations "to undertake efforts to modify circumstances in their external environments." The second, or implementive stage, is that in which nations decide on "purposeful actions directed at modifying objects in the international environment." The third, or responsive stage, is that in which other nations react to such actions.[56]

Put another way, just as it may be argued that in many cases the cause that produces an effect which then becomes a cause for a subsequent effect, and so on, creates a viable progression, so does the policy action that produces a reaction which then becomes an action that evokes another reaction. Thus, if one country institutes a policy, and other countries react by generating policies of their own, the first country may view these responses as actions to which it needs to react, producing the next stage of actions and reactions--which represents a continuous sequence of policies and interactions.

Another feature of foreign policy--which the policy maker must take into account, but which is infrequently noted by the analyst or the public--is its cost, or the commitment of resources. Charles Burton Marshall puts it most cogently: "The use of means involves costs . . . . The cost aspects of a foreign policy are the aspects despite which a course of action is taken. The gain aspects are those because of which a course of action is undertaken." And he adds that, for those who are responsible for deciding on policy, balancing these two aspects is usually difficult and close.[57]

Aside from those costs that require appropriations--such as providing foreign assistance or paying assessments levied on members by international organizations--direct costs may entail the mobilization of a variety of human and material resources: institutional, political, economic, social, military, and psychological.[58] Other costs--indirect or intangible--entail time spent in policy-making and implementation; the degree of compromise or offsetting consequences resulting from negotiations; the effect on credibility, influence, prestige, popularity, and electoral outcome; and the capacity of policy makers to deal with only a limited number of problems at a time. As Marshall sees it, "the limits of foreign policy are determined not alone by our inherent finiteness and not alone by our extrinsic capability but also by the degree of our steadfastness in shouldering the burdens. That, rather than the righteousness of unexecuted wishes" is the true test of "a great nation."[59]

Since World War II many volumes have been devoted to the role of public opinion in the formulation of the nation's foreign policy and the need for popular acceptance and consensus.[60] In 1950 Gabriel Almond wrote that, despite disunity and conflicts among American elites, "there is, nevertheless, a general ideological consensus in the United States in which the mass of the population and its leadership generally share. At the level of basic attitudes this is largely an unconscious consensus of feeling with regard to values and reactions regarded as suitable in response to certain political cues." In a democracy, he believes, such consensus exists on the main themes of foreign policy, both ends and means, but such attitudes "are contingent rather than absolute."[61]

Two decades later it was reported that whereas previously differences between the people and their leaders focused on "policy means" rather than on "the aims, objectives, and procedures of American relations with other countries." But this degenerated into the rhetoric of "great debates," confrontation, and public demonstrations rather than simply a dialogue between contrasting perspectives. As a result, "consensus has been displaced by acerbic controversy and opposition that frequently seems to be irreconcilable."[62]

Nevertheless, in a pamphlet on foreign policy published for the general public in 1976, the Department of State observed: "Our Task is to define--together--the contours of a new world and to shape America's contribution to it. Our foreign policy cannot be effective if it reflects only the sporadic and esoteric initiatives of a small group of specialists. It must rest on a broad national base and reflect a shared community of values." On the matter of consensus, however, it cautioned: "No genuine democracy can or should obtain total unanimity. But we can strive for a consensus about our national goals and chart a common course."[63]

Because the roles of the media, public opinion, and popular consensus are not really reducible to absolute and universal judgments and precepts for all nations at all times, it is difficult to generalize on the role that has been or should be played by them in the establishment and implementation of foreign policy. In his widely read study of public opinion and American democracy, V. O. Key acknowledges that "the sharp definition of the role of public opinion as it affects different kinds of policies under different types of situations presents an analytical problem of extraordinary difficulty."[64]

Two generalizations seem to emerge, namely, that the leaders of the government have responsibility for, and do in fact formulate foreign policy, and that they seek to generate official and popular support and consensus for such policies, which is less manageable or certain in pluralistic and democratic than in autocratic societies. Even so, the ultimate issues are whether the necessity of gaining popular consensus hamstrings policy initiative and responsibility of leadership, whether policy is made on the basis of rationality rather than emotional popular endorsement,[65] and whether policy is formulated from the perspective, not of vocal and demonstrative vested, parochial, or partisan interests, but of promoting the ideals, security, and welfare of the nation as a whole.

Resolving this leadership-followership dichotomy raises a good many thorny issues. These include the meaning and functioning of the "general will" and governance of, by, and for the people; the credibility of the leaders; the extent to which foreign policy determination should be left to experts; the manner in which consensus percolates down from above or emanates up from below; the degree of negativism or adverseness rampant in the society; the knowledgeability, mood, and fickleness of the populace; the fashion in which the people evidence a sense of responsibility; the motives and tactics of opinion makers and influencers; the ways in which public opinion is manipulated, and by whom and for what reasons; the validity and value of opinion surveys and polls; and the extent to which the people insist not only on the right to know but also to participate and to decide.[66]

In considering such matters, certain guidelines may be helpful. In his volume on foreign relations maxims, diplomatic historian Thomas Bailey maintains that the government as the agent of the people is expected to frame policy that is not incompatible with their aspirations and desires, that in

principle "public opinion shapes foreign policy in a democracy" but that "the public must be educated to its responsibilities," and that, while the government needs to pay attention
to them, "opinion polls cannot conduct foreign policy."[67]

As an operational expedient it would seem that in the
relationship between policy makers and the public, the leaders need to be understood to formulate policy with the welfare of the country and its people at large in mind, that
they are the stewards of the interests and objectives of the
nation, that they be allowed flexibility in their determinations, and that they remain credible and respected in the
performance of their task.

On the other hand, the people establish the outer parameters of viable policy which the leaders exceed at their
peril; they serve as ultimate guardians of the general goals
and policy principles, and in a democracy eventually they
control through the electoral process.[68] But they do not
need to be consulted directly during the policy-making process, nor should they expect recurring referenda on either
policies or tactics. In short, minimally the public's role
is permissive--often characterized less by overt acceptance
than by receptivity--and preferably it is supportive, but it
need not be decisional.

Finally, note must be taken of the problem of judging
the value and success of foreign policy, or what has been
called the "positive achievements for the nation."[69] Simply
stated, the nation is successful if it attains its policy
aims. F. S. Northedge suggests that "'success' in foreign
policy may be broadly defined as the achievement of declared,
publicized or recognized objects of state policy, the maintenance or advancement of prestige or influence abroad, and
the abandonment of interests only in return for the gaining
of comparable or if possible weightier interests."[70] The
problem is deciding, which is bound to be largely subjective,
whether and how well the objectives are reached, whether or
not national prestige has been enhanced and in whose eyes,
and what has been the effect on which national interests.

Addressing the public in its pamphlet on foreign policy
in 1976, the Department of State declared: "But no nation can
choose the timing of its fate. The tides of history take no
account of the fatigue of the helmsman. Posterity will regard not the difficulty of the challenge, only the adequacy
of the response."[71] Based on years of personal experience,
Henry Kissinger warns: "Each success only buys an admission
ticket to a more difficult problem."[72]

In concluding his volume on a new foreign policy for the
United States, Hans Morgenthau also cautions that, despite
the greatest of care, "however sound in itself" no foreign
policy "can guarantee success" because "foreign policy is always at the mercy of accidents and, more particularly, of the
foreign policies of other nations." A nation "will discharge
its responsibilities toward itself and mankind only if it
maximizes the chances for success by putting into practice
the principles on which a sound foreign policy must rest."
Again the issue is debatable--what are those principles?[73]

To facilitate judgment in deciding whether a foreign policy is successful, certain questions need to be asked. Among the most salient are do the conditions and circumstances require reaction in the form of foreign policies; do the policies warrant the risks and costs essential to their implementation; is the nation prepared and equipped to employ the resources needed to achieve its objectives; will the attainment of the ends sought militate against others that are more important or consequential; and, in summary, to return to Walter Lippmann's dictum (quoted at the close of the preceding chapter), are the nation's objectives and power, its aims and means, and its commitments and resources in equilibrium?

Supplementing these requirements, Northedge prescribes the following tests: is policy based so far as possible on an accurate assessment of the facts; is it timely both in the short and the long run; is it as self-consistent as the nature of foreign policy allows it to be; is it understood and sufficiently backed by interest groups and the people at large; is it implemented with appropriate resources; and is it "smiled on by fortune?" To these requirements he adds: "But, above all, a foreign policy is most likely to succeed if it is moving with the tide of affairs and weaving itself into the positive volition of other states rather than pitting itself against their resistance."[74]

In many cases the judgments on success are bound to differ because there is no absolute way of evaluating it, because the criteria are subjectively developed and applied, and because a sense of success, or its rationalization, may not accurately reflect reality. Determinations are bound to be influenced by the knowledgeability and rationality of the observers, as well as by their biases, predispositions, experiences, and personal interests, and by the degree to which they share responsibility for the objectives pursued and the execution of the policies.[75] In judging the judgments it may be well to remember the postulate of British statesman Viscount John Morley: "Success depends on three things: who says it, what he says, how he says it; and of these three things, what he says is the least important."[76]

CATEGORIES OF POLICIES

Having in mind that public policy consists of two phases--domestic and foreign--little needs to be said about the domestic segment except that it is clearly interlinked with foreign policy. Attitudes on this matter vary from "what we are, here at home, conditions and determines what we do as a nation outside of our own borders,"[77] and "domestic factors largely determine the course of foreign policy and relations"[78] to "foreign policy is a phase of domestic policy, an inseparable phase,"[79] "foreign policy begins where domestic policy ends,"[80] and in contemporary world affairs "the traditional distinction between foreign and domestic policies tends to break down."[81]

In other words, foreign and domestic policies may be regarded as virtually indistinguishable in their effects or as

a composite consisting of three components--foreign, domestic, and an intermediary composite in which they are mixed.
Or they may be viewed as distinct--two sides of the same
coin--with domestic policy applying internally and foreign
policy applying externally, or as twin segments of a common
policy complex consisting of an amalgam of functional applications (to agricultural, commercial, economic, political,
security, and other substantive areas) many of which have
both external and internal ramifications. The critical differentiating factor is the policy's implementation beyond
the jurisdiction of the nation. Another major difference is
that domestic policy is usually converted into binding laws
and regulations, whereas foreign policy applies to an area
that lacks a common lawmaking institution and in which policy
is implemented by negotiation among legal equals that, according to international law and practice, are not bound by
that to which they do not consent.[82]

An alternative aspect of this relationship consists of
what are called domestic sources of foreign policy. Rosenau
has probed the premise that such sources of foreign policy
"are no less crucial to its content and conduct than are the
international situations toward which it is directed." He
concedes that "domestic factors may be of considerable significance even if they are not primary sources of foreign
policy, and on some issues they may well be dominant."[83]

Theoretically and for purposes of policy-making and
analysis, although much of foreign policy is cummulative or
incremental, individual policies may be particularized, applied to specific circumstances at a given time. Most policies are formulated in this manner, but logically they
should be related to the existing policy spectrum in order to
minimize incongruity. These policies may also be functionally or geographically oriented, applied either to particular
topics (such as security, trade, immigration, or nuclear
weapons) or to geographic areas (such as Western Europe, Latin America, or the Middle East).

Other concrete categories appose verbal versus actualized, positive versus negative, unilateral versus multilateral, and substantive versus procedural policies. The distinction between simple declaratory policy, which requires no
explicit implementation or only when the reaction of other
nations necessitates it, and policies that clearly mandate
overt action is readily understandable. But, according to
Stanley Hoffmann, this differentiation appears to be declining as nations lack the will or the resources to influence
others and because policies that are merely enunciated nevertheless come to be regarded as lines of action insofar as
they affect other governments' understanding of a nation's
policy.[84]

It is simple to distinguish positive policy (to do something) from negative policy (not to do anything). But the
policy maker should be aware of the difference between doing
nothing as a result of dereliction and doing nothing by virtue of overt decision. Often it is not easy for the outside
analyst to be sure which negative aspects really are matters
of policy and which cases of inaction are not.

The distinction between unilateral and multilateral foreign policy reflects differing orientations and intentions.
Unilateralism denotes the nation's disposition to act independently, to be free to "go it alone," without requiring
either identical, parallel, or confirmatory policy on the
part of other nations, or their negotiated cooperation--such
as a policy of neutrality in time of war or independent policy for dealing with international terrorism. Multilateral
policy involves the intent of demonstrative cooperation with
other nations, which usually requires negotiated accommodation with them, thereby restricting the nation's freedom of
action and sometimes necessitating open diplomacy in multipartite forums, with ultimate determination by formal voting.[85]

The relation of substantive and procedural policies is
not readily apparent. By substantive is meant policies that
evidence content, essence, or substantiality--that which is
to be done--whereas procedural policies concern how or when
it is to be done. Nevertheless, in practice the dividing
line between them may be obscure. The procedural are normally supportive of substantive policies, they are more flexible, and they vary in practice. If one state wishes to con-
summate a trade treaty with other nations, it may achieve
this by various methods and may establish different procedural policies to govern such negotiations with each of the
other governments.

The most material distinction among policy categories,
however, pertains to the structuring of the corpus of foreign
policies on the basis of duration and importance (see Figure
1). In terms of durability, at the forefront stand the long-
range or strategic policies which, though not immutable are
relatively constant and long-lived. These may be areally
and functionally oriented. Thus, a country may institute a
policy of abstentionism respecting the affairs of a non-con-
tiguous part of the world while becoming intimately involved,
perhaps even interventionist, in its own geographic area. It
may simultaneously pursue such functional policies as self-
determination, democratization, free trade, human rights,
modernization, freedom of the seas, and reciprocal commercial
air rights without geographic restrictions or time limits.

The second level, for want of a more precise delineation, may be designated as intermediate-range foreign policies. These are distinctive and material elements of the
policy spectrum which, although they have not acquired the
maturity or status of strategic policies, tend toward constancy and significance, but they may differ for geographic
areas or other particular groups of states. And in the long
run they may evolve into strategic policies. Finally, there
is the panoply of short-range, tactical policies, intended to
refine, support, or implement the more fundamental and permanent, and they are subject to variation and change from time
to time, place to place, and situation to situation.

Based solely on importance, especially the first two
categories (the strategic and intermediate) consist of policies not only of a primary but also of a secondary or subsidiary nature. On this scale, lesser policies may be desig-

nated tertiary, which are usually both less consequential and
constant. As a result, they are likely to be identical with
short-range, tactical policies. To illustrate, a basic policy
respecting the establishment of jurisdiction in outer space
may consist of separate sub-policies concerned with jurisdiction, respectively, over interplanetary space, active space
vehicles, deactivated or dormant space instrumentalities,
persons, other living beings, man-made electronic phenomena
or facilities, the heavenly bodies, and the like (see Table
IV in Chapter 9).

Similarly a given policy, such as promoting the right of
legation (that is, the right of independent nations to diplomatic representation abroad and to receive foreign emissar-
ies), supported by international custom and legal ordination
in the 1961 Vienna Convention on Diplomatic Relations, may be
long-range, geographically unrestricted, and also primary.
But the practical extension of this right to a particular
type of state at a given time under specific circumstances
may involve a mixture of intermediate and subsidiary policies. Each significant policy component, therefore, may be
buttressed by a number of supporting policies. Thus, the
foreign policy cosmography, which can at least hypothetically
be extrapolated extensively, is an intricate but sometimes
unsystematized complex of strategic/intermediate/tactical and
of primary/secondary or subsidiary/tertiary elements.

FOREIGN POLICY COMPLEX

Documentation on a nation's policies is readily available in a variety of materials. Official policy statements
are presented in thousands of addresses and other public
papers, and their practical applications are prescribed in a
great many legislative enactments, executive orders, administrative regulations, committee reports, and such other end
products as treaties, agreements, mutual declarations, resolutions, and other negotiated decisions. These are supplemented with hundreds of historical, descriptive, and analytical volumes, monographs, and essays produced by historians,
social scientists, diplomats, biographers, and other commentators.

Despite this plethora of material--in order to take account of the history, traditions, political structures, geographic factors, and commercial, political, and many other
interests, to say nothing of the persuasions and ambitions of
political leaders and the exigencies of the moment--perhaps
no one can produce a complete, systematic, and comprehendible
depiction of the full range of foreign policy even for a giv-
en country. For the United States it would take volumes to
achieve this, and much of their content would necessitate
revision before this monumental task could be completed. As
a result, the best that can be hoped for is a partial representation, perhaps for a single policy, or more likely for
some supporting sub-policy.

For the sake of convenience or ostensible facilitation
of comprehensibility, all too often foreign policy is viewed
as an agglomeration of components. However, to achieve com-

prehensive understanding, both the decision maker and the
outside analyst need to perceive foreign policy as an interrelated totality. While difficult, this should not be impossible and may be essential. Using the general patterning
described earlier, the foreign policy spectrum may even be
structured graphically, as depicted generically in Figure 1.
At the base of the spectrum are the day-to-day tactical and
the tertiary policies to implement the more fundamental elements of the system. In addition to extrapolating the entire
complex in this fashion, for analytical and decision-making
purposes each primary or secondary, as well as each strategic
and intermediate, policy may be structured independently in
this manner.[86]

Examination of such foreign policy systematization suggests the following generalizations. To recapitulate, in
terms of longevity three main policy categories are delineat-
ed--namely, the strategic/fundamental, the intermediate, and
the tactical/implementing. The principal distinction is between the strategic and intermediate, on the one hand, and
the tactical on the other. The more highly refined or complicated the layerings, the more difficult it is to define
precisely the dividing line between them.

Even with only three principal types, the question
arises as to when a policy ceases being tactical and becomes
intermediate and when it changes from the latter to the long-
range strategic. The distinguishing qualities are duration
and mutability, and often precise and historically valid
judgment requires hindsight, although the attempt at such
structuring may at any stage be founded on logic and intent.
Sometimes it is equally difficult to judge if, on the basis
of importance, specific policy is primary or secondary, or
whether it is the latter or is less significant. In this case
differentiation is based on intrinsic value or degree of relevance, and, because determinations may not be scientifically
discoverable, they may depend rather upon systematic reasoning and subjective value judgments.

Second, precise delineations respecting both of these
sets of policy relationships are impossible to program in
state practice because, in an inconstant world, conditions,
intentions, aims, probabilities, capabilities, and people
change. At best, therefore, it is only possible to systematize the policy spectrum in detail as of a given moment in
relation to a particular set of circumstances. Or it is necessary to elevate the projection to one of abstract rather
than concrete applicability. This being the case, the farther
the extrapolation proceeds from the broad and general to the
precise and specific, the more ephemeral is the hierarchical
depiction.

Third, the more definitive the supporting secondary and
tertiary policies, the more likely are they to be confused,
if not actually identified, with tactical policies. To state
it another way, the more specific and minute the policies are
that support a primary policy, the more they assume the character of tactical policies. Coalescing of policy constituents, as a consequence, is centrifugal rather than centripe-
tal. Logic warrants determining this distinction of "tacti-

Figure 1
Foreign Policy Complex—
Hypothetical Model

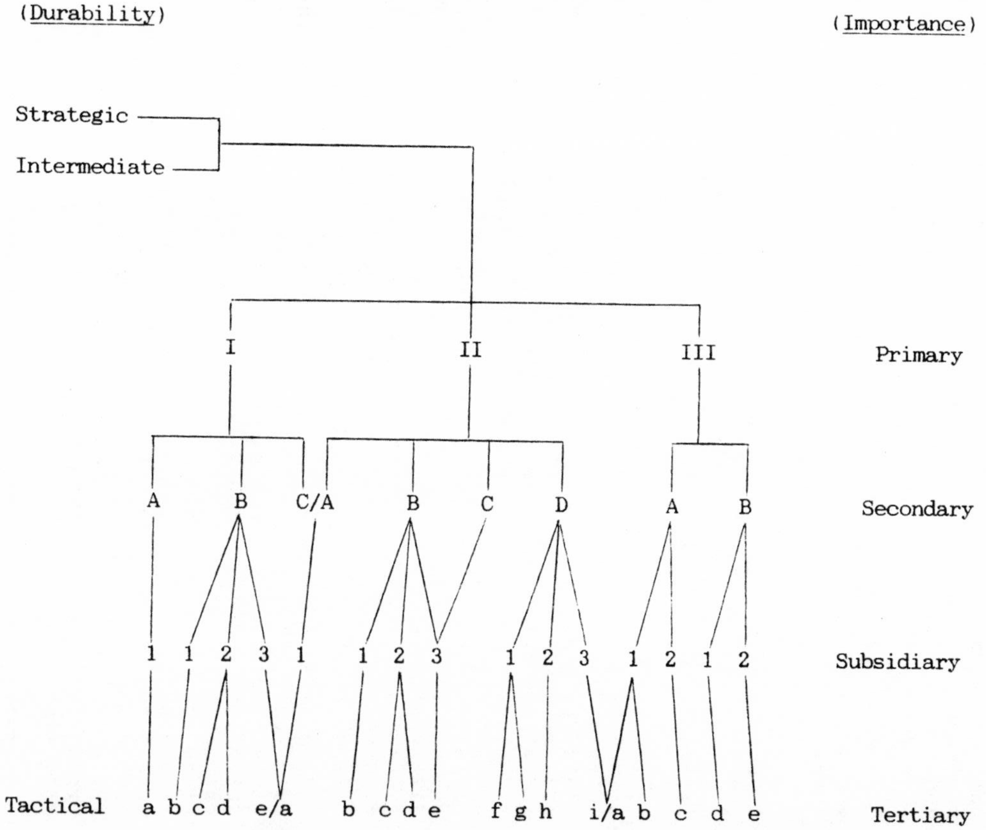

(Durability)
(Importance)
Strategic
Intermediate
I
II
III
Primary
A
B
C/A
B
C
D
A
B
Secondary
1 1 2 3 1
1 2 3
1 2 3
1 2 1 2
Subsidiary
Tactical
a b c d e/a
b c d e
f g h
i/a b c d e
Tertiary

cality" principally on the basis of impermanence, temporariness, and brevity. Regardless of a policy's finiteness, therefore, if it is relatively unchanging, it may be regarded as supportive of fundamental policy rather than as being tactical. Even though this matter may appear to be exaggerated, the policy maker needs to be aware of it in order to minimize policy schizophrenia--or a semblance of the malady--which is referred to more fully later. The citizen and sometimes even the expert analyst appears to compound his confusion by focusing largely upon the tactical. "Refined policy" according to Edmund Burke, "ever has been the parent of confusion; and ever will be so."[87]

Fourth, in shaping the foreign policy design, differing priorities may be decided upon in keeping with the application of varying criteria. The latter, for example, may be long-term merit, short-range importance, expediency, cost, practicability, or national prestige and ego satisfaction. Naturally, complete agreement may be impossible among leaders or outside commentators as to the degree of relevance of or preference for particular criteria. As a result, conclusions concerning priorities will differ, and this will be reflected in the resulting configuration of the foreign policy cosmography. Moreover, as conditions change, or as minds are persuaded to modify the role of criteria, shifts will occur in the policy spectrum, which may convey the impression of policy instability.

Fifth, certain policies and sub-policies are fulfillable in the sense that they can be consummated by some precise action, whereupon they no longer constitute compelling needs or desires. Illustrations include the attainment of diplomatic recognition and international status on gaining independence, the acquisition of a piece of territory or the satisfactory resolution of a boundary question, the creation of or acceptance into an international organization, the formulation of an alliance, and the negotiation of a treaty. On the other hand, the strategic and many of the primary policies are of a continuing nature and are rarely completely achievable, such as averting the outbreak of war, the peaceful settlement of international disputes, preventing foreign intervention, promoting trade relations, engaging in international cooperation, and maintaining national power and prestige. In general, it seems, the more fundamental the policy--except for the attainment of independence and national identity--the less likely is it to be fully executable. As such needs and objectives remain unfulfilled, policy making comes to constitute a continuum, whereby a fixed set of basic policies are forged that form the central core of the nation's policy complex.

Sixth, the various segments of an integrated policy structure overlap and are not entirely mutually exclusive. As it is projected level by level in increasing detail, overlapping and a good deal of interaction occurs. In some cases, a secondary or sub-policy under one primary, long-range policy may be virtually identical with another sub-policy supporting another primary policy (see Figure 1, items I/C and II/A). For example, a policy of supplying military aid to a foreign government to buttress an alliance pursuant to a basic na-

tional defense policy may also support foreign trade and international cooperation policies. It is not unnatural that
elements of the foreign policy systems of many nations are so
inextricably intertwined that the successful implementation
of one policy cannot be projected without affecting the
achievability (or unachievability) of others. Analysis and
determinations respecting one foreign policy component cannot, therefore, be sagacious or prescient in isolation from
all others.

In some cases the interrelationship of policy elements
is "bijunctural"--that is, coordinate policies may be directly and immediately correlative and mutually supportive. Such
interconnection may exist between parallel policies of military alliance and maintaining international stability, and
between averting hostilities and resolving international disputes by amicable means through negotiation, conciliation,
arbitration, and adjudication. Nevertheless, multiple interrelationships also occur, in that not only are sub-policies
that support a more primary policy ipso facto intermeshed,
but the more fundamental may themselves be interrelated. The
Monroe Doctrine of the United States, by way of illustration,
was closely linked with strategic, long-range policies providing for the promotion of self-determination and international political stability, together with the enhancement of
regional security, national capability, and international
prestige, while at the same time it was supported by non-
colonization, non-interference, and non-interposition secondary policies.

Seventh, a foreign policy network may be viewed from a
particular, predetermined perspective--such as from the point
of view of international status (i.e., leadership, power,
image, and prestige), international cooperation, national security, and the like. Foreign policy decision-making may
function under the aegis of a total environmental psychology, with the policy maker assuming an overall perspective.
If this is done deliberately and consistently, the perspective will remain broad and relatively constant. This is more
feasible for the lesser power which has fewer international
interests, responsibilities, and commitments. Significantly,
it also appears to be easier to approximate in the political
system within which the internal function of decision-making
is highly centralized. But this generalized focus may not
always be possible or desirable, as in times of major crisis.
Consequently, when the perspective shifts, kaleidoscopically
the policy matrix also changes in form and content.

In actual practice, the decision maker is frequently
confronted with a problem within a specific set of circumstances requiring policy formulation at a given time, and he
is apt to frame his perspective in terms of that limited environmental perception, which causes him to visualize the
policy scheme from a fixed and restricted point of view. The
same or another decision maker focusing attention upon another issue involving a different set of circumstances may view
the policy design from an entirely different perspective. As
a result, inconsistencies--real or apparent--are bound to occur, and priorities may become uncertain. Needless to say,
a warped perspective, unless expertly handled within the pan-

oply of the total policy complex, invites the production of
faulty policy.

In analyzing and judging foreign policy, it is necessary
for the historical or analytical reviewer to be aware of the
perspective employed by the policy maker. Subsequent questioning or criticism of his decision may be as attributable
to his perspective as to his policy determination. Review
and assessment of policy-making with hindsight have the advantage, among others, of enabling the analyst to approach
the matter from a broader perspective and with knowledge of
the consequences which, therefore, permits the reaching of
conclusions at considerable variance with those of the decision maker. Yet, as Lippmann notes in the preface to his
volume on foreign policy, there may be a considerable gap
between hindsight and insight.[88]

Eighth, some foreign policy elements may be accorded a
particular sequential relevance. Competing governments pursuing their respective objectives in the international arena
may actually adopt antithetical ordering of time or sequence
priorities--producing foreign policy "contrasequences." Sometimes, particularly in crises, this is reflected in secondary
or derivative diplomatic disputes over preconditions to negotiation, and history reveals examples where such resultant
disputes become as heated as do the primary controversies.

For example, in the matter of resolving the "European
question" following World War II, to oversimplify, the Soviet
government and its allies demanded that, in order to attain
relaxation of East-West tensions, it was essential to first
settle the German question (naturally to the satisfaction of
the Kremlin and East Germany), and then negotiate a disarmament settlement. The Western powers, on the other hand, insisted upon the opposite sequence. They stipulated that a
change of Soviet attitude--through deeds rather than rhetoric
--had to come first, followed by a reduction of the Soviet
military posture in Central Europe, whereupon German reunification could then be negotiated and East-West tensions molli-
fied. These contravening sequences were based, in part, on
differing views respecting the relation of political prerequisites to the negotiability of policy.

Ninth, there are recognizable limits, not always appreciated by the outsider, within which foreign policy can be
formulated and implemented. In other words, the foreign
policy maker is far from a completely free agent. Such limits exist in both the external and internal environments.
The principal external factors may be generalized as the
very nature of the society of nations composed of theoretically sovereign equals, each with its own sets of interests,
goals, objectives, policies, and strategy; the established
and extraordinary processes whereby nations are expected to
deal with one another, including the craft of diplomacy; the
rule of law to the extent to which it is embodied in general
international juridical precepts and specific law-creating
treaty obligations; the large number of global and regional
institutionalized forums, such as the United Nations, the
Arab League, and the Organization of American States, within
which a member country is committed to participate in keeping

with stated purposes and pursuant to established processes;
and the global, regional, and more immediate power relationships of one country with another.

The internal delimiting factors may be grouped as ideological (the traditions and ideals), constitutional (the
legal decision determinants), the institutional (the decision-making mechanism), and the socio-political (the decision
influencers). The last two elements embrace the organizational fabric of the polity; its system of governance; and
particularly in democracies the extra-governmental pluralistic structuring of the people, with their differing concerns
and competing desires, and whose interests are presumed to be
reflected by political parties, vested interest and action
groups, and the instrumentalities of the mass media. These
and other external and internal restrictive elements impinge
upon the freedom of action of a government in formulating its
foreign policy and affect if not reduce the options of the
decision maker.

Tenth, the foreign policy systems of nations contain
actual or apparent schizophrenia. That is to say, countries
generally pursue some antithetical or seemingly divergent
policies. This is most conspicuous in the realm of tactical
and tertiary policies, which are expected to remain fluid and
are frequently changed. Thus, one country may grant foreign
aid to another but not to its neighbor, it may supply assistance to a particular government one year and deny it the
next, or it may provide one kind of support but not another.

Juxtapositional dichotomies also occur in the areas of
more fundamental policies, however, and it is here that the
achievability of one may be impeded by the pursuance of
another. To illustrate, a newly emergent country may adopt a
series of policies designed to preserve its recently gained
independence and international posture, while at the same
time it pursues policies which run the risk of undermining or
threatening this status. Or a country may adhere to policies
intended to preserve peace, involving the unilateral or collective condemnation of other countries for warlike actions,
while itself engaging in aggressive policies toward, or even
launching hostilities upon, a neighbor. Both West and East
Germany have espoused the policy of national reunification,
and yet they have established policies of individual international identity and status, involvement as sovereign members
in regional as well as global international cooperative arrangements, and active participation in opposing military
alliances--which have rendered their reunification less feasible.[89]

Finally, also contributing to policy complexity, the relationship of aims and means varies with respect to the nature of the policy issue. In practice--on the basis of operational methodology--there are four distinguishable types of
policy. In terms of increasing significance or criticality,
some issues concern ordinary day-to-day activities and problems, both substantive and procedural. Many policies of this
nature fall into the tertiary/tactical categories.

The next level of issues relate to anticipatory, long-range policies, in the planning of which policy makers enjoy lead time to refine both objectives and methods of implementation in keeping with national purposes and basic goals. Another level involves contingency planning--either advance planning for probable contingencies, or designing preferred policy to attain concrete objectives that support the nation's purposes and goals, accompanied by rationalized alternatives should such choices prove to be undesirable, unachievable, or hazardous (see Chapter 8).

The remaining level of policy issues pertains to crisis management and resolution, in which lead time is normally limited, and for which crisis mitigation becomes the principal immediate objective. The nature and pertinence of both the policy objectives and the policies initiated to achieve them, and their correlation with national purposes and goals in keeping with national interests, therefore, vary considerably in relation to the type of policy issue involved.

In short, given all of its manifestations, the foreign policy complex is intricate and, in its more finite constituents, the interests-ends-means mosaic is not only incremental, inclusive, convoluted, and multiplex, but also mutant. Inability to comprehend this leads inevitably to fragmentary, unsynthesized, and unrealistic policy-making and warped assessments.

The foreign policy network of a nation is perplexing, and systematic inquiry, though difficult, is challenging and may possibly be exciting. Such analysis is facilitated, however, if the matrix is systematized. The resultant extrapolation not only assists in distinguishing the important from the less important, the permanent from the temporary, the relevant from the extraneous, the valid from the unsound, and the reasonable from the prohibitive. It also obliges the policy maker or commentator to define and distinguish among policy missions, levels of policy, and criteria for priorities, as well as policy preferences. And it encourages them to develop an awareness of gaps in the policy spectrum, irrelevancies, countervailances, and redundancies--thereby facilitating the normative function of looking toward foreign policy redefinition, rectification, and improvement.

NOTES

1. Diplomacy is defined, more precisely, as "the political process" by which nations "establish and maintain official relations, direct and indirect, with one another, in pursuing their respective goals, objectives, interests, and substantive and procedural policies in the international environment . . . and involves essentially, but is not restricted to, the functions of representation, reporting, communicating, negotiation, and maneuvering, as well as caring for the interests of nationals abroad." For a comprehensive analysis of the concept of diplomacy, see Elmer Plischke, "The Optimum Scope of Instruction in Diplomacy," in *Instruction in Diplomacy: The Liberal Arts Approach*, Monograph No. 13 (Philadelphia: American Academy of Political and Social Science, 1972), pp. 1-25, with definition on p. 20.

British diplomatist Harold Nicolson clearly distinguishes foreign policy from diplomacy, which he restricts to the execution of policy, or negotiation.   See his *Diplomacy* (London: Oxford University Press, 1965), pp. 12-14. See also Charles W. Thayer, *Diplomat* (New York: Harper, 1959), p. 82.   Most commentators agree that the primary responsibility for policy implementation lies with diplomats; in addition to Nicolson and Thayer, see William Macomber, *The Angels' Game: A Handbook of Modern Diplomacy* (New York: Stein and Day, 1975), p. 59.   H. Bradford Westerfield in *The Instruments of America's Foreign Policy* (New York: Crowell, 1963) discusses some of the applications of diplomacy, including isolationism, total and limited warfare, information, trade and other economic programs, and interventionism.

2. Jeane Kirkpatrick, editorial, November 23, 1986.   See also *American Strategy for the Nuclear Age*, edited by Walter F. Hahn and John C. Neff (New York: Doubleday, 1960), p. 4.

3. Hugh Gibson, *The Road to Foreign Policy* (Garden City, N.Y.: Doubleday, Doran, 1944), p. 2.

4. Walter Lippmann, *U.S. Foreign Policy: Shield of the Republic* (Boston: Little, Brown, 1943), p. 7.   He was seriously concerned with the relationship of resources and capability, which are discussed later.

5. See commentary in Norman Hill, *Contemporary World Politics* (New York: Harper, 1954), p. 38.   For examples, see Hugh Gibson and Dean Acheson below (notes 9 and 10) and Lippmann's interpretation quoted at the end of the preceding chapter.

6. See comment in Hill, *Contemporary World Politics*, p. 38. Early in their administrations Presidents often proclaim that they are going to institute propitious changes in foreign policy. Thus, in his first state of the union message, President Eisenhower declared that he would establish "a new, positive foreign policy;" see *Papers of the Presidents: Dwight D. Eisenhower, 1953*, p. 13.

7. See Wallace Irwin, Jr., *America in the World: A Guide to U.S. Foreign Policy* (New York: Praeger, 1983), p. x.

8. Quoted in Edgar Ansell Mowrer, *The Nightmare of American Foreign Policy* (New York: Knopf, 1948), p. 43.

9. Gibson went so far as to say: "We stand alone as a Great Power without a policy" and "we have no continuity of foreign policy because we have no comprehensive, recognized policy to continue." *The Road to Foreign Policy*, especially pp. 6, 9, 11, 45.   His first two chapters are devoted to the questions of whether or not the United States has a foreign policy and why it needs one. See also commentary in Feliks Gross, *Foreign Policy Analysis* (New York: Philosophical Library, 1954), pp. 44-48.

10. Dean Acheson, *Power and Diplomacy* (Cambridge, Mass.: Harvard University Press, 1958), p. 2.

11. For example, Walter Lippmann has argued that although the United States does not lack foreign policies, they have "become dangerously inadequate"; *U.S. Foreign Policy*, p. ix. Others regard foreign policy as too liberal or too conservative, too static or too changing, too unsystematic, too magnanimous or too self-centered, or too impractical. Former Undersecretary of State Sumner Welles has written: "A government's foreign policy must be judged far more by its results than by its intentions. Innumerable foreign policies, like the road to hell, have been

paved with good intentions." See *Where Are We Heading?* (New York: Harper, 1946), p. 334. For additional commentary on such critics of American foreign policy as Hans Morgenthau and George Kennan, see Dexter Perkins, "American Foreign Policy and Its Critics," in *American Foreign Policy and American Democracy*, edited by Alfred H. Kelly (Detroit: Wayne University Press, 1954), pp. 65-88. See also Cecil V. Crabb, Jr., *Policy-Makers and Critics: Conflicting Theories of American Foreign Policy* (New York: Praeger, 1976).

12. See John W. Davis' essay on United States foreign policy in *The Foreign Policy of the Powers*, edited by Hamilton Fish Armstrong (New York: Harper, 1935), pp. 143-61.

13. Henderson maintained that whereas the charge is frequently made that the United States lacks foreign policies and drifts aimlessly, "I want to assure you that we do have well-established foreign policies. We have long-term foreign policies which are as stable and as permanent as the traditions and way of life of the American people. We are also constantly formulating shorter-term policies in order to meet the ever-shifting world situation." Loy W. Henderson, *Foreign Policies: Their Formulation and Enforcement* (Washington: Government Printing Office, 1946), pp. 2-3.

14. Hill, *Contemporary World Politics*, p. 38.

15. Gross, *Foreign Policy Analysis*, p. 47.

16. Charles O. Lerche calls foreign policy "a social and political process"; *Foreign Policy of the American People*, 3d ed. (Englewood Cliffs, N.J.: Prentice-Hall, 1967), pp. 4-5. However, Charles P. Schleicher insists that the concept of foreign policy differs from the more generic foreign affairs and international relations because they denote interactions which result from policy; *International Relations: Cooperation and Conflict* (Englewood Cliffs, N.J.: Prentice-Hall, 1962), p. 130.

17. Secretary of State Dean Rusk has argued, however, "that an idea is not a policy and that the transformation of an idea into a policy is frequently an exhausting and frustrating process." See Department of State, "The Formulation of Foreign Policy," *American Foreign Policy: Current Documents*, 1961 (Washington, Government Printing Office, 1965), p. 27.

18. Cecil V. Crabb, Jr., defines foreign policy "as those external goals toward the achievement of which the nation is prepared to commit its resources," and he specifies that foreign policy consists of two elements, "objectives and the means for attaining them," which he conceives as national power. See *American Foreign Policy in the Nuclear Age*, 4th ed. (New York: Harper and Row, 1983), p. 16. Also see usage of Marshall Knappen who says that foreign policy consists of goals and objectives as well as "the methods by which they are to be approached"; *An Introduction to American Foreign Policy* (New York: Harper, 1956), p. 1. See also Harold and Margaret Sprout, *Foundations of International Politics* (Princeton, N.J.: Van Nostrand, 1962), pp. 107-8.

19. Melquiades J. Gamboa calls them a "plan of action"; *Elements of Diplomatic and Consular Practice: A Glossary* (Quezon City, Philippines: Central Lawbook Publishing, 1966), p. 202. On the contrary, Schleicher states that foreign policy cannot be equated with policy plans; see *International Relations*, p. 130.

20. Charles Osgood calls foreign policy "essentially strategy for maintaining or changing the existing status quo in terms of self interest"; *Perspective in Foreign Policy*, 2d ed. (Palo Alto, Calif.: Pacific Books, 1966), p. 9. See also *The International Relations Dictionary*, edited by Jack C. Plano and Roy Olton (Santa Barbara, Calif.: ABC-Clio, 1982), p. 7. As noted earlier, Dean Acheson goes so far as to label it a "grand strategy" in *Power and Diplomacy*, p. 2.

21. This is evidenced by some of the references cited in notes in this and other chapters and by a great many other volumes in the field of foreign affairs and diplomatic history.

22. See John Gange, *American Foreign Relations: Permanent Problems and Changing Policies* (New York: Ronald, 1959), p. 24.

23. See Charles A. Beard, *A Foreign Policy for America* (New York: Knopf, 1940), p. 4; Knappen, *An Introduction to American Foreign Policy*, p. 1; and Edgar S. Furniss, Jr., and Richard C. Snyder, *An Introduction to American Foreign Policy* (New York: Rinehart, 1955), p. 28. Harold and Margaret Sprout, *Foundations of International Politics*, pp. 107-11, prefer the term "patterns," as do Kenneth Thompson and Roy Macridis in "The Comparative Study of Foreign Policy," in *Foreign Policy in World Politics*, 5th ed., edited by Roy C. Macridis (Englewood Cliffs, N.J.: Prentice-Hall, 1976), pp. 21-23.

24. See Gange, *American Foreign Relations*, p. 24, who calls policies "means to advance or satisfy these national interests or objectives," and George Kennan declares: "Our foreign policy, in short, is only a means to an end"; *Realities of American Foreign Policy* (Princeton: Princeton University Press, 1954), p. 5. Charles Burton Marshall has written: "Ends are concepts. Means are facts. Making foreign policy consists of meshing concepts and facts in the field of action." See "The Nature of Foreign Policy," *Department of State Bulletin* 26 (March 17, 1952): 416. See also his *The "Limits" of Foreign Policy* (New York: Holt, 1954), pp. 31-34.

25. Lerche calls policy a method for attaining objectives; *Foreign Policy of the American People*, p. 21. See also Knappen's statement in note 18 above. This term is often used interchangeably with means; for a discussion of ends and means, see Chapter 4, pp. 74-77.

26. Dean Rusk, Address, December 10, 1963, in Department of State, *American Foreign Policy: Current Documents, 1963* (Washington: Government Printing Office, 1967), p. 36.

27. Rusk, "The Formulation of Foreign Policy," p. 23.

28. William G. Carleton, *The Revolution in American Foreign Policy: Its Global Range* (New York: Random House, 1963), p. v.

29. See Louis Henkin, *How Nations Behave: Law and Foreign Policy* (New York: Praeger, 1968), p. 13. On the matter of foreign policy regarded as the sum of more than an aggregate of policies, see the section on usage below.

30. K. J. Holsti, *International Politics: A Framework for Analysis* (Englewood Cliffs, N.J.: Prentice-Hall, 1967), p. 21.

31. Sprout, *Foundations of International Politics*, pp. 107-108.

32. Beard, *A Foreign Policy for America*, p. 4.

33. Seabury, *Power, Freedom, and Diplomacy* (New York: Random House, 1963), p. 5; see also pp. 289-90.

34. Kurt London, *How Foreign Policy Is Made* (New York: Van Nostrand, 1949), p. 12.   See also his *The Making of Foreign Policy: East and West* (Philadelphia: Lippincott, 1955), p. 1.

35. Marshall, "The Nature of Foreign Policy," p. 415.

36. The Brookings Institution report on American foreign policy published in 1956, influential in refining interpretation, states that policies are "specific courses of action designed to achieve *objectives* . . . . The distinction between *policies* and *objectives* is that between means and ends"; see William Reitzel, Morton A. Kaplan, and Constance G. Coblenz, *United States Foreign Policy, 1945-1955* (Washington: Brookings Institution, 1956), p. 473. Similar interpretations as courses of action are provided in a good many studies, such as Thomas A. Bailey, *The Art of Diplomacy: The American Experience* (New York: Appleton-Century-Crofts, 1968), p. 89; Ellis Briggs, *Anatomy of Diplomacy: The Origin and Execution of American Foreign Policy* (New York: McKay, 1968), p. 6; Gamboa, *Elements of Diplomatic and Consular Practice*, p. 202; Gross, *Foreign Policy Analysis*, p. 50; Charles O. Lerche, Jr., and Abdul A. Said, *Concepts of International Politics: In Global Perspective*, 3d ed. (Englewood Cliffs, N.J.: Prentice-Hall, 1979), p. 32; *The International Relations Dictionary*, p. 7; and many others. As indicated earlier, Dean Acheson prefers the expression "lines of action"; see Chapter 5, note 50.

37. Gross, *Foreign Policy Analysis*, p. 50. He also defines foreign policy in the singular as "both an ideology and a complex"; for discussion on the foreign policy complex, see the last section of this chapter. Compare this with Lerche's view quoted later.

38. Irwin, *America in the World*, p. x. Also compare with the views of Henkin cited earlier. Similarly, Ernest Lefever argues that "Foreign policy is the sum of a nation's efforts to affect the world beyond the borders of its legal jurisdiction"; see *Ethics and United States Foreign Policy* (New York: Meridian Books, 1957), p. 10.

39. London, *The Making of Foreign Policy*, p. 1, and for an earlier version see his *How Foreign Policy Is Made*, p. 12.

40. *Dimensions of American Foreign Policy: Readings and Documents*, edited by Martin Needler (Princeton: Van Nostrand, 1966), p. 31.

41. T. B. Millar, on the other hand, states that "Foreign policy is presumably something less than the sum of all policies" which have an effect on the foreign relations of the nation.   "Many kinds of domestic policies have external effects but are not foreign policy." See "On Writing About Foreign Policy," *Australian Outlook* 21 (1967): 71-84, in *International Politics and Foreign Policy: A Reader in Research and Theory*, edited by James N. Rosenau (New York: Free Press, 1969), pp. 57-64.

42. Rusk, "The Formulation of Foreign Policy," p. 22.

43. For commentary on this distinction, see Furniss and Snyder, *An Introduction to American Foreign Policy*, p. 28.

44. Beard, *A Foreign Policy for America*, pp. 6-7.

45. Lerche, *Foreign Policy of the American People*, pp. 4-6, 21.   See

also Lerche and Said, *Concepts of International Politics*, p. 32, in which
they indicate that the principal distinction is founded on policy formulation in terms of goals and objectives. Similarly, Schleicher claims
that foreign policy is variously defined broadly as a process consisting
of objectives, plans, and actions, and more narrowly simply as actions;
International Relations, pp. 129-30. Also compare these views with those
of Feliks Gross cited earlier.

46. Thompson and Macridis, "The Comparative Study of Foreign Policy," pp. 1-4.

47. See Bernard C. Cohen, "Foreign Policy," *International Encyclopedia of the Social Sciences* (New York: Macmillan, 1968), V, 530. This
article deals primarily with approaches to foreign policy decision-making, rather than the essence or nature of policy. See also discussion
on decision-making in Chapter 9.
    For additional commentary on ideology, see Jorge Larrain, *The Con-
cept of Ideology* (Athens: University of Georgia Press, 1979), which discusses the origin of the concept, historical tradition, and structural
analysis; M. Seliger, *Ideology and Politics* (New York: Free Press, 1976),
which treats ideology versus pragmatism, types of ideology, and ideological change; and Calvin J. Larson and Philo C. Washburn, eds., *Power, Participation, and Ideology: Readings in the Sociology of American Life* (New
York: McKay, 1969).

48. Gibson, *The Road to Foreign Policy*, p. 1.

49. Acheson, "A Conversation with Dean Acheson," CBS-TV interview,
September 28, 1969, in *The Quotable Quotation Book*, edited by Alex Lewis
(New York: Crowell, 1980), p. 103.

50. Felix Morley, *The Foreign Policy of the United States* (New York:
Knopf, 1951), p. 7.

51. Seabury, *Power, Freedom, and Diplomacy*, pp. 10-11.

52. Relating policy to interests, the Department of State maintains
that "Although our basic interests remain the same over the years, the
means by which we express and advance those interests change from generation to generation, and sometimes even from year to year. They change in
response to new situations at home and abroad." Department of State,
American Foreign Policy, 1952 (Washington: Government Printing Office,
1952), p. 7. London contends that "A workable foreign policy can never
be static" because international conditions "are subject to constant
change" so that "to build a policy on the basis of the *status quo* is an
illusion that can only lead to disappointment, if not disaster." *The
Making of Foreign Policy*, p. 13. On policy flexibility, see also Lerche,
Foreign Policy of the American People, pp. 22-23.

53. For example, Gibson, who claims that such scraps "are not policies" but are rather "in some cases, no more than phrases indicating
aims, purposes, or aspirations," which "begin to have value only when
they are put to work." Consequently, the diplomatic practitioner is
obliged to "deal with questions as they arise and clamor for his attention." *The Road to Foreign Policy*, pp. 7-9. See also note 9 above.
Mowrer's criticism is that "American foreign policy was regularly one
jump behind the times"; *The Nightmare of American Foreign Policy*, p. 247.

54. Roger Hilsman, *To Move a Nation* (New York: Dell, 1967), pp. 548-
49.

55. Rosenau also notes that while the observer is obliged to segment this sequence for analytic purposes he risks exaggerating the segment under review and assessing it out of its broader context. See *International Politics and Foreign Policy*, p. 167. For commentary on the "cyclical theory of American foreign policy," see Dexter Perkins, *The American Approach to Foreign Policy* (Cambridge: Harvard University Press, 1962), Chapter 7.

56. James N. Rosenau, *The Scientific Study of Foreign Policy* (New York: Free Press, 1971), p. 80.

57. Marshall, *The "Limits" of Foreign Policy*, p. 33.

58. For commentary on the mobilization of resources for policy-making and implementation, see Howard H. Lentner, *Foreign Policy Analysis: A Comparative and Conceptual Approach* (Columbus, Ohio: Merrill, 1974), pp. 199-214.

59. Marshall, *The "Limits" of Foreign Policy*, p. 34.

60. In addition to those cited below, examples include Thomas A. Bailey, *The Man in the Street: The Impact of American Public Opinion on Foreign Policy* (New York: Macmillan, 1948); Max Beloff, *Foreign Policy and the Democratic Process* (Baltimore: Johns Hopkins Press, 1955); Bernard C. Cohen, *The Public's Impact on Foreign Policy* (Boston: Little, Brown, 1973); Edwin P. Hoyt, *American Attitude: The Story of the Making of Foreign Policy in the United States* (New York: Abelard-Schuman, 1970); Brian Klunk, *Consensus and the American Mission* (Lanham, Md.: University Press of America, 1985); Walter Lippmann, *Public Opinion and Foreign Policy in the United States* (London: Allen and Unwin, 1952); Lester Markel, et al., *Public Opinion and Foreign Policy* (New York: Harper, 1949); Richard A. Melanson and Kenneth W. Thompson, eds., *Foreign Policy and Domestic Consensus* (Lanham, Md.: University Press of America, 1985) on consensus in the United States since the 1940s; George H. Quester, *American Foreign Policy: The Lost Consensus* (New York: Praeger, 1982) on the "Vietnam syndrome;" and James N. Rosenau, *Public Opinion and Foreign Policy* (New York: Random House, 1961).
Earlier studies were published by James Bryce (1922), Harold Lasswell (1943), Walter Lippmann (1922 and 1925), Abbott L. Lowell (1913), Arthur Ponsonby (1915), Quincy Wright (1933), and others. These are supplemented with considerable essay literature. For a comprehensive bibliography on public opinion, the media, and interest groups as they relate to foreign policy matters, see Elmer Plischke, *U.S. Foreign Relations: A Guide to Information Sources* (Detroit: Gale Research, 1980), pp. 348-64.

61. Gabriel A. Almond, *The American People and Foreign Policy* (New York: Harcourt, Brace, 1950), pp. 158-59.

62. See *Consensus at the Crossroads: Dialogues in American Foreign Policy*, edited by Howard Bliss and M. Glen Johnson (New York: Dodd, Mead, 1972), p. v. For commentary on post-World War II changes in attitudes and approaches contributing to this retrogression, see Ralph B. Levering, *The Public and American Foreign Policy, 1918-1978* (New York: Morrow, 1978), especially pp. 154- 59.

63. Department of State, *United States Foreign Policy, 1976* (Washington: Government Printing Office, 1976), pp. 5, 48. On this matter see also Max Beloff, *Foreign Policy and the Democratic Process*, especially Chapter 1.

64. V. O. Key, Jr., *Public Opinion and American Democracy* (New York: Knopf, 1961), p. 7; see also Chapter 2, "Consensus," in which he distinguishes among supportive consensus, permissive consensus, multiple consensus, and consensus of decision. For commentary on consensus as it relates to the characteristics of American foreign policy, including the tendency to rely more on consensus than rationality, see Joseph de Rivera, *The Psychological Dimension of Foreign Policy* (Columbus, Ohio: Merrill, 1968), Chapter 8, especially pp. 300-301.

65. Examining whether a single overarching policy concept can be devised to build domestic support in the United States, James Chace concludes: "We may simply have to learn to conduct foreign policy for a very long time without a single unifying theme on which to base a broad national consensus." See "Is a Foreign Policy Consensus Possible?" *Foreign Affairs* 57 (Fall 1978): 1-16. For representation of the view that reliance on popular support weakens foreign policy-making, see Hans J. Morgenthau, *Politics Among Nations: The Struggle for Power and Peace*, 4th ed. (New York: Knopf, 1967), pp. 7, 141-43.

Ambassador George Kennan, columnist Walter Lippmann, and others also support the benefit of rational policy making by governments and question the overemphasis on popular endorsement. Thus, Kennan questions whether the government should be "beholden to short term trends of public opinion," which involve "emotionalism and subjectivity which make it a poor and inadequate guide for national action." See *American Diplomacy, 1900-1950* (Chicago: University of Chicago Press, 1951), p. 93. For his comment that "only a government can speak usefully and responsibly in foreign affairs," see his *Realities of American Foreign Policy* (Princeton: Princeton University Press, 1954), p. 43. Lippmann holds that normally "voters cannot be expected to transcend their particular, localized and self-regarding opinions" and that "their opinions and interests should be taken for what they are and for no more. They are not--as such--propositions in the public interest." *Essays in the Public Philosophy* (Boston: Little, Brown, 1955), p. 41.

66. The issue, generally insisted upon by the media, as a right, is to know "what" and "how much" and "when?" These questions raise additional issues of confidentiality, confidence, and secrecy in making and implementing foreign policy in addition to revealing the policy that has been made. In defining "the public," additional questions need to be posed as to whether this means the mass public, or the knowledgeable or attentive public, or a foreign relations expert or leadership public, or merely a vocal, demonstrative, or activistic minority.

On active popular participation there are those who argue for greater democratization of foreign policy, citizen diplomacy, or as put by Beloff, "popular control of foreign policy"; see his *Foreign Policy and the Democratic Process*, Chapter 1, especially pp. 19-20, 25. For additional commentary on democratic diplomacy, see Elmer Plischke, *Conduct of American Diplomacy*, 3d ed. (Princeton: Van Nostrand, 1967; reprinted by Greenwood Press, Westport, Conn., 1974), pp. 38-43.

67. Bailey, *The Art of Diplomacy*, Chapter 10.

68. Henry Kissinger has warned: "The statesman's duty is to bridge the gap between his nation's experience and his vision. If he gets too far ahead of his people he will lose his mandate; if he confines himself to the conventional he will lose control over events." *Years of Upheaval* (Boston: Little, Brown, 1982), p. 169.

69. See London, *How Foreign Policy Is Made*, p. 11.

70. F. S. Northedge, *The Foreign Policies of the Powers* (New York: Free Press, 1968), p. 37.

71. Department of State, *United States Foreign Policy, 1976*, p. 47.

72. Henry Kissinger, *Wilson Library Bulletin* 53 (March 1979).

73. Hans J. Morgenthau, *A New Foreign Policy for the United States* (New York: Praeger, 1969), p. 244.

74. Northedge, *The Foreign Policies of the Powers*, pp. 37-40, with summary on p. 40.

75. See general commentary of Bliss and Johnson, *Consensus at the Crossroads*, pp. 318-20, and for discussion of the difficulty of scientific or systematized evaluation, see Thompson and Macridis, "The Comparative Study of Foreign Policy," pp. 23-29.

76. John Morley, *Recollections*, vol. II, Book 5, Chapter 4.

77. James P. Warburg, *Foreign Policy Begins at Home* (New York: Harcourt, Brace, 1944), p. v.

78. This is the thesis of Richard N. Rosecrance, *Action and Reaction in World Politics: International Systems in Perspective* (Boston: Little, Brown, 1963), in which he reviews a series of case studies and develops nine behavioral "systems."

79. Beard notes that three questions need to be asked concerning issues in foreign policy considerations, namely, what relation does it bear on specific interests at home and their connection abroad, how does the policy affect those interests and the national interest at large, and who formulates it? See *A Foreign Policy for America*, pp. 9-10.

80. Henry A. Kissinger, "Domestic Structure and Foreign Policy," *Daedalus* 95 (Spring 1966): 503.   He stresses the impact of domestic structure and administrative organization on foreign policy and world relations; see pp. 503-29.

81. Morgenthau, *Politics Among Nations*, p. 144.   Morgenthau also discusses the matter of policy promotion by influencing the minds of the people through the use of propaganda and psychological warfare; see pp. 324-31.   From a broader perspective, shortly after World War II the Department of State declared: "There is no longer any real distinction between 'domestic' and 'foreign' affairs"; see Department of State, *Our Foreign Policy* (Washington: Government Printing Office, 1950), p. 4.

82. For additional commentary, see Seabury, *Power, Freedom, and Diplomacy*, pp. 7-9. Rosenau, in *The Scientific Study of Foreign Policy*, pp. 410-13, examines foreign and domestic policy as distinct issue-areas for analytical purposes.

83. *Domestic Sources of Foreign Policy*, edited by James N. Rosenau (New York: Free Press, 1967), pp. 2, 4.   Among the domestic sources examined are personality, attitude change, social position and party identification, mass communication, interest groups, electoral and voting factors, and others. For the application of linkage theory to the relationship of domestic and foreign relations factors and developments, see *Linkage Politics: Essays on the Convergence of National and International Systems*, edited by James N. Rosenau (New York: Free Press, 1969,.

84. For additional commentary, see Stanley Hoffmann, *Gulliver's Troubles: Or the Setting of American Foreign Policy* (New York: McGraw-Hill, 1968), pp. 63-64.

85. For comment on these categories as related to interventionism and non-interventionism, see Westerfield, *The Instruments of America's Foreign Policy*, pp. 33-35.

86. For analysis of such a depiction, with illustrative tables and diagrams, see Elmer Plischke, "West German Foreign and Defense Policy," *ORBIS* 12 (Winter 1969): 1098-136. For additional case studies of policy development in German affairs, see Elmer Plischke, "Integrating Berlin and the Federal Republic of Germany," *Journal of Politics* 27 (February 1965): 35-65; "Resolving the 'Berlin Question'--An Options Analysis," *World Affairs* 131 (July-September 1968): 91-100; and "Reunifying Germany--An Options Analysis," *World Affairs* 132 (June 1969): 28-38.

87. Burke, Speech on conciliation with America, March 22, 1775, quoted in *Putnam's Complete Book of Quotations*, edited by W. Gurney Benham (New York: Putnam, 1927), p. 40a.

88. Lippmann, *U.S. Foreign Policy*, pp. x-xiii.

89. For commentary, see pertinent references cited in note 86.

7

NATIONAL POWER
AND CAPABILITY

Without mechanical power--the ability to move mass
--there can be no technology. Without political
power--the ability to move men--technology cannot
serve a social purpose. All civilized life rests,
therefore, in the last instance on power.
Nicholas J. Spykman, *America's Strategy
in World Politics* (1942)

The statesman, who means to maintain peace, can no
more ignore the order of power than an engineer can
ignore the mechanics of physical force.
Walter Lippmann, *U.S. Foreign Policy* (1943)

The power of the state can be justified only in
terms of what it seeks to do.
Harold J. Laski, *Politics* (1931)

Power and capability, as practical political phenomena, are
as historic as the social interrelations of human society and
political institutions. British philosopher Bertrand Russell
has declared: "Every man would like to be God . . . . Of the
infinite desires of man, the chief are the desires for power
and glory."[1] In one of his earlier works Hans J. Morgenthau,
speaking of the *animus dominandi*--or the desire for power--
claims that "The lust for power manifests itself as the desire to maintain the range of one's own person with regard
to others, to increase it, or to demonstrate it." It concerns itself "not with the individual's survival but with
his position among his fellows once his survival has been
secured."[2] And to Robert Dahl the concept of power "is as
ancient and ubiquitous as any that social theory can boast."[3]

As applied to foreign relations, Frederick L. Schuman
maintains that "All politics is a struggle for power," that
persons who possess it "usually relish the joy of commanding
others to do their will," and that "foreign policy is an expression of a State's will-to-power."[4] Morgenthau, who has
written extensively on the subject, puts it even more strong-
ly in his *Politics Among Nations*:

International politics, like all politics, is a

struggle for   power. Whatever   the ultimate aims of
international politics, power is always the immediate aim.   Statesmen and peoples may ultimately seek
freedom,   security, prosperity,   or   power itself.
They   may   define   their   goals in terms of a religious,   philosophic,   economic,   or   social   ideal
. . . . But whenever   they strive to   realize their
goal by means of international politics, they do so
by striving for power.[5]

Two decades   later, representing widespread consensus on
the matter, British analyst J. W. Burton concluded: "There is
probably no greater common factor in all thinking on international relations than the   assumption that   States depend for
their existence   upon power," which is essential to achieving
their objectives,   "thus making   the management   of power the
main problem to be solved."[6]   In short, national power is one
of the transcendant   characteristics of   nation-states.   It
ranks   among   the   most   common concepts of foreign relations
and, like the sun in the solar system   or energy   in physics,
it is a key motivating force in and a major tool for analysis
of international politics.

Though sovereign and therefore equal "in the eyes of the
law," according   to Harold   and Margaret Sprout, nations differ, sometimes   considerably, in   their ability   to exert and
resist pressure, negotiate and bargain, deliver and withstand
attack, and make their policies prevail. Their power   and capabilities vary   with time and rates of change.   Furthermore,
they are often identified   as types   of "powers"--lesser powers, great powers, and superpowers. Or they are distinguished
politically as Western, Communist, and neutralist   powers, or
geographically   as   Asian,   Atlantic,   European, Sub-Saharan,
Latin American, and other regional power   aggregates. Econom-
ically they   may also be grouped as "have" and "have not," as
industrialized and unindustrialized, or as developed and less
developed, and   Third World   nations, and historically as ancient, modern,   and contemporary,   or as   traditional and new
states.   Pragmatically, they may be viewed as satiated versus
unsatisfied, as dynamic versus static, as   status quo versus
revisionist, and   as peace loving versus warlike or aggessive
powers.[7]

Concern with national   power   evokes   related considera-
tions--those   of   national   influence and capabilities, power
politics,   balance   of   power,   and   national responsibility,
character, credibility, respect, and prestige.   Stanley Hoffmann regards it as an exceedingly complex concept   in that it
is impossible   "to subsume   under one word" such variables as
power as a "condition" and as a "criterion of policy," as an
actuality and   a potentiality, as "a sum of resources" and an
assortment of "processes."[8]

Analysis also involves issues   of   the   applicability of
power to   ideals and values, interests and policy objectives,
ends and means, commitments and feasibilities,   national will
and morality,   and external   and internal affairs, and of its
pragmatic application in the conduct of foreign affairs.

INTERPRETATIONS OF CONCEPTS

Power is held to be a crucial concomitant of politics in that, in the opinion of Joseph Frankel, "all politics, by definition, revolve around the exercise and pursuit of power," and therefore power has been central to the study of political theory throughout history. In international politics, he adds, power "is considerably more in evidence and less circumscribed than in domestic politics."[9] Cecil V. Crabb calls national power a "pivotal concept," Charles P. Schleicher observes that it "occupies a central place in international affairs," and Edgar Furniss and Richard Snyder acknowledge that it "looms large in most contemporary writing on international politics."[10] It is deemed to be a "supreme value," a "deference value,"[11] and as "much more influential than the concept of national interest."[12]

Because of differences in essence and usage, it is difficult to define as a political phenomenon. Applied to human affairs, writes Frankel, it is not a power "over nature, or material, or oneself, but over the minds and actions of other men," and it "denotes the capacity to produce intended effects" in human interrelations.[13] In foreign affairs, to some it denotes intrinsic substance, recognized as national ability, capacity, strength, might, or character.[14] To most it is essentially relational, applying to the interactions of one nation with another. In this respect interpretations connote a variety of perspectives.

So far as bases or sources of power are concerned, some stress unity, consensus, and national purpose and will,[15] or authority, responsibility, credibility, status, and prestige.[16] A great many, concerned with non-forceful processes, emphasize influence, inducement, persuasion, or cooperation and collaboration. For forceful processes and effects, most also add coercion or compulsion and domination, imperialism, aggrandizement, and hegemonism. Of these, notions of influence, persuasion, force, and coercion receive the greatest amount of literary attention.

Additional concepts important in practice and analysis include such variants as a power vacuum,[17] power games,[18] and negotiating from strength.[19] But the key concepts essential for understanding the role of power in foreign affairs are national power, national capabilities, power politics, and balance of power.

National Power

Inasmuch as power is recognized as critical in all politics, it is essential to understand what it means in both this general context and, more precisely, in the international relations of nations. It has been considered as a component of both practice and social theory since ancient times,[20] but extensive and intensive explication and analysis began in the twentieth century, especially after World War II. In the literature on power as a factor of politics in general it is perceived as "the primary and most inclusive variable of political life," "an activity--the effort to influence others,"

and "the heart of political research."[21] Generically, as a
matter of human affairs, it is defined simply as "a common
pattern of impulse," "the production of intended effects," or
"the process of affecting policies of others" and "a control
over value practices and patterns."[22] It also is conceived
as "the criterion of international politics."[23]

Examples of more comprehensive treatment are provided by
James March, who examines the concept in relation to human
discretion and describes three approaches to the study of
power and six models of application to human choice,[24] and
William Riker, who outlines five "formal definitions of power" ranging from the process of inducing others to do something they would not otherwise do, to voting in systems where
votes determine outcome.[25] Morgenthau views political power
as "a psychological relation between those who exercise it
and those over whom it is exercised," which gives "the former
control over certain actions of the latter through the influence which the former exert over the latter's minds."[26]

As a component of the foreign relations anatomy, national power--or "powerhood"[27]--is defined either as an ability,
as a means to achieve ends, or both. Emphasizing ability,
for example, it has been described as "the general capacity
of a state to control the behavior of others," "the capacity
to impose one's will upon others or, at least, to resist the
demands of others," and "the capacity to do, make or destroy."[28] It also is called "the ability to influence others"
and "the ability to control and manipulate the actions of
others."[29] Put more theoretically, it is "the ability to
shift the probability of outcomes."[30] Combining ability,
capacity, and opportunity, Schuman provides multiple interpretations: "the ability to impose one's will on others,
capacity to dictate to those who are without power or who
possess less power, opportunity to achieve the gains which
power makes possible of attainment."[31]

Considering power as a means, Nicholas Spykman, denomi-
nating it a technique, points out that it consists of persuasion, purchase, barter, and coercion as applied to the
processes of cooperation, accommodation, and conflict.[32] K.
J. Holsti, distinguishing four usages, insists that "it is a
means, it is based on capabilities, it is a relationship and
a process, and can also be a quantity."[33]

Many commentaries combine ability with purpose in their
perceptions. To illustrate, power is portrayed as "the capacity to produce intended effects," "the ability to influence
the behavior of others in accordance with one's own ends,"
and, more precisely, "the sum total of the strength and capabilities of a state harnessed and applied to the advancement
of its national interests and the attainment of its national
objectives."[34] Others define it even more comprehensively,[35]
or more simply as "part of the framework of all diplomacy."[36]

Some analysts differentiate power from force (which
often is primarily employed to represent military power) and
influence (which connotes persuasion rather than threats or
sanctions), regarding power as an intermediate concept between the poles of forceful action and persuasion.[37] Al-

though related to authority and responsibility, there are
those who distinguish between them and power, considering
authority as implying the exercise of command over others[38]
and responsibility as applicable to those accountable for
exercising national power.

National Capability

Employed in the plural, national powers are generally
conceived as national capabilities, but in the singular the
latter is also used synonymously with national power. Whereas the notion of power has been given widespread credence in
historical, descriptive, and theoretical analysis, in foreign
policy studies and diplomatic and military practice the expression "national capability" is often preferred.

Several writers discuss both power and capability, but
some clearly emphasize the latter.[39] The reasons given are
that capability is held to be more concretely definable,[40]
and that power is often discredited as symbolizing the capacity or willingness to coerce, which is usually reduced to the
use or the threat to use military force which therefore may
be considered an end in itself rather than a means of achieving something or acting purposefully.[41] Also, according to
Harold and Margaret Sprout, power as a quantifiable mass has
given way in contemporary thinking both to a broader perception of behavioral relationships and to diagnosing the qualities of political influence, force, and military potential.[42]
As a consequence, some analysts are inclined to primarily
equate the term "power" with military force or coercion.[43]

In the singular, national capability has been variously
interpreted. Aside from sweeping identification with power
as a means or instrument employable to achieve ends, it is
defined as a nation's "capacity to affect changes in the
global environment in its own interest," "ability to do something in relation to other countries," or "ability to inter-
vene in the affairs of others."[44] Howard Lentner simply prefers to call it "national capacity."[45]

However, most commentaries on capability use the concept
in the plural, construing capabilities as capacities, potentials, qualities, or elements or ingredients of power. For
example, capabilities are described as factors that "determine the successful pursuit of objectives and the capacity to
resist the demands and actions of other states," or that "enable one entity to threaten sanctions vis-à-vis another,"
"the quantifiable human and nonhuman resources which are
available . . . in the pursuit of foreign policy objectives,"
and "any physical or mental object or quality available as an
instrument of inducement, to reward, threaten, or punish."[46]
Thus interpreted, in both the singular and plural, the concept differs little from national power.

Distinguishing Power and Capability

Aside from those who equate power and capability or regard capabilities as components of power, there are neverthe-

less some who seek to differentiate between them. One opinion
is that capabilities are the "attributes" of nations that
"permit" them "to exercise various degrees of power" in their
relations with other states.[47] Another view considers capabilities largely as potentialities to be powerful or those
factors that "*could be* mobilized and brought into play" as
distinguished from "the actual effort and effect," which are
characterized as power--thereby converting potential into applied power.[48] On the other hand, Charles Lerche and Abdul
Said, in addition to expressing reluctance to use the term
"power" because of its adverse connotations (although they
agree that the two terms may be used interchangeably), hold
that power is "a status to which states aspire" and only a
few achieve, whereas capability is any capacity "to do some-
thing--to act purposefully in an actual situation."[49]

Consequently, if the concepts of power and capability
are to be differentiated, several possibilities warrant consideration. Capabilities or power components (in the plural)
determine the nature and extent of the nation's overall power
or capability (in the singular). Or capability represents
the potential to be powerful, whereas power constitutes the
status and effect of the actual mobilization of the nation's
capability. Or, if related to national action, power denotes
the essence of capacity to influence, persuade, or coerce
whether the nation does so or not and therefore exists independently of the necessity for, or the decision to act, while
capability is the capacity to actually perform--that is, to
act in specific circumstances with respect to concrete conditions. Moreover, in statecraft and analysis the word "power"
is invariably employed in considerations of power politics
and balance of power, but capability is preferred in the
arena of diplomacy--the making and implementing of foreign
policy. In such matters as military affairs and weaponry,
both expressions are employed.

Definition

To summarize, the terms "national power" and "national
capability" are frequently perceived as identical and interchangeable. In the singular they constitute aggregates--power
connoting the sum of the ingredients that represent physical,
psychological, and moral strength, and capability consisting
of capacities of the same order. Both concepts pertain to the
treatment of national ideals and values. They signify both
actualities and potentials. Both are applicable to the determination of national ends and means, and are relevant to,
if not decisive, in the framing of national goals and concrete objectives, the formulation of policies, and the designing of national strategies.

In addition, both involve a spectrum of applications,
minimally reducible to political, economic, and military
factors. Both imply the necessity of dual actions--the allocation of resources for the purposes intended, and the
maintenance and enhancement of such resources in readily
usable forms. Both play a critical role in decision-making
and therefore are indispensable components of the foreign
affairs anatomy.

Despite the disparate uses of the term "national power" in international politics and the confusion concerning its relation with "national capability," for operational and ana- lytical purposes it is manifest that:

National power is the sum total of the abilities of the nation--both persuasive and coercive, peaceful and forceful, actual and potential--to preserve its interests, attain its goals and objectives, and promote its policies and strategies in its rela- tions with other nations. Comprised of a complex of qualities, elements, and factors--or capabili- ties--it constitutes a primary means of influencing other nations in achieving its aims and implement- ing its policies, and forestalling those nations from impinging upon it to its disadvantage.

Elements of Power and National Capabilities

A great deal of attention in both practice and analysis is devoted to the components of power and identifying and as- sessing power capabilities. These are generally called qual- ities, elements, factors, or ingredients, and they are some- times referred to as prerequisites or indicators. In sweep- ing terms, the essentials are identified simply as political, economic, and military capacities.[50] However, Morgenthau, representing many thoughtful studies, lists nine primary cat- egories: geography, natural resources, industrial capacity, military preparedness, population, national character, na- tional morale, the quality of diplomacy, and the quality of government.[51]

Others refine these components by adding such factors as common values, ideological commitment, societal cohesiveness, national consensus and unity, national character, national style, leadership, reputation, confidence, skill in the use of propaganda, access to foreign supplies of strategic mater- ials, scientific inventiveness, technological "know-how," foreign support, and even agricultural production and foreign air and naval bases.[52] Treated in this fashion, the list is virtually endless, and any one of these factors may be crit- ical in a given set of circumstances. To these must be added what Feliks Gross calls "Factor X," by which he means chance, irrational elements in human considerations, and similar un- predictable conditions and developments that affect foreign relations.[53]

Analysts differentiate among them in broad descriptive categories. Some distinguish between prerequisites and fac- tors,[54] tangible and intangible components,[55] and constrain- ing and facilitating elements, as well as highly stable, mod- erately stable, and unstable or flexible domestic determin- ants.[56] Others compare unitary and segmented power, and many emphasize the distinction between internal and external strength.

Ray Cline proposes a system of what he calls "politec- tonics" for appraising the capability of nations, consisting of five components: critical mass composed of population and

territory, economic capability, military might, strategic
purpose, and the will to use national strategy.[57] Surprisingly, few commentaries incorporate national will in such
inventories.[58] Although some writers speak of "the will to
power" they fail to address themselves to "the will to employ
it." In the exercise of power politics, the calculation or
miscalculation by others of a nation's will to utilize its
power may be as crucial as its very existence. Equally remarkable, even fewer commentaries include national credibility as a component of the nation's power.

POWER POLITICS

The concept power politics--or *Machtpolitik*--is as old
as the development and analysis of interpolitical relations.
Despite its widespread use, both as a practical function and
a theory, Thomas Cook and Malcolm Moos view it as "a facile
but largely meaningless phrase, with overtones of healthy
realism or sinister immoralism."[59] Norman Hill observes that
its general nature "is easily understood, but a more exact
specification of its meaning will encounter difficulties" because both "power" and "politics" are "inexact words, so that
a combination of the two is particularly baffling."[60]

Thomas Etzold calls it "one of the more equivocal terms
in the lexicon of international affairs." For many, including historians, it is value-laden in a negative sense, whereas for others, especially some political scientists, it is a
more neutral expression descriptive of the process of inter-
governmental affairs. Confronted with the problem of defining it both as a concept and as a description of relations,
in part because there is "no precise equivalent . . . whether
linguistic, theoretical, or traditional"--among English,
French, and German commentaries--differences of interpretation and understanding vary greatly.[61] Paul Seabury adds
that it is difficult to build a theory of international relations upon a basis of power politics, if by the latter is
meant "a system composed of states, each of which seeks to
augment its own power in relation to other states."[62]

Some writers, including Hans Morgenthau, Quincy Wright,
and Ernest Lefever, regard power as indigenous in human affairs so that, in essence, all international politics is
power politics. Morgenthau declares that because the "lust
for power" is "common to all men," it is "inseparable from
social life itself" and therefore is inevitable in international politics. Wright maintains that "all politics is
power politics." Similarly, Lefever writes: "Taken literally, the term 'power politics' is an accurate but redundant
statement of fact--all politics are power politics because in
all politics power is an inescapable element."[63]

In its most rudimentary version the term merely signifies the use of power--whether denominated influence, persuasion, or coercion--in the interrelations of nations.
Martin Wight generalizes it as "the relations between independent Powers," which equates it with international affairs.[64] When used in this fashion, it is claimed that "international politics is of necessity power politics" and

that the term "power," in effect, is patently a synonym of
"international." Whereas the purpose of such usage is to
identify the international scene, analytically the expression
is often applied primarily to the interaction of the more
important states--or *the Powers*.[65]   Quincy Wright conjoins
power and politics by noting that the former is "the capacity to accomplish ends" and politics is "the art of adapting
means to accomplish group ends against the opposition of
other groups."[66]

More complex, Lerche and Said distinguish two interpre-
tations--as *Machtpolitik*, applying to the relations of nations governed largely by force or threat, which they reject,
and as a purely descriptive characterization of the way in
which the global political process actually works, which they
prefer.[67] Raymond Aron is inclined to draw a rudimentary distinction between the politics of force and the politics of
influence.[68] Grayson Kirk contends that in the United States,
where it has been fashionable to view power politics as
Machtpolitik and therefore to disparage it, the concept means
"the cynical and ruthless use of power to advance national
interests at the expense of others."[69]

Alan James also identifies two usages. One interpretation, essentially pejorative, suggests a "power game" in
which states are anxious to stand, in relation to other nations but particularly their rivals, in a favorable power
posture, and that they will not consciously act to reduce
their power significantly, but will constantly be concerned
about their relative, preferably superior, power status. The
alternative conception emphasizes methods nations adopt to
achieve their aims, which differ from those of domestic politics in that the ultimate international method is the threat
of the use of armed force which, he suggests, warrants the
reference to power in the concept.[70]

Norman Padelford and George A. Lincoln emphasize the
difference between the use of power by a nation "to achieve
its goals and satisfy its interests" and "the struggle for
power" to attain preponderance.[71] Burton maintains that power politics has always been "a game of chicken"--with one
side either backing down or being confronted with a resulting
"head-on collision." He asserts, however, that criticisms of
the power approach to the study of international relations
"are merely matters of emphasis," and he questions the degree
to which power itself constitutes a prime motivation of nations.[72]

Some observers, notes Holsti, believe that governments
have a choice between using power politics and other means to
achieve their objectives, but he argues that this dichotomy
is "at best a crude normative generalization" because no nation "fails to seek to influence the behavior" of others in
their interrelations except for routine administrative trans-
actions. Joining others, he also acknowledges that "all international politics are in a sense power politics."[73] Pursuing this line of reasoning, the alternative is to avoid
using the expression whenever possible and to simply use the
terms "foreign relations" and "international politics."[74]

As a matter of national practice, in the opinion of Lerche and Said, power politics is founded on a set of assumptions "that are consciously accepted and deliberately implemented" by all nations. These include: "a climate of moral relativism" in which there are no absolutes of right or justice in the relations of nations; the only common value of all countries is the desirability of preserving the nation-state system; nations must rely on "self-help as a rule of action;" nations are dependent on their own strength and the capability of their leaders for their own rewards and benefits; and the relations of nations are determined "not by the application of general principles" but by their own capabilities, which they call "the crux of power politics." Operationally, therefore, they add, "factors of power determine questions of right," so that, in this sense, "might (broadly interpreted) actually makes right."[75]   It is this progression of assumptions--consonant with political realism (realpolitik)--that evokes fervid criticism of the nature and use of power politics and leads to attempts to develop alternative normative interpretations, analyses, and theories.[76]

BALANCE OF POWER

The concept of balance of power, on which much has been written over the centuries,[77] is also "indispensable to the understanding of international relations, despite the very different meanings and uses of the notion, and the equally divergent assessments of the political realities to which it refers."[78]   Common to all politics, it is critical to international affairs, and its meaning is often presumed to be understood.   It is variously called a "cornerstone" of the modern state system,[79] "at once the dominant myth and fundamental law of interstate relations,"[80] and both a "condition" and "relationship of interaction," as well as a principle, process, device, or system--and it may be embodied or implied in the foreign policies of nations.[81]

Morgenthau declares that balance of power "is only a particular manifestation of a general social principle to which all societies composed of a number of autonomous units owe the autonomy of their component parts" and that both the principle and policies seeking its preservation "are not only inevitable but are an essential stabilizing factor in a society of sovereign nations."[82]   Morton Kaplan, on the other hand, maintains that it is only one of six types of international systems.[83]

In essence, the expression "balance of power" simply connotes power balancing power.   Emphasizing its relation to international equilibrium and stability, it is defined as "a tendency toward equilibrium,"[84] "the maintenance of an equilibrium so that no State or States can without good cause be an aggressor,"[85] and a state system in which "no one of its members must ever become so powerful as to be able to coerce all the rest put together."[86]

Raymond Aron describes international equilibrium as an arrangement in which each nation "tries not to be at the mercy of the others."[87]   Morgenthau notes that the terms "bal-

ance" and "equilibrium" are commonly employed in many sciences, signifying "stability within the system composed of a
number of autonomous sources." He adds that the notion of
equilibrium is founded on two assumptions--that the elements
to be balanced "are necessary for society or are entitled to
exist" and that "without a state of equilibrium among them
one element will gain ascendancy over the others, encroach
upon their interests and rights, and may ultimately destroy
them."88

Arthur Lee Burns hypothesizes that a two-power process
"can reach only an unstable equilibrium" whereas a three-or-
more process, "other things being equal, tends toward stable
equilibrium."89 Such emphasis on equilibrium in international
affairs has engendered a unique school of "equilibrists,"90
which gives greater credence to international equilibrium
than to strict balance of power.91

Morgenthau identifies two main prototypes of operation
of power balance--the "pattern of direct opposition" in which
nations counter one another in having their respective interests and policies prevail, and the "pattern of competition"
in which they vie with one another in their interaction with
other nations.92 "The balancing process," he observes, "can
be carried on either by diminishing the weight of the heavier
scale or by increasing the weight of the lighter one." The
power method is embodied in the "divide and rule" maxim. Alternative means employed to maintain balance, aside from increasing military power, he says, embrace the promotion of
alliances and counteralliances, and the emergence of a balancer or "third force."93

Similarly, discussing the means of implementing balance
for purposes of preserving the independence of nations and
the state system, Edward V. Gulick prescribes several basic
corollaries. These include the exercise of national vigil-
ance to conserve the society of nations, alliances to counter
imbalance, intervention to preserve nations and the state
system, third party "holding the balance" which provides mobility of action in the balancing process, and coalitions
which generally are created in times of war crises that
threaten the state system.94 To some the balance of power
arrangement is believed to be genuine and viable primarily,
or only, if there is a third party balancer, which is powerful and mobile and is able to shift to keep the system in
balance.95

Recognizing the multiple usages of the expression, Harold and Margaret Sprout emphasize the distinction between
balance of power as a political concept, as a basis of foreign policy, and as a pragmatic state of affairs.96 Inis
Claude also identifies three meanings--as a situation (a
purely descriptive term indicating the character of an arrangement in which power relationships are based on rough or
precise equality), as a policy (either an established policy
or "a principle capable of inspiring the policy of states"),
and as a model for the operation of international politics.97

Hoffmann specifies three basic substantive uses of the
term--to designate any distribution of power among nations,

whether it represents equilibrium or disequilibrium; to indicate a policy on the part of nations that "deliberately
aims at preventing the preponderance of any one state and at
maintaining an approxmiate equilibrium among the major rivals"; and to signify a system of international politics in
which the pattern of relations among nations "tends to curb
the ambitions or the opportunities of the chief rivals and to
preserve the approximate equilibrium of power among them."[98]
Thus, many commentaries describe balance of power as a method
of achieving and promoting international equilibrium. Alternatives to balance and equilibrium include equivalence, parity, stability, and equipoise.[99]

    The fundamental interlocking purposes of maintaining a
balance of power encompass the preservation of independence
and security of the nation, the conservation of the state
system, and the prevention of the achievement of preponderance by any one country and its dominating or destroying the
society of nations. Other aims, such as the preservation of
peace, the averting of war, and the sustainment of the status
quo, which have frequently been alleged, in the opinion of
Gulick and Schuman are secondary in the sense that the maintenance of peace really is sought by nations to conserve
their sovereignty and status within the state system.[100]

    Since World War II, however, the prevention of the out-
break of nuclear war--by means of nuclear parity, balance,
equilibrium, and deterrence--in order to preserve humanity
and civilization might be conceived as a sufficiently vital
goal to be sought in and of itself. But this, as both a
process and a policy, can also be justified as conserving the
very existence of nations.[101]

    As a matter of principle as well as practice, a balance
of power may connote parity--an exact or roughly equivalent
balance. Or it may constitute some equilibrium even though
not an absolute or approximate balance,[102] or it may produce
or manifest stability, even if it falls short of providing
such a balance but nevertheless affords a "livable equilibrium."[103] Often the last of these permeates the juxtaposition of nations and provides stability, so long as no attempts are made to substantially change the power relationship and thereby threaten the equilibrium.

    In other words, frequently governments are less likely
to create a perfect balance than to achieve a livable equilibrium, and thus are more concerned with averting precipi-
tate, major power changes that produce substantial advantage
that they know will upset stability and impel competitors or
adversaries to react so sharply as to undo the advantage intended. As a result, often a livable equilibrium, rather
than an exact or approximate balance, is the best that can be
attained, and the struggle for power is converted into the
production and maintenance of a power relationship which,
though not preferred, nevertheless does not threaten the nation's existence, its vital interests, or its fundamental
national goals.

    Finally, it needs to be noted that the concepts of pow-
er, balance, equilibrium, and stability are usually applied

to general or global politics, or to those of the major powers or blocs of nations. The same considerations, however,
pertain to regional and local politics. For example, they
are equally applicable to such areas as Europe, the Middle
East, Southern or Eastern Asia, Central or Southern Africa,
or the Caribbean, and often to neighbor-to-neighbor relations, as in the case of India and Pakistan, China and the
Soviet Union, and Canada and the United States.

DEVELOPMENT OF ANALYSIS

Power, power politics, and balance of power have been
discussed in scores of historical, analytical, and philosophical volumes and essays down through the centuries. What
Robert Dahl calls "an endless parade of great names" from
Plato and Aristotle through Niccolo Machiavelli and Thomas
Hobbes to social philosophers Vilfredo Pareto and Max Weber
devoted attention to the matter. To the sixteenth century
most thinkers were concerned mainly with power relations
within a given community, or society, but the rise of the
modern nation-state, in Dahl's view, stimulated political
theorists and other analysts to also realize the importance
of power in international relations. In this transition
Machiavelli marked a turning point from classical-normative
to modern empirical theory, and Weber sparked the move to
political realism in his treatment.[104] During the nineteenth
century power was extolled in the writings of such thinkers
as Heinrich von Treitschke and Friedrich Nietzsche.[105]

Power Politics

It was not until the twentieth century, however, that
extensive and intensive attention has been paid to the study
of the nature, historical application, and abstract considerations of national power. Eric Kaufmann, in his study of
international law, contends that the essence of the nation-
state is *Machtenfaltung* (the development and display of power), reflected as the power theory of international politics.[106] Shortly before World War II Bertrand Russell examined power as a general political phenomenon, applied to
both individuals and groups, as well as to nations.[107]
Others, including British historian Edward H. Carr, and American political scientist Frederick L. Schuman, who published
comprehensive studies of international affairs, also contributed to this emergent literature.[108] In the meantime, over
the years many histories, biographies, and other studies examined the pursuit and exercise of power in modern times by
such pre-twentieth-century European practitioners as Bismark,
Castlereagh, Frederick William III of Prussia, Louis XIV and
XVI of France, Metternich, Napoleon, William Pitt, Richelieu,
and Talleyrand.[109]

In the United States conflicts over theory and practice
date back to the founding of the Republic. On the one hand,
the issue of distributing political power was fundamental in
designing the American system of governance, which was resolved by creating a unique balance of power arrangement--
actually a dual system of division and separation of powers,

as specified in the Constitution.[110] On the other hand, so far as international politics is concerned--despite a long-standing policy of isolationism, or non-involvement in Europe's political affairs--the United States became involved in power relations with Britain, France, Russia, and Spain in developing its continental expansion beginning in the late eighteenth century, and with the politics of Europe and the Far East in the War of 1812 and World Wars I and II.[111]

Contemporary with the disquisition of Russell, in the United States a major effort to analyze political power resulted in the theoretical analyses of George Catlin, Charles Merriam, Harold Lasswell, and others.[112] Parallelling this development, Morgenthau launched a movement to address the role of power in the relations of nations. His thesis, quoted earlier, is that international politics, like all politics, is a struggle for power.[113] Most of the American textual studies in international politics joined this movement during the 1950s and 1960s, and some of these have subsequently continued their concern with the subject.[114]

As in the case of reaction to Morgenthau's views on national interest, discussed in Chapter 2, opponents of his analysis of power sought to propound alternative interpretations and theories, arguing that power is primarily a means to achieve other ends or that the nation's aims need to be more morally estimable than its interests.[115] Others either disagree with specific aspects of Morgenthau's reasoning or, questioning the reliability or propriety of power politics, suggest alternatives for promoting international stability, balance, equilibrium, and peace, or propose the mitigation of power politics by means of redistributing power among nations.[116]

Beginning in the 1950s dozens of others have probed the anatomy and functioning of national power.[117] Aside from general studies of power in contemporary politics and foreign affairs, this literature consists of comprehensive surveys,[118] shorter essays,[119] systematic and theoretical analyses,[120] and a variety of more specialized treatises.[121]

In the aggregate these materials explore such matters as the origin, adequacy, escalation, preponderance, and mortality of power; philosophies and ideologies of power; its applicability to negotiation, conflict resolution, crises, and war; legitimacy and responsibility of power; and its relationship to foreign policy, morality, international law and organization, and expansionism, hegemonism, and imperium. It also includes disquisitions on research design and scientific methodology, assessment of national power as an analytical tool, and formulation of constructs, models, and paradigms. Moreover, as in the case of national interest, national power is related to political realism, providing a melange of analyses, a good deal of endorsement, and some rejection.[122] In addition, attention is devoted to theories of the dynamics, statics, and humanizing of power politics,[123] problems of investigation and the designing of acceptable operational definitions,[124] and comparisons of power politics (as both a concept and theory) with its alternatives.[125]

Balance of Power

The idea of balance of power to preserve the nation-
state system, international order, and tranquility also
emerged in classical thought. The works of Aristotle and
Demosthenes were concerned primarily with internal balance of
political power,[126] and Machiavelli expanded application to
the interrelations of principalities. David Hume's historical essay on operationalizing the concept, which traces its
origins and usage from Greek to modern times, indicates that
it existed throughout Western history. And he claims that it
had "an influence on all the wiser and more experienced
princes and politicians" and that the notion of preserving a
balance among nations "is founded so much on common sense and
obvious reasoning" as to be undeniable.[127] An anthology of
selected historical accounts of developments is provided by
Seabury. These essays deal with the operation of the strategy in the seventeenth century, in European affairs, and in
the practices of particular statesmen--Metternich, Bismarck,
and others.[128]

Many volumes have been published specifically on the
theory and application of alliances and the balance of power
in Europe and the role played by Great Britain.[129] To illustrate, in the eighteenth century Johann von Justi and Franz
Josias von Hendrich disparaged the application of the balance
principle in international affairs.[130] On the other hand,
Jean Jacques Rousseau and Immanuel Kant addressed themselves
largely to balance of power within the nation, although Kant,
not generally regarded as a conventional writer on the subject, also treats some of the ideas on the concept that later
came under consideration.[131] Among the many nineteenth-century analysts of power balance, major contributions supporting the principle were provided by Friedrich von Gentz and
Lord Brougham and Vaux, who were concerned with preserving
the state system and esteemed balance of power as a meritorious and enlightened precept.[132] These were supplemented with
a substantial flow of descriptive and biographical accounts
of specific practitioners and histories of the application of
balance in Europe's politics down through the century.[133]

But it was not until after World War I, and particularly
since 1945, that inquiry into the nature, functioning, and
future viability of balance of power became commonplace in
the United States. Complementing an array of general essays,
largely theoretical and analytical,[134] dozens of international politics and foreign relations general texts[135] and monographs,[136] and a host of journal articles deal with the subject. So do a good many studies on peace keeping, alliances,
international law, treaties, and especially international
stability and equilibrium.[137]

Some contemporary literature is also devoted to the concept of the superpowers and their relations. This deals with
their domestic power basis, their political interrelations
and orbits, and especially their nuclear capacity.[138] These
materials pay special attention to superpower balance and
stability; nuclear strategy, weaponry, and arms limitation;
and what has been called "nuclear peace." They also introduce
such notions as nuclear equilibrium, equality, parity, suffi-

ciency, and both "tactical" and "strategic" nuclear balance.

Aside from historical surveys, this balance of power literature delves into a variety of topics. Buttressing general considerations--assumptions, aims, and means of implementation[139]--these embrace the nature of the balance system, the process of redressing imbalance, justification for and rejection of the balance principle, its impact on the status quo,[140] and United States policy and attitudes respecting the precept.[141] More precise considerations range from the relationship of balance of power and neutralization, the treatment of minor powers, and stability in East-West bipolar affairs,[142] to specialized aspects of theory and methodology.[143] Moreover, the application of the balance of power formula to nuclear capability and warfare generated a separate body of literature centering on concepts of nuclear deterrence and the "balance of terror." The latter has been characterized briefly as "the equilibrium of power among nuclear states stemming from common fear of annihilation in a nuclear war."[144]

Despite the inadequacies of balance of power theory, difficulties of establishing and sustaining balance in practice, and the arguments levied against it, including those of Woodrow Wilson,[145] the fact remains that in international relations the notions of balance and equilibrium to maintain stability and the nation-state system have endured for a long time. In practice, balance and equilibrium may be static or dynamic, and in particular cases they may prove to be reliable or unreliable. Nevertheless, attested to by centuries of usage, they have functioned with some success to stabilize international politics and in the absence of reliable alternatives they are likely to be relied upon in the future conduct of foreign affairs.

CHARACTERISTICS AND COMMENTARY

It is well known that in the eighteenth century William Pitt declared: "Unlimited power is apt to corrupt the minds of those who possess it," and a century later Lord Acton refined this to: "Power tends to corrupt; absolute power corrupts absolutely."[146] No doubt with Hitler in mind, in 1946 Morgenthau wrote: "Where the lust for power seizes upon the state as the vehicle on which to ride to hegemonial power among the nations, absolute corruption follows in the wake of this drive for absolute power."[147] Similarly, Norman Cousins contends that power is disposed "to become a theology, admitting to no gods before it."[148]

On the other hand, in 1826 Benjamin Disraeli insisted that "all power is a trust." This perception has permeated the views of many American statesmen, exemplified by the Founding Fathers and illustrated by Harry Truman's statement in 1945 that "The responsibility of the great states is to serve and not to dominate the world."[149]

This is not to say that all power wielding is inherently noxious or evil, but rather that the manner and degree in which it is wielded may be evil, that the very possession of superior power may both permit and invite its overuse, and that the benefits that flow from its successful application may whet the drive for increased power and even greater use. Charles Schleicher makes the point that national power is inherently neutral--neither good nor bad--and that "it is its use that can be termed justifiable or unjustifiable." It may engender a sense of responsibility, but in their inter-relations in which they exercise power, nations are inclined to view its possession and control by themselves as wholesome and its possession by others as creating an international power problem.[150] In one of his later works, Morgenthau discusses two factors that govern what he calls "greatness" in the pursuit of power--namely, to a certain degree "the sacrifice of intellectual and moral virtues" or the subordination of "the pursuit of power to transcendent intellectual and moral values." The former characterizes those who pursue power and the latter characterizes those who possess it but are not possessed by it.[151]

Scope and Purpose

Over time the international scope of power has both increased and decreased. The increase is represented by such matters as population growth, changing technology, expansion of investment capital and industrial production, advancement of management expertise, and perfection of advanced weaponry, including nuclear missilery. Decrease, at least in a relative sense, is caused by the sizeable proliferation of independent nations following World War II, by extensive global and regional institutionalization, and by increasing interdependence of nations. Nevertheless, it remains ubiquitous, valued, advantageous, and crucial in international affairs.

The descriptive qualities of national power that analysts seek to comprehend are its magnitude, distribution within the political system, application (whether general or specialized), and "domain" or "extension." These are differentiated from such explanatory characteristics as resources or base values, skill in utilizing such resources, motivation, and costs.[152]

The functional purposes of power, as noted earlier, are normally expressed as influence or coercion or, as Holsti discerns them, to persuade, offer or grant rewards, threaten or inflict non-violent punishment, or utilize force in the pursuit of objectives and the implementation of policies.[153] Because the acquisition and possession of power are operationalized politically within a system of equilibrium, the aims of power differ little from those discussed under the balance of power.

As noted in Chapter 5, substantively the fundamental goals of nations include independence and identity, national security, human welfare, honor and prestige, and peace and stability. At times they may be oriented toward preserving or changing the status quo, promoting or obstructing expansion and imperialism, and advancing national values, ideals, and ideology. Power appears to exhilarate those nations that seek to promote change, expansion, and ideals or ideology, which seems to suggest that in such cases power exercised for positive purposes may be more motivating than power exercised for negative or constraining reasons.

Ends or Means

One of the major debates concerning national power and capability focuses on perceptions as to whether they are ends or means. Frankel observes that the "ends-means relation constitutes the most frequently analyzed aspect of decision-making."[154] One school of thought, led by Morgenthau and other exponents of realism, views power as both an end and a means. Those who see the ends of the nation as preserving its primary interest--or survival--consider power, essential to maintaining national security, as an end in itself.[155] Schuman categorically states that "the enhancement of state power is always the goal."[156]

From this power-based perspective, according to Burton, it may be held that as a nation employs power in its relations with others, in terms of results it matters little whether it is used as a means or an end or whether, on the other hand, it is employed simply "because men and States naturally seek it." Moreover, he argues, power may be pursued as an end in balance of power considerations and, in a static model of international politics, even though nations are satisfied with the world situation "there would still be drives for power for its own sake."[157]

However, most statesmen and analysts consider power as a means to achieve ends, and certainly its capability connotation denotes a means.[158] This is also implied in many definitions of both power and capability, especially those that specify that their purpose is to pursue national interests and attain national goals and objectives. To the extent that power and capability may be sought by nations in order to accomplish such ends, at most they become combined sub-goals (or pre-goals) and means to reach more important and transcendent goals. Nevertheless, when power proves regularly to be useful in attaining ends, there is a risk--as evidenced by history--that power may come to be accepted as an overriding, national ego-satisfying end in itself, especially for aggressive, autocratic nations.[159]

Relationship and Relativity

Power and capability are relational in several ways. They are related to the other major components of the foreign affairs anatomy discussed in earlier chapters, to such additional factors as morality, leadership, national character, and responsibility, and to feasibility and commitments. Walter Lippmann epitomizes the relationship of power and commitment when he writes: "a foreign policy consists in bringing into balance, with a comfortable surplus of power in reserve, the nation's commitments and the nation's power."[160] Lerche and Said, supporting this thesis, maintain that policy makers are bound by "existing commitments and precedents" within which they must act."[161]

Such commitments are both internal and external, and expectations and reactions to them have both national and international ramifications. But it is the international to which Lippmann and others address their attention. These may involve unilateral promises, joint policy statements that need to be elaborated by negotiation, and treaty obligations --especially those embodied in collective security and mutual defense arrangements, coalitions and alliances, trade and other agreements, and international organizations. Concern with the matter of overcommitment has aroused the anxiety of a number of Americans since World War II.[162]

Another important characteristic of national power, universally acknowledged, is its relativity. Even though it may be agreed that a nation's gross power or aggregate capabilities may be conceived as existing per se and therefore may be regarded as intrinsic, in international relations the perception gains significance only when it is applied to the nation's interactions with others--when it is calculated and applied in practical foreign affairs situations. For example, the stipulation that a nation has certain resources--population, industrial capacity, or military manpower and equipment --is meaningless in terms of power relations unless these are juxtaposed with those of other nations in a concrete context.[163]

On this matter Harold and Margaret Sprout contend that "there is no meaningful way to characterize a state's power in a political vacuum" because it is only relevant to international politics when applied to the interrelations of one nation with another.[164] Speaking of political significance, Vernon Van Dyke maintains that not its "absolute power," but the nation's power position in relation to other states is material in international affairs, and that "power calculations must encompass all those states whose power may or will be brought to bear when a test of power comes."[165] In other words, the power posture of the nation depends ipso facto upon that of its competitors and adversaries--upon those it intends to influence.

Application of this factor of relativity is integral to the concepts of the balance of power and equilibrium, and to foreign relations decision-making. Lerche and Said point out that it applies in two obvious ways, with respect to the nation's capacity to act in pursuit of a previously determined objective, and as the basis of comparing its capability with those of other nations. In both cases the decision must be made that the capability is sufficient to achieve the end desired and that the nation is prepared to commit its power in the face of that of other states. If its actions are likely to be obstructed or neutralized by those of others, its capability is obviously inadequate.[166]

Types of Power and Patterns of Relationship

Aside from such generalized distinctions as those based on essence (components or ingredients), analysts distinguish a number of categories of power. These include influence or persuasion versus coercion, force, domination, or manipula-

tion--based on severity or the degree of power vis-à-vis other nations; coercive versus legitimate (legal, traditional,
and charismatic powers)--based on manifestation; positive
versus negative or offensive versus defensive--based on
changing or preserving the status quo;[167] direct versus indi-
rect--based on the manner of application; explicit versus im-
plicit--based on articulation;[168] unilateral (one-way) versus
bilateral or contralateral (two ways) and multilateral (mul-
ti-directional)--based on the number of nations involved; and
others.[169]   Although these may be useful in certain types of
power analysis, Dahl concludes that "no single classification
system prevails," that titles of categories are unstandard-
ized, and that in the abstract "it is impossible to say why
one   classification   system   should   be   preferred over
another."[170]

     Discussing the patterns of power politics, Lerche and
Said differentiate among situations involving substantial
agreement of the great powers committed to a generalized
status quo orientation, splitting of great powers into competing and hostile camps, coalescence of smaller nations
(both medium and lesser powers) in their strategy for dealing
with great powers, and disorganization of small states in
which they become isolated and are subject to pressure from
medium and great powers. Commenting on the methods of balancing power, they discuss intervention, territorial compensation, spheres of influence, and the creation of buffer
zones--that are territorially oriented, as well as the principle of divide and rule, the formation of alliances, and
armaments (the principal means of maintaining and reestab-
lishing balance in the nation's favor).

     On patterns of equilibrium they identify three basic ar-
rangements: multiple balance of power or uncentralized power
relations, characterized by widespread dispersal of action
capability; the simple balance of power formula in which relations center on two great powers or power blocs; and integrated power radiating from a single source (or imperium,
which has not been fully realized since the fall of the Roman
Empire).[171]   From the structural/organizational perspective,
Frederick H. Hartmann provides a simple differentiation among
unilaterialism, alliances, balance of power (of individual
nations and blocs), collective security, world government,
and world conquest.[172]

     Addressing himself to political power in general, to
systematize thinking and usage, Adolf Berle projects what he
calls the five "natural laws" of power. These include "power
invariably fills any vacuum in human organization," it "is
invariably personal," it "is invariably based on a system of
ideas or philosophy," it "is exercised through, and depends
on institutions," and it "is invariably confronted with, and
acts in the presence of, a field of responsibility."[173]

RATING AND MEASUREMENT

     The system of international politics has frequently been
characterized by stratifying nations--as great, medium, and
small powers, with the great powers often presuming to regu-

late certain matters in keeping with their interests, and lesser powers representing several differing levels of gradation. Until recent times the study of international relations usually centered around the relations of a small number --ranging from four to eight--of the more powerful states. Membership in this elite group, according to Lerche and Said, has been founded less on "mathematical calculations of power components" than on "international practice and consensus," formalized through some mechanism they call the "concert of power."[174] Thorsten V. Kalijarvi bases such rudimentary gradation largely on the ability to wage war and the measure of independence of action nations possess, which influence the respect they enjoy in their interaction with one another.[175]

Before World War II the consensus was that France, Germany, Italy, Japan, the Soviet Union, the United Kingdom, the United States, and possibly China were held to be great powers. By 1944 France and Italy were dropped from the list, and within a year Germany and Japan surrendered and were also dropped, leaving only three or four great powers. Subsequently the United States and the Soviet Union emerged as superpowers, and France, Germany, and Japan joined the United Kingdom and China as significant world powers. A few others attained notable regional power status.[176]

On the question of the extent of power, in one of his early commentaries, contemplating the desire of individuals for power, Morgenthau took the position that although the selfishness of human beings has limits, their "will to power has none" and, while their vital needs are capable of satisfaction, their "lust for power would be satisfied only" when they achieve domination--"there being nobody above or beside them" if they "became like God."[177] In international affairs, however, the very existence of other nations in multifurcated competitive relations juxtaposes the power of nations and creates inherent limitations on each individual country. Holsti contends that the amount of influence one state wields over another is restricted in many ways, including its capacity to mobilize its power in support of its objectives.[178]

A great deal is written about the methods and problems of calculation or measurement of national power and capability.[179] In the relationships of nations, before undertaking an initiative, decision makers at least theoretically assess the capability of the state to achieve its objectives under existing and potential circumstances--which is known as capability assessment. Analysts agree that such calculation requires the determination of not only an estimation of the nation's current power status but also its potential. Distinctions are drawn between actual or currently mobilizable, realizable, and operationalizable, as contrasted with latent capabilities.[180] This comparison is applied in two ways. The assessment recognizes either the difference between the total available capabilities and those that the nation is willing to apply in a given context, or the differential between its currently existing and such modified capabilities or nascent capacities as it is able to muster, or develop, if necessary to implement its policies.[181] Calculation, therefore, must be concerned with potentiality as well as actuality.

Coping with cohesiveness and divisibility of national power, Carr has written that "in its essence, power is an indivisible whole" and that "it is difficult in practice to imagine a country for any length of time possessing one kind of power in isolation from the others."[182] However, as noted, he and other analysts segment the concepts of power and capability (in the singular) into a variety of elements or ingredients (in the plural) for descriptive and measurement purposes.

But if they are synthesized as an aggregate measure of power, capacity, or status, such a unified measure would, nevertheless, lack reliability so far as intangibles and certain psychological characteristics are concerned.[183] At best, therefore, in most practical situations the nation is inclined to calculate those qualities or ingredients of its power that bear most directly upon the objective to be achieved and the circumstances at hand. In some cases these may be primarily territorial, economic, military, psychological, or diplomatic, but usually they are intertwined.

Discussion of national power as a "quantifiable mass," derived by concentrating on certain well-defined, key factors that have been freely explicated in considerations of balance of power and international equilibrium, in the view of Harold and Margaret Sprout, became popular in the eighteenth century, was challenged in the next century, but nevertheless persisted into the twentieth century.[184] In the meantime, some schools of thought extolled single-factor prescriptions, including historical or economic determinism and geopolitics.[185] Certain analysts have weighted national power largely in relation to what they regard as the most crucial capability component--concentrating on the operational environment or milieu (both physical and psychological),[186] or on demographic,[187] industrial,[188] or military (including nuclear)[189] sources of power. Others focus on dual or multiple dimensions of capability,[190] and still others emphasize such additional matters as national status or "issue area" purtenance.[191]

To illustrate, A. F. K. Organski has devised a rule of thumb "index to power" of tangible components, a formula which he considers as useful though imperfect for assessing national power status. Arguing that whereas all capability components are interrelated, they boil down to three "most important determinants"--namely, population size, political performance, and economic development. Admitting that certain features, including aspects of political performance, are not quantifiable, his index, he maintains, nevertheless implies something about political efficiancy, enabling him to further constrict his index to the two most critical components--population size and economic development. These, in turn, are reducible to the gross national product (GNP). This, he concedes, does not confer powers upon the nation but simply reflects the status and virility of the other factors. Employing this prescription, he constructs a comparative table of seventy nations, giving their GNP status in 1950 and 1965, but he recognizes its limitations.[192]

Appraising power measurement, statesmen and commentators

generally agree that national powers and capabilities are numerous, varied, and fluctuating.[193]   Although assessment is indispensable for both the practitioner and the student of foreign affairs, warns Frankel, the mechanical or arbitrary calculation of the sum total of national capability is inadequate for explaining the actual amount of power wielded by a nation.[194] Despite the technical progress made in attempts to assess power, because of its mutations, relativity, and uncertainties, there is little agreement on a common, realistic formula for reliable measurement. The task is so huge and complicated that, Van Dyke points out, there is a temptation to avoid objective calculation in favor of short cuts which, he concedes, "may produce results that have an equal degree of reliability."[195]   These short cuts are generally of three types--restricting capability assessment to the objectives sought,[196] relying on proven accomplishment[197] or, like Organski, fabricating an overall index of national power.

The following conclusions may be drawn concerning the matter of power calculation: the ingredients are multiple, interrelated, and complex, and interact with one another; they are dynamic and subject to change; their pragmatic value depends upon their comparison with those of other nations; some are of a material nature whereas others are human and psychological; some may be considered as basic raw resources of power (such as geographic, demographic, economic, and social ingredients) while others need to be developed or operationalized to translate potentials into realized power (such as organizational, administrative, and military establishments); and some (including population, agricultural and industrial production, and gross national product) are quantifiable, but others are not (such as national will, national morale, and international credibility of leaders and foreign policies).

In addition, views differ on the gradation of capability components in formulating power estimates; formulas for weighing individual capacities are equivocal and often inadequate, and many intangibles may be largely subjective; calculation must be applied not only to actual but also to potential power factors, and to the will to employ them; and, given the complexity of the task of assessment, there is considerable temptation to oversimplify, to depend on short cuts, and to produce rudimentary indexes.

Finally, despite efforts to reduce power assessment to scientific principles and treatment, as Hartmann suggests, the techniques available are as yet imperfect and fail "to measure historical experience, social causation, and attitudinal responses" or "to isolate them one from another without distortion."[198] William C. Olson and Fred A. Sondermann maintain that "grand estimates" cannot be precise. "All that one can hope for is that the questions that are asked will be defined as precisely as possible, that the data provided to answer these questions is as complete as possible, and that the assumptions which are made will be as explicit as possible." However, the unsatisfactory nature of power assessment, they add, must not "be a reason to abandon the effort altogether."[199]

And yet, even if a universal and operational formula existed for a nation to calculate its own power posture in a given situation, and for ways to determine the assessments of other nations concerning their status, there is no guarantee that all calculations will be correct. When nations seek to calculate not only their own assessments of their own capabilities, but also attempt to determine the calculations by other nations of their respective estimates of their capabilities, there exists ample opportunity for self-deception and error. Consequently, there is always the possibility and risk that action may be based on serious miscalculation.

OPERATIONALIZING POWER

In practical situations as well as with theoretical considerations, as indicated in Chapter 9, decision makers must juxtapose their national interests and aims with their capabilities, expectations, feasibilities, and commitments in formulating their policies and strategies.[200] They also need to relate power to national will and international responsibility and morality. Frankel observes that "power is never now completely divorced from responsibility" which "in any form, imposes the necessity of explanation; indeed no decisional sequence is complete without it."[201]

In operationalizing analysis and assessment, the power exercised by a nation depends not only on its actual power status at the moment and its capability potential, but also the countervailing power of other nations. This necessitates an intricate triple-staged process of calculating interrelationships. To illustrate, focusing simply on calculable existing capability, state A needs to determine its own power status (its "X" factor) and state B does the same for itself. But state A, as best it can, also needs to calculate "X" for state B, and vice versa. Then state A needs to estimate state B's estimation of its own "X", and state B does the same for state A. Next state A calculates state B's estimation of state A's assessment of state B's power, and again state B does this for state A's estimation.

In the second stage, if power potentials are involved and lead time is available, this same calculation process needs to be repeated for latent power probabilities. The result is a delicate network of multi-phased capability estimates and potentials. Eventually a third stage of the deliberation assesses the nation's willingness to use its power, with each state calculating its position for each of the considerations specified for the first phase, and if potentials are critical, for them as well.

This depiction applies merely to bilateral relations. If other nations are involved, state A must undertake these calculations not only with respect to its relations with state B, but also for states C, D, E, and others, as well as for a series of interrelated calculations among all the other nations, such as the relations of state B with states C, D, and E, and the like. Even if limited to quantifiable and other material elements, and intangibles and uncertainties are left aside, judgments concerning concrete power relations are not only complicated and contingent, but in many cases are precarious if not impossible. Yet, policy makers must make the best policy and strategy decisions they can, founded on the best power determinations they are able to devise. Miscalculation, especially with respect to the going to war, and issues of nuclear power, may be catastrophic.[202]

In addition, such power calculations need to take account of both the alternative methods to be employed in operationalizing capabilities and the limits within which they are exercisable. From one perspective the methods--or uses--include variations respecting the flexibility of policy options and the maintenance of mobility of action, direct and indirect negotiations, the formation of coalitions and alliances, the management of crises, and many others.[203]

Calculations of, and decisions about, these may also be as difficult and critical as the quantity and quality of the nation's power components. On the choice of methods, Organski notes that determination will be based essentially on the degree of agreement that exists between the nations. Choice of methods employed, he believes, fall into five categories. These embrace the unusual case in which nations are in complete agreement, their disagreement is slight or superficial, disagreement is somewhat greater but the general relationship is fundamentally friendly, disagreement is widespread and severe, and disagreement is profound. On this scale coercion and the application of sanctions increase in intensity from category to category.[204]

It is obvious that no nation is omnipotent. Every state's power is subject to constraints that may be both internal and external. The domestic considerations include national ideals and mores, constitutional and legal principles and requirements, governmental division and separation of political powers and authority, political cohesion and popular consensus, and public opinion. Aside from the limitations growing out of the very nature of the international society composed of competitive nations, alluded to earlier, the external constraints encompass the sovereign rights of nations, their opposing interests, objectives, and policies, and their commitments as well as their capacities in a competitive environment, which confirms that national power is relative rather than absolute.[205]

Reflecting on the matter, in his volume of maxims for the conduct of foreign affairs, Thomas Bailey lists a number of precepts for practical guidance in wielding power. Among them, he declares: "policy without power is impotent," "the will to use power can be as important as power itself," "power abhors vacuums," and the "abuse of power breeds resentment." He also cautions: "turn on the heat by degrees," "make allowances for the strength of weakness" because weak states "can often count on forces outside themselves," and he concludes that the proper use of power "can preserve the peace."[206]

POWER AND MORALITY

A major concern of practitioners and theorists is the relationship of power politics and international morality. Distinctions are drawn between the personal morality of peoples (and their leaders) and political morality.[207] Reinhold Niebuhr declares that "Politics will, to the end of history, be an area where conscience and power meet, where the ethical and coercive factors of human life will interpenetrate and work out their tentative and uneasy compromises."[208]

Bertrand Russell devotes considerable attention to this matter. Discussing "moral codes," he contends that morality is considered as both "a social institution analogous to law"--or "positive morality"--and "a matter for the individual conscience"--or "personal morality," and that the two are related with each other in principle and with the exercise of power in practice. He asserts that moral codes restrain power wielding, but they change from civilization to civilization and from era to era. He believes that the ethics of power "cannot consist in distinguishing some kinds of power as legitimate and others as illegitimate," and that whatever is good or bad "is embodied in individuals, not primarily in communities" such as nations.[209]

Morgenthau has written that, as a political animal, "man is born to seek power, yet his actual condition makes him a slave to the power of others. Out of this discord between man's desire and his actual condition arises the moral issue of power, that is, the problem of justifying and limiting the power which man has over man. Hence, the history of political thought is the history of moral evaluation of political power."[210]

Conjoining power and morality, Edward A. Carr maintains: "The utopian who dreams that it is possible to eliminate self-assertion from politics and to base a political system on morality alone is just as wide of the mark as the realist who believes that altruism is an illusion and that all political action is based on self-seeking . . . . Political action must be based on a coordination of morality and power." In international affairs, to which he devotes most of his analysis, he notes that the role of morality "is the most obscure and difficult problem in the whole range of international studies," he makes a strong case for distinguishing "between individual and state morality," and he declares that "it is as fatal in politics to ignore power as it is to ignore morality."[211]

Nicholas Spykman argues that from an ethical point of view "power can be considered only as a means to an end" and that its use "should be constantly subjected to moral judgments." But, he warns, "to hope for a world that will operate without coercion and to decry man's desire to obtain power is an attempt to escape from reality into a world of dreams." He goes on to say that the leader who conducts foreign relations can concern himself with values of justice, fairness, and tolerance "only to the extent that they contribute to or do not interfere with the power objective," that the search for power "is not made for the achievement of moral values," and that the latter "are used to facilitate the attainment of power."[212]

In international politics, while Morgenthau rejects subverting national interest to international morality, he also disclaims the notion that power politics is inherently immoral. He cautions against the two extremes of either overrating the influence of ethics upon foreign affairs or underestimating it by denying that leaders are motivated by anything but considerations of power. Those who engage in moral condemnation of power politics view it as "so thoroughly evil" that it is useless to seek moral limitations on the aspirations of power in foreign relations.[213]

In a more positive way, Seabury holds that although many "openly despair of morality in public life, none but the cynical or disillusioned would deny that ethics is relevant to the international behavior of states." He believes that ethics "is concerned with moral problems of human choice and action . . . not just the choice between good and evil, but often with the choice between lesser good and lesser evil."[214]

Lerche and Said emphasize that, aside from the relationship of morality and national interest, the most troublesome conceptual distinction is that between morality and power, particularly if the latter is regarded as "brute force"--a connotation that "deprives power of moral neutrality." They reject this perception as illogical and indefensible, "there being no reason to equate power with force or to strip it of moral content," because power may be used for either moral or immoral purposes, in either moral or immoral ways.[215]

John G. Stoessinger suggests that because "power and morality are inseparable," they may be considered as two concentric circles. Sometimes power is the larger and encompasses morality, whereas at other times morality may include power and, significantly, greater power may accrue to a nation from its moral behavior. Discussing personal and political morality, he professes that leaders, however lofty their purposes, "dare not ignore the reality of power," but equally they dare not disregard "the existence of morality." The basic difference between interpersonal and international relations, he believes, resides "in the fact that personal behavior is usually judged by an ethic of *intention*" whereas that of the political leader "is essentially one of *consequence*."[216]

In summary, most commentaries recognize differences--substantial differences--between the morality of individuals and nation-states. The bottom line, writes Carr, is: "The view that the same ethical standard is applicable to the behaviour of states as to that of inividuals is, however, just as far from current belief as the view that no standard at all applies to states." Recognizing incompatibilities between personal and professional, commercial, and national morality, "most people, while believing that states ought to act morally, do not expect of them the same kind of moral behavior which they expect of themselves and one another."[217]

ALTERNATIVES TO POWER

Realists reject utopianism, legalism, and sentimentalism as fundamental guidelines for the conduct of foreign relations.[218] At the same time, practitioners and philosophers repudiate hegemonism, world conquest, and imperium as reasonable or justifiable international objectives. For centuries they have sought alternatives to power politics and the balance of power that lie between extreme realism founded on brute force--or "naked" or "raw" power[219]--and the substitution or supercession of power in the relations of nations based on some process of international integration or the complete elimination of the state system. Their alternatives fall into three main categories: changing the manner of the conduct of diplomacy, reorganizing the international community and modifying the international "division of powers," and replacing power politics with a system of collective security.[220]

Little need be said about the diplomatic options of nations, except that they are manifold with respect not only to formulating and implementing foreign policies, but also to foreign affairs processes, bilateral versus multilateral interaction, levels of applicability (handled at the summit or by foreign ministers, professional diplomats, or technical experts), and forms and degrees of persuasion or coercion applied. Discourse on the subject ranges from the nature and function of diplomacy as an instrument of international politics to the methods of bargaining and negotiation, the production of treaties and agreements, and the means of promoting interests, pursuing objectives, and implementing policies.[221]

Proposals to restructure the society of nations, or specific regional groupings, permeate the realms of political theory and international law and organization--all requiring some realignment of the division of political powers. The resulting syncretized international organization is a mechanism for conducting international politics through continuing or fairly permanent agencies to which member nations ascribe specified governmental authority and responsibility--but not necessarily their sovereignty--within which nations wield their power through formal and informal techniques, and through which they espouse their interests and policies. The mechanism may constitute either a multipartite diplomatic forum or, if member nations surrender their sovereignty, it may be converted into a genuine federal union (in which case constituent relations and power wielding, though they continue, are no longer international).

In ascending order of change in the division of governmental power and authority, these include three basic types-- the international confederation, the supranational organization, and the global federal union or world government.[222] In the confederation member nations retain their sovereign status but surrender limited authority and functions (not including lawmaking or independent taxing powers) to a collective institution.[223] A second type, known as supranational, was established on a limited regional basis in Europe following World War II. In this system member states retain

their sovereignty but surrender authority over certain limited functions to an integrated mechanism, including specified
lawmaking and taxing authority.[224]

In the third type, the supernational system or genuine
federation, nations unite to create a federal union to which
they surrender their sovereignty and substantial governmental
authority. It has the power to enact laws, levy taxes, and
exercise a variety of functions, usually including the maintenance of a military establishment and the preservation of
national security.[225] The process of amalgamation is federative, but the end product may either be a federation, in
which the constituent components remain in existence with
residual powers, or an integrated "unitary" (or non-federal)
nation in which the constituent components cease to exist as
political entities possessing the inherent right to self-ex-
istence. In other words, in such cases the process is federative and its resultant may or may not be federal, so that
the concept "international federation" can apply only to the
process, not to the end product, in which case it constitutes
a non sequitur.[226]

Since World War II many suggestions have been made to
establish a global federation or world government.[227] These
propose, by the federative process, to eliminate the nation-
states as sovereign entities (with their independent national
power and war making capability) and supersede them with a
universal federal union, with governmental authority divided
between it and the federating nations. Proposals vary from
simple espousal of eliminating international power politics,
primarily to maintain peace and stability, to complex arrangements for a global constitution and governmental mechanism, in some plans consisting of federations within federations within a superfederation. Supporters of these schemes
embrace internationalists, integrationists, supernational-
ists, transnationalists, globalists, universalists, and other
exponents of related forms of interdependence and a new international order in which nation-states would cease to exist.[228]

Some integrative propositions incorporate the principle
of collective security, the third category of alternatives to
replace power politics among independent nations. According
to Kenneth W. Thompson, collective security "is a method of
managing the power relations of nation states through a
partially centralized system of security arrangements" in
which "ultimate power remains diffused among independent
sovereign states" and authority respecting the "spheres of
maintenance and enforcement of peace is vested in an international body."[229] Thus, observes Van Dyke, a collective
security system is simply one "in which a number of states
are bound to engage in collective efforts on behalf of each
other's individual security" or, according to Hartmann, it
constitutes "a universal collective security scheme in which
every member theoretically assumes some obligation to go to
the aid of *any* member against whom aggression is committed."[230]

Collective security is presumed to be inherent in the
national federation, applicable among its constituent members

and also between the federal union and other nations. It has
also been attempted, without success, in the international
confederation and supranational agency--similarly expected to
be applied both among member nations within the collectivity
and between it and non-members.

For several centuries, down through World Wars I and II
and since, another alternative has also been tried, consisting of "coalitions" or "concerts" of powers, by which nations
temporarily join against aggressors during times of crisis,
to aggregate their national power in ad hoc collective defense systems.[231] These need to be distinguished from collective security. In the post-World War II collective de-
fense--or mutual security--arrangement, based on formal treaty or agreement, nations agree in advance to support one another in maintaining their security against other nations.
Such treaties may provide for alliances, with or without collective machinery and military forces in being, represented
by the North Atlantic Alliance, the Western European Union,
the Rio Pact for the Western Hemisphere, and the Warsaw Pact
for the European Communist orbit. In view of their acknowledged purposes, they can scarcely be regarded as obviating or
superseding the exercise of national power or power politics.

The most far-reaching attempts in modern times to provide for an alternative to power politics and the balance of
power, and for a centralized method of lawmaking and the settlement of international disputes, were embodied in the theoretical conceptualization, constitutions, and institutions
of the League of Nations and the United Nations.[232] Woodrow
Wilson, who denounced the principle of the balance of power,
as part of his World War I peace settlement supported a plan
for the unity of nations to collectively come to each other's
aid if attacked, thus making the security of individual
League participants an obligation of all members.[233]

Following World War II, led by Franklin Roosevelt, the
United Nations was established to supersede the League. It
differs from the latter in several respects. Initially it
was planned as an anti-Axis aggregation to coalesce national
power and provide for collective security against the wartime
aggressors. But eventually it became a universal organization intended to ensure the security of all nations.

Despite these and other attempts to rely on collective
security, the general consensus is that they have failed to
eliminate power politics, balance of power, international
conflict, and hostilities. And they failed to provide reliable international equilibrium. The history of implementing collective security both in the League and the United
Nations, therefore, has been disappointing. As a consequence,
the universal judgment is that, while collective security may
be logical, defensible, and desirable in theory, it does not
work in practice.

In his comprehensive study of the balance of power, Gulick contends that collective security, "far from being alien
to the age-old tradition of the balance of power, not only
derives out of the latter, but also must be seen as the logical end point of the balance-of-power system, the ideal to-

ward which it has been moving, slowly and haltingly, for several hundred years."[234]   Morgenthau agrees that "the logic of collective security is flawless, provided it can be made to work under the conditions prevailing on the international scene."[235] Similarly, Norman Palmer and Howard Perkins maintain that, although collective security "is one of the most popular terms in the jargon of international diplomacy," it remains "one of those desirable goals which under present conditions are distant and unattainable"--an "illusive myth."[236]

Another, more pessimistic view, expressed by Robert Strausz-Hupé and Stefan Possony, is that "systems of collective security have always been short-lived" and invariably break down simply because "the aggressor does not want compromise or settlement, but change and conflict."[237] Much the same pessimism is expressed by Seabury, who finds that collective security is "not operative, not a part of the collective common law of states, or not respected by states, particularly when vital interests are at stake."[238] Lerche and Said go even further in asserting that neither the international integration of power nor collective security "have ever been real successes" because they "may function only upon the basis of massive consensus among the world's leading powers."[239]

Several commentaries that identify the assumptions on which collective security is founded admit that in the real world they are unrealizable. These assumptions provide that aggressors will be clearly identified, all nations will join in action against an aggressor, they are equally willing to participate actively in stopping aggression, the collective system will muster overwhelming strength against the aggressor, and participating nations will subordinate their own interests to the common good.[240]

In the absence of viable and trustworthy alternatives, power remains a fundamental component of the foreign relations anatomy and is, in fact, a primary energizing feature of its functioning. Insofar as international relations are political relations within the nation-state system and power is a motivating force in all politics, it will be sought and employed in the international arena. As long as alternatives, however logical and desirable in principle, falter in practice, the impact of national power, exercised by small states as well as the more powerful, will not be ignored in state practice, and consequently cannot by disregarded in either theory or analysis.

Aside from disestablishing or superseding the state system, the principal issues are not whether national power exists and will be used, but rather, whether it remains primarily a means to other more noble ends, whether those ends are compatible with the nature of the international community, the state system, and the nations that compose them, whether power functions adequately to preserve that system and constrains aggrandizement and aggression, and whether balance of power arrangements can produce essential stability and livable equilibrium in international politics.

The main argument against power politics must be directed at either its inadequacies or the manner of its uses and
abuses.   J. William Fulbright has warned that a nation may
lose its perspective and regard "its power as a sign of God's
favor, conferring upon it a special responsibility for other
nations," may confuse power with virtue, and may experience a
psychosis that drives it, though generous and benevolent in
intent, to overcommit itself, to gratify its ego, and to seek
to prove itself as "bigger, better, or stronger than other
nations."[241]   Some critical commentaries, such as those of
Thomas Cook and Malcolm Moos, Frank Tannenbaum, Norman Cousins, and others question the national desires, purposes, and
motivation of the United States.   Others are troubled by the
niceties of the relation of international power and morality.
And there are those, assessing the concept of balance of power, who are convinced that it fails to provide adequate international equilibrium and to avert war,[242] and therefore
seek institutional changes to replace balance with collective
security arrangements and world government.

There are also those who are pursuaded that power is
misperceived,[243] or that it has reached its apogee in international affairs and is beginning to decline.[244] Still
others argue that its essence is changing so substantially
since World War II that world politics is assuming a new
character,[245] that as a result of its contemporary role it
needs to be reassessed[246] and that the concepts of political
capability, power politics, and equilibrium take on special
meaning in the missile age.[247]

On the other hand--aside from those who view national
power as a natural, long-lived, ubiquitous, and essential
feature of international affairs, or as a proven instrument
for maintaining equilibrium and stability[248]--there are many
who defend power politics and the balance of power as inevitable if not desirable in theory as well as in practice. Such
defenses, for example, are provided by Carr,[249] Gulick,[250]
Schleicher,[251] and others.

In addition, Dewitt C. Poole contends that a complex
balance of power system is the best, perhaps the only, guarantee of human freedom.[252] Spykman notes the absence in the
international community "of a governmental organization capable of preserving order and enforcing law" and contends
that the society of nations has never "guaranteed the member
states either life, liberty, property, or the pursuit of happiness" irrespective of "paper provisions of international
conventions" and that political equilibrium "is neither a
gift of the gods nor an inherently stable condition," but
results rather from "the operation of political forces."[253]
Hoffmann maintains that, although "assessments of power become progressively more difficult," balance of power is still
essential "in order to prevent war," and Max Beloff holds
that balance of power is a necessary, even a healthy, principle in the nuclear age.[254]

Finally, the alternative of superseding power politics
and balance of power by creating confederations, supranational agencies, collective security arrangements, and world government merely alters the forum in which power is wielded.

In a federal union, including a federated world government, it is converted from international to internal power politics. While such alternatives may alleviate some of the most highly criticized or feared aspects of power wielding in international affairs, they will not eliminate power wielding in politics. For, as Carr has written, power is an essential instrument of government, so that "To internationalise government in any real sense means to internationalise power; and since independent power is the basis of the nation-state, the internationalisation of power is really a contradiction in terms. International government is, in effect, government by that state which supplies the power necessary for the purpose of governing."[255]

NOTES

1. Bertrand Russell, *Power: A New Social Analysis* (New York: Norton, 1938), p. 11. He adds that these, though not identical, are closely allied, that the easiest way to obtain glory is to obtain power, that the drive for glory prompts the same actions as are prompted by the desire for power, and that the two motives may, for most practical purposes, be regarded as one.

2. Hans J. Morgenthau, *Scientific Man vs. Power Politics* (Chicago: University of Chicago Press, 1946), pp. 192-93.

3. Robert Dahl, "The Concept of Power," *Behavioral Science* 2 (July 1957): 201. See also James G. March, "The Power of Power," who refers to its obviousness, in *Varieties of Political Theory*, edited by David Easton (Englewood Cliffs, N.J.: Prentice-Hall, 1966), p. 68; and Russell, *Power*, Chapter 1.

4. Frederick L. Schuman, *International Politics*, 3d ed. (New York: McGraw-Hill, 1941), pp. 261, 265. It is interesting to note that this view was dropped in his later editions.

5. Hans J. Morgenthau, *Politics Among Nations: The Struggle for Power and Peace* (New York: Knopf, 1948), p. 13. This quotation is repeated in his later editions.

6. J. W. Burton, *International Relations: A General Theory* (Cambridge: Cambridge University Press, 1967), p. 46. For discussion of this fundamental assumption, see pp. 46-50. This feature of ubiquity is also commented on by other authors.

7. For general commentary, see Harold and Margaret Sprout, *Foundations of International Politics* (Princeton: Van Nostrand, 1962), p. 136, and *Toward a Politics of the Planet Earth* (New York: Van Nostrand, Reinhold, 1971), p. 163. See also Charles P. Schleicher, *Introduction to International Relations* (New York: Prentice-Hall, 1954), pp. 95-98.

8. Stanley Hoffmann discusses the "Realist Theory" of international politics in his *Contemporary Theory in International Relations* (Englewood Cliffs, N.J.: Prentice-Hall, 1960), p. 32.

9. Joseph Frankel, *International Relations* (New York: Oxford University Press, 1964), p. 96.

10. See respectively, Cecil V. Crabb, Jr., *American Foreign Policy*

in the Nuclear Age, 4th ed. (New York: Harper and Row, 1983), p. 20; Schleicher, *Introduction to International Relations,* p. 129; Edgar S. Furniss, Jr., and Richard C. Snyder, *An Introduction to American Foreign Policy* (New York: Rinehart, 1955), p. 23.

11. Harold D. Lasswell and Abraham Kaplan, *Power and Society: A Framework for Political Inquiry* (New Haven, Conn.: Yale University Press, 1950), p. 74. In Chapter 5 they relate power to decision-making and choice, influence, and coercion (see pp. 74-102). See also Steven Lukes, *Power: A Radical View* (London: Macmillan, 1974), p. 26, in which he maintains from the sociological perspective that "power is one of the concepts which is ineradically value-dependent."

12. This is the view of John A. Vasquez, *The Power of Power Politics: A Critique* (New Brunswick, N.J.: Rutgers University Press, 1983), p. 54.

13. Frankel notes different usages of the concept of power. In mathematics it is the product produced by the continued multiplication of a number by itself, in physics it means the rate of transfer of energy, and in human affairs it is a relational phenomenon, not something that one possess; see his *International Relations,* p. 97.

14. The notions of national ability, capacity, and strength or might appear in many interpretations, and George F. Kennan refers to the "state of national character" in dealing with the Soviet Union; see his *American Diplomacy, 1900-1950* (Chicago: University of Chicago Press, 1951), p. 154.

15. Schuman, for example, has written that Americans are "incapable of stating and acting upon their national interests as they actually exist" and are prone to believe that foreign affairs are not "concerned with problems of power . . . but with questions of ethics." See his *International Politics,* 7th ed. (1969), p. 597. On national will, see also note 58.

16. For commentary on the relation of power and responsibility, see pp. 170, 174, and notes 173, 201, and 214; and for discussion of the relation of power and authority, see David V. J. Bell, *Power, Influence, and Authority: An Essay in Political Linguistics* (New York: Oxford University Press, 1975). See also comments on responsibility in Chapter 2, and note 114.

17. To illustrate, see *American Foreign Policy: An Analytical Approach,* edited by William C. Vocke (New York: Free Press, 1976), pp. 14, 115, 117, 119; Norman J. Padelford and George A. Lincoln, *The Dynamics of International Politics* (New York: Macmillan, 1962), pp. 175, 183-84 (as applied to boundaries) and pp. 562-63 (in Europe at end of World War II). See also the extensive literature on power politics, balance of power, and diplomatic history.

18. See Alan James, "Power Politics," in *International Political Analysis: Readings,* edited by David V. Edwards (New York: Holt, Rinehart, and Winston, 1970), pp. 206-25; and John Spanier, *Games Nations Play,* 3d ed. (New York: Holt, Rinehart, and Winston, 1978). On power games see also notes 108, 123, 134, 145.

19. See Coral Bell, *Negotiating from Strength: A Study in the Politics of Power* (New York: Knopf, 1963), which reviews the formulation of policy and procedures for negotiating with the Soviet Union after World

War II; see especially Chapters 2 and 5 on the constituents of negotiating strength. See also William P. Rogers, "The Necessity for Strength in an Era of Negotiations," *Department of State Bulletin* 68 (May 14, 1973): 581-92; Walter W. Marseille, "Negotiating from Strength," *Bulletin of the Atomic Scientists* 11 (January 1955): 13-18, which deals with nuclear negotiations; and Alexander L. George, David K. Hall, and William E. Simons, *The Limits of Coercive Diplomacy: Laos, Cuba, Vietnam* (Boston: Little, Brown, 1971) on American efforts to use force as an instrument of diplomacy, as related to doctrine and strategy. For general studies on negotiation, see Fred Charles Ikle, *How Nations Negotiate* (New York: Praeger, 1964); *The Negotiation Process: Theories and Applications*, edited by I. William Zartman (Beverly Hills, Calif.: Sage, 1978).

20. See the section on the development of analysis below.

21. For these interpretations, especially by George Catlin, Harold Lasswell, and David Easton, see David Easton, *The Political System: An Inquiry Into the State of Political Science* (New York: Knopf, 1959), section on "The Concept of Power," pp. 115-24, especially pp. 116, 118, 121.

22. See respectively, Charles E. Merriam, *Political Power: Its Composition and Incidence* (New York: McGraw-Hill, 1934), p. 7; Russell, *Power*, p. 35; and Lasswell and Kaplan, *Power and Society*, p. 76.

23. See Hoffmann, *Contemporary Theory in International Relations*, p. 5.

24. March, "The Power of Power," pp. 39-70.

25. William H. Riker, "Some Ambiguities in the Notion of Power," *American Political Science Review* 58 (June 1964): 341-49. He illustrates each of the five definitions with mathematical formulas, and discusses their differences on pp. 343-48.

26. Morgenthau, *Politics Among Nations*, 4th ed. (1967), p. 27. Subsequent references are to this 4th ed. See also David C. McClelland, *Power: The Inner Experience* (New York: Irvington, 1975), and David G. Winter, *The Power Motive* (New York: Free Press, 1973), which is a theoretical analysis of power as a motive and its relation to social interactions.

27. "Powerhood" is the expression used by Arthur Lee Burns, *Of Powers and Their Politics: A Critique of Theoretical Approaches* (Englewood Cliffs, N.J.: Prentice-Hall, 1968), Chapter 14.

28. See respectively, K. J. Holsti, *International Politics: A Framework for Analysis* (Englewood Cliffs, N.J.: Prentice-Hall, 1967), p. 193; Robert Rienow, *Contemporary International Politics* (New York: Crowell, 1961), p. 18; and Raymond Aron, *Peace and War: A Theory of International Relations* (Garden City, N.Y.: Doubleday, 1966), p. 47.

29. See respectively, Wayne H. Ferris, *The Power Capabilities of Nation-States: International Conflict and War* (Lexington, Mass.: Heath, 1973), p. 4; and Schleicher, *Introduction to International Relations*, p. 87. Similarly, it is called "the ability to affect the actions, thoughts, and feelings of others"; see Vernon Van Dyke, *International Politics*, 2d ed. (New York: Appleton-Century-Crofts, 1966), p. 185.

30. See Dahl, "The Concept of Power," pp. 201-15. In this study,

acknowledging "subtly and grossly different meanings," Dahl seeks to establish "the intuitively understood meaning" of the term which "must inevitably result in a formal definition" which, because it is "not easy to apply in concrete research problems," must be reduced to "operational equivalents of the formal definition"; see pp. 201-2. See also his article on "Power," *International Encyclopedia of the Social Sciences* (1968) XII, 405-15.

31. Schuman, *International Politics*, 3d ed. (1941), pp. 262-63.

32. Nicholas J. Spykman, *America's Strategy in World Politics: The United States and the Balance of Power* (New York: Harcourt, Brace, 1942), pp. 12-15.

33. Holsti, *International Politics*, p. 194.

34. See respectively, Frankel, *International Relations*, p. 97; A. F. K. Organski, *World Politics*, 2d ed. (New York: Knopf, 1968), p. 104; and Norman J. Padelford and George A. Lincoln, *International Politics: Foundations of International Relations* (New York: Macmillan, 1954), p. 193, but see also their revised interpretation in their *The Dynamics of International Politics*, p. 36.

35. For example, see Burns, *Of Powers and Their Politics*, pp. 86-87, who specifies some fourteen elements in defining "A Power."

36. See Norman Hill, *Contemporary World Politics* (New York: Harper, 1954), p. 235.

37. To illustrate, see Theodore A. Couloumbis and James H. Wolfe, *Introduction to International Relations: Power and Justice* (Englewood Cliffs, N.J.: Prentice-Hall, 1978), p. 57. For an alternative, more general view, see Lasswell and Kaplan, *Power and Society*, Chapters 4 and 5, in which they compare power with influence and coercion, regarding influence as a "value position and potential" that affects the politics of others, and the outcome of conflict and coercion as varying from constraint to deprivation. See also note 11.

38. See Ferris, *The Power Capabilities of Nation-States*, pp. 4-6, in which he compares power with influence, force (which he interprets as the actual application of sanctions), and authority, but he admits to serious difficulty in distinguishing among them in practice.

39. Such as Ferris, *The Power Capabilities of Nation-States*, especially pp. 6-8.

40. See Furniss and Snyder, *An Introduction to American Foreign Policy*, pp. 23-24.

41. See Charles O. Lerche, Jr., and Abdul A. Said, *Concepts of International Politics in Global Perspective*, 3d ed. (Englewood Cliffs, N.J.: Prentice-Hall, 1979), p. 61. Although this posture is taken in Chapter 3, the authors deal separately with power politics, balance of power, and equilibrium of power in Chapter 5.

42. Sprout, *Toward a Politics of the Planet Earth*, Chapter 8. For their earlier version, see *Foundations of International Politics*, Chapter 4. They suggest that it would be better if the concept of power could be stricken from the vocabulary of statecraft altogether, but admit that this is impossible; see *Foundations of International Politics*, p. 141 and

Toward a Politics of the Planet Earth, p. 168.

43. Examples of emphasis on the military perspective are contained in Inis L. Claude, Jr., *Power and International Relations* (New York: Random House, 1962), especially p. 6; Thomas K. Finletter, *Power and Policy* (New York: Harcourt, Brace, 1954); Harold and Margaret Sprout, *Foundations of International Politics*, p. 141, and *Toward a Politics of the Planet Earth*, p. 168. See also note 189.

44. See respectively, Lerche and Said, *Concepts of International Politics*, p. 58; Howard H. Lentner, *Foreign Policy Analysis: A Comparative and Conceptual Approach* (Columbus, Ohio: Merrill, 1974), p. 25; and J. W. Burton, *Systems, States, Diplomacy and Rules* (Cambridge: Cambridge University Press, 1968), p. 119.

45. Lentner, *Foreign Policy Analysis*, pp. 25-32.

46. See respectively, Furniss and Snyder, *An Introduction to American Foreign Policy*, p. 24; Ferris, *The Power Capabilities of Nation-States*, p. 6; Charles F. Hermann, *Crisis in Foreign Policy: A Simulation Analysis* (Indianapolis: Bobbs-Merrill, 1969), p. 125; and Holsti, *International Politics*, p. 194.

47. See Couloumbis and Wolfe, *Introduction to International Relations*, p. 57. See also Ferris, *The Power Capabilities of Nation-States*, p. 6, who holds that capabilities are "a prerequisite for the assertion of a power relationship but are not synonymous with such a relationship."

48. See Charles A. McClelland, *Theory and the International System* (New York: Macmillan, 1966), p. 70.

49. Lerche and Said, *Concepts of International Politics*, pp. 60-61.

50. For example, see William Reitzel, Morton A. Kaplan, and Constance G. Coblenz, *United States Foreign Policy, 1945-1955* (Washington: Brookings Institution, 1956), Chapter 3. To these primary categories may be added the psychosocial; see Frankel, *International Relations*, pp. 116-18, and Frederick H. Hartmann, *The Relations of Nations*, 5th ed. (New York: Macmillan, 1978), pp. 56-59.

51. Morgenthau, *Politics Among Nations*, Chapter 9. In his first edition (1948) he did not include the quality of government. See also his *In Defense of the National Interest* (New York: Knopf, 1952), p. 175, and *Principles and Problems of International Politics: Selected Readings*, edited by Hans J. Morgenthau and Kenneth W. Thompson (New York: Knopf, 1950), p. 75. Many general textual volumes on international politics published in the 1950s and 1960s provide similar lists.

52. See, for example, the lists of M. Margaret Ball and Hugh B. Killough, *International Relations* (New York: Ronald, 1956), pp. 86-97, and for their table of twenty items see p. 86; Couloumbis and Wolfe, *Introduction to International Relations*, pp. 64-71; Crabb, *American Foreign Policy in the Nuclear Age*, pp. 22-25; Hartmann, *The Relations of Nations*, Chapter 3; Lentner, *Foreign Policy Analysis*, Chapter 6 on "Domestic Determinants"; William C. Olson and Fred A. Sondermann, *The Theory and Practice of International Relations*, 2d ed. (Englewood Cliffs, N.J.: Prentice-Hall, 1966), pp. 99-102; Schleicher, *Introduction to International Relations* (1954), Chapter 5 and *International Relations: Cooperation and Conflict* (Englewood Cliffs, N.J.: Prentice-Hall, 1962), pp. 253-58 and Chapter 13. See also "Elements of National Power," *The*

International Relations Dictionary, 3d ed. (Santa Barbara, Calif.: ABC:Clio, 1982), pp. 169-70.

53. Feliks Gross, *Foreign Policy Analysis* (New York: Philosophical Library, 1954), pp. 124-25.

54. See Ferris, *The Power Capabilities of Nation-States*, pp. 6-7.

55. See Couloumbis and Wolfe, *Introduction to International Relations*, pp. 65-71; Fred Greene, *Dynamics of International Relations: Power, Security, and Order* (New York: Holt, Rinehart, and Winston, 1964), Chapter 7; Lerche and Said, *Concepts of International Politics*, pp. 68-75.

56. See Lentner, *Foreign Policy Analysis*, pp. 57-65, 135-70.

57. Ray S. Cline, *World Power Trends and U.S. Foreign Policy for the 1980s* (Boulder, Colo.: Westview, 1980), Chapter 1.   See also notes 179 and 191.

58. For commentary on national will or resolve to pursue national will to implement policy--in addition to Cline, *World Power Trends and U.S. Foreign Policy*, pp. 22, 143-45, and especially pp. 166-78--see Couloumbis and Wolfe, *Introduction to International Relations*, p. 58, who observe that the "greatest intangible" in power relationships "is one's 'will' to employ one's power"; Morgenthau, *In Defense of the National Interest*, Chapter 8, who discusses the consequences of the failure of national will; and Hartmann, *The Relations of Nations*, pp. 157-59, who considers "The Will to Power as a Cause of War" as a negative misnomer or a rationalization "behind a respectable facade."   See also note 15.

59. Thomas I. Cook and Malcolm Moos, "Foreign Policy: The Realism of Idealism," *American Political Science Review* 46 (June 1952): 347.   See also their *Power Through Purpose: The Realism of Idealism as a Basis for Foreign Policy* (Baltimore: Johns Hopkins Press, 1954), pp. 106-13.

60. Hill, *Contemporary World Politics*, p. 237.

61. Thomas H. Etzold, "Power Politics," *Encyclopedia of American Foreign Policy* (New York: Scribner, 1978) III, 784.   See also note 11. Others also note the equating of power politics with international politics; for example, see Terry Nardin, *Law, Morality, and the Relations of States* (Princeton: Princeton University Press, 1983), p. 35.

62. Paul Seabury, *Power, Freedom, and Diplomacy: The Foreign Policy of the United States of America* (New York: Random House, 1963), pp. 95-96.   For commentary on contemporary theories of power politics and alternative theories, see Burton, *International Relations*, especially pp. 14-20.

63. See respectively, Morgenthau, *Scientific Man vs. Power Politics*, pp. 9-10; Quincy Wright, *The Study of International Relations* (New York: Appleton-Century-Crofts, 1955), p. 140; and Ernest Lefever, *Ethics and United States Foreign Policy* (New York: Meridian, 1957), p. 8.

64. R. J. Martin Wight, *Power Politics* (London: Royal Institute of International Affairs, 1946), p. 7.

65. See James, "Power Politics," p. 207.

66. Wright, *The Study of International Relations*, p. 140.

67. Lerche and Said, *Concepts of International Politics*, p. 104.

68. Aron, *Peace and War*, pp. 47-52.

69. Grayson L. Kirk, "The Problem of American Security," in *American Foreign Policy*, edited by Lawrence H. Chamberlain and Richard C. Snyder (New York: Rinehart, 1948), p. 417. But he adds that despite this depiction power politics cannot "be disregarded or even minimized" in either practice or analysis. For additional comments on power politics as a sinister expression, see Greene, *Dynamics of International Relations*, pp. 150-51.

70. James, "Power Politics," pp. 207-25, especially pp. 207-8, 214.

71. Padelford and Lincoln, *The Dynamics of International Politics*, p. 24. They reject the second interpretation for dealing with the shaping of international political behavior.

72. Burton, *International Relations*, pp. 50-53. When power is relied upon, he says, "in terms of results it matters little whether power is employed as a means, or whether . . . it is employed because men and States naturally seek it." On power games, see also notes 18, 108, 134, 145.

73. Holsti, *International Politics*, pp. 192-93.

74. See comments of the Sprouts in note 42. The relationship of the concept of power politics to international morality is discussed later in this chapter.

75. Lerche and Said, *Concepts of International Politics*, p. 105. For commentary on other sets of assumptions respecting the relationship of power politics to the source of international conflict, including "the drive for power," and on analysis of resultant structures, see Burton, *International Relations*, pp. 32-54 and Chapter 5.

76. For additional citations to literature on power politics, see below, the section on development of analysis.

77. Inis Claude observes that the concept of balance of power "is, by any standard, an ancient notion in the field of international relations" and that the issue of whether "it is also an honorable one is a question to which the history of thought provides no uniform and consistent answer." See his *Power and International Relations*, p. 11.

78. See Stanley Hoffmann, "Balance of Power," *International Encyclopedia of the Social Sciences* (1968) I, 506-10, with quote on p. 506. For an earlier version, see Sidney B. Fay, "Balance of Power," *Encyclopedia of the Social Sciences* (1930) II, 395-99. For a general descriptive essay on the concept as related to the United States, see Dewitt C. Poole, "Balance of Power," *Life* 23 (September 22, 1947): 77-80, 85-92.

79. See Schuman, *International Politics*, 7th ed. (1969), pp. 67, 71. He contends that, together with sovereignty and the principles of international law, it may be regarded as one of the three "cornerstones" of the Western state system, and that it has emerged in every system of states in which the latter competed with one another.

80. See George Liska, *Quest for Equilibrium: America and the Balance of Power on Land and Sea* (Baltimore: Johns Hopkins University Press, 1977), p. 5. For additional commentary on the balance of power as law, see Kenneth W. Thompson, "Toynbee and the Theory of International Relations," in Hoffmann, *Contemporary Theory in International Relations*, pp. 99-104.

81. Ernst B. Haas, nevertheless, admits that the concept of balance of power is not "free from philological, semantic, and theoretical confusion," and he provides a useful inventory of definitions and usages; see his "Balance of Power: Prescription, Concept, or Propaganda," *World Politics* 5 (July 1953): 442-77.

82. Morgenthau, *Politics Among Nations*, p. 161. In Chapter 14 he discusses balance of power both as a device for self-defense and as an ideology. In this volume he uses the term in four ways--as a national policy, as an actual state of affairs, as an approximately even distribution of power, and as any distribution of power; see p. 161, note 1.

83. Morton A. Kaplan, *System and Process in International Politics* (New York: Wiley, 1957), p. 21. He also presents six rules that characterize balance of power, p. 23.

84. See Frankel, *International Relations*, p. 156. He prefers, however, to restrict the term to the European international system between 1648 and 1914, which he describes briefly on pp. 156-62. For citations to additional commentary on the European balance of power arrangement, see notes 95, 129-33.

85. See Burton, *International Relations*, p. 56.

86. See Friedrich von Gentz, *Fragments Upon the Balance of Power in Europe* (London: M. Peltier, 1806), pp. 61-62, quoted in Edward V. Gulick, *Europe's Classical Balance of Power* (Ithaca, N.Y.: Cornell University Press, 1955), p. 34.

87. Aron, *Peace and War*, p. 146.

88. Morgenthau, *Politics Among Nations*, pp. 161, 163.

89. Burns, *Of Powers and Their Politics*, p. 249. On the third party balancer arrangement, see also note 95.

90. For an illustration of the use of this expression, see *The Balance of Power and Nuclear Deterrence: A Book of Readings*, edited by Frederick H. Gareau (Boston: Houghton Mifflin, 1962), Introduction.

91. For additional commentary on equilibrium, see Sten S. Nilson, "Political Equilibrium," *Journal of Conflict Resolution* 3 (December 1959): 383-90.

92. Morgenthau, *Politics Among Nations*, Chapter 11.

93. Morgenthau, *Politics Among Nations*, Chapter 12, with quotation on p. 172.

94. Gulick, *Europe's Classical Balance of Power*, Chapter 3.

95. For summary description of the classical balance of power arrangement in Europe, with Britain serving as "balancer," see Crabb, *Amer-*

ican *Foreign Policy in the Nuclear Age*, pp. 6-8; Spykman, *America's Strategy in World Politics*, pp. 103-21. For general commentary on the nature and functioning of third party balancer, see Gulick, *Europe's Classical Balance of Power*, pp. 65-70; Morgenthau, *Politics Among Nations*, pp. 187-90; and Organski, *World Politics*, pp. 279-80, 285-88, 290-1. For a brief reference to "balancer power," see also Liska, *Quest for Equilibrium*, pp. 123-24. See also notes 84, 129-33.

96. Sprout, *Foundations of International Politics*, pp. 95, 115, 118, 119.

97. Claude, *Power and International Relations*, pp. 13-25. For Morgenthau's four usages of the concept, see note 82.

98. Hoffmann, "Balance of Power," pp. 506-7. See also Stanley Hoffmann, "Weighing the Balance of Power," *Foreign Affairs* 50 (July 1972): 618-43.

99. For example, Liska, *Quest for Equilibrium*, especially pp. 21-22, compares balance, parity, equilibrium, equality, and equivalence; he also uses the expression "equipoise," which was also used by President Woodrow Wilson (see notes 145, 233). Robert B. Mowat also prefers this term for balance of power as periodically readjusted; see Harold and Margaret Sprout, *Foundations of International Politics*, pp. 94-95.

100. Preserving peace and the status quo are given as the purposes of balance of power by Fay, "Balance of Power," p. 397. For arguments denying the theoretical and practical validity of these as the goals of balance of power, see Gulick, *Europe's Classical Balance of Power*, pp. 30-34, 209-10. Schuman makes this explicit in his *International Politics*, 7th ed. (1969), p. 71, where he writes that the balance of power principle is "designed not to preserve peace, as later rationalizations would have it, but simply to maintain the independence of each unit of a State System by preventing any one unit from so increasing its power as to threaten the rest."

101. For additional citations to literature on the balance of power, see the section on development of analysis.

102. Claude uses the neutral expression "the distribution of power" to represent balance/imbalance and equilibrium/disequilibrium; see his *Power and International Relations*, p. 16.

103. For comprehensive studies on the development and analysis of the United States and international equilibrium, or equipoise, see George Liska, *International Equilibrium: A Theoretical Essay on the Politics and Organization of Security* (Cambridge, Mass.: Harvard University Press, 1957), in which he emphasizes the international organization of collective security, focusing in part on the smaller powers in the international arena; and Liska, *Quest for Equilibrium*, in which he amalgamates history, doctrine, and diplomacy, stressing great power balance and equilibrium. See also Nilson, "Political Equilibrium."

104. For general commentary, see Dahl, "Power," pp. 406-7. Burns, discussing "powerhood," makes the point that while notions of internal power come for the most part from Roman and Stoic philosophers, the concept of the relations of nations emanates rather from Biblical and theological than from classical and philosophical sources; see *Of Powers and Their Politics*, pp. 77-85.

105. See Arnold Brecht, *Political Theory: The Foundations of Twentieth Century Political Thought* (Princeton: Princeton University Press,
1959), p. 345.

106. Eric Kaufmann, *Das Wesen des Völkerrechts und die Clausula
Rebus Sic Stantibus* (Tübigen, Germany: Mohr, 1911).

107. Russell, *Power*. Aside from forms of power, Russell deals with
such matters as power and moral codes, power philosophies, the ethics of
power, and the taming of power in Chapters 15-18.

108. Edward Hallett Carr, *The Twenty Years' Crisis, 1919-1939: An
Introduction to the Study of International Relations* (London: Macmillan,
1939), Part 3 of which deals with "Politics, Power, and Morality;" and
Schuman, *International Politics*, first published in 1933; see 3d ed.
(1941), Chapter 7 of which deals with "The Politics of Power," and 7th
ed. (1969), Chapter 8 of which is entitled "The Game of Power Politics."
On the power game see also note 18.

109. For summary commentary on the views and practices of these and
other leaders, see Gulick, *Europe's Classical Balance of Power*.

110. Debates on these distribution of power principles are to be
found in *The Federalist* papers, and comments concerning United States
political strength are contained in presidential inaugural addresses,
messages to Congress, and other public statements. In the twentieth
century many general studies of politics and political science deal with
internal distribution of power, such as James Wilford Garner, *Introduction to Political Science* (New York: American Book Co., 1910), Chapter 13
(and later editions); Raymond G. Gettell, *Introduction to Political
Science* (Boston: Ginn, 1910), Chapter 17; Francis G. Wilson, *The Elements
of Modern Politics* (New York: McGraw-Hill, 1936), especially pp. 341-42,
377-81; and many others. For a summary statement on the framing and
nature of the separation of powers system and foreign affairs, see Daniel
S. Cheever and H. Field Haviland, Jr., *American Foreign Policy and the
Separation of Powers* (Cambridge, Mass.: Harvard University Press, 1952),
especially Chapters 1-3. See also Francis O. Wilcox, *Congress, The Executive, and Foreign Policy* (New York: Harper and Row, 1971).

111. For a summary of early American thought and action involving
power relations with foreign nations, see Etzold, "Power Politics." For
commentary of American leaders supporting and rejecting the concept of
national power, see Norman A. Graebner, *Ideas and Diplomacy: Readings in
the Intellectual Tradition of American Foreign Policy* (New York: Oxford
University Press, 1964), materials cited in index, pp. 884-85.

112. See George E. Catlin, *The Science and Methods of Politics* (New
York: Knopf, 1927), *A Study of the Principles of Politics* (New York: Mac-
millan, 1930), and *Systematic Politics* (Toronto: University of Toronto
Press, 1962), especially Chapter 3; Merriam, *Political Power*; Lasswell
and Kaplan, *Power and Society*; and Harold Lasswell, *Power and Personality*
(New York: Norton, 1948).

113. In 1948 Morgenthau stressed the individual's "desire for power
(*animus dominandi*);" see his *Scientific Man vs. Power Politics*, pp.
192-95. He develops his basic thesis respecting power politics in his
later works, particularly *Politics Among Nations*, Chapters 3-10, and
Truth and Power: Essays of a Decade, 1960-1970 (New York: Praeger, 1970),
Chapter 1.

114. Such as Hartmann, *The Relations of Nations*, Chapters 3, 13-21; and Harold and Margaret Sprout, *Toward a Politics of the Planet Earth*, Chapters 8, 9, 14. Many later writers of the 1970s and 1980s have also joined their ranks.

115. To illustrate, see the views of Cook and Moos, *Power Through Purpose*; in Chapter 2 they reveal that they are less concerned with analyzing power than with discussing purpose. See also their "Foreign Policy: The Realism of Idealism," pp. 343-56. For his analysis of the concept of the coordinate state as an alternative to national power and interests, see Frank Tannenbaum, *The American Tradition in Foreign Policy* (Norman: University of Oklahoma Press, 1955); "The American Tradition in Foreign Relations," *Foreign Affairs* 30 (October 1951): 31-50; and "The Balance of Power Versus the Coordinate State," *Political Science Quarterly* 67 (June 1952): 173-97.
See also Ephraim D. Adams, *The Power of Ideals in American History* (New Haven, Conn.: Yale University Press, 1926); Gabriel Kolko, *The Roots of American Foreign Policy: An Analysis of Power and Purpose* (Boston: Beacon, 1969), on the political and economic dimensions of power in American society; and Norman Cousins, *The Pathology of Power* (New York: Norton, 1987) who, in Chapter 13, discussing the purposes of military power, argues that conflicts need to be resolved "in terms of first principles"; see also note 243.

116. See the final section of this chapter.

117. For a comprehensive analysis of the development of ideas, approaches, and treatments of power and power politics, see Vasquez, *The Power of Power Politics*, which surveys American literature in depth since World War II. See also the "Bibliographical Essay" on power and balance of power in Gulick, *Europe's Classical Balance of Power*, pp. 311-25. For a general bibliography of materials on power as related to national security, see Arthur D. Larson, *National Security Affairs: A Guide to Information Sources* (Detroit: Gale Research, 1973), pp. 54-55.

118. Such as Dean Acheson, *Power and Diplomacy* (Cambridge, Mass.: Harvard University Press, 1958); George Ball, *The Discipline of Power: Essentials of a Modern World Structure* (Boston: Little, Brown, 1968); Adolf A. Berle, *Power* (New York: Harcourt, Brace, and World, 1967); J. William Fulbright, *The Arrogance of Power* (New York: Random House, 1966); Harlan Cleveland, *The Obligations of Power* (New York: Harper and Row, 1966); Francis H. Hinsley, *Power and the Pursuit of Peace: Theory and Practice in the History of Relations Between States* (Cambridge: Cambridge University Press, 1963).

119. These are illustrated by Dahl, "The Concept of Power"; Dorothy Emmet, "The Concept of Power," *Proceedings of the Aristotelian Society* 54 (1953-1954): 1-26; Etzold, "Power Politics"; Herbert Goldhamer and Edward A. Shils, "Types of Power and Status," *American Journal of Sociology* 45 (September 1939): 171-82; James, "Power Politics"; March, "The Power of Power"; Charles A. McClelland, "Power and Influence," in his *Theory and the International System*, pp. 61-89; Riker, "Some Ambiguities in the Notion of Power"; and Trevor Taylor, "Power Politics," in his *Approaches and Theory in International Relations* (London: Longman, 1978).

120. In addition to Burns, *Of Powers and Their Politics* and Vasquez, *The Power of Power Politics*, examples include Peter Bachrach and Morton S. Baratz, "Two Faces of Power," *American Political Science Review* 56 (December 1962): 947-52; *Power*, edited by John R. Champlin (New York: Atherton, 1971), which provides an anthology of essays on the nature and

study of power; Lukes, *Power: A Radical View*, which proposes one, two, and three-dimensional views of power and analyzes their applicability; Cousins, *The Pathology of Power*; R. J. Martin Wright, *Power Politics* (London: Royal Institute of International Affairs, 1946); and such segments as Arnold Brecht, *Political Theory*, pp. 345-48, and Burton, *International Relations*, pp. 46-59, and *Systems, States, Diplomacy and Rules*, pp. 30-31, 113-16.

121. In addition to other works cited earlier in this chapter, see Herbert Agar, *The Price of Power: America Since 1945* (Chicago: Chicago University Press, 1957); M. Blechman and Stephan S. Kaplan, *Force Without War: U.S. Armed Forces as a Political Instrument* (Washington: Brookings Institution, 1978); Burton, *International Relations*, Chapter 12, on "From Power to Steering"--or gradations of power other than force; Seyom Brown, *The Changing Essense of Power* (Washington: Brookings Institution, 1973), reprint from *Foreign Affairs* 51 (January 1973): 286-99, and *The Faces of Power: Constancy and Change in United States Foreign Policy from Truman to Johnson* (New York: Columbia University Press, 1968); Ferris, *The Power Capability of Nation-States*, Chapters 2, 3, 5, which deal with conflict and war; John H. Herz, "Power Politics and World Organization," *American Political Science Review* 36 (December 1942): 1039-52; Joyce Kolko and Gabriel Kolko, *The Limits of Power: The World and U.S. Foreign Policy, 1945-1954* (New York: Harper and Row, 1972).

122. For an analysis of power and its relation to idealism, the realist tradition, and the behavioral perspective, see Vasquez, *The Power of Power Politics*, Chapter 2, and for his realist paradigm, see Chapters 3-7.

123. See Burns, *Of Powers and Their Politics*, Chapters 5-13, which deal with criteria and explanations of systematic change, the dynamics of power relations, the theory of statics, probability, games, alliance theory, negotiation, and philosophic humanizing of power politics. On power games also see note 18.

124. For example, see comments by Dahl, in "Power," pp. 409-14.

125. See Arend Lijphart, "The Structure of the Theoretical Revolution in International Relations," *International Studies Quarterly* 18 (March 1974): 41-74. See also the final section of this chapter.

126. See commentary of Paul Seabury, ed., *Balance of Power* (San Francisco: Chandler, 1965), Chapter 1. Seabury also discusses the earlier contribution of the Hindu philosopher Kantilya (4th century, B.C.).

127. David Hume, "Of the Balance of Power," *Essays and Treatises on Several Subjects* (Edinburgh: Bell and Bradfute, 1825) I, 331-39, and *Essays: Moral, Political, and Literary*, edited by T. H. Greene and T. H. Grose (London: Longmans, Green, 1875) I, pp. 348-56. This is also reproduced in *World Politics: The Writings of Theorists and Practitioners, Classical and Modern*, edited by Arend Lijphart (Boston: Allyn and Bacon, 1966), pp. 228-34; and in Seabury, *Balance of Power*, pp. 32-36.

128. See Seabury, *Balance of Power*, Chapters 5-7.

129. For a comprehensive survey of the development of the concept and theory respecting balance of power to World War II, see Gulick, *Europe's Classical Balance of Power*, especially Chapters 1-3.

130. See Johann Heinrich von Justi, *Die Chimare des Gleichgewichts von Europa* (Altona, Germany: Iversen, 1758); and Franz von Hendrich, *Historischer Versuch über das Gleichgewicht: Der Macht bei den alten und neuen Staaten* (Leipzig: [n.p.], 1796).

131. See Rousseau's essay on perpetual peace in *The Political Writings of Jean Jacques Rousseau*, edited by C. E. Vaughan (Cambridge: The University Press, 1915), Volume I; and Immanuel Kant, *Zum Ewigen Frieden* (Königsberg, Germany: Nicolovius, 1795) translated as *Perpetual Peace: A Philosphical Essay* (London: Allyn and Unwin, 1903). Also note A. F. Kovacs, "The Development of the Principle of the Balance of Power from the Treaty of Westphalia to the Congress of Vienna," (unpublished manuscript, University of Chicago Library, cited in Gulick, *Europe's Classical Balance of Power*, p. 20).

132. See Friedrich von Gentz, *Fragments Upon the Balance of Power in Europe*, translation (London: Peltier, 1806), and Henry, Lord Brougham and Vaux, "Balance of Power," in *Works* (London: Griffin, 1855-61) VIII (1857): 1-50. Lord Brougham also regarded war as an instrument of balancing power.

133. For example, see Ludwig Dehio, *The Precarious Balance: Four Centuries of the European Power Struggle*, translated by Charles Fullman (New York: Knopf, 1962) which chronicles developments from the contest of the Papacy and the Holy Roman Empire to World War II; Sir Howard Esme, "British Policy and the Balance of Power," *American Political Science Review* 19 (May 1925): 261-67; Gulick, *Europe's Classical Balance of Power*, Chapters 4-11; Arthur Hassal, *The Balance of Power, 1715-1789* (New York: Macmillan, 1896); Gould Francis Leckie, *An Historical Research Into the Nature of the Balance of Power in Europe* (London: Taylor and Hessey, 1817); Nicholas Mansergh, *The Coming of the First World War: A Study on the European Balance, 1878-1914* (New York: Longmans, Green, 1949); R. A. Rosecrance, et al., "Power, Balance of Power, and Status in Ninteenth Century International Relations," *Sage Professional Papers in International Studies* (Beverly Hills, Calif.: Sage, 1974); Theodore H. von Laue, "History of the Balance of Power, 1494-1914," unpublished manuscript cited in Gulick, *Europe's Classical Balance of Power*, p. 25; Quincy Wright, "Balance of Power," in *Compass of the World*, edited by Hans W. Weigert and Vilhjalmur Stefansson (New York, Macmillan, 1944), pp. 53-60. See also *Europe's Catechism* (London: 1741), which provides a series of questions and answers on the balance of power principle, mentioned in Gulick, *Europe's Classical Balance of Power*, p. 315. For the balance in Europe following World War II, see A. W. DePorte, *Europe Between the Superpowers: The Enduring Balance* (New Haven, Conn.: Yale University Press, 1979). See also notes 84, 95.

134. Such as Sidney B. Fay, "Balance of Power," pp. 395-99; and Hoffmann, "Balance of Power," pp. 506-10. See also Brian Healy and Arthur Stein, "The Balance of Power in International History: Theory and Reality," *Journal of Conflict Resolution* 17 (March 1973): 33-61; Morton A. Kaplan, Arthur Lee Burns, and Richard E. Quandt, "Theoretical Analysis of the 'Balance of Power'," *Behavioral Science* 5 (1960): 240-52, which presents a competitive game as a device for applying models and theories; A. F. Pollard, "The Balance of Power," *Journal of the British Institute of International Affairs* 2 (March 1923): 53-64; Alfred Vagts, "The Balance of Power: Growth of An Idea," *World Politics* 1 (October 1948): 82-101; Arnold Wolfers, "The Balance of Power," *SAIS Review* 3 (Spring 1959): 9-16; Dina A. Zinnes, "An Analytical Study of the Balance of Power Theories," *Journal f Peace Research* 4 (No. 3, 1967): 270-88; and Dina A. Zinnes, et al., "Formal Analysis of Some Issues in Balance of Power The-

ories," *International Studies Quarterly* 22 (September 1978): 323-56.

135. Such general texts published in the 1950s and 1960s, include Morgenthau, *Politics Among Nations*, Chapters 11-14; Organski, *World Politics*, Chapter 12; Padelford and Lincoln, *International Politics*, pp. 197-222; Norman D. Palmer and Howard C. Perkins, *International Relations*, 2d ed. (Boston: Houghton Mifflin, 1953), Chapter 9; Schleicher, *International Relations*, Chapter 17; Van Dyke, *International Politics*, Chapter 12. Some, such as Schuman, *International Politics*, 3d ed. (1941), pp. 51-70, 280-82, and Chapter 11, and 7th ed. (1969), pp. 270-76, bridge the period of World War II; and Hartmann, *The Relations of Nations*, Chapters 16-19, continued his treatment into the 1970s.

Less attention was devoted to the subject in basic foreign affairs texts; exceptions include Crabb, *American Foreign Policy in the Nuclear Age*, pp. 6-8 (see also his more extensive treatment in his earlier editions); Kurt London, *The Making of Foreign Policy: East and West* (Philadelphia: Lippincott, 1965), pp. 78-83; and Richard C. Snyder and Edgar S. Furniss, Jr., *American Foreign Policy: Formulation, Principles, and Programs* (New York: Rinehart, 1954), pp. 716-18. A few recent monographs also touch on the subject, such as Lentner, *Foreign Policy Analysis*, and Seabury, *Power, Freedom, and Diplomacy*.

136. In addition to many historical accounts, these include Gareau, *The Balance of Power and Nuclear Deterrence*; Seabury, *Balance of Power*; Marshall R. Singer, *Weak States in a World of Powers: The Dynamics of International Relationships* (New York: Free Press, 1972); and others, including Burns, Burton (*International Relations*), Ferris, and Vasquez.

137. On equilibrium, see citations in notes 95 and 103.

138. For example, see Walter C. Clemens, *The Superpowers and Arms Control: From Cold War to Interdependence* (Lexington, Mass.: Heath, 1973), which deals with balance of power (pp. 23-29) and the nuclear arms control road to peace (Chapter 4); John M. Collins, *U.S.-Soviet Military Balance: Concepts and Capabilities, 1960-1980* (New York: McGraw-Hill, 1980), providing a balance sheet on Soviet-American power relations; A. W. DePorte, *Europe Between the Superpowers: The Enduring Balance*; William T. R. Fox, *The Super-Powers: The United States, Britain, and Soviet Union--Their Responsibility for Peace* (New York: Harcourt, Brace, 1944), which discusses the "high politics" of the impending post-World War II era, emphasizing military power; Edy Kaufman, *The Superpowers and Their Spheres of Influence: The United States and the Soviet Union in Eastern Europe and Latin America* (New York: St. Martin's Press, 1976), which concerns superpower relations with Third World countries; and *The Superpowers in a Multinuclear World*, edited by Geoffrey Kemp, Robert L. Pfaltzgraff, Jr., and Uri Ra'anan (Lexington, Mass.: Heath, 1974), which contains essays on the Soviet-American relationship and the changing strategic balance.

On other aspects, see Robert Hargreaves, *Superpower: A Portrait of America in the 1970's* (New York: St. Martin's Press, 1973), which concentrates on domestic characteristics and problems as they affect superpower status; Thomas G. Paterson, *Soviet-American Confrontation* (Baltimore: Johns Hopkins Press, 1973); and Charlotte Waterlow, *Superpowers and Victims: The Outlook for World Community* (Englewood Cliffs, N.J.: Prentice-Hall, 1974).

139. See Gulick, *Europe's Classical Balance of Power*, Chapters 1-3.

140. See Seabury, *Balance of Power*, Chapters, 3, 4, and 6.

141. For example, see Ernst B. Haas, "The Balance of Power as a Guide to Policy-Making," *World Politics* 15 (August 1953): 370-98; Poole, "Balance of Power," pp. 77-80, 85-92; Seabury, *Balance of Power*, pp. 68-74, 136-43, 177-84; Robert Strausz-Hupé, "The Balance of Tomorrow," *ORBIS* 1 (April 1957): 10-27; Alfred Vagts, "The United States and the Balance of Power," *Journal of Politics* 3 (November 1941): 401-49.

142. See respectively, Fred Greene, "Neutralization and the Balance of Power," *American Political Science Review* 47 (December 1953): 1041-57, to achieve East-West equilibrium in Europe; Singer, *Weak States in a World of Powers*; and Kenneth N. Waltz, "The Stability of a Bipolar World," *Daedalus* 93 (Summer 1964): 881-909. See also P. Dale Dean, Jr., and John A. Vasquez, "From Power Politics to Issue Politics: Bipolarity and Multipolarity in Light of a New Paradigm," *Western Political Quarterly* 29 (March 1976): 7-28, on the scientific inadequacy of the concepts of bipolarity and multipolarity.

143. See Ernst B. Haas, "Balance of Power," pp. 442-77, and "Balance of Power as a Guide to Policy-Making," pp. 370-98; Morton A. Kaplan, "Balance of Power, Bipolarity, and Other Models of International Systems," *American Political Science Review* 51 (September 1957): 684-95; Donald L. Reinken, "Computer Explorations of the 'Balance of Power': A Project Report," in *New Approaches to International Relations*, edited in Morton A. Kaplan (New York: St. Martin's Press, 1968), pp. 459-81; Zinnes, "An Analytical Study of the Balance of Power Theories," pp. 270-88. See also commentary by Vasquez, *The Power of Power Politics*, especially pp. 32-33, 80-81, 87-88, 97-101, 183-94.

144. On deterrence, see Gareau, *The Balance of Power and Nuclear Deterrence*. See also Bernard Brodie, "The Anatomy of Deterrence," *World Politics* 11 (January 1959): 173-91; Arthur Lee Burns, "From Balance to Deterrence: A Theoretical Analysis," *World Politics* 9 (July 1957): 494-529; Winston Churchill, "Defense Through Deterrents," *Vital Speeches of the Day* 21 (March 15, 1955): 1090-94; Frederick H. Gareau, "Nuclear Deterrence: A Discussion of the Doctrine," *ORBIS* 5 (Summer 1961): 182-97; Carl Kaysen, "Keeping the Strategic Balance," *Foreign Affairs* 46 (July 1968): 665-75.

On the balance of terror, see Glenn H. Snyder, "The Balance of Power and the Balance of Terror," in Seabury, *Balance of Power*, pp. 184-201; Albert Wohlstetter, "The Delicate Balance of Terror," *Foreign Affairs* 37 (January 1959): 211-34. For the definition of balance of terror, see *The International Relations Dictionary*, 3d ed. (1982), p. 161.

145. Woodrow Wilson repudiated the principle of balance of power and sought to replace it with a system of collective security, which is discussed in the final section of this chapter. Among other things, Wilson called balance of power a "great game, now forever discredited" and "a historic game of pawns and peoples . . . the old balances of power," he denounced "equipoises of power," and he declared that the United States would "join no combination of power which is not a combination" of all nations. See Saul K. Padover, *Wilson's Ideals* (Washington: American Council on Public Affairs, 1942), pp. 72, 100, 107, 109. See also note 233.

146. Respectively William Pitt, Earl of Chatham, in a speech on January 9, 1770; Lord Acton in a letter to Bishop Creighton.

147. Morgenthau, *Scientific Man vs. Power Politics*, p. 200. For his comments on the corruption of political action, see pp. 195-96.

148. Cousins, *The Pathology of Power*, p. 23.

149. Benjamin Disraeli in *Vivian Grey* (1826) I, Chapter 2; Harry S. Truman, first Message to Congress, April 16, 1945.

150. Schleicher, *Introduction to International Relations*, p. 87.

151. Morgenthau, *Truth and Power*, p. 133.

152. See Dahl, "Power," pp. 407-9.

153. Holsti, *International Politics*, pp. 204-5.

154. Probably, Frankel says, because this ends-means dichotomy is more amenable to rational analysis than are other aspects, and most foreign policy is concerned with means, especially with power; see Joseph Frankel, *The Making of Foreign Policy: An Analysis of Decision-Making* (New York: Oxford University Press, 1963), p. 142.

155. See Morgenthau's statement quoted on pp. 151-52. See also Van Dyke, *International Politics*, p. 186, who claims that nations, whatever their goals, need power and they may need to employ it to achieve these aims, and therefore "it may well be an end in itself." But he also writes that power is sometimes held to be a theoretical goal whereas in reality it is a means "to achieve more ultimate objectives," see pp. 11-12. Seabury notes that even in cases in which power appears to be paramount, nations also pursue other ends and therefore seek power to achieve them; see *Power, Freedom, and Diplomacy*, pp. 97-98.

156. Schuman, *International Politics*, 3d ed. (1941), p. 275.

157. Burton, *International Relations*, p. 53. Others who belong to this school, according to Burton, include Reinhold Niebuhr, Nicholas Spykman, and Kenneth Thompson. Nevertheless, in a later volume, Burton states categorically that power "is not an end in itself"; see *Systems, States, Diplomacy and Rules*, p. 140.

158. Lerche and Said, *Concepts of International Politics*, p. 59, maintain that "capability is thus a shorthand reference to the 'means' aspect of the ends-means continuum." For others who regard power as a means, see Couloumbis and Wolfe, *Introduction to International Relations*, p. 57; John Gange, *American Foreign Relations: Permanent Problems and Changing Policies* (New York: Ronald, 1959), p. 39; Harold and Margaret Sprout, *Foundations of International Politics*, pp. 171-72, who discuss "means-providing" and "means-utilizing" functions of power.

159. For commentary on this possibility, see Van Dyke, *International Politics*, pp. 186-87. He notes that power may also become an end "as a result of psychological forces at work in those who participate in the decision-making process."

160. This is the thesis of Walter Lippmann, *U.S. Foreign Policy: Shield of the Republic* (Boston: Little, Brown, 1943) p. 9. See also his statement that foreign policy can be framed only when commitments and power are brought into balance, referred to in Chapter 6.

161. See commentary in Lerche and Said, *Concepts of International Politics*, pp. 56-57.

162. As illustrations, see J. William Fulbright, *The Arrogance of*

Power, together with analysis of this volume in Eugene V. Rostow, *Peace in the Balance: The Future of American Foreign Policy* (New York: Simon and Schuster, 1972), Chapter 6; and George W. Ball, *The Discipline of Power: Essentials of a Modern World Structure* (Boston: Little, Brown, 1968).

163. See Frankel, *International Relations*, p. 103. But he warns that in his judgment mere quantification is of little value.

164. Sprout, *Toward a Politics of the Planet Earth*, p. 155.

165. Van Dyke, *International Politics*, p. 217.

166. Lerche and Said, *Concepts of International Politics*, pp. 65–66.

167. For commentary on positive and negative powers, see Organski, *World Politics*, pp. 118–19.

168. See Russell, *Power*, Chapters 2 and 3.

169. In addition to earlier references to distinctions, see Goldhamer and Shils, "Types of Power and Status," pp. 172–76. Other types identified by Lasswell and Kaplan vary from inducement (promise of indulgence) and constraint to censorship, injunction, compulsion, intimidation, chatisement, violence, terrorism, and "naked force." They also recognize more nebulous forms of power, including homage, fealty, regard, and charisma. See *Power and Society*, especially pp. 83–85, 88–94, 139–41, and table on p. 87.

170. Dahl, "Power," p. 412.

171. Lerche and Said, *Concepts of International Politics*, pp. 107–14.

172. Hartmann, *The Relations of Nations*, Chapter 15. World government and federation are discussed in the last section of this chapter and are mentioned in Chapter 8. *The International Relations Dictionary*, 3d ed. (1982) similarly discusses militarism, alliances, collective security, and world government.

173. Berle, *Power*, summarizes his five laws on p. 37 and discusses them on pp. 37–140, and he amplifies his analysis of international power in Book V, pp. 403–529.

174. For commentary, see Lerche and Said, *Concepts of International Politics*, pp. 106–7.

175. Thorsten V. Kalijarvi and associates, *Modern World Politics*, 3d ed. (New York: Crowell, 1953), pp. 48–49. On the matter of independence as a measure of power status, he lists ten categories, such as fully sovereign states, protectorates, suzerainties, trusteeships, neutralized states, and several quasi-dependencies.

176. For descriptive and historical summary analysis of power relations and developments, see Schuman, *International Politics*, 3d ed. (1941), Chapters 7 and 9, especially pp. 274–99, and 4th ed. (1948), Chapters 7, 10, and 11. An earlier study of Leopold von Ranke on "The Great Powers" as of 1833 is provided in Seabury, *Balance of Power*, Chapter 12, and a brief comment on the great powers is contained in Frankel, *International Relations*, pp. 100–2. For materials on superpowers

see citations in note 138. Parenthetically, when the United Nations was established, only five nations were given "permanent" seats on the Security Council--China, France, the Soviet Union, the United Kingdom, and the United States--reflecting the attitude on the major world powers at the time.

177. Morgenthau, *Scientific Man vs. Power Politics*, p. 193.

178. Holsti, *International Politics*, pp. 198-99. Holsti also notes how strong states often fail to attain their objectives and sometimes weak states do achieve theirs; see pp. 199-200. For additional commentary on constraints on power, see Russell, *Power*, Chapter 18 on "The Taming of Power" in human relations, especially pp. 294-305 on psychological aspects; and Berle, *Power*, pp. 61-62, 88-91, and 144-45 on economic and philosophical aspects. On limitations and constraints see also notes 205, 206, 209, 213, 216, 243.

179. For illustrative studies, see Ferris, *The Power Capabilities of Nation-States*; Stephen B. Jones, "The Power Inventory and National Strategy," *World Politics* 6 (July 1954): 421-52; Jack Sawyer, "Dimensions of Nations: Size, Wealth, and Politics," *American Journal of Sociology* 73 (July 1967): 145-72; Herbert A. Simon, "Notes on the Observation and Measurement of Political Power," *Journal of Politics* 15 (November 1953): 500-16 (on materiality of the actual existence of power, not merely the resources of the nation). For a comprehensive analysis of a cross-national comparison of nations, with emphasis on a substantial number of variables and their relation to national behavior, see R. J. Rummel, *The Dimensions of Nations* (Beverly Hills, Calif.: Sage, 1972).

180. See Couloumbis and Wolfe, *Introduction to International Relations*, p. 58, for actual versus potential power; Lentner, *Foreign Policy Analysis*, pp. 206-8, for mobilizable resources; Hartmann, *The Relations of Nations*, p. 66, for realizable power; and Ferris, *The Power Capabilities of Nation-States*, pp. 33-36, for discussion of operationalizing capabilities.

181. On the latter usage, see Harold and Margaret Sprout, *Toward a Politics of the Planet Earth*, pp. 171-72. For an assessment of power potential as a war-making capacity at the time of outbreak of World War II, see Schuman, *International Politics*, 3d ed. (1941), pp. 291-99.

182. Carr, *The Twenty Years' Crisis*, p. 139.

183. See commentary in Couloumbis and Wolfe, *Introduction to International Relations*, p. 72.

184. Sprout, *Toward a Politics of the Planet Earth*, pp. 164-65. For Frankel's view on quantifying power, see note 163.

185. For discussion of geopolitics, see Chapter 8.

186. See Harold and Margaret Sprout, *Foundations of International Politics*, pp. 46-58, and *Toward a Politics of the Planet Earth*, Chapters 11 and 15.

187. See Organski, *World Politics*, 1st ed. (1958), pp. 137-47, and 2d ed. (1968), pp. 144-54, in which he claims that population is the primary determinant of a nation's power; and A. F. K. Organski and Katherine Organski, *Population and World Power* (New York: Knopf, 1961), especially Chapters 1, 2, 8, and 9, in which they conclude that population is "a na-

tion's greatest resource" and "a modern nation's power rests largely on
the size of its population." Additional references are provided in their
extensive bibliography, pp. 253-63. See also note 192. Also Kingsley
Davis, "The Demographic Foundations of National Power," in *Freedom and
Control in Modern Society*, edited by Morroe Berger, Theodore Abel, and
Charles H. Page (New York: Van Nostrand, 1954). For additional citations
on manpower, see Larson, *National Security Affairs*, pp. 184-85.

188. For example, see Acheson, *Power and Diplomacy*, which focuses on
industrial productivity; see emphasis given on p. 29.

189. Such as Gareau, *The Balance of Power and Nuclear Deterrence*,
especially Chapters 14-17; John H. Herz, *International Politics in the
Atomic Age* (New York: Columbia University Press, 1959), especially
Chapter 8; Klaus E. Knorr, *Military Power and Potential* (Lexington,
Mass.: Heath, 1970), with discussion of the nature of military power in
Chapter 1.   Brown, *The Faces of Power*, focuses on the military-tech-
nological aspects of power as applied to balance of power, crises, and
wars by Presidents Truman, Eisenhower, Kennedy, and Johnson. See also
note 43.

190. These conjoin such factors as economic resources and force capability; economic development and military might; demographic, industrial, and military strength; or size, economic development, and polity.

191. For an overall survey of developing contemporary analysis of
the calculation of national power, see Vasquez, *The Power of Power
Politics*, pp. 54-64, and for a comprehensive treatment, see Jack Sawyer,
"Dimensions of Nations," which studies 236 social, economic, political,
and other characteristics of 82 independent nations, and concludes that
three factors are paramount in determining national power, namely, population, gross national product and per capita income, and political
orientation.   Also, for illustrations of more than fifty scoring tables
of selected power components and the power politics capacities of
nations, see Ferris, *The Power Capabilities of Nation-States*, "List of
Tables," pp. xi-xvii. Cline, *World Power Trends and U.S. Foreign Policy*,
contains thirty-six comparative tables of power resources ranging from
population, territory, critical mass, gross national product, military
and nuclear strength, and final assessment of perceived power, to
petroleum, food, and steel and cement production (see list, pp. xi-xii).
See also reference to Rummel, *The Dimensions of Nations*, in note 179.

192. See Organski, *World Politics*, pp. 207-15, with table of ranking
of seventy nations given on pp. 210-12. As of 1965 the United States
ranked first, whose GNP was twice that of the Soviet Union and seven
times greater than that of China, and the combined GNP of the United
States, France, West Germany, and the United Kingdom exceeded those of
all of the rest of the world--which scarcely provides a reliable basis
for the making of policy and the exercise of power in international
relations. An earlier version, simply listing and comparing the population of the Western and Soviet orbit powers is provided in Edward V.
Gulick, "Our Balance of Power System in Perspective," *Journal of International Affairs* 14 (1960): 15.

193. For example, see Schuman, *International Politics*, 3d ed.
(1941), p. 291. Hartmann, *The Relations of Nations*, p. 67, notes that
nations change constantly in both potential and realized power and that
such changes are both absolute and relative; and Seabury, *Power, Freedom,
and Diplomacy*, p. 112, calls national power "highly unstable and certainly transitory."

194. Frankel, *International Relations*, p. 102. Hans J. Morgenthau, *A New Foreign Policy for the United States* (New York: Praeger, 1969), p. 141, also argues that national overall power "is not susceptible to quantification." Simon, discussing the matter of apprehending and calculating power, differentiates the assessment of power from the actual exercise of power; see "Notes on the Observation and Measurement of Political Power," pp. 500-516.

195. Van Dyke, *International Politics*, pp. 216-17.

196. For example, see Holsti, *International Politics*, p. 199, who writes that power "is always the capability to do something . . . within a framework of certain goals and for political objectives." See also Gross, *Foreign Policy Analysis*, pp. 94-95.

197. To illustrate, Frankel, *International Relations*, pp. 102-3, states that power "can be realistically estimated only in action" and discussion of assessment of a nation's potential must be limited to "its capacity for such action." On the other hand, Hartmann, *The Relations of Nations*, p. 68, contends that the view that power only has meaning if results are observable "from its existence or use"--that is, "no effects, no power"-- while of some value, fails to account neither for the subtleties of the power equation nor for the validity of policy based on the existence of nuclear weapons without detonating them. For a similar view, see William R. Kintner, *Peace and the Strategy Conflict* (New York: Praeger, 1967), Chapter 9. By comparison, William O. Chittick, editor of *The Analysis of Foreign Policy Outputs* (Columbus, Ohio: Merrill, 1975), pp. 178-81, prefers to focus on measuring outputs and outcomes of the possession and use of national capability which, he insists, in calculations must be related to both costs and benefits.

198. Hartmann, *The Relations of Nations*, p. 67. For summaries of problems and conclusions, see pp. 66-68.

199. Olson and Sondermann, *The Theory and Practice of International Relations*, p. 102.

200. For special emphasis on the relationship of power and national interests, see Morgenthau, *In Defense of the National Interest* and *Politics Among Nations*. See also Seabury, *Power, Freedom, and Diplomacy*, p. 83.

201. Frankel, *The Making of Foreign Policy*, p. 214. See also Joseph C. Grew, "The Responsibility of Power," *Department of State Bulletin* 12 (June 24, 1945): 1145-49, who discusses United States statesmanship and responsibility following World War II; and Lerche and Said, *Concepts of International Politics*, p. 106, who allude to principles of alleged "responsibility of power." See also Walt W. Rostow, "Limits and Responsibilities of American Power," *Department of State Bulletin* 60 (January 6, 1969): 4-7. See also note 214.

202. During the Cold War miscalculation became a frequently emphasized concern in United States negotiations with the Soviet Union.

203. Kalijarvi generalizes these techniques as embracing strategy and diplomacy (to adjust power relationships), recourse to tribunals (to resolve conflicts by adjudicatory processes), "methods short of war" (such as embargoes, nonintercourse, pacific blockade, and intervention), and ultimately war. See *Modern World Politics*, pp. 51-53.

204. Organski, *World Politics*, pp. 115-18.

205. For commentary on limits and constraints, for example, see Crabb, *American Foreign Policy in the Nuclear Age*, pp. 25-29; Greene, *Dynamics of International Relations*, pp. 155-58; Rostow, "Limits and Responsibilities of American Power." See also notes 178 and 216. For a general statement on the means of operationalizing military power, see Ferris, *The Power Capabilities of Nation-States*, pp. 31-36. For commentary on "first principles" as transcending the exercise of national power, see Cousins, *The Pathology of Power*, pp. 202-3. See also note 243.

206. Addressing himself to ethical considerations and restraints on power, Bailey adds: "moral disapprobation breaks no bones," and "morality covers a multitude of sins," but he also counsels "honor all commitments." See *The Art of Diplomacy: The American Experience* (New York: Appleton-Century-Crofts, 1968), Chapter 18 and pp. 160-61.

207. For example, on morality and the politics of national rules, see Merriam, *Political Power*, pp. 215-20. He also touches on morality in world relations, p. 218. See also Pitirim A. Sorokin and Walter A. Lunden, *Power and Morality: Who Shall Guard the Guardians* (Boston: Porter Sargent, 1959), who emphasize the morality of rulers, especially in Chapters 2, 3, and 5, and the decline of values, in Chapter 9, including the need for moral leadership, pp. 174-83, and Noam Chomsky, *American Power and the New Mandarins* (New York: Pantheon, Random House, 1967), which contains essays critical of the role Americans played in policy-making leading to the Vietnam War.

208. Reinhold Niebuhr, *Moral Man and Immoral Society: A Study in Ethics and Politics* (New York: Scribner, 1932), p. 4; see also his *Christianity and Power Politics* (New York: Scribner, 1940).

209. Russell, *Power*, Chapters 15, 17. Moral codes are also referred to in Lasswell and Kaplan, *Power and Society*, pp. 82, 83. See also Percy E. Corbett, *Morals, Law, and Power in International Relations* (Los Angeles: Haynes Foundation, 1956); and Nardin, *Law, Morality, and the Relations of Nations*. For additional specialized studies, see Edgar Bodenheimer, *Power, Law, and Society: A Study of the Will to Power and the Will to Law* (New York: Crane, Russak, 1972), in which he emphasizes the domination of the will to law and stability in societal relations and minimizes the will to power; and Adrienne Koch, *Power, Morals, and the Founding Fathers: Essays in the Interpretation of the American Enlightenment* (Ithaca, N.Y.: Cornell University Press, 1975).

210. Morgenthau, *Scientific Man vs. Power Politics*, pp. 168-69; see also his commentary on ethics, science, and politics, pp. 35-37. For his views on the dichotomy of intellectuals seeking truth and politicians seeking power, see his *Truth and Power*, Chapter 1, especially p. 14.

211. Carr, *The Twenty Years' Crisis*, Chapter 9 on "Morality in International Relations," with quotes on pp. 125, 126.

212. Spykman, *America's Strategy in World Politics*, pp. 12, 18.

213. Morgenthau, *Politics Among Nations*, pp. 224-25. In Chapter 15 he discusses morality, mores, and law as constraints on domestic power, and in Chapter 16 he comments on the moral aspects of the protection of human life in peace and war, and on total war, and he acknowledges the deterioration of international morality after World War II. See also

notes 206, 209, 216.

214. Seabury also emphasizes that ethics presupposes "the very idea of responsibility"; see *Power, Freedom, and Diplomacy*, pp. 138-39. On responsibility see also note 201.

215. Lerche and Said, *Concepts of International Politics*, pp. 156-57. They conclude that morality may be exterior to capability or be one of its components, and that power and morality, as concepts, belong to different "analytical frames of reference and cannot be conjoined in any prescriptive way."

216. John G. Stoessinger, *The Might of Nations: World Politics in Our Time*, 3d ed. (New York: Random House, 1969), pp. 28-29, 228-35. For additional philosophical commentary on international morals and morality as a constraint on the actions of persons and nations, and the qualities of international morality, see Nardin, *Law, Morality, and the Relations of Nations*, especially pp. 223-50, 305-8. For earlier references to constraints on power, see notes 178, 206, 209, 213.

217. Carr, *The Twenty Years' Crisis*, p. 199. Also comparing power and national interests, one of the principal differences, he says on p. 201, is that states, by common consent, are morally bound to promote and protect the interests of the nation.

For additional commentary on morality and international politics, see Gordon A. Craig and Alexander L. George, *Force and Statecraft: Diplomatic Problems of Our Times* (New York: Oxford University Press, 1983), especially Part III; *The Moral Dimensions of International Conduct*, edited by James A. Devereux (Washington: Georgetown University Press, 1983); Fred M. Frohock, "Rationality, Morality, and Impossibility Theorems," *American Political Science Review* 74 (June 1980): 373-84; J. E. Hare and Carey B. Joynt, *Ethics and International Relations* (New York: St. Martin's Press, 1982); Stanley Hoffmann, *Duties Beyond Borders: On the Limits and Possibilities of Ethical International Politics* (Syracuse, N.Y.: Syracuse University Press, 1981); James V. Schall, *Christianity and Politics* (Boston: St. Paul, 1981); Kenneth W. Thompson, *Ethics and National Purpose* (New York: Council on Religion and International Affairs, 1957) on the moral dilemma of ethics in relation to rationalism, legalism, and ideals; *Ethics and International Relations: Ethics and Foreign Policy*, edited by Kenneth W. Thompson (New Brunswick, N.J.: Transaction, 1985); *Traditions and Values: American Diplomacy, 1945 to the Present*, edited by Kenneth W. Thompson (Lanham, Md.: University Press of America, 1984).

218. See earlier commentary on this matter in Chapter 2. For comments on hegemonism as an alternative, see Berle, *Power*, Book V, Chapter 4 entitled "Is Empire Avoidable?" See also comments on geopolitics in Chapter 8.

219. These expressions are used, respectively, by Russell, *Power*, Chapter 6, and Greene, *Dynamics of International Relations*, p. 150. Others use similar terms, such as brute force. See also note 169.

220. For general commentary on "international integration," see the *International Encyclopedia of the Social Sciences* (1968) VII, 522-47, which contains separate sections on regional and global integration, functional integration, and economic unions. See also notes 222, 228.

221. One of the specialized aspects of diplomacy is the negotiation of treaties to outlaw the going to war, such as the Pact of Paris, signed

in 1928. See Quincy Wright, *The Role of International Law in the Elimination of War* (New York: Oceana, 1961). For bibliographical resources on diplomacy, negotiations, and diplomatic practices and practitioners, see Robert B. Harmon, *The Art and Practice of Diplomacy: A Selected and Annotated Guide* (Metuchen, N.J.: Scarecrow Press, 1971), Chapters 1-3, pp. 132-56, and Chapter 5; and Elmer Plischke, *U.S. Foreign Relations: A Guide to Information Sources* (Detroit: Gale Research, 1980), Chapters 2-5, pp. 139-47, and Chapters 9 and 17.

222. There is extensive literature on these basic systems. For general commentary, see *Systems of Integrating the International Community*, edited by Elmer Plischke (Princeton: Van Nostrand, 1964), which contains separate chapters on international confederation (focusing on the United Nations), the European Community, international federalism in theory and practice, and integrating the Communist East-European bloc. See also Elmer Plischke, "Reflections on International Integration: Problems of Organizational Institutionalization," *World Politics* 129 (April-June 1966): 20-27.

223. Examples include the American coalescence under the Articles of Confederation, the League of Nations, the United Nations, and dozens of other contemporary global and regional, general and specialized, agencies. Hundreds have been established during the past two centuries, but the most extensive development of international integration was launched during and after World War II. The Department of State identified some 400 such organizations (including many bilateral agencies) with which the United States participated during the 1940s, and the United States is currently a member of some 75 major multipartite agencies. But the Department of State emphasizes that these organizations, taken together, do not compose any world government. For background see Department of State, *International Organizations in Which the United States Participates* (Washington: Government Printing Office, 1950).

224. This is exemplified by the European Communities. Treaties were drafted for the European Coal and Steel, Economic, and Atomic Energy Communities, which were ratified and implemented, and for the European Defense and Political Communities, which were signed but not ratified.

225. Current examples, in addition to the United States, include Australia, Canada, India, Maylasia, Switzerland, West Germany, and others, and in some respects also the Soviet Union and Yugoslavia.

226. For general commentary on federalism, see Max Hilbert Boehm, "Federalism," and Arthur W. Macmahon, "Federation," *Encyclopedia of the Social Sciences* (1931) VI, 169-78; and Daniel J. Elazar, "Federalism," *International Encyclopedia of the Social Sciences* (1968) V, 353-67. On theoretical aspects, see Carl Joachim Friedrich, *Man and His Government: An Empirical Theory of Politics* (New York: McGraw-Hill, 1963), Chapter 32.

227. See comments in Chapter 8. See also Berle, *Power*, Book V, Chapter 5, and for philosophical prospects after World War II, see Reinhold Niebuhr, "The Illusion of World Government," *Foreign Affairs* 27 (April 1949): 379-88, who declares: "We may have pity upon, but can have no sympathy with, those who flee to the illusory security of the impossible from the insecurities and ambiguities of the possible," p. 388.

228. H. N. Brailsford, defining "internationalism," calls it "the ideal of an organic, supernational society which would include within itself constituent national societies controlled from above but endowed

with independent functions and vitality." He distinguishes it from "cos-mopolitanism" which may be interpreted as a subjective state of mind that is posited on the unity of mankind. See *Encyclopedia of the Social Sciences* (1932) VIII, 214-19.

For additional perspectives on post-World War II world order, see Lionel Gelber, *Peace by Power: The Plain Man's Guide to the Key Issue of War and the Post-War World* (New York: Oxford University Press, 1942) and Lionel Gelber and Robert K. Gooch, *War for Power and Power for Freedom* (New York: Farrar and Rinehart, 1940); Robert O. Keohane and Joseph S. Nye, *Power and Interdependence: World Politics in Transition* (Boston: Little, Brown, 1977), who stress international economic integration as a transcendent analytical concept; and Ervin Laszlo, *A Strategy for the Future: The Systems Approach to World Order* (New York: Braziller, 1974), which discusses three phases for designing a contemporary world system.

229. Kenneth W. Thompson, "Collective Security," *International Encyclopedia of the Social Sciences* (1968) II, 565-67. He discusses development of the concept and a series of basic operational problems. See also his "Collective Security Reexamined," *American Political Science Review* 47 (September 1953): 753-72, in which he deals with preconditions and the unreality of two approaches to collective security. For additional, brief commentary, see Lerche and Said, *Concepts of International Politics*, p. 111. See also *Collective Security*, edited by Marina S. Finkelstein (San Francisco: Chandler, 1966); Ernst B. Haas, *Collective Security and the Future International System* (Denver: University of Denver, 1968); Willard N. Hogan, *International Conflict and Collective Security: The Principal Concern of International Organization* (Lexington: University of Kentucky Press, 1955). See also Schleicher, *International Relations*, pp. 314-29, who discusses conditions for success, institutionalization, and sanctions; Hartmann, *The Relations of Nations*, Chapter 20, who applied collective security in the Italo-Ethiopian and Korean crises. These case studies are also discussed by Morgenthau, *Politics Among Nations*, Chapter 24; and Palmer and Perkins, *International Relations*, pp. 277-87.

230. See respectively, Van Dyke, *International Politics*, pp. 410-11; and Hartmann, *The Relations of Nations*, p. 301. For additional variations of interpretation, see Hill, *Contemporary World Politics*, pp. 621-22; Palmer and Perkins, *International Relations*, pp. 270-71; Schleicher, *International Relations*, p. 315; Schuman, *International Politics*, 7th ed. (1969), pp. 203-4. See also Organski, *World Politics*, who not only defines the concept on pp. 407-9, but also discusses the assumptions on which it is founded, pp. 409-19.

231. For commentary, see Sidney B. Fay, "Concert of Powers," *Encyclopedia of the Social Sciences* (1931) IV, 153-54. He describes it as the arrangement "by which the Great Powers sought to establish a common policy of cooperation to prevent war and the spread of revolutionary tendencies." In the nineteenth and twentieth centuries it operated by means of diplomacy, largely through international conferences.

232. For commentary on the principle of collective security in the League of Nations and United Nations, see Morgenthau, *Politics Among Nations*, pp. 285-98, 397-408; Organski, *World Politics*, Chapter 16; Palmer and Perkins, *International Relations*, Chapter 10; Schleicher, *International Relations*, pp. 314-29; and Van Dyke, *International Politics*, pp. 410-21.

233. For selected statements of Wilson's critical views on balance of power and collective security, see Padover, *Wilson's Ideals*, pp. 100,

109. He proclaimed that "every matter which is likely to affect the peace of the world is everybody's business," and that mankind is seeking "freedom of life," not "equipoises of power." Collective security was sought to be achieved by Article 10 of the League Covenant. See also note 145.

234. Gulick, *Europe's Classical Balance of Power*, pp. 307-8.

235. Morgenthau, *Politics Among Nations*, p. 398.

236. Palmer and Perkins, *International Relations*, pp. 285-86.

237. Robert Strausz-Hupé and Stefan T. Possony, *International Relations* (New York: McGraw-Hill, 1950), p. 264.

238. Seabury, *Power, Freedom, and Diplomacy*, p. 383. For an explanation of the principal reasons for the failure of collective security, see Van Dyke, *International Politics*, pp. 413-17.

239. Lerche and Said, *Concepts of International Politics*, p. 111.

240. Morgenthau concludes that "collective security cannot be made to work in the contemporary world"; for his assumptions, see *Politics Among Nations*, pp. 398-400, and for quotation, see p. 401. See also Organski, *World Politics*, p. 424, who maintains that the assumptions on which collective security is founded are themselves invalid.

241. Fulbright, *The Arrogance of Power*, Chapter 1, especially pp. 3-5, 9. See also J. William Fulbright, *Prospects for the West* (Cambridge, Mass.: Harvard University Press, 1963), p. 76, in which he insists that success breeds arrogance; and his *The Crippled Giant: American Foreign Policy and Its Domestic Consequences* (New York: Random House, 1972), in which like Woodrow Wilson, he condemns "the liturgy of 'realism'," and "the empty system of power," pp. 153, 275-79. Especially critical, Frank Tannenbaum calls balance of power "this dreadful doctrine," which is "make-believe" because it is not founded on a scientific basis, and he regards it as amoral and anathema to American heritage and ideals. See his *The American Tradition in Foreign Policy* and "The Balance of Power Versus the Coordinate State," especially pp. 173, 175.

242. For example, Fay maintains that balance of power "has never achieved a satisfactory equilibrium for any long period of years and has signally failed in its purpose of preserving peace and the status quo." See his "Balance of Power," p. 398.

243. See Cousins, *The Pathology of Power*, Chapter 2. On pp. 202-3 he lists his "six first principles"--such as the "human commonwealth" exceeds the nation-state, "mankind" outranks the nation, the "rights of man" transcend the rights of the nation, and "private conscience" is superior to "public edict."

244. See Berle, *Power*, Book 6, Chapter 1; and Max Mark, "The End of Power Politics," *Virginia Quarterly Review* 44 (Summer 1968): 353-68.

245. See Brown, *The Changing Essence of Power*, especially pp. 286-99. He notes significant changes from bipolar Cold War politics and classical balance of power, and he envisages an emergent "five-sided balance of power."

246. See Ball, *The Discipline of Power*, Chapter 1.

247. See Glen H. Snyder, "Balance of Power in the Missile Age," *Journal of International Affairs* 14 (1960): 21-34.

248. See references to Burton, Carr, Ferris, Frankel, Hume, Lippmann, Liska, Morgenthau, Rostow, and others, cited earlier.

249. In his concluding chapter, Carr contends that "power is a necessary ingredient in every political order" and even if the system changes, political power wielding will continue; see *The Twenty Years' Crisis*, Chapter 14, especially p. 297.

250. Gulick assesses the theory of equilibrium, its assumptions, special aims, and means in *Europe's Classical Balance of Power*, Chapter 13, and specifies that the theory is not a causal, haphazard matter of self-interest, but rather "a moderately well-defined and relatively systematic approach to the problems of statecraft," p. 298.

251. Schleicher concludes his analysis of power by noting: "One, perhaps the principal, reason for the international struggle for power is that power is essential to security in an anarchistic world--one without world government." See his *International Relations*, p. 261.

252. Poole, "Balance of Power," p. 78. Poole also claims that balance of power is a thoroughly American idea, pp. 86-90.

253. Spykman, *America's Strategy in World Politics*, pp. 16-17, 25. See also the arguments of the French scholar Leonce Donnadieu, who contends that the balance of power protects the majority of states and that it promotes the common interest and security of the international community as a whole. See *Essai sur la theorie d'equilibre* provided in English in Gareau, *The Balance of Power and Nuclear Deterrence*, pp. 82-88.

254. See respectively, Hoffmann, "Balance of Power," p. 509, and Max Beloff, "Balance of Power," *Interplay* 1 (August-September 1967): 14-18. See also Grayson Kirk's view given in note 69.

255. Carr, *The Twenty Years' Crisis*, p. 137. Many others who assess alternatives to power politics and balance of power agree that change in the nation-state system is difficult if not impossible, and question the viability of alternatives. For example, *Globalism vs. Realism: International Relations Third Debate*, edited by Ray Maghroori and Bennett Ramberg (Boulder, Col.: Westview, 1982) provides essays that espouse globalism and others that defend realism on the ground that the nation-state remains the most important "global fixture" in the international system; John Donald B. Miller, *The World of States: Connected Essays* (New York: St. Martin's Press, 1981) argues that the sovereign state is still the most powerful and able institution in the world and admits little possibility of world federalism; and Ivo D. Duchacek, *The Territorial Dimension of Politics: Within, Among, and Across Nations* (Boulder, Col.: Westview, 1986) rejects revisionists who, for the sake of peace and development, would supersede the nations with regional and global world order.

8

NATIONAL PLANNING AND STRATEGIES

Our "mode of thinking" must seek a sustainable strategy geared to *American* goals and interests . . . . We must learn to pursue a strategy geared to long-term thinking and based on both negotiation and strength simultaneously.
George P. Shultz, *Foreign Affairs* (1985)

The complex of foreign policy actions will assume coherence and purpose only if it conforms to a grand strategy.
Melvin R. Laird, Foreword, G. Warren Nutter, *Kissinger's Grand Design* (1975)

In strategy, as elsewhere, effective policy requires some measure of both content and consensus. Strategic programs . . . are both prescriptions for future action and ratifications of existing power relationships. A strategy which is so vague or contradictary that it provides no prescription for action is no strategy. So too, a strategy whose prescriptions are so unacceptable that they are ignored is no strategy.
Samuel P. Huntington, *Foreign Affairs* (1960)

As is the case with other foreign relations concepts, everyone presumes to understand the meaning of the terms "planning" and "strategy"--in their nominative and adjectival senses, and in their singular and plural versions. And yet, probing analysis of these expressions reveals their intrinsic interaction with other components of the foreign relations process, their complexities and mutations, and the confusion that reigns in their interpretation and usage.

In assessing their nature and applications, consideration needs to be given to whether planning is an art and/or a science and to the relevance of strategy to purposes and policies in the ends-means relationship. Attention also needs to be paid to the role played by strategy in the determination of foreign policies and the conduct of international affairs, to the difference between strategy and tactics, and to resulting pragmatic and theoretical constructs.

Planning and strategy formulation constitute the process and its end product by which all of the components previously discussed are interrelated--intellectually for purposes of analysis and assessment, and pragmatically for purposes of national action--to arrive at and execute foreign relations decisions. These may concern matters of broad scope, primary importance, and anticipated longevity, or of lesser significance and time relevance. They apply to basic, initiatory actions, reactive responses, and contingency planning, and although they constitute means rather than ends, they relate to both. Their criticality to the management of foreign affairs is freely recognized. The viability and competence of the process and the feasibility and value of the end product may spell the difference between success and failure. (The concrete methods of decision-making, central to such planning, are discussed in Chapter 9.)

DEVELOPING INTEREST IN PLANNING AND STRATEGY

Planning and strategy have historically been common components of foreign relations as well as military affairs. Whereas statesmen and diplomats have developed means for incorporating them into their operational repertoires, only in recent decades have they been subjected to intense analytical scrutiny. Aside from memoirs, biographies, and histories, earlier writings focused primarily on warfare, international law and institutionalization, diplomacy, and the methods, principles, and agencies for establishing and maintaining peace.

Except for occasional theoreticians, much of the descriptive and probative literature produced is of twentieth-century vintage, emerging in an array of studies on international politics, foreign policy, and diplomatic practice. Most of these deal either with planning as a process or with strategy as a type of plan. But, strangely, few are equally concerned with both. However, distinctions are drawn between planning and operations and between policy-making and implementation as separable aspects of foreign affairs. Another factor that permeates diagnosis is the matter of the strata or levels of both planning and strategy.

FOREIGN RELATIONS PLANNING

For a nation to manage its foreign relations effectively and expeditiously, it would seem logical that its leaders would plan systematically. The need for planning has been widely recognized. Herodotus has said that "a well laid plan is ever to my mind most profitable." At the time of World War II, Hugh Gibson, a career American diplomat, equated foreign policy-making with planning. He argued that a government must deliberately devise its policy fundamentals, and that long-range planning is essential to avoid approaching international affairs from the standpoint of the status quo and to produce continuity of action.[1] More recently, George Allen Morgan has written: "The urgency of planning in our age of international flux and danger needs no argument."[2] In their commentaries, Feliks Gross and James L. McCamy contend that governments must have plans because foreign policy-making is an ongoing affair, requiring continuous study of changing situations and reinterpretation of such plans.[3]

A number of analysts, primarily practitioners and observers of diplomacy, acknowledge planning to be an art. On the other hand, very few proclaim it to be a science, perhaps because in the real world it is not reducible to laboratory tests. Those who address the planning function with a view to the prediction of outcomes, regard them as uncertain at best, thus belieing the scientific treatment of the conduct of foreign affairs. And yet, the very purpose of planning is to systematize rational behavior by interrelating all of its components in order to avoid more haphazard and hazardous policy-making and implementation. While planning, therefore, is clearly an art, it also represents an attempt to approximate the techniques and benefits of scientific method, and may also be regarded as a craft.

Interpretations of Planning

The essence of planning--to devise or project a method or course of action--is a rational procedure, according to Joseph Frankel, for "ascertaining the possibility or the degree of likelihood of the need for taking decisions in the future" or for the making "of decisions in advance, on the assumption that the situation would be more or less as envisaged by the planners."[4] Others describe it as "thinking ahead with a view to action," or "an organic ingredient in the whole process of conducting foreign affairs;" as relating current actions "to future consequences and objectives;" and as conceiving of "specific objectives in particular theaters of activity" and determining "how to move forward towards those objectives under rapidly changing operational circumstances."[5]

"Planning like any other intellectual activity," observes Morgan, discussing policy planning in the United States, "can be viewed as a process of problem solving."[6] Franklin Lindsay, who analyzes foreign relations program planning, defines it as "the process by which policy objectives are translated into action programs of the scope, magnitude, and timing required for their realization." Relating this to requisite resources, he adds: "Because today's policies require massive applications of manpower, money and facilities--and because it takes time to bring these assets into being--we must increasingly *anticipate* the needs posed by our objectives."[7]

Robert L. Rothstein, examining the matter of planning in some detail, calls it an abstraction ordained "to control or limit uncertainty" in a field that is "dominated by a high degree of uncertainty," to conceptualize the "why," "what," and "how" questions in international affairs, and to assist the policy maker in his task of producing "specific policy decisions." It is "distinguished by a deliberate and conscious effort to make choices on the basis of rationality" which he interprets as the "judicious attempt to choose the best alternative to reach a given goal."[8]

From a more technical perspective, in the opinion of the Department of State planning is "the process of decision-making for the future." Whether a specific planning operation deals mainly with setting objectives, predicting contingencies, or devising programs of action, "the actual process" needs to be geared "to meet the requirements previously set out for decisionmaking generally, including issue identification, 'adversary analysis,' and recommendations, requirements for implementation, and continued review and appraisal."[9]

Thus, so far as its primary ingredients are concerned, such planning constitutes the rationalization of the nation's ends and means, concrete objectives, resources, and capacities in deciding upon measures and methods to achieve desired consequences in the international environment.[10] In short:

> *Foreign relations planning is a future-oriented rational process engaged in to decide on foreign policies and other courses of action to be taken by a nation in keeping with its national interests and capabilities to achieve its basic goals and specific objectives, and on the commitment of resources required to attain them, as related to the potential consequences and the reactions of other nations.*

Characteristics and Commentary

It has been said that "planning suggests a systematic attempt to shape the future" and that it consists of four phases. These consist of specification and clarification of goals and objectives, evaluation of the condition or situation to be met, the selection of courses of action and the weighing of probable consequences of the various alternatives, and the determination of the optimum methods of carrying out the action decided upon.[11]

Listing intellectual and procedural steps in planning, regarding it largely as problem solving, Morgan describes it as selecting and formulating a problem, gathering and sifting pertinent data, developing probable solutions, and concluding with the solution judged best. If the outcome is a design for attaining a stated objective, the problem becomes how to achieve it, and the chosen solution is the course of action recommended for its accomplishment. "The conceptions of ends and means," he suggests, "grow by interaction throughout the planning process; ends take the lead in general, but it is the increasing grasp of means which shapes the pattern in detail because it is the key to solving the problem."[12]

Dealing more precisely with the sequence of steps involved in planning, and interrelating costs with needs, objectives, and commitments, Lindsay lists: the preparation of preliminary estimates of needs, an estimate of the degree to which essential requirements can be met from the resources already available, an estimate of the remaining needs that must be accommodated if the minimum objectives are to have a reasonable chance of success, and a preliminary estimate of costs and time required to provide a test of the feasibility of achieving such objectives. Only then is it reasonable to develop detailed plans.[13]

Planning is intended to enhance the conduct of foreign affairs by elevating it beyond the simple coping with day-to-day needs, reaction to current events as they occur, or contemporary crisis situations.   It is designed especially to enable a government to effectively deal with existing conditions and, with lead time, to manage future international relations.[14]   As a process it is characterized as intellectual rather than operational, and therefore is concerned more with assumptions and ideas--involving information, insights, analysis, projection, and assessment--than with the details of pragmatic methodology.[15]

In his study of basic precepts, diplomatic historian Thomas A. Bailey acknowledges that "policy planning is a complicated art" and declares that statesmen should strive for long-range major benefits rather than short-term minor gains, that although they cannot look too far ahead with assurance they should nevertheless try, and that "improvisation is a risky procedure," which may lead to cross-purposes. Like others, he also endorses the principle that "basic policies should be reexamined periodically." Wise political leaders, he believes, will constantly review the "portfolios of policies" entrusted to their care, regarding them "as evolutionary and fluid, not static and frozen."[16]

Walt W. Rostow, who directed planning in the Department of State for some years and has produced a number of essays on the subject, notes that in foreign affairs planning there is no neat beginning, middle, and end. Rather, it is an ongoing task which requires not merely "analysis and invention" but also "close attention to operational problems that have to be solved." Planners therefore must have "a true sensibility for the burdens and responsibilities" that operating colleagues must bear. On the matter of consequences, he declares that the test of the planners "lies in the results achieved rather than in abstract notions of method and procedure," that sometimes their contributions turn out "to be dry creeks" but more frequently produce results which flow "directly and promptly into the stream of national policy," and that such consideration "can contribute marginally" by providing "a tactical reserve of energy and creative initiative" and may "help develop perspective and clarify the longer-run objectives towards which the flow of policy should move."[17]

Commenting on "the attempt to plan" in projecting the future, Joseph de Rivera also develops a critique of planning by the Department of State. He claims that "very few people are concerned with coordinating one policy with another," that relatively little planning takes place in the Department largely because the bureaucracy is so busy handling the problems of the moment so that little attention is devoted to overall relationships and long-range policy, and because foreign relations planning is far more comprehensive and complex than certain other forms of planning. He also maintains that too much planning results in consensualization and compromise among particularized interests and agencies, and that incrementally much American foreign policy is simply rationalized existing policy.[18]

     The lack of planning in the foreign field, Lindsay ar-
gues, is   due to   skepticism concerning   its practical value,
produced partly by misconception of its role, and by the "operational orientation of most of the top foreign policy officials."   Executive agents   are generally   obliged by circumstances to devote their energies to practical problems that
demand immediate attention. Furthermore, he says, professional diplomats   are motivated   by the traditional perception of
diplomacy, with   negotiation--in keeping with British diplomatist Harold Nicolson's interpretation--as the core of foreign relations, but this pertains   to policy implementation
rather than   its formulation.[19]   These and other attitudinal
impediments militate against healthy   and   vigorous planning
and can be overcome only by engaging planners who are re-
lieved of operational responsibilities, but   who are nevertheless accepted by the operational bureaucracy.

     Though regarded as fashionable and important by policy
analysts, and despite its merits, planning is plagued by limitations,   difficulties,   and   obstacles.   Commenting on its
value and feasibility, Charles Burton Marshall, who served in
Department of State planning, acknowledges the complexity and
uncertainty of foreign relations as compared with other types
of policy analysis, and the fact that problems often exceed a
nation's power of ordaining and management.   He therefore
questions "the notion of the attainability of perfect foresight in the planning and perfect efficacy in the execution
of foreign policy."   He contends that "foreign policy, attempting to cope with the future, must be speculative and
chancy" and   that utility rather than perfection is the true
test of planning.[20]

     Marshall also insists that the idea that all the na-
tion's problems can be solved through "total planning" is
fallacious because, while it is feasible to plan at a given
moment on   the basis of the data at hand, it is not possible
to predetermine the planner's perspective at a later stage.
And he ridicules the exaggeration that "planning can make
everything tidy,   answer   all   problems before they happen,
foresee all   eventualities, and   prepare in advance the pat
answer for every exigency."[21] In other words, it is not a
cure-all--nor is it a substitute for common sense.

     Often a nation's foreign policy process and bureaucracy
are not readily adapted to planning, predictability is regarded as unreliable, and the nature of the views and interactions of thinkers and practitioners, and of generalists and
specialists, militate against its efficacy and success. These
and similar factors induce Rothstein to conclude: "Planning
has never been a very successful or important enterprise in
foreign affairs . . . for it is difficult to imagine an area
in which the obstacles could be more formidable."[22] Foreign
relations planning, warns Frankel, should not be exaggerated,
especially in relation to past actions, because it often a-
mounts to little more "than an analysis of past mistakes,"
in which case it may be described as "trial following the
commission of errors."[23]

Noting the difficulty that flows from divesting planning from operations in the Department of State, George Kennan, a career diplomat who also had engaged actively in planning in the Department, has written that it "has simply been a fail-ure, like all previous attempts to bring order and foresight into the designing of foreign policy by special institutional arrangements within the department . . . . The formulation of policy is the guts of the work of the department, and none of it can successfully be placed outside the hierarchy which governs operations."[24]

Institutionalization

To be useful in state practice, the planning function needs to be structured. Development was accelerated materi-ally during World War II. At the national level, the British government created FOES (Forward Operation Enemy) to coor-dinate its military and foreign offices. In the United States interdepartmental cooperation was directed by Cabinet commit-tees, SWNCC (State, War, Navy Coordinating Committee, or "Swink"), superseded by SANACC (State, Army, Navy, Air Coor-dinating Committee), and other agencies. Allied joint plan-ning was handled at the highest level at a series of summit conferences and meetings and by the United States/British Combined Chiefs of Staff (for military planning), the Euro-pean Advisory Commission, and other components of intergov-ernmental occupation machinery.

After the War, the National Security Council was created by a statute enacted by Congress in 1947 to plan and advise the President on national security affairs.[25] That same year the Policy Planning Staff was established in the Department of State (converted into the Policy Planning Council in 1961), to advise the Secretary and other ranking members of the State Department.[26] Its functions are to formulate and develop long-term programs for the attainment of policy ob-jectives, anticipate problems in foreign affairs, undertake studies and prepare reports on politico-military issues, evaluate the adequacy of current policies and make advisory recommendations on them, and integrate planning activities within the Department.[27]

Commenting on optional organizational structuring, Lind-say specifies a number of guidelines for a national planning process. These include centralized overall direction and su-pervision to guarantee completeness, balance, and timeliness; decentralization of detailed planning, to be sure that plans are grounded in reality; full-time attention to planning by a small, highly competent group; accurate estimation of costs as plans are made to provide adequate bases for budgetary de-cisions; and follow-up and review to ensure that plans are properly implemented.[28]

CONTINGENCY PLANNING

Foreign relations planning, as indicated, may serve to provide systematic consideration of interests, objectives, policies, capabilities, resources, and potential consequences in the framing of courses of action to be pursued. But much of this planning may also be applied to future contingencies --whether caused by changing conditions, new developments, or potential crises, as well as for unforeseen reactions to the nation's policy implementation.

In brief, such planning is described as: "systematic advance planning of policy and action to be pursued if and when contingencies occur,"[29] planning "which considers what should be done if some event occurs which radically departs from expectations and which may require . . . urgent action,"[30] dealing with "situations where advance planning may substantially improve this country's ability to respond effectively to the event and even exploit it to its own advantage,"[31] or simply a scheme or arrangement to cope with happenings or developments which are uncertain.

Contingency planning is common in national security and military affairs. Comparing it with foreign affairs planning, it is apparent that military problems are reasonably clear cut and are generally reducible to a manageable number of practical solutions because such factors as time, space, geography, and logistics tend to confine or restrict the number of possible courses of action to deal with them. Moreover, inasmuch as these "force factors" are calculable with some precision, the military planning process, as it relates to the ponderables of real or hypothetical situations, may result in carefully prescribed and viable results.[32] The military definition, which applies planning to major contingencies that can reasonably be anticipated, is therefore relatively simple.[33]

In foreign affairs, on the other hand, the limiting factors are more nebulous and intricate, including human elements that are difficult to isolate and prejudge, so that the number of foreseeable contingencies is greater, the specification of resources is more varied, and the task of planners is more complicated and equivocal.[34] Morton Kaplan points out that when all the important factors are considered, which themselves are contingent--such as personality, economic and political conditions, technological developments and inventions, and other intranational and transnational contributory considerations--"the complexity becomes so great that serious efforts systematically to discuss them all . . . would become lost in the detail."[35]

In practice and analysis the expression "contingency planning" is given differing interpretations, depending on whether it applies to existing, potential, or changed assumptions, circumstances, objectives, or policies. The most obvious connotation is that a contingency plan is an alternative to a basic plan and is activated only if it is necessary or desirable to deviate from the fundamental plan. In this sense it is designed to prepare to the maximum extent possible for dealing with a situation under conditions deemed less likely to materialize than those anticipated on the basis of which the original plan is prepared. Or it may be viewed as an alternative plan (or set of coequal plans) for a given contingency that may change as situational factors, interests, or policies change.

But the concept may also be held to mean that separate plans are devised to be applied to different sets of contingencies, and these may be either linked or unlinked. Salience and value in judging contingency planning depends on which of these interpretations is applied, and whether such planning pertains to policy-making or to its implementation. Acknowledging the desirability of policy elasticity, Winston Churchill has observed: "The best method of acquiring flexibility is to have three or four plans for all the probable contingencies, all worked out with the utmost detail. Then it is much easier to switch from one to the other as and where the cat jumps."[36]

Relating the present to the future, according to Burton Sapin, contingency planning energizes "thinking ahead systematically and in depth about some problem or situation with a view to doing something about it in the present." It is posited on the assumption that such thinking promises enough practical policy payoffs to warrant substantial investment in time and effort.[37] Opinions differ, however, on the merits of its practical application. For example, Rostow, who adopts a limited view, contends that it is not applicable to "certain abstract future circumstances," but rather "to conceive of specific objectives" and to determine "how to move forward towards those objectives under rapidly changing operational circumstances."[38] Rothstein claims that it deals "neither with strategic alternatives nor policy guidance" but only with "possible responses to likely and unlikely specific events."[39]

Others apply the concept not merely to contemporary problems and circumstances, but also to long-term projections and hypothetical probabilities. Thus, Morgan states categorically that "contingency planning is akin to long-range planning in that it may reach years ahead, though against an unspecified date rather than across an approximate time span,"[40] and John Ausland and Hugh Richardson declare that contingency plans "examine possible alternative responses to hypothetical events or situations" and prescribe preferences respecting possible responses.[41]

Nevertheless, there is considerable consensus that it is unnecessary and wasteful, if not unrealistic, to expect planners to prepare for every conceivable international contingency.[42] As a consequence, intelligence must be applied both to preparing for contingencies and to the matter of selecting the most likely, important, and critical contingencies--so that planning does not degenerate into an end in itself.

RESULTS OF PLANNING

To generalize, the progeny of planning is obviously a design for action--a program or scheme that specifies courses of conduct that relate to the other factors in the policy-making equation--or it comprises the rationalized measures or means projected to achieve the ends desired by the nation. This end product may be simple or complex, it may be articulated as a basic precept or distilled proposition, or it may provide an intricate exposition of primary and lesser foreign

relations objectives and substantive and procedural policies.
It may apply globally, regionally, or more specifically to
individual countries, or to functional topics or individual
situations and crises. It is clear that no plan is likely to
be perfect and that, no matter how well it is designed, its
value hinges on how determined its implementers are to make
it succeed.[43]

Among the most serious criticisms of foreign affairs
planning is the contention that all too often the outcome
represents a synthesized and watered down compromise among
competing perspectives, interests, and purposes produced by
bargaining and concession among opposing pressures and
groups. Many perceive the planning process as possessing
such distinct advantages as reasoned and deliberate initiation, the systematizing of policy-making, and the consideration and assessment of alternatives. But some consider the
consensualized results extenuated and diluted. The issue,
therefore, is not the intrinsic merit of planning, but rather
the manner in which it is employed.[44] To some extent this is
a problem of strengthening the coordination of design and operations, and of aligning the thinking of the conceptualist
and theorist with that of the practitioner.

Another criticism is that prediction is scientifically
impossible. It must be realized that the very nature of international politics renders "scientific" prognostication
with certainty as visionary, which, at best, is uncertain and
fallible. Nevertheless, it constitutes an integral ingredient
of the planning process--with respect to developments, foreign reactions, outcomes, and other factors. It is incumbent
on the planners, in coping with innumerable "if-then" equations, to apply human intelligence to produce rational judgments concerning their choices and the probabilities.[45]

"Sensible decision-making," notes Rothstein, "is impossible without a serious commitment to planning, and planning
is impossible without a serious commitment to prediction."
Moreover, planning prediction "is one of the areas in which
collaboration between theorists and practitioners is most
likely to be fruitful," he maintains, because "prediction is
a practical necessity that is done best when it rests on
sound theoretical principles or at least uses the best knowledge and methods that the theoretical world can offer."
Even though limitations and uncertainties permeate forecasting in international affairs, there is little choice but to
attempt to plan and predict as well as possible, "for the
alternative is not to eliminate the need for planning and
prediction but to do them without skill, without commitment,
and without understanding."[46]

Evaluating foreign affairs planning in general, Morgan
concludes that it is necessary and dynamic, and can be energizing, and the quest for excellence must be pursued with
sincerity and vigor. To be most meritorious, it must be for
the benefit of the nation--not for the enhancement of some
lesser interests. "Its finest fruit," he believes, "may be
troubles that never occur." At the same time, as suggested,
planning is no panacea. "We must shun delusions of omnipo-
tence which project habits of domestic mastery into expecta-

tions of perpetual prosperity abroad. Our strongest effort, however brilliantly planned," Morgan cautions, "can only be a fractional factor in the total sweep of historic causation. But that fraction may make the difference between success and failure."[47]

FOREIGN RELATIONS STRATEGIES

Today the term "strategy" is widely and variously employed. Initially derived from the Greek, it meant "the art of the general" or "generalship" and was conceived as the art and science of employing armed forces to secure the objects of public policy by the application of force or the threat of force. On the other hand, the expression "tactics" refers to the factors or measures set in motion by strategy. Alfred T. Mahan, American naval historian, bases his distinction on the operational contact of military forces, applying tactics to localized hostilities when adversaries are in actual contact, whereas strategy denotes the basic disposition of forces that contribute to the entire conduct of a campaign or a war. Strategy analyst Bernard Brodie interprets this comparison as complementary aspects of actual fighting and the planning of the fighting.

Development of the Concept

Merely surveying some highlights, early contributions to strategic analysis include the maxims of Sun Tzu (*The Art of War*, 500 B.C.), and the chronicles of Xenophon and Thucydides (on Greek generalship), Vegetius (*The Military Institutions of the Romans*, 390 A.D. which deals more with tactics than strategy), and Niccolo Machiavelli (*Art of War*, 1521).[48] Napoleon Bonaparte's postulates pertain more validly to modern times. Karl von Clausewitz, Prussian general and writer on land warfare in the early nineteenth century, originated the notion of limited war, distinguished between strategy and tactics, and by his frequently quoted statement that "war is a mere continuation of politics by other means," introduced the philosophic perception that stressed the primacy of the nation's political objectives.

Mahan, who produced a major geopolitical theory of strategy, analyzed the principle of the command of the sea, distinguishing between attaining command and exercising it. Giulio Douhet (Italian), Billy Mitchell (American), and Lord Trenchard (British) early developed principles of air strategy. Subsequently dozens of others contributed to the refinements of military science and, since World War II, to superpower and nuclear strategy.

Beginning in the early twentieth century, such contributions were supplemented with officially prescribed "principles of warfare," codifying basic maxims for military strategy and tactics. Currently military establishments and institutional research agencies engage in intensive scrutiny of a host of military issues, strategic theories and doctrines, policy models and paradigms, and strategic planning, as well as more concrete matters such as balance of forces,

nuclear and conventional weapons systems, nuclear and limited
warfare, guerilla and unconventional hostilities, the arms
race, massive and minimal deterrence, strategic sufficiency
and flexibility, conflict management, and the teaching of
strategic studies.[49]

Although some earlier military analysts related military
operations to political objectives and policies, it was not
until recent times that the understanding of strategy was
both broadened and multifurcated. Since World War II intense
interest has developed in the planning and analysis of foreign relations strategy, adding new concepts of "national
strategy" and "grand strategy" to differentiate them from
purely military affairs. Military strategy has been generically defined as a planned mode of action or operation, but
attention has also been paid to many nonmilitary institutions
and fields of inquiry and activity. To cite a few of the more
obvious, these embrace politics, parliamentary and bureaucratic procedure, diplomacy, negotiation and bargaining, law
enforcement and litigation, business and corporate affairs,
management theory and practice, labor relations, sports and
games, and the study of "policy science" and decision-making.

In a broad sense, strategy now permeates all phases of
human face-to-face interrelations, calculated gamelike aspects of human dealings which sociologist Erving Goffman
calls "strategic interaction," and human performance in competition, contests, and conflicts.[50] And it is the subject
of attention, not only of statesmen, politicians, and foreign
affairs experts, but also of those concerned with economics,
philosophy, psychology, sociology, and even medicine and
evangelism. As a result, since World War II scores of volumes, dozens of studies, reports, and addresses, and hundreds
of articles and other commentaries have been produced enrich-
ing the mushrooming literary resources on the subject.

Interpretations

The dictionary definition of strategy describes it as a
plan, method, or series of maneuvers or strategems to obtain
a specific objective or result. It is perceived as "an overall plan" for accomplishing the nation's goals and objectives,[51] "an overall view" of a situation "to offer criteria
for distinguishing useful from less useful means, and criteria for organising these means into a coherent and purposeful
whole,"[52] "a plan for the employment of resources for the attainment of a predetermined end,"[53] "the art of using power
for the attainment of goals in competition,"[54] and "an inherent element of statecraft at all times."[55]

The purposes of strategy are to pursue or change the
status quo and to distribute and apply "means to fulfill the
ends of policy,"[56] "to advance the interests" of the nation
while preventing other countries "from impinging on such interests,"[57] and to maximize net gains and minimize net losses.[58] It "connotes perspective, the selection of the right
priorities, relating the parts to the whole."[59] It is "seldom revealed in any one decision," but grows out of "a series
of cumulative decisions."[60]

Strategy is distinguishable from foreign policy, but there are those who treat them synonymously[61] or call strategy a "policy of execution."[62] Whereas policy is recognized as a course of action to achieve objectives, strategy is a broader concept in that it constitutes a plan for putting the policy into operation and therefore correlates policy to the determination of locus, timing, issue, and commitment of resources. As a matter of fact, Henry Kissinger asserts that "Policy and strategy merge at every point."[63]

Until World War II the term strategy was largely a military concept, but as noted by Harold and Margaret Sprout, "Today the term is applied to operational plans in all sorts of situations involving the interaction of adverse parties." In the field of international politics, they say, "strategy has come to denote the operational plans in accord with which governments manipulate *all kinds* of instrumentalities--nonmilitary as well as military--in their efforts to accomplish desired objectives vis-à-vis other nations."[64] This broadened depiction, according to John P. Lovell, "can be used to refer to any predesigned set of moves, or series of decisions, in a competitive situation where the outcome is not governed purely by chance."[65]

Consequently these and other interpretations intimate that in international relations strategy is a plan for the preparation of which all of the components of the anatomy of foreign affairs are integrated into a rationalized operational program. In other words:

> *Foreign relations strategy is a plan of action to promote a nation's interests and ideals in the pursuit of its purposes, basic goals, and concrete policy objectives, by means of substantive and procedural foreign policies for the implementation of which the nation commits its political, economic, diplomatic, military, psychological, and moral resources.*

Differentiation from Foreign Policy Plans and Tactics

Thus interpreted, strategy needs to be distinguished not only from foreign policy, but also from tactics and, in its generic form, from specific types of strategies. The expressions "plans" and "strategies" are used interchangeably and, if they are to be differentiated, the former is regarded as broader in scope in that all foreign relations strategies are plans, but many plans cannot be designated as strategies.

Plans may vary from goal articulation to implementation, from substantive to procedural policy, and from short-range to long-term, situational to broad-scale, and localized or regional to global considerations. The concept of strategy, on the other hand, is applied to the more important, concretized plans designed to achieve predetermined objectives in a particular way. While as lexicographical expressions "plans" and "strategies" may be differentiable, in practical and analytical usage they are often synonymized.

More significant, as suggested earlier, is the distinction between strategy and tactics. In military parlance tactics are sub-plans or maneuvers prescribed to effectuate a
strategy. The military deliberately distinguishes between
strategic and tactical forces, weapons systems, and plans. In
foreign relations literature the concept of tactical plans
and techniques is rarely discussed either at length or in
depth, perhaps because it is taken for granted that they sup-
plement fundamental policy strategy. Karl Deutsch mentions
in passing that "tactical moves" are components of strategy.[66]   John E. Kieffer calls tactics "the process of conducting single actions" (which combined with others constitute strategy),[67] and Harry Howe Ransom maintains they are
methods of "execution of strategic plans in an operational
sense,"[68] whereas Frederick Hartmann views "tactical plans"
as supportive of a "strategic conception."[69]

Despite this simple conceptual difference between strategy and tactics, in the actual practice of designing foreign
policy their interrelation is often confusing. As the policy
complex is extrapolated (as indicated in Chapter 6), each
sub-component may be perceived as tactical in that it is intended to support and implement or operationalize a more general or important element. Procedural policies usually fall
into this category, and perhaps to minimize confusion some
writers prefer to speak of fundamental strategic doctrines
and tactical means of execution.

National Strategies

In the realm of foreign affairs the most material variation to be noted is "national strategy" as a distinct form of
strategy. Ransom has observed that following World War II, as
distinctions were drawn between military strategy and "higher," "grand," and "national" strategy, their scope was extended to encompass non-military areas of policy planning.[70]
In the United States the military also acknowledges this by
expanding its purview to amalgamate political, economic, and
psychological with military factors--to which some commentators add social, cultural, moral, spiritual, and other considerations.

At times the terms "general," "higher," "national,"
"grand," and "global" strategy are used interchangeably.
"General strategy" is described as the art and science of
controlling the sum total of the nation's powers in time of
war or peace, "higher strategy" simply denotes a more basic
and general form than purely military strategy, and "global
strategy" carries a geographic connotation.[71]

Most analysts who distinguish foreign relations from
military strategy prefer the expressions "national strategy"
and "grand strategy." The French commentator André Beaufre
calls national strategy an American innovation and claims
that the British prefer "grand strategy," for which the
French use "total strategy."[72] These denote the mobilization
and use of all the resources of the nation to achieve its
goals and objectives. By these designations some writers
imply a single, overall or completely integrated plan,[73]

whereas others, although they employ the concept in the singular, infer that a country may simultaneously have more
than one national strategy. To   illustrate, it may be feasible for it to have separate but related national strategies
for particular geographic areas and diverse functional topics, such as national security, arms proliferation and control, trade, alliances, international integration, outer
space exploration and utilization, and others.

     As applied to foreign affairs national strategy has been
described as "a redoubtable and significant agent of policy"
which "sets the direction of national effort, marshalls national resources," and prescribes "operations necessary for
the attainment of national political objectives."[74] Such an
interpretation differs little from definitions of strategy in
general except that national strategy is more basic, comprehensive, and long-range, in pursuit of important political as
well as security results, involves the totality of the nation's capabilities, non-military as well as military, for
its implementation, and is formulated at the highest political levels.

     A country's national strategy is rarely embodied in a
single document.   Nor is a single, integrated, and inclusive
national strategy likely to be fabricated to cover the gamut
of contemporary international issues.   For example, a nation's strategies might prescribe noninvolvement in one geographic area and active involvement in another, or they may
provide for endorsement of unilateral action respecting one
type of activity and multilateral endeavors in others. Norman Padelford and George Lincoln suggest that to promote national security they range from nonresistance, neutralism,
nonalignment, and unilateral programs, through various forms
of collective security, to the aggressive use of military
force.[75] Multiple national strategies afford the nation
greater flexibility respecting its disparate objectives, policies, and procedures, but are bound to be most effective if
they are sufficiently extensible or general to allow for
pragmatic treatment of lesser day-to-day problems, the development of tactical methods, crisis management, and contingency planning.

     Grand Strategies

     Some writers prefer the expression "grand strategy" but
fail to distinguish it from national strategy.[76] British usage and the French employment of "total strategy" denote a
single, all embracing, higher national strategy which differentiates it in terms of "scope," "significance," and "duration." In military analysis, grand strategy constitutes an
over-all plan to win a war, as compared with winning in a
particular theater of hostilities or a specific battle or
skirmish.

     Liddell Hart, British analyst who is primarily concerned
with military affairs, and is alleged to have conceived the
notion of "grand strategy," delineates it as "higher strategy," embodying both military plans and political policies
ordained to establish the kind of settlement the nation de-

sires to govern post-hostilities peace. In this sense grand strategy entails the practical necessity of adapting overall military planning to the political objectives of war and the nation's fundamental goals and policies.[77]

Michael Howard perceives it more liberally as covering "those industrial, financial, demographic, and societal aspects of war that have become so salient in the twentieth century" thought of the Western powers.[78] West German statesman Helmut Schmidt defines grand strategy even more broadly to encompass the interrelated political, economic, and military goals of the nation that are embodied in "a unifying concept" to guide the nation's international relations, but he also applies it as a higher strategy than that of a single nation.[79]

A different interpretation regards grand strategy as special in terms of importance. In this guise it is often employed as a basic politico-military strategy for the nation's survival, defense, and security--sometimes related specifically to post-World War II nuclear power and relations.[80] Edward M. Earle describes it as: "The highest type of strategy . . . which so directs and integrates the policies and armaments of the nation that the resort to war is either rendered unnecessary or is undertaken with the maximum chances of victory."[81] Implicit in this version is the notion of "total diplomacy," which Richard Snyder and Edgar Furniss depict as "a general policy" and mode of international conduct "that is designed to produce those external political conditions most conducive to the security needs of the nation."[82]

This version of grand strategy may be pragmatically elaborated as a "grand alliance" or "grand design." Examples include the Grand Alliance of 1689 (consisting of England, Austria, and other states that fought against Louis XIV of France), the "Grand Coalition" (England and those continental European powers that were at war with Napolean early in the nineteenth century), and the anti-Axis coalition or "Grand Alliance" of World War II.[83]

Equally relevant is the "Grand Design," or Henry IV's seventeenth-century strategy to organize Europe into fifteen relatively equal powers united in an international system to maintain the peace among them and to jointly achieve ascendency over outside powers.[84] More recent strategies propounded for organizing the society of nations to stabilize geopolitical relations and maintain the peace embrace the nineteenth-century Holy Alliance (the brainchild of Czar Alexander I of Russia) and the Concert of Europe, as well as the twentieth century plans for the League of Nations and the United Nations,[85] the global integration strategies of Clarence Streit and other World Federalists,[86] the North Atlantic Alliance, and the proposals of the 1950s for European unification.[87]

In addition, there are the post-World War II "grand designs" identified with such statesmen as Franklin Roosevelt (collective security and political integration of the wartime anti-Axis aggregation), Josef Stalin (Russian hegemonism and

political control in Eastern Europe and north Asia), Harry
Truman (containment and the Truman Doctrine), George Marshall
(assistance for post-World War II European reconstruction),
Charles de Gaulle (revival of French grandeur by creating a
United Europe, dissolving of the North Atlantic Alliance and
the Warsaw Pact, and neutralizing Central Europe), and Richard Nixon and Henry Kissinger (detente, rapprochement, creating a stable world order based on negotiations along a broad
front, and the linkage principle).[88]

To a large extent, regardless of intent, only with hindsight will these strategies warrant the designation "grand"
designs. Nevertheless, they and other grand strategies coalesce certain national policies and override others, and they
may change from era to era, country to country, and even administration to administration, but they may produce historic
legacies.

Characteristics and Commentary

Contemplating the calculating nature of purposeful
strategy, it is held to differ from other approaches to national verbal behavior "in that it proposes the planned, deliberate development and use of principles, concepts, and
enunciated norms as a conscious part of the conduct of foreign policy." Such articulated strategy, like other aspects
of foreign relations decision-making "introduces into the
weighing of policy options an awareness that actions taken
must also be explained and that the explanation may be in the
long run more costly or more beneficial to the national interest than the act itself."[89] In other words, strategies
must be consciously and teleologically devised, with attention paid to feasibility and consequences as well as to desires and substance.

The principal conditions or variables in determining
foreign affairs strategies, notes K. J. Holsti, include the
structure of the international system, the nature of the nation's domestic attitudes and socio-economic needs, the degree to which policy makers perceive a persistent external
threat to the nation's own values and interests, and its geographic location, topographical characteristics, and endow-
ment in natural resources.[90]

Aside from assessing the status and import of these factors, the policy maker must ask and respond to a series of
pertinent questions that entwine the nation's ends and means.
For example, what national interests are at stake, and are
they vital to the welfare of the nation? What are its general goals and concrete policy objectives? Which nations can
realistically contravene these objectives, and which may support them? In terms of resources, is the nation capable of
implementing the strategies under consideration, and is the
nation's will devoted to the fulfillment of its commitments?
How can the nation succeed in achieving its aims at a minimum
cost? Equally important, according to Frederick Hartmann, is
the sequence in which the questions are raised. Deciding on
the nation's interests and objectives is critical and must
come first, he says, before any attempt is made to formulate

policy and decide what should be done.[91]

The rationale of foreign affairs strategy, observes Lovell, who considers it largely as denoting a contest, requires assiduous attention to "cost-gain estimates." In his view strategy is essentially a plan for achieving success in a competitive international environment--a scheme by which policy makers seek to advance the interests and aims of the nation while preventing others from impairing them. In such contestation, therefore, there are two coordinate ingredients of strategy: an offensive component ("the design for making gains") and a defensive element ("the design for preventing losses"). The offensive strategy needs to embody considerations of "not only the possible rewards to be derived from particular actions, but also the chances of success and the estimated costs of the actions." The defensive strategy, in addition to these factors, also addresses the prevention of actions by others that would threaten the nation's interests, and responses to such threats in the event that prevention fails.[92]

Georg Schwarzenberger suggests seven fundamental pragmatic foreign affairs strategies of nations--he calls them "strategic objects of foreign policy" or "patterns of action"--that have varied little in the course of modern history. These embrace isolationism (and nonalignment or neutralism)--postures that are most innocuous and inoffensive in international politics; alliances--arrangements providing for mutual assistance and alignment of national policies and power; guarantees--commitments by greater powers to maintain the independence, neutrality, or noninvolvement of lesser nations; balance of power--equilibrium among competing and contesting nations (discussed in Chapter 7); imperialism--territorial annexation, colonial subjugation, or domination by indirect means; hegemonism--discreet imperialist control that obliges a weaker nation to regard compliance with the wishes of the stronger power as preferable to insistence on unquestioned sovereign independence and rights; and universalism--the supersession of international society and its replacement by a universal state or some lesser integrative form of unification.[93]

Volumes have been written on the nature of strategic inquiry--much of it centering on military and national security affairs.[94] Bernard Brodie summarizes the basic categories of analysis as the formulation and intellectual testing of new strategic concepts by a variety of analytical schemes (including gaming), the formulation of national security policy recommendations concerning particular regions, and recommendations on the selection of weapons systems on the basis of "cost-effectiveness"--how to achieve the greatest value for any given sum of money or, conversely, how to get a high level of potential at minimum cost.[95] These same categories are applicable to foreign affairs strategy, whether it focuses on territorial jurisdiction, alliance formation, international amalgamation, crisis management, trade, foreign assistance, international terrorism, or other issues, subject to interpreting Brodie's reference to weapons systems as diplomatic, negotiatory, and similar techniques.

Also relating costs to benefits, Hartmann presents a series of guidelines for success by discussing ways in which foreign relations strategies may fail. These, he suggests, are if alternative strategic conceptions are not explored, if the strategy "is no real plan but simply a jumble of incompatible hopes," if the strategy departs from the fundamental values of the nation and eventually fails to be supported, if it is frustrated by lack of coordination or by defects in the governmental mechanism, if there is inadequate national power backing, if the strategy is designed to deal with an imaginary world rather than the real world or if reality changes and the plan is not flexible enough to adjust, or if it runs into impedient or overwhelming opposition by other nations. "Failures in organization and application," he concludes, "will be very important but failures in conceptualization will be critical."[96]

Paralleling these interrogatory canons, Thomas A. Bailey prescribes, in addition to those specified in earlier chapters, such guiding precepts for planning and executing strategy as sound information is the taproot of sound policy, internal disunity devitalizes and criticism at home weakens foreign relations abroad, flexibility facilitates and consistency clarifies policy, keep the diplomatic initiative, come to terms with the inevitable, nations that drift with events may become their victims, naivety is the foe of reality, never slam doors, make reasons realistic and pretexts plausible, know your adversary, and take advantage of your adversary's domestic difficulties.[97]

The instruments of strategy harmonize with the instruments of international affairs and diplomacy. These run the gamut from negotiation, bargaining, and compromise to economic (trade and aid), psychological (information and disinformation programs, propaganda, and psychological warfare), power (capability, influence, and persuasion), and military (force and the threat of force) methods of implementation. When pragmatized these constitute either substrategies or tactics.[98]

Discussing the strategy of conflict, Thomas Schelling defines "strategic moves" as those actions that influence other nations' choices in a favorable manner by affecting the other nations' expectations on how the operative nation will behave. The object, he contends, is to "communicate persuasively" to other nations "a mode of behavior" that leaves to the other nation "a simple maximization problem whose solution . . . is the optimum for one's self, and to destroy the other's ability to do the same."[99]

PRAGMATIZATION OF STRATEGIES

Turning from analysis of the concept to usage, many illustrations may be cited. For example, in *The Prince* Machiavelli espoused a sixteenth-century strategy for Italian principalities to unify in order to regain the stature and domination of ancient Rome, which he regarded as the high point of human achievement.[100] Subsequently Richelieu, Sebastien de Vauban, Frederick the Great, Napoleon Bonaparte, Antoine

Henri Jomini, Karl von Clausewitz, and a host of other military theorists and planners amplified and modified strategic doctrine.[101]

During the past century a series of broad-scale geopolitical strategies were also propounded to augment rulership and national security.[102] Friedrich Ratzel, a German geographer, posed most of the major subjects embodied in geopolitics and considered warfare as an integral subject of both politics and geography.[103] More philosophical in his theorizing, Mahan, American apostle of naval might, wrote widely between 1890 and World War I on the impact of maritime strength upon history and he endorsed the principle that, to be a great nation, it had to be a great naval power.[104]

During the decade prior to World War I, British geographer Sir Halford Mackinder proposed an antipodal geopolitical theory in which he conceived the concept of the Eurasian Heartland (extending from the Elbe River to the Ural Mountains) which would be self-sufficient. He claimed that the nation that controlled it could dominate the Afro-Eurasian landmass--or the "World Island"--and therefore the rest of the world, because it would be secure against sea power.[105] In 1922 Karl Haushofer, a German geographer, founded an Institute of Geopolitics in Munich, launched the monthly *Zeitschrift für Geopolitik (Journal of Geopolitics)* two years later, and developed his "new science" of geostrategy. Hitler based his pan-Germanism and *Lebensraum* expansionism on Haushofer's doctrines, seeking to implement Mackinder's original proposition.[106]

Nicholas Spykman, American desciple of geopolitics, writing at the time of World War II and reacting to the Heartland theory, propounded his "Rimland" strategy. He asserted that enduring peace depends on a stable balance and concert among such "island nations" as the United States and Britain and such Heartland powers as Russia and China--the Big Four coalition during the early 1940s--to prevent any nation from gaining control of the Heartland.[107]

Since World War II some geopolitical enthusiasts have turned to the idea that in the current era the decisive powers will need to be important continental nations, such as China, the Soviet Union, and the United States. Even in the case of the Soviet Union, although Communist doctrine is essentially grounded on Marxist-Leninist dialectic theory of historical inevitability as applied to "socialism," it appears that, so far as its imperialism and hegemonism are concerned, it acts on the basis of a modified mixture of the Heartland and continental power doctrines.[108] Today most thinkers disavow the validity and reliability of geopolitics as a credible science and ridicule geographic determinism. But this fails to deny either its past production of geostrategic propositions or their influence on then contemporary leaders and history.

Inasmuch as they are held to be plans of action to achieve determined objectives, the diplomatic history of nations and their international politics provide many examples of national strategies--whether they are called basic poli-

cies, doctrines, plans, or strategies. In the case of the
United States, in addition to the Monroe Doctrine (enunciated
in 1823 to apply to the independent countries of the Western
Hemisphere and amplified by treaty commitment in the Rio Pact
in 1947) and the nexus of policy statements, diplomatic
notes, agreements, and actions commencing in 1899 known as
the "Open Door," more recent history records a series of
American "doctrines." These bear the names of specific Pres-
idents--Truman, Eisenhower, Johnson, Nixon, Carter, and Reagan. Occasionally they are associated with a Secretary of
State, such as the Stimson Non-Recognition Doctrine.[109]

Others, in recent years, called plans,[110] are attributed
to Henry Morgenthau, Jr. (to reduce post-World War II Germany
to an agrarian state), and George C. Marshall (to assist the
free nations of Europe in their postwar economic recovery and
rehabilitation). Or they are designated as programs, such as
Lend-Lease (during World War II), Technical Assistance (Truman's Point Four Program), and the "Alliance for Progress"
(development assistance for the Western Hemisphere). Occasionally strategies are embodied in legislative resolutions,
represented by the Fulbright (1943), Vandenberg (1948), Ton-
kin Gulf (1964), and War Powers (1973) resolutions.

Frequently strategies are simply called policies. They
may be general, as evidenced in American diplomatic history
by self-determination, isolationism, inter-Americanism and
good neighborism, continental expansion and manifest destiny,
free trade and the most-favored-nation principle, freedom of
the seas and airspace, peaceful settlement of disputes (good
offices and mediation, conciliation, arbitration, and adjudication), collective security and international cooperation,
open diplomacy, and arms limitation. All of these have been
widespread and complex in application, but not all have been
consistently implemented in specific instances when they were
not regarded as consonent with American national interests.[111]

Others have been applied in post-World War II East-West
relations, such as containment, liberation of East European
Communist countries, coexistence, bipolarity and tripolarity,
detente, and rapprochement. Specific strategies have dealt
with arms control and nuclear power and weaponry, including
massive retaliation, deterrence, limited assured destruction,
first and second strike capabilities, and flexible response
in United States/Soviet relations. Still others apply to
nuclear nonproliferation; arms limitation and reduction (un-
derground, limited, and total test bans, strategic offensive
and lesser range nuclear arms, anti-ballistic missile systems, and the strategic defense initiative); nuclear weapons
in the Antarctic, on the seabed, and in outer space; and the
prevention of the outbreak of nuclear war.

So long as it is a planned course of action that is
overtly implemented, each of these and similar doctrines,
declarations, programs, and policies may be held to constitute a national strategy. They may be rendered operational
by repeated articulation, legislation, executive proclama-
tion, or treaties and agreements. Some are fundamental and
long range (i.e., self-determination and freedom of the

seas), others are basic but intermediate in range (i.e., containment and massive retaliation), and a few may be of limited duration or be rapidly superseded. At times they are complementary (i.e., isolation and neutrality or international integration and peaceful settlement), and occasionally they may be antithetical (i.e., non-involvement and alliances).

A few of these may come to bear the rank of grand strategies, and others may be long range in intent but short lived in practice. Most are flexible in that they are subject to interpretation and adjustment as conditions change. And, as suggested in Chapter 6, some are general and comprehensive, supported by subsidiary substantive and procedural elements, comprising intricate complexes of policies and specific methods for carrying them into effect.

NOTES

1. Hugh Gibson, *The Road to Foreign Policy* (Garden City, N.Y.: Doubleday, Doran, 1944), pp. 11-12; see also his Chapter 2.

2. George Allen Morgan, "Planning in Foreign Affairs: The State of the Art," *Foreign Affairs* 39 (January 1961): 271.

3. Feliks Gross, *Foreign Policy Analysis* (New York: Philosophical Library, 1954), p. 45; and James L. McCamy, *Conduct of the New Diplomacy* (New York: Harper and Row, 1964), pp. 39-42.

4. Joseph Frankel, *The Making of Foreign Policy: An Analysis of Decision Making* (New York: Oxford University Press, 1963), pp. 180-82.

5. See, respectively, Morgan, "Planning in Foreign Affairs," p. 271; Robert R. Bowie, *Shaping the Future: Foreign Policy in an Age of Transition* (New York: Columbia University Press, 1964), p. 82; and Walt W. Rostow, "The Planning of Foreign Policy," Chapter 3 in *The Dimensions of Diplomacy*, edited by E. A. J. Johnson (Baltimore: Johns Hopkins Press, 1964), p. 43. For commentary on these, see Robert L. Rothstein, *Planning, Prediction, and Policymaking in Foreign Affairs* (Boston: Little, Brown, 1972), pp. 82-83.

6. Morgan, "Planning in Foreign Affairs," p. 272.

7. Franklin L. Lindsay, "Program Planning: The Missing Element," *Foreign Affairs* 39 (January 1961): 280.

8. Rothstein, *Planning, Prediction, and Policymaking in Foreign Affairs*, pp. 89-96.

9. Department of State, *Diplomacy for the 70's: A Program of Management Reform for the Department of State* (Washington: Government Printing Office, 1970), p. 348.

10. It is interesting to note that interpretations of planning usually emphasize objectives, policies, resources, and consequences, and that it is future oriented, but few include national interests and national power in discussing planning.

11. See Charles E. Rothwell, foreword to *The Policy Sciences*, edited by Daniel Lerner and Harold D. Lasswell (Stanford: Stanford University

Press, 1951), p. ix.

12. Morgan, "Planning in Foreign Affairs," pp. 272-74.

13. Lindsay, "Program Planning," pp. 287-88.

14. See Rothstein, *Planning, Prediction, and Policymaking in Foreign Affairs*, pp. 93-94. For additional commentary on the purpose of planning, see Lindsay, "Program Planning," p. 283. In practice the planner, according to Rostow, does not face a choice between long-term and short-term interests, but "must combine them" because to produce desired results in the future he "must concern himself not merely with goals but also with how to get from here to there." See Rostow, "The Planning of Foreign Policy," pp. 42-43.

15. See Rothstein, *Planning, Prediction, and Policymaking in Foreign Affairs*, p. 93. See also commentary in *American Strategy for the Nuclear Age*, edited by Walter F. Hahn and John C. Neff (Garden City, N.Y.: Doubleday, 1960), pp. 442-43, which stresses lead time for survival; and Rothstein, *Planning, Prediction, and Policymaking in Foreign Affairs*, pp. 83-84, 92-99 on short- and long-term planning.

16. Thomas A. Bailey, *The Art of Diplomacy: The American Experience* (New York: Appleton-Century-Crofts, 1968), pp. 90-91, 95, 99-100.

17. "The Planning of Foreign Policy," pp. 41, 47, 49-52, 54.

18. Joseph de Rivera, *The Psychological Dimension of Foreign Policy* (Columbus, Ohio: Merrill, 1968), pp. 98-104.

19. "Program Planning," pp. 282-83. For criticism of the aversion of professional diplomats to planning, see also Smith Simpson, *Anatomy of the State Department* (Boston: Houghton Mifflin, 1967), pp. 24, 41.

20. Charles Burton Marshall, *The Limits of Foreign Policy* (New York: Holt, 1954), pp. 15, 17-18, 25, 27.

21. Charles Burton Marshall, "The Nature of Foreign Policy," *Department of State Bulletin* 26 (March 17, 1952): 418-19.

22. Rothstein, *Planning, Prediction, and Policymaking in Foreign Affairs*, pp. 3-4, 12, 97, 110-13, 191. See his Chapter 2 for discussion of such obstacles.

23. Frankel, *The Making of Foreign Policy*, pp. 182-83.

24. George F. Kennan, *Memoirs, 1925-1950* (Boston: Little, Brown, 1967), p. 467. For criticism of State Department planners' failure to produce a basic foreign policy plan, see Simpson, *Anatomy of the State Department*, pp. 24, 122, 246, and for commentary on the distinction between planning and operations and criticism of planning by "Country Directors," see William I. Bacchus, *Foreign Policy and the Bureaucratic Process: The Department of State's Country Director System* (Princeton: Princeton University Press, 1974), pp. 92-96.

25. For bibliographical guidance to literature on the National Security Council system, see Elmer Plischke, *U.S. Foreign Relations: A Guide to Information Sources* (Detroit: Gale Research, 1980), pp. 241-47. For a Congressional study, see the reports of the Jackson Subcommittee of the Senate Committee on Government Operations, *Organizing for National*

Security, 3 vols. (Washington: Government Printing Office, 1961) and *Administration of National Security* (Washington: Government Printing Office, 1963-1964). See also *The National Security Council,* edited by Henry M. Jackson (New York: Praeger, 1965).

26. On the development of the Policy Planning Staff/Council, see Rostow, "The Planning of Foreign Policy," pp. 41-55; Roger Hilsman, *To Move a Nation* (New York: Dell, 1967), Chapter 36; Elmer Plischke, *Conduct of American Diplomacy,* 3d ed. (Princeton: Van Nostrand, 1967), pp. 186-87, 189, 191, 199-200; and Rothstein, *Planning, Prediction, and Policymaking in Foreign Affairs,* pp. 51-66, 87, 97-98. For discussion of the Policy Analysis and Resource Allocation System (PARA), introduced in 1971, see John H. Esterline and Robert B. Black, *Inside Foreign Policy: The Department of State Political System and Its Subsystems* (Palo Alto, Calif.: Mayfield, 1975), pp. 82-83.

27. Described in Kennan, *Memoirs, 1925-1950,* p. 327.

28. Lindsay, "Program Planning," p. 290.

29. Plischke, *Conduct of American Diplomacy,* p. 645.

30. *The National Security Process* (Washington: Institute for Defense Analysis, 1968), p. 82.

31. Burton M. Sapin, *The Making of United States Foreign Policy* (New York: Praeger, 1966), p. 295.

32. See Robert Strausz-Hupé, William R. Kintner, and Stefan T. Possony, *A Forward Strategy for America* (New York: Harper, 1961), p. 384.

33. This is essentially the definition prescribed in various United States and other military manuals.

34. See Strausz-Hupé, Kintner, and Possony, *A Forward Strategy for America,* pp. 384-90, including suggestions for a "high-level" mechanism for planning foreign affairs. Discussing policy planning as a complicated art, Bailey has quipped: "The official planners devise proposals for meeting all likely contingencies, except, as cynics have observed, those that actually develop"; see *The Art of Diplomacy,* p. 100.

35. *New Approaches to International Relations,* edited by Morton A. Kaplan (New York: St. Martin's Press, 1968), p. 389.

36. Winston Churchill, report to the House of Commons, in *The Second World War,* vol. V, *Closing the Ring* (Boston: Houghton Mifflin, 1951), p. 162.

37. Sapin, *The Making of United States Foreign Policy,* p. 294.

38. Rostow, "The Planning of Foreign Policy," p. 43.

39. Rothstein, *Planning, Prediction, and Policymaking in Foreign Affairs,* p. 96.

40. Morgan, "Planning in Foreign Affairs," p. 278.

41. John C. Ausland and Hugh F. Richardson, "Crisis Management: Berlin, Cyprus, Laos," *Foreign Affairs* 44 (January 1966): 300-301.

42. See Morgan, "Planning in Foreign Affairs," p. 278; Lindsay, "Program Planning," p. 290; and Ausland and Richardson, "Crisis Management," p. 303.

43. In 1969 President Nixon told Congress: "Merely making proposals takes only a typewriter; making workable proposals takes time." Message to Congress, April 14, 1969, in *Public Papers of the Presidents: Richard Nixon, 1969*, p. 285.

44. See commentary in Gross, *The Making of Foreign Policy*, pp. 182-83.

45. For comment on the practical difficulties of projecting the future in foreign policy-making, see de Rivera, *The Psychological Dimension of Foreign Policy*, pp. 103-4; and Frankel, *The Making of Foreign Policy*, pp. 185-90. See also Daniel Bell, "Twelve Modes of Prediction," in *International Political Analysis: Readings*, edited by David V. Edwards (New York: Holt, Rinehart, and Winston, 1970), pp. 378-408. On "scientific" prediction and probabilities, and on academic fashions and forecasting, see Rothstein, *Planning, Prediction, and Policymaking in Foreign Affairs*, pp. 161-63, 186-90, and on "scientism" and prediction, see Gross, *Foreign Policy Analysis*, pp. 155-66. On psychological aspects, see Anthony A. D'Amato, "Psychological Constructs in Foreign Policy Prediction," *Journal of Conflict Resolution* 11 (September 1967): 294-311. For a general survey, see Nazli Choucri and Thomas W. Robinson, *Forecasting in International Relations: Theory, Methods, Problems, Prospects* (San Francisco: Freeman, 1978).

46. *Rothstein, Planning, Prediction, and Policymaking in Foreign Affairs*, pp. 18-19, 190, and all of Chapter 4.

47. Morgan, "Planning in Foreign Affairs," p. 278.

48. For greater detail, see Bernard Brodie, "Strategy," *International Encyclopedia of the Social Sciences* (1968) XV, 281-88, and for a comprehensive survey, see B. H. Liddell Hart, *Strategy*, 2d ed. (New York: Praeger, 1967). See also Edward Mead Earle, *Makers of Modern Strategy: Military Thought from Machiavelli to Hitler* (Princeton: Princeton University Press, 1971). In "The Forgotten Dimensions of Strategy," Michael Howard offers a framework for analysis based on a study of the way in which both strategic doctrine and warfare developed since the days of Napoleon, emphasizing their operational, logistical, social, and technological dimensions; see *Foreign Affairs* 57 (Summer 1979): 975-86.

49. For example, see Colin S. Gray, *Strategic Studies: A Critical Assessment* (Westport, Conn.: Greenwood, 1982). For his summary of waves of post-World War II American strategic studies, especially on nuclear weaponry and doctrine, see pp. 15-23; and for his views on the relationship of strategy to politics, culture, and ethics, see Chapters 4 to 6. See also Colin S. Gray, *Strategic Studies and Public Policy: The American Experience* (Lexington: University Press of Kentucky, 1982).

50. Erving Goffman, *Strategic Interaction* (Philadelphia: University of Pennsylvania Press, 1969). In recent years a substantial literature has been produced on contestation, simulation, gaming, and gamesmanship, including that which pertains to diplomatic encounter, crisis situations, and war. For an illustration of analysis of strategy in sports, see Paul Weiss, *Sport: A Philosophic Inquiry* (Carbondale, Ill.: Southern Illinois University Press, 1969) and for comparisons of application of strategy to several fields, see John D. McDonald, *Strategy in Poker, Business and War*

(New York: Norton, 1950).

For bibliographical suggestions on simulation and gaming, see Arthur D. Larson, *National Security Affairs: A Guide to Information Sources* (Detroit: Gale Research, 1973), especially pp. 252-58, and Plischke, *U.S. Foreign Relations*, especially pp. 489-92.

51. John E. Kieffer, *Strategy for Survival* (New York: McKay, 1953), p. 14.

52. Anders Boserup and Andrew Mack, *War Without Weapons: Non-Violence in National Defense* (New York: Schocken, 1975), p. 148.

53. Charles O. Lerche, Jr., and Abdul A. Said, *Concepts of International Politics in Global Perspective*, 3d ed. (Englewood Cliffs, N.J.: Prentice-Hall, 1979), p. 50. In the field of business management, a typical definition is that strategy consists of "the guiding philosophy of the organization in the commitment of its resources to attain or fulfill its goals." See D. L. Bates and David L. Eldredge, *Strategy and Policy: Analysis, Formulation, and Implementation*, 2d ed. (Dubuque, Iowa: Brown, 1984), p. 11.

54. Stephen B. Jones, "The Power Inventory and National Security," *World Politics* 6 (July 1954): 422. Strategy, in the broad sense, is also defined by him as "the art of using power"; see Stephen B. Jones, "Global Strategic Views," *Geographical Review* 45 (October 1955): 492.

55. Earle, *Makers of Modern Strategy*, p. viii. For additional commentary on interpretations, see John B. Best, "Notes Toward a Formal Definition of Strategy," *Psychological Report* 54 (April 1984): 513-14, which relates strategy to problem solving; and William L. Shanklin, *Strategic Planning: Concepts and Implementation* (New York: Random House, 1985).

56. Liddell Hart, *Strategy*, p. 335.

57. John P. Lovell, *Foreign Policy in Perspective: Strategy, Adaptation, Decision Making* (New York: Holt, Rinehart, and Winston, 1970), p. 66.

58. Karl W. Deutsch, discussing games, or rational conflicts characterized by strategy, in *The Analysis of International Relations* (Englewood Cliffs, N.J.: Prentice-Hall, 1968), p. 115.

59. Hahn and Neff, *American Strategy for the Nuclear Age*, p. 443.

60. K. J. Holsti, *International Politics: A Framework for Analysis*, 2d ed. (Englewood Cliffs, N.J.: Prentice-Hall, 1972), p. 102.

61. As noted in Jones, "The Power Inventory and National Security," pp. 422-23, but he prefers to use strategy as meaning the art of achieving objectives.

62. Liddell Hart, *Strategy*, p. 335.

63. Henry A. Kissinger, *Problems of National Strategy: A Book of Readings* (New York: Praeger, 1965), p. 477. Others, represented by Frederick Hartmann, claim that strategy incorporates policy, and that foreign policy "as an overall program for action in world affairs, must indeed reflect a strategic concept." See Frederick H. Hartmann, *The New Age of American Foreign Policy* (New York: Macmillan, 1970), p. 9. For Kissin-

ger's definition and analysis of "strategic doctrine," by which he means
the pattern of responses to the challenges of other nations, see his
Nuclear Weapons and Foreign Policy (New York: Harper, 1957), pp. 403-23.
For additional commentary on the relation of strategy and policy, see
John Bayliss, *Contemporary Strategy: Theory and Policies* (New York:
Holmes and Meier, 1975); Robert E. Schellenberger and Glenn F. Boseman,
Policy Formulation and Strategy Management: Text and Cases (New York:
Wiley, 1982); Robert C. Shirley and Michael H. Peters, *Strategy and
Policy Formulation: A Multifunctional Orientation* (New York: Wiley,
1981).

64. Harold and Margaret Sprout, *Foundations of International Politics* (Princeton: Van Nostrand, 1962), p. 58.

65. Lovell, *Foreign Policy in Perspective*, p. 65. For additional
commentary, see J. M. Higgins, *Strategy Formulation, Implementation, and
Control* (Hinsdale, Ill.: Dryden, 1985); Henry Trofimenko, "The 'Theology' of Strategy," *ORBIS* 21 (Fall 1977): 497-515, with additional discussion in 21 (Winter 1978): 975- 79; William C. Waddell, *The Outline of
Strategy* (Oxford, Ohio: Planning Forum, 1986). For analysis of the relation of strategy and ethics, see J. L. Allen, "Relation of Strategy
and Morality," *Ethics* 73 (April 1963): 167-78; and Anatol Rapoport,
Strategy and Conscience (New York: Harper and Row, 1964).

66. Deutsch, *The Analysis of International Relations*, p. 115.

67. Kieffer, *Strategy for Survival*, p. 13.

68. Harry Howe Ransom, "Strategy," *Dictionary of Political Science*
(New York: Philosophical Library, 1964), p. 503.

69. Hartmann, *The New Age of American Foreign Policy*, p. 8. By comparison, Feliks Gross views long-range policies as strategies and supportive short-range policies as tactics; see his *Foreign Policy Analysis*,
pp. 126-28.

70. Ransom, "Strategy," p. 503.

71. For example, see Edgar J. Kingston-McCloughry, *Global Strategy*
(New York: Praeger, 1957) in which the author asserts that contemporary
strategy must amalgamate national, individual military service, and joint
and combined military strategies to produce the highest common denomina-
tor, pp. 36-38.

72. André Beaufre, *An Introduction to Strategy*, translated by R. H.
Barry (New York: Praeger, 1965), p. 30. Beaufre maintains that at the
apex of the pyramid of a nation's strategies is "total strategy," determined by the highest political authority. For an illustration of grand
strategy, see James R. M. Butler's *Grand Strategy*, 7 vols. (London: H. M.
Stationary Office, 1956-1976), which is a comprehensive historical analysis of British strategy during World War II.

73. See, for example, Kieffer, *Strategy for Survival*, p. 14, and
Strausz-Hupé, Kintner, and Possony, *A Forward Strategy for America*, p.
13.

74. Strausz-Hupé, Kintner, and Possony, *A Forward Strategy for America*, p. 13.

75. Norman J. Padelford and George A. Lincoln, *The Dynamics of In-*

ternational Politics (New York: Macmillan, 1967), p. 400.

76. For example, see Albert Wedemeyer, *Wedemeyer Reports* (New York: Devin-Adair, 1958), p. 81; he defines grand strategy as "the art and science of employing all of a nation's resources to accomplish objectives defined by national policy." See also *Strategic Terminology: A Trilingual Glossary*, edited by Urs Schwarz and Laszlo Hadik (New York: Praeger, 1966), p. 94, and Patrick W. Powers, *A Guide to National Defense* (New York: Praeger, 1975), p. 31. A more restricted usage is confined to the concept "grand policy" by Robert Strausz-Hupé and Stefan T. Possony, *International Relations* (New York: McGraw-Hill, 1950), p. 487.

77. Liddell Hart, *Strategy*, Chapter 22, especially pp. 335-36, 366. See also Henry A. Sargeaunt and Geoffrey West, *Grand Strategy: The Search for Victory* (New York: Crowell, 1941).

78. Howard, "The Forgotten Dimensions of Strategy," p. 975.

79. Helmut Schmidt, *A Grand Strategy for the West: The Anachronism of National Strategies in an Interdependent World* (New Haven, Conn.: Yale University Press, 1985), pp. 5-7. His convictions lead him to question the efficacy if not the validity of national strategies in contemporary international politics and to argue not for revolutionary international institutionalization, but for the establishment of a common Western grand strategy.

80. See, for example, Beaufre, *An Introduction to Strategy*; Hahn and Neff, *American Strategy for the Nuclear Age*; Kieffer, *Strategy for Survival*; Henry A. Kissinger, *The Necessity for Choice: Prospects of American Foreign Policy* (New York: Harper, 1961), *Nuclear Weapons and Foreign Policy,* and *Problems of National Strategy*; *Grand Strategy for the 1980s*, edited by Bruce Palmer (Washington: American Enterprise Institute, 1978); Urs Schwarz, *American Strategy: A New Perspective--The Growth of Politico-Military Thinking in the United States* (Garden City, N.Y.: Doubleday, 1966) on the variety of American strategic doctrines; Strausz-Hupé, Kintner, and Possony, *A Forward Strategy for America*; David W. Tarr, *American Strategy in the Nuclear Age* (New York: Macmillan, 1966); and *National Security in the Nuclear Age: Basic Facts and Theories*, edited by Gordon B. Turner and Richard D. Challener (New York: Praeger, 1960).

81. Edward Mead Earle, "Political and Military Strategy for the United States," *Proceedings of the Academy of Political Science* 19 (January 1941): 7.

82. Richard C. Snyder and Edgar S. Furniss, Jr., *American Foreign Policy: Formulation, Principles, and Programs* (New York: Rinehart, 1954), p. 55.

83. To illustrate, Winston Churchill, in his six volume biographical account, *The Second World War*, titles volume III *The Grand Alliance* (Boston: Houghton Mifflin, 1950), but he also describes it as the "Tripartite Coalition."

84. For a survey of pre-twentieth-century plans for world organization to maintain the peace--including those of Pierre Dubois, Emeric Crucé, Alighieri Dante, William Penn, Abbé de St. Pierre, Rev. Noah Worcester, and others, see Elmer Plischke, *Systems of Integrating the International Community* (Princeton: Van Nostrand, 1964), pp. 10-12; see also Elmer Plischke, "Reflections on International Integration," *World Affairs* 129 (April-June 1966): 20-27.

85. For example, see the plans for the League of Nations sponsored by Lord Robert Cecil, Sir Walter Phillimore, and Sir Cecil Hurst of Great Britain; General Jan Christian Smuts of South Africa; and David Hunter Miller and especially Woodrow Wilson of the United States. For a comprehensive study on the development of plans for the United Nations, preceding the San Francisco Conference of 1945, see Department of State, *Postwar Foreign Policy Preparation, 1939-1945* (Washington: Government Printing Office, 1949).

86. Clarence K. Streit, *Union Now* (New York: Harper, 1939). Following the outbreak of World War II he published *Union Now With Britain* (New York: Harper, 1941), and his postwar version is entitled *Freedom's Frontier: Atlantic Union Now* (New York: Harper, 1961). See also commentary in Plischke, *Systems of Integrating the International Community*, pp. 13-14.

Illustrative proposals for world integration and government, which mushroomed in the 1940s and 1950s, include: Ruhl J. Bartlett, *The League to Enforce Peace* (Chapel Hill: University of North Carolina Press, 1944); George A. Birdsall, *A Proposed World Government* (Washington: Shaw Press, 1944); Ely Culbertson, *Total Peace* (Garden City, N.Y.: Doubleday, Doran, 1943); William B. Curry, *The Case for Federal Union* (New York: Penguin, 1940); *Federation: The Coming Structure of World Government*, edited by Howard O. Eaton (Norman: University of Oklahoma Press, 1944); Joseph P. Kamp, *We Must Abolish the United States: The Hidden Facts Behind the Crusade for World Government* (New York: Constitutional Education League, 1950); O. Newfang, *World Federation* (New York: Barnes and Noble, 1939) and *World Government* (New York: Barnes and Noble, 1945); Emery Reves, *The Anatomy of Peace* (New York: Harper, 1945); Edith Wyner, *World Federal Government in Maximum Terms* (Afton, N.Y.: Fedonat Press, 1954). Representative of more recent literature on world interdependence is Richard A. Falk, *A Study of Future Worlds* (New York: Free Press, 1975), and for a summary essay on international integration, see Steven Rosen and Walter S. Jones, *The Logic of International Relations* (Cambridge, Mass.: Winthrop, 1974), Chapter 11.

Sponsors of the movement for world federation include such agencies as: Federal Union, Ltd. (founded in 1938), Federal Union, Inc. (1939), Committee to Frame a World Constitution (1945), World Movement for World Federal Government (1946), Atlantic Union Committee (1949), and the more recent World Order Models Project (WOMP).

87. The integration of Western Europe is based on the Robert Schuman, Rene Plevin, Jean Monet, and Paul-Henri Spaak Plans for the creation of the European Coal and Steel, Political, Economic (Common Market), Atomic Energy, and Defense Communities. See, for example, the extensive literature on European unification and Joseph Kraft, *The Grand Design: From Common Market to Atlantic Partnership* (New York: Harper, 1962).

88. For comments on "Stalin's Strategy," see Gross, *Foreign Policy Analysis*, pp. 128-30. For a critique of Kissinger's grand strategy, see G. Warren Nutter, *Kissinger's Grand Design* (Washington: American Enterprise Institute, 1975). For general commentary, see Seyom Brown, "An Alternative to the Grand Design," *World Politics* 17 (January 1975): 232-42.

On the linkage principle, see Richard Nixon, *The Real War* (New York: Warner, 1980), pp. 267-69 and Henry Kissinger, *For the Record: Selected Statements, 1977-1980* (Boston: Little, Brown, 1981), pp. 87-91. Also see Michael G. Fry and Arthur N. Gilbert, "A Historian and Linkage Politics," *International Studies Quarterly* 26 (September 1982): 425-44; John A. Hamilton, "To Link or Not to Link," *Foreign Policy* 44 (Fall 1981): 127-44; James N. Rosenau, ed., *Linkage Politics: Essays on the*

Convergence of National and International Systems (New York: Free Press, 1969); Arthur A. Stein, "The Politics of Linkage," *World Politics* 33 (October 1980): 62-81.

89. Thomas M. Franck and Edward Weisband, *World Politics: Verbal Strategy Among the Superpowers* (New York: Oxford University Press, 1971), p. 7. This volume deals with aligning strategic concepts with national interests--with saying things that, in the long run, contravene the nation's interests and therefore bear long-term costs at the expense of short-term gains.

90. Holsti, *International Politics*, p. 103.

91. For a simpler version of such basic questions, and his commentary, see Hartmann, *The New Age of American Foreign Policy*, pp. 9, 10, 259. He insists that these questions must be asked at the outset to decide not what the nation should do, but what it wants done. The matter of sequence, he stresses, is the single greatest procedural cause of failure.

92. Lovell, *Foreign Policy in Perspective*, pp. 66-69. Lovell also discusses types of strategies and patterns of interactions; see especially pp. 98-101, 129-31.

93. Georg Schwarzenberger, *Power Politics: A Study of World Society*, 3d ed. (New York: Praeger, 1964), pp. 160-82; on international federation and unification see also note 86 above. For an interpretation of United States patterns of action, see Gene E. Rainey, *Patterns of American Foreign Policy* (Boston: Allyn and Bacon, 1975, especially Chapters 13-19 which deal with patterns related to functional issues.

94. For a selected bibliographical compilation, see Larson, *National Security Affairs*, especially pp. 154-56, 161-64, 166-74, and Plischke, *U.S. Foreign Relations*, pp. 277-83.

95. Brodie, "Strategy," p. 287.

96. Hartmann, *The New Age of American Foreign Policy*, pp. 8-9.

97. Bailey, *The Art of Diplomacy*, pp. 84, 88, 91-95, 97-98, 114-15, 117-19, 129-30, 143, 147, 150-52, 161-62. For a list of positive and negative basic maxims pertaining to military strategy, see Liddell Hart, *Strategy*, pp. 347-50.

98. For discussion of the inventory of strategic instruments in foreign relations, see H. Bradford Westerfield, *The Instruments of America's Foreign Policy* (New York: Crowell, 1963), and for the instruments of national strategy, see Strausz-Hupé, Kintner, and Possony, *A Forward Strategy for America*, Chapters 4-9. See also William R. Kintner, *Peace and the Strategy Conflict* (New York: Praeger, 1967), Chapter 4 for an assessment of assets and liabilities and Chapter 9 for his comments on power and persuasion.

99. Thomas C. Schelling, *The Strategy of Conflict* (New York: Oxford University Press, 1963), pp. 160-61.

100. Machiavelli maintained that the state is amoral and a force, not an inherent benevolent entity, and that nationalism is a transitional phase of the trend toward expansionism. See *The Prince* (New York: New American Library, 1952), especially Chapters 5-7, which deal with govern-

ing dominions that, prior to being occupied, lived under their own laws, new dominions that are acquired by arms and other forces, and new dominions acquired by the power of others or by fortune.

101. For a survey of the most prominent contributors from Machiavelli to World War II, see Earle, *Makers of Modern Strategy*, Chapters 2-11.

102. The Swedish geographer Rudolf Kjellen, who coined the term "geopolitics" in 1916, defined it as the theory of the state as a geographic organism in space. Subsequently it came to mean the approach to the study of the power and policies of nations from the perspective of geographic considerations.

103. See Friedrich Ratzel, *Politische Geographie* (Munich: Oldenbourg, 1897), 3d ed. (1923). Considered to be the founder of contemporary political geography, he developed a series of "geographical laws." Also see James M. Hunter, *Perspective on Ratzel's Political Geography* (Lanham, Md.: University Press of America, 1983).

104. See also Chapter 2 for Mahan's views on national interest and note 30 of Chapter 2 for a list of his principal works. For commentary, see Margaret Tuttle Sprout, "Mahan: Evangelist of Sea Power," in Earle, *Makers of Modern Strategy*, Chapter 17.

105. See Sir Halford J. Mackinder, *Britain and the British Seas* (New York: Appleton, 1902) and especially "The Geographical Pivot of History," *Geographical Journal* 23 (1904): 421-44, and *Democratic Ideals and Reality* (New York: Holt, 1919, republished by Holt, 1942).

106. See Karl Haushofer, especially *Wehr Geopolitik: Geographische Grundlagen Einer Wehrkunde* (Berlin: Junker, 1932), and *Weltpolitik von Heute* (Berlin: Zeitgeschichte Verlag, 1934); also many monographs and articles. See also Derwent Whittlesy, "Haushofer: The Geopoliticians," in Earle, *Makers of Modern Strategy*, pp. 388-411. For an analysis of Haushofer's influence on Hitler and German policy in the 1930s, with bibliography, see "Geopolitics," *Encyclopedia Britannica* (1973), X, pp. 203-206.

107. See Nicholas Spykman, "Geography and Foreign Policy," *American Political Science Review* 32 (February 1938): 28-50 and (April 1938): 213-36, which relates such factors as size, world location, and regional location to a nation's foreign policy and relations. Also Nicholas Spykman and Abbie A. Rollins, "Geographic Objectives in Foreign Policy," *American Political Science Review* 33 (June 1939): 391-410 and (August 1939): 591-614, and Nicholas Spykman, *America's Strategy in World Politics* (New York: Harcourt Brace, 1942).

108. See James Burnham, *The Struggle for the World* (New York: Day, 1947) which is a plea for a worldwide United States empire to counter Soviet hegemonism. For additional analyses on geopolitics, see Russell H. Fifield and George Etzel Pearcy, *Geopolitics in Principle and Practice* (Boston: Ginn, 1944); Colin S. Gray, *The Geopolitics of the Nuclear Era: Heartland, Rimlands, and the Technological Revolution* (New York: Crane, Russak, 1977), Chapter 3 on the Soviet Union; Andrew Gyorgy, *Geopolitics: A New German Science* (Berkeley: University of California Press, 1944); Richard Hennig, *Geopolitik: Die Lehre vom Stadt als Lebewesen* (Leipzig: Teubner, 1928 and 1931); Jones, "Global Strategic Views," pp. 492-508; John E. Kiefer, *Realities of World Power* (New York: McKay, 1952), Chapters 2-4, 7; Nurit Kliot and Stanley Waterman, eds., *Pluralism and Political Geography: People, Territory and State* (New York: St. Martin's

Press, 1983); Ronan Paddison, *The Fragmented State: The Political Geography of Power* (New York: St. Martin's Press, 1983); Robert Strausz-Hupé, *Geopolitics: The Struggle for Space and Power* (New York: Putnam, 1942); *Compass of the World*, edited by Hans W. Weigert and Vilhjalmur Stefansson (New York: Macmillan, 1944), especially Chapters 2, 3, 11-14, 18, 25. Also see Ladis K. D. Kristof, "The Origins and Evolution of Geopolitics," *Journal of Conflict Resolution* 4 (March 1960): 15-51, and Harold Sprout, "Geopolitical Hypotheses in Technological Perspective," *World Politics* 15 (January 1963): 187-212.

109. See Cecil V. Crabb, Jr., *The Doctrines of American Foreign Policy: Their Meaning, Role, and Future* (Baton Rouge: Louisiana State University Press, 1982) and William H. Overholt and Marylin Chou, "Foreign Policy Doctrines," in *Foreign Policy Analysis*, edited by Richard L. Merritt (Lexington, Mass.: Heath, 1975), Chapter 18.

110. An early American strategy, called the "Plan of 1776," devised by the Congress, as amplified by the "Plan of 1784," provided a model for American diplomatic agents in Europe to negotiate initial bilateral treaties of amity and commerce with friendly European powers. When the "Armed Neutrality" plan was created under the leadership of Catherine II of Russia in 1780, to protect the maritime interests of the weaker European nations, the "United States" supported its trade principles and employed the strategy of attempting adherence in order to gain recognition of its independent status but failed to achieve acceptance as a signatory of the plan.

111. A number of these precepts have been embodied in historic collective policy statements, including Wilson's Fourteen Points (1918), the eight points of the Atlantic Charter (1941), and the twelve points contained in Truman's Navy Day Address (1945).

9

DECISION-MAKING

Decision making is not a science but an art. It
requires, not calculation, but judgment. There is
no unit of measure which can weigh the substantive
consequences of a decision against the political
consequences, or judge the precise portions of public opinion and congressional pressure, or balance
domestic against foreign, short-range against long-
range, or private against public considerations.
Theodore C. Sorensen, *Decision-Making
in the White House* (1963)

In any event he [the decision maker] knows that an
idea is not a policy and that the transformation of
an idea into a policy is frequently an exhausting
and frustrating process. He is aware of the difference between a conclusion and a decision . . . the
policy officer must move from conclusion to decision and must be prepared to live with the results,
for he does not have a chance to do it again. If he
waits, he has already made a decision, sometimes
the right one, but the white heat of responsibility
is upon him and he cannot escape it, however stren-
uously he tries.
Dean Rusk, Address, February 20, 1961

Decision-making in foreign relations is the process whereby
the nation's leaders select problems, objectives, policies,
and procedures for decision, consider alternatives for dealing with them, and choose among preferred options for application and execution. Such decision-making, as well as theories of international relations and explications of particular perspectives of the interrelations of national aims and
means have become the subjects of substantial inquiry and an
extensive literature. Hypotheses, conceptualizations, analyses, and case studies of both actual and potential experiences, worthy ventures in themselves, contribute to an awareness of the complexity, and an understanding of the craft of
conducting international affairs.

To be realistic it may be assumed that governments and

their leaders must make decisions within the context of the
existing functional, institutional, and political environment. If they are wise and responsible, they will put the
needs of the national community above more parochial interests and seek to make sound and meritorious determinations
and, therefore, their decision-making will be--or at least
should be--deliberately and prudently managed.

Decision-making is generally regarded as a process, although it is also called a function, method, and technique.
It applies to societal interactions at all levels, to both
the public and the private sectors, to internal and external
affairs, and to substantive and procedural matters. So far
as substance is concerned, it is broader in scope than the
production of public policy while, in terms of pragmatic
functioning, it is narrower than what is usually conceived as
the overall function of policy-making. In the realm of foreign affairs, it pertains not only to the essence of policy,
but also to the national interests served, the national purposes, goals, and concrete objectives to be achieved, the
mechanisms and methods whereby both the ends and means to attain them are designed, the resources to be committed, and
the strategies of internal and international implementation.

Decision-making analysis and literature examine the subject from differing perspectives. These portray organizational or mechanistic, elitist, institutional, bureaucratic, operational, communicatory, and other approaches, or some combination of them. Or they concentrate on action flow, or on
methodological modularization, emphasizing individual cases,
gamesmanship, simulation, quantification, computerization,
and the like. Or the motivation reflects theory development.
Selected functional areas of applicability are treated, such
as general societal relations, institutional management, or
particular aspects of governance, including parliamentary and
judicial procedure, public policy-making and, more precisely,
security and foreign policy determination. Some studies, especially those that are psychologically oriented, develop the
intellectual or rational aspects of the process.

At the outset it is essential to realize that human beings, not institutions, make decisions. Harold and Margaret
Sprout point out that leaders, not states, devise foreign
policy. When such human agents reach their decisions, however, the latter become the prescriptions of the nation.
This means that prior to consummation the psychological ante-
cedents--desiring, perceiving, and analyzing--together with
the concrete act of choosing or judging are the functions of
human beings, but once they are made, determinations are attributable to the corporate entities--the nations which "can
rarely escape the consequences of their rulers' decisions."[1]

Because decision-making is central to the prescription of
a nation's concerns and aims, the framing of its foreign policies, planning, and designing its strategies, and because it
involves the mental process of exercising choice, there are
those who regard it as an art. Quincy Wright, reviewing qualities essential for practical action in international politics, for example, claims that it is more an art than a science.[2] Whereas diplomacy usually is portrayed as an art[3] and

most interpretations of decision-making define it as a process, a few studies of foreign relations also characterize it as an art.[4]

On the other hand, since the 1950s many attempts have been made to systematize analysis with a view to prescribing or at least eliciting basic hypotheses, precepts, and formulas and to apply scientific techniques to explain the application of decision-making to the conduct of foreign affairs. Discussing the premises and promises of decision-making, James Rosenau traces the study of foreign relations from its initial traditional version, through its "take-off" phase, to its "maturation" stage--with increasing application of scientific procedures.[5] In other fields--principally mathematics, statistics, economics, administration, and various forms of gamesmanship--the march to "scientize" has advanced much faster and farther, some suggesting that decision-making needs to be, while others claim that it already approximates, or has even been converted into a science.[6]

In short, depending on one's focus, a case can be made that, like planning, decision making is an art, a science, or both. In addition, when highly developed and frequently engaged in, from the perspective of viewing it as a mental rather than an institutional process, it may also be denominated as a craft.[7]

INTERPRETATIONS

Often the concepts "decision-making" and "policy-making" are confused and used interchangeably, by both practitioners and analysts. The expression "policy-making" customarily tends to denote the political process for formulating foreign policies and prescribing their means of application. In this broad version it embraces the full complement of the ingredients in the conduct of international affairs, emphasizing the matter of determination respecting each of these components, but differentiating them from policy implementation. An alternative usage embraces the complex of the factors and agencies that contribute to the management of foreign relations, often stressing the nature and operation of the policy machinery and also distinguishing it from policy execution. A third, more restricted delineation simply regards foreign policy-making as the pragmatic act of devising policies, both substantive and procedural, to achieve the nation's goals and objectives.[8]

Decision-making, on the other hand, is more narrowly conceived as the particular method of arriving at decisions. Yet, it may be broader in scope than policy-making in that it may apply individually to each of the components and steps in the foreign relations equation, ranging from the specification of issues and facts, through consideration of alternative interests, aims, and foreign policies, to pragmatic operational procedures and eventually to reappraisal.

Surprisingly few studies of international politics and foreign affairs define such concepts as decision-making, decisions, and choice. Joseph Frankel generically describes de-

cision-making as "a process ending in an act of will of a
person or a group of persons who choose between two or more
alternatives." Before the final act of will, he maintains,
"many other choices are involved--of information sources, interpretation methods, values, objectives, means," and others,
so that normally multiple choices or decisions will be made
in arriving at principal decisions.[9]

Others interpret it as "a social process that selects a
problem for decision . . . and produces a limited number of
alternatives, from among which a particular alternative is
selected for implementation and execution,"[10] and as "a process in which events, circumstances, and information precipi-
tate a choice designed to achieve some desired result" or "a
process of narrowing down a body of information, identifying
primary problems, and choosing among alternative solutions."[11] Similarly, Graham Allison characterizes the study
of decision-making as "the attempt to explain international
events by recounting the aims and calculations of nations or
governments."[12] Although it is involved in them, as a process
decision-making must be differentiated not only from the parallel conception of foreign policy-making, but also from such
matters as problem solving, crisis handling, and foreign relations planning.

There is universal agreement that the keystone of decision-making is the matter of choice--the exercise of discretion among possibilities. A nation is confronted with a decision problem whenever there is a choice between at least
two options, even though the responses may literally be "yes"
or "no" to each proposition. According to Howard Lentner, it
presumes the rejection of alternatives, including the defer-
ral of choice, and he argues that while decision makers are
motivated by the desire to produce benefits, they also must
consider disadvantages and costs.[13]

Naturally the end products of decision-making are the
decisions made. In addition to Frankel's depicting them as
acts of will, as applied to foreign affairs they are defined
as "the choice to pursue certain goals with certain means"[14]
which, at a minimum, "provides for doing something or doing
nothing."[15] Also emphasizing human volition, Charles Lerche
and Abdul Said assert that choice is the "key concept" in
policy-making and that the decision maker "must preserve, at
any stage in the process, the maximum range of choice," which
"results in formulating opportunities (or imperatives) as a
set of alternatives for action."[16] Lerche also declares sum-
marily that "Choice is the essence of decision, and decision
is the heart of policy."[17]

Although decision-making applies to many factors other
than the formulation of policies, and although the function
of deciding may itself be viewed as an action taken by leaders on behalf of their nations, the decisions made need to be
distinguished from those "courses of action" that are decided
upon. Frankel notes that the distinction between decisions
and actions "lies in their spheres of operation." Decisions
are made "in the decision-maker's mind," whereas actions or
the implementation of courses of action "take place in his
environment." By decision-making, in other words, "is under-

stood an act of determining in one's own mind a course of action" and by decision "is understood that which is thus determined," or the deed performed, or the perpetration "of
acting or doing."[18]

Lentner contends that a clear analytical delineation
must be drawn between what he calls the psychological and the
operational--or the decisional and execution phases of decision-making.[19] Joseph de Riviera draws attention to the necessity of differentiating psychologically among such attitudinal matters as bias ("the initial emotional predisposi-
tion a person may have towards the favored alternative"), decision ("the moment when the alternative is developed enough
. . . to permit the first action to take place"), and commitment ("the effect of a number of factors that make a decision
non-reversible"). As a consequence, the decision maker generally progresses from viable preference, to decision (the
exercise of discretion overtly to adopt the preferred option), to determination to effectuate it pragmatically.[20]
In foreign relations, to summarize:

> Decision-making is an intellectual process whereby
> human beings define, analyze, assess, and determine
> the interests, aims, policies, procedures, capabil-
> ities, and strategies of nations, in coping with
> developments and problems in their relations with
> other countries. In doing so, decision makers con-
> sider alternatives and, by deliberate choice, or
> acts of will, they decide on the preferred op-
> tion(s) for application or implementation that are
> intended to result in optimum benefits at minimum
> risk and disadvantage.

CHARACTERISTICS AND COMMENTARY

Most analysts agree upon the complexities and difficulties of decision-making.[21] These are environmental, psychological, and institutional. According to Dean Rusk, from
another perspective, they are also political, military, economic, financial, legal, legislative, procedural, and administrative. Former Assistant Secretary of State Harlan Cleveland has jokingly said that the making of foreign policy is
frequently like trying to nail jelly to the trunk of a tree,
and Under Secretary Nicholas deB. Katzenbach has quipped that
he found the foreign policy process to be more like a taffy
pull.

The criteria of discretion, observes Lerche, are so
eroded by time and change that as a consequence American decision makers "often seek refuge in a synthetic but comfort-
ing illusion of inevitability"--a development that impedes or
even obviates the necessity for the exercise of choice.[22]
Similarly, notes de Rivera, those responsible often find it
easier to do nothing than to come to grips with deciding. Not
only does it take energy to make a judgment--and thereby in-
tervene in the flow of events--but in actual practice it is
also difficult to reconcile differing assessments of facts,
interests, aims, and capabilities with costs and benefits,
and at the same time to overcome the "fear of making the

wrong decision."[23]

Phases and Aspects

Decision-making is complicated, in part, by the linking
of preceding and succeeding phases of a sequence. These are
described by Frankel as threefold.   The first consists of
pre-decisional acquisition and assessment of information, advice and recommendations to the decision maker, and deliberation.   The second constitutes the rendering of decisions. The
third, or post-decision phase, involves implementation.   In
practice, however, it is misleading to regard the decision
phase as a clear-cut dividing juncture in the sequence.   "It
is more realistic," he suggests, "to consider the process as
one continuous whole with no rigid distinction between its
parts."[24]

For purposes of analysis, another depiction, provided by
Michael Haas, identifies four stages or "decision-making cy-
cles" and four facets in each decisional problem. Aside from
the point of deciding, the stages consist of the "prestimu-
lus" period (during which decision makers are not yet concerned with making decisions), the "stimulus" stage (which
triggers them to consider the need to act), the "information
processing" phase, and the final stage in which the impact or
outcome of the determination is reviewed.   The four facets
embrace the structural, cognitive, affective, and moral or
evaluative aspects of making decisions.   These eight stages
and facets are intertwined in a complex of interrelated components which suggest a matrix of sixty-five variables in the
decision-making process.[25]

The importance of adequate and reliable information cannot be overemphasized.   Frankel calls it the critical "link
between the decision-makers and their environments, or as the
means of transforming the operational environment into the
psychological one," which is not only inherently of "great
importance" but also "has led to a proliferation of information services in all governments."[26]   Thomas Bailey presents
as one of his guiding precepts that "sound information is the
taproot of sound policy," adding that a foreign relations decision "is no sounder than the validity and completeness of
the facts on which it is based."[27]   Feliks Gross maintains
that the quantity of facts is unlimited so that it is essential to establish a "hierarchy of importance," and that the
proper selection of facts, which itself requires decisions to
be made, "is the test of craftsmanship," as are "intelligence
and wisdom in understanding of mutual relationship between
facts."[28]

In addition, it is essential to understand the difference between perceptions and facts, the need for verification
to convert apprehensions into facts, and the significance of
decision-making in the critical process of such conversion.[29]
In short, some of the most crucial decisions may apply to the
determination of facts, on the basis of which all other decisions may rest.

So far as the psychological aspects of decision-making

are concerned, de Rivera prescribes four factors that affect
the production of a viable decisional end product. These include projecting each alternative possibility "into the future" in order to envision probable outcomes; reacting to
such assessment concerning the future by weighing each potential outcome against "some pre-existing frame of reference";
considering additional possibilities and predicting their
outcomes; and determining "a preference that permits one to
act"--or the emergence of a "unified preference" from among a
series of possibilities, manifested in intent or commitment
to effectuate it.[30]

Categories

Decision-making literature analyzes many categories of
both the decision-making process and the decisions made. William Chittick prescribes three general types of processes:
the descriptive or explanatory (which seeks to identify key
elements and indicate how they are combined in arriving at
judgments); the prescriptive or normative (which attempts to
reflect the choice of values--as beliefs rather than facts--
and to prescribe decisional rules for choosing among them);
and the engineering or design version (which focuses particularly on the inputs, proceedings, and outputs to achieve
objectives).[31] Ralph Keeney and Howard Raiffa identify not
only the descriptive versus the prescriptive categories, but
also distinguish between formal versus informal and individual versus group decision-making.[32] A major consideration,
given substantial attention in literature dealing with mathematical and psychological approaches, contrasts decision-making under conditions of certainty, risk, and uncertainty.[33]

Analysis also distinguishes among various categories of
the decisions made. The more common distinctions are based
on either purpose and content or importance, timing, and duration. To illustrate, some who deal with policy-making in
general, note the obvious comparison between substantive and
procedural decisions.[34] Others differentiate among minor,
routine, significant, fundamental, and critical decisions,[35]
or some similar delineation founded on importance. Still
others, concerned with timing, sequence, and longevity, compare long and short-range, initial and sequential, basic and
supportive, or fundamental and incremental decisions.[36]

Relating decisions to action, Frankel believes that
they fall into two general classes--those that do and those
that do not lead to action,[37] which might also be recognized
as positive and negative decisions. In terms of purpose or
dynamics rather than sequential stages, Lentner prescribes
three categories: initiatory (those that are intended to ini-
tiate action), responsive (those that produce reactions to
events occurring outside the nation), and "drift decisions"
(those that merely reiterate previously made decisions).[38]
Additional criteria on which distinctions are based include
degrees of intensity[39] and the flexibility[40] of decisions.

As the study of foreign affairs decision-making accelerated after World War II, many additional aspects evoked
attention. Aside from the intellectual or rational and the

political or bureaucratic approaches to analysis and practice, illustrations include diverse formulations of constants
and variables, coding of data, matters of cognition, communication, dissonance, and distortion, internal and external
pressures, decision channels, inputs and outputs (and outcomes), levels and the pace of decision-making, micro- and
macroanalytic methodologies, governmental structures and procedures, responsibility and decisional authority, and the
personality and methods of decision makers.[41] And those who
seek to "scientize" decision-making introduce a host of more
esoteric features.[42]

DECISION-MAKING ANALYSIS

In a practical sense decision-making dates back to the
origin of mankind. Concern with analyzing it systematically
as a process, however, derives its origins from two sources--
the study of mathematical economics (beginning in the eighteenth century) and public administration (originating at the
turn of the nineteenth century). Within a hundred years, it
is said, Woodrow Wilson in the United States and Max Weber in
Germany launched academic studies of organizational decision-
making.[43]

But it was not until after World War II that widespread
study of foreign relations decision-making emerged.[44] In
1946 the Brookings Institution inaugurated a program of research and education, emphasizing current foreign policies
of the United States and analysis of its policy process. It
contributed studies of both the governmental mechanism for
the conduct of foreign affairs and a series of annual volumes
concerned with contemporary problems of foreign policy. The
latter developed a method of attacking selected issues--which
Brookings called the "problem approach"--for the purpose of
applying decision-making techniques, accentuating choice a-
mong alternative courses of action, and promoting understanding of the role of rational thinking in the decision process.[45]

Approaches and Treatments

Considerable stimulus to decision-making analysis was
provided by Richard Snyder, H. W. Bruck, and Burton Sapin,
who in their studies devote attention to such matters as
data categories for studying foreign affairs decisions, propositions for empirical projection and assessment, conjoining
psychological with political and sociological levels of explication, and issues of methodology and international relations theory. They also outline ways in which their propositions may be applied to other aspects of the political process.[46]

Extensions of analysis have subsequently been developed
by others, providing a variety of approaches. Some concentrate on the role of those making decisions, either from the
perspective of decision makers in general[47] or from that of
more limited factors, including their "belief systems" and
"operational codes,"[48] and a good many volumes are addressed

to biographical--in some cases stressing psychological--
analysis.[49]   Other treatments develop decision-making "incrementalism" and "rationalism," which are examined later.[50]
Another category, consisting of what has been labelled "bureaucracy watchers," bridges the traditionalist-scientific
chasm, exponents of which concentrate on the functioning of
bureaucracies in the decision process, which is also considered later.[51]

Using the Cuban missile crisis of 1962 to explore alternative decision-making processes, Graham Allison projects
three comparative models of analysis. These consist of the
classical "rational actor" or "black box" model, which explains events by accentuating the aims and animus of nations,
determined by "purposeful agents" or deciders who maximize
national interests; the "organizational process" model, which
focusses on institutional performance and on motives (akin to
the political approach, discussed later); and the "bureaucratic politics" model, which evokes a mix of the alternatives espoused by the various agents and agencies involved in
the nation's decision process.[52]

Additional approaches emphasize other factors.   These
embrace political,[53] psychological,[54] and practical operational[55] perspectives, and some treatises on series of critical or historic decisions.[56]   Several thinkers, not specifically concerned with foreign relations, also contribute
to decision-making analysis.   These are illustrated by
Herbert Simon, who propounded the concept of "bounded rationality" or the mental and physiological limits of decision-making;[57] Harold Lasswell, who developed a descriptive
model of seven functions in making decisions;[58] and the exponents of incrementalism and rationalism, already noted.[59]

A substantial number of commentaries reflect a broad
perspective, treating decision-making generally[60] or concentrating specifically on foreign affairs.[61] A good many constitute concrete case studies,[62] including some on the decision to drop the atom bomb.[63]   Other contributions, by comparison, concerned with methodology, relate decision-making
to problem solving and crisis handling, systems analysis, information processing and automation, survey techniques, and
gaming (both human and computerized).[64]

These are supplemented in the literature by many examples of other more finite considerations. They vary, for
example, from studies specifically concerned with information, intelligence, and communication[65] to prediction and
risk,[66] from those that deal with domestic structures and
leadership[67] to quantification, psychotechnical matters, and
model building,[68] and from group decisions or "groupthink"
and "panel consensus"[69] to intraorganizational and interorganizational decision-making,[70] and others, even the impact
of ethics on the decision process.[71] As a result, the list of
approaches and investigatory treatment is virtually endless.

The Search for Decision Theory

Many analyses are concerned with developing and testing

hypotheses and producing "decision theory."[72] They constitute a mode of analysis intended to explain the correlation
of the elements that influence, and the process which leads
to, making decisions. The objective is a comprehensive
scheme that reveals and systematizes the process, propounds
fundamental functional precepts, and renders it possible to
predict how determinations are, or should be, rendered under
a variety of conditions. Theoretical analysis is concerned
with such questions as what is the decision, why is it made,
how is it determined, what is its impact on the environment,
what reactions may ensue and why, and especially what do the
answers reveal concerning the functioning of the system that
produces the decision and what principles or rules may be extrapolated to govern the future of decision-making? Some theorists seek to produce universally applicable designs reducible to formal models, paradigms, and mathematical equations.

     Although in 1967 James Rosenau acknowledged the need for
theory in foreign relations and observed, as noted, that
analysis of policy had advanced beyond the original "traditional" into the intermediate "take-off" stage and was rapidly approaching the "transition to maturity," there still is
no generally accepted theory or common overall model.[73] The
reasons range from competing perspectives to differing motives, approaches, and methods. Opposing schools of thought
have emerged, demonstrating their respective patterns of
analysis and criticizing or rejecting others, and sometimes
merging one with another or splintering off on some tangent.
Revisionists attack the orientation and premises of behavioralists, traditionalists question normativists and disagree
with positivists, and, because functions like the conduct of
foreign affairs are so complex, there is usually more conflict than agreement on political values and treatment. As a
consequence, analysis has generated a series of disparate hypotheses, theories, models, and analytical tools, but has
failed to produce a single, overriding, and universally applicable and acceptable doctrine.

RATIONAL, INCREMENTAL, BUREAUCRATIC, AND OTHER ANALYTICAL
APPROACHES

     The most controverted aspect of foreign relations de-
cision-making centers on the nature and import of rationality, which is central to two sets of appositional methods of
analysis, as applicable both to practice and scholarly inquiry. On the one hand, there are those who differentiate
among incremental, rational, and eclectic decision-making.[74]

     Incrementalists maintain that the decision process pro-
ceeds slowly and progressively, at each stage building on
previous determinations, producing minimal changes from the
status quo. Decision makers are viewed primarily as problem
solvers who make series of decisions, each designed to take
corrective action required by the consequences of those previously made, thus proceeding by means of "trial and error."
They often fail to methodically assess the whole range of
possibilities and are prone to accept the most politically
expedient solutions--which is characterized as "muddling
through."[75]

The rational approach--also called the "rational actor" and the "rational-comprehensive" method of analysis--founded on logic and reasoning, seeks to systematically define the problem, develop alternative solutions, assess the probability of the consequences of the options, and by reasoning produce decisions founded on logical principles. It is concerned with producing a balance between values and the environment or, as Walter Lippmann put it, between what is desired and the realistic possibilities.[76] Rational decision-making and analysis applies to the entire range of components in the conduct of foreign relations, including ends and means, feasibilities, and likely outcomes. In other words, it can be said to concentrate on the achievement of national aims, within the limits imposed by given conditions and constraints.

Some maintain that this usage assumes the perspective of a fixed situation in which, at the time of consideration, conditions do not change and which, others contend, is more applicable to certain other fields (especially those involving concrete cost-benefit relations) than to political considerations.[77] Many works on decision-making, largely descriptive and explanatory, which usually pay little attention to justifying their treatment as an analytical tool, fall into this category.

The intermediate eclectic consideration--called "mixed scanning"--attempts to integrate the incremental and rational-comprehensive approaches. It recognizes the limits of human capability to guarantee purely rational decisions and also of the value of methodical analysis, but it applies them primarily to the more important decisions, while employing this arrangement as a context for engaging in incrementalism for less consequential judgments. It therefore bridges the usefulness of both incrementalism and rationalism and seeks to overcome some of their principal deficiencies.[78]

The second paralleling set of distinguishable methods of decision-making and their analysis consists of what are denominated the political, bureaucratic, and pragmatic rational approaches. They are not necessarily mutually exclusive with those previously described.

Briefly, the political interpretation--or the politics of decision-making--popular in the 1950s and 1960s, encompasses the spectrum of agencies, pressures, and other factors--including ideals and ideologies, executive, legislative, and judicial agencies, leaders and elites, diplomatic practice, interest groups, the media, public opinion, governmental procedures, legal and moral constraints, and the like --that have an impact on the making of foreign relations decisions.[79]

In this mode of analysis attention is paid to governmental functioning and output partially coordinated by an interrelated group of leaders, particularly emphasizing political behavior and processes. Many studies of specific policy issues and developments, including those produced by traditionalist historians and social scientists, utilize this method, as do many practitioners, especially at the higher levels.[80]

Often exploratory, descriptive, and explanatory historical
accounts of decisions fall into this category.[81]

The bureaucratic approach became especially popular in
the 1970s, beginning with Allison's analysis. His third model, which he favors, focuses on the influence of participants, their interests, their positions and their interactions within the bureaucracy that is concerned with making
decisions.[82] This method of analysis tends to emphasize
"bureaucratic politics"--the role and pursuasive power of
bureaucratic participants, instrumentalities, and procedures
--and underrates some of those extra-bureaucratic factors
included in the broader political treatment or accentuated in
rational analysis. By the late 1970s analysts developed more
than half a dozen non-traditional approaches to decision-making inquiry including, aside from basic bureaucratic politics, such more specialized treatments as data processing,
cognition, cybernetics, "groupthink," and multiple advocacy
(which is discussed later).

In contrast to these analytical interpretations of decision-making as a process, Cecil V. Crabb, addressing himself
directly to the historical philosophy of American policy and
operational method, contends that the United States has traditionally pursued a pragmatic problem solving approach. He
maintains that this is in keeping with the fact that the
philosophical school of thought known as pragmatism achieved
its highest literary expression and practical application in
America, which affects foreign relations as well as internal
affairs. He claims that the principal "consistency" of
American foreign relations lies "in the high degree of correspondence with pragmatic tenets." While objectives, policies, and procedures may change, this constancy nevertheless
remains manifest in the manner if not the process of making
foreign relations decisions in the United States.[83]

In this context the final approach again concentrates on
rationality--the application of reason, or how the human mind
is actually made up--in arriving at decisions.[84] Such ration-
alism--utilizing an intellectual or cerebral process--perme-
ates all decision-making in some way in that those involved
exercise discretion in making choices and judgments, even
those who are regarded as effective intuitive deciders.

This does not mean that in practice the process external
to the decision maker is necessarily definable as rational,
or that the policies and other determinations made are defensible as rational in the sense that, in terms of conditions and consequences, especially with hindsight, they can
be judged as the most logical and meritorious.[85] Nor does it
mean that reason alone is the source of choice even though
rationalism is the process used in choosing, or that decision-making must fall into the category of the "rational actor's" model to the exclusion of others. In this permeative
sense rationalism in the practice of making decisions cannot
be disregarded, whether the analytical treatment constitutes
historical reanalysis or traditional, political, bureaucratic, multiple advocacy, or any other system of analysis--in
all of which ultimately human beings are presumed to apply
discretion and judgment.

Put another way, it is logical that at key stages of decision-making in international affairs, as in other fields,
deciders must engage in the mental process of choosing among
alternatives. This may occur at the initial or lowest levels
of decision-making, at various intermediate levels, and at
the primary or ultimate level. Therefore the reasoning process is central to the exercise of choice by those who recom-
mend or make the decisions and, as a consequence, cannot be
ignored in decision-making analysis, even though many commentaries deny either that foreign relations decision-making
by practitioners is a rational process or that it is a legitimate method of analysis. In other words, despite the view
that "rational-actor" decision-making analysis fails to lead
to a viable model of foreign policy reanalysis or to an empirically substantiable and generally acceptable theory of
foreign affairs, the role of rationality in the process cannot be denied.

RATIONALISM AS OPERATIONAL PROCESS--ADVOCATORY AND OPTIONS
ANALYSIS METHODS

So far as substance is concerned, as noted, decision-
making is broader in scope than the devisal of public policy
while, in terms of pragmatic functioning, it is narrower than
the overall task of policy-making. In the   realm of foreign
affairs, it pertains not only to the essence of policy, but
also to such related elements as the national interests
served, the national purposes, goals, and objectives to be
achieved, the mechanisms and methods whereby both the ends
and the means to attain them are prescribed, the resources to
be committed, and the strategies of internal and international implementation.

As a matter of practice, distinguishing it from alternative methods of analysis, in essence the intellectual dimension of decision-making, in whatever milieu, entails a logical exercise in perceiving, assessing, and choosing among alternatives. As an organized scheme, it concentrates on the
matter of determining choices and is consequently designed to
coalesce the conception, articulation, and evaluation of, as
well as judicious election among, options. In performing this
undertaking, whereby human minds arrive at judgments, there
are two basic operational techniques--the "advocatory" and
the "options analysis" methods.   These need not be mutually
exclusive and they may be conjoined as correlative modes of
action, even as applied to particularized circumstances.[86]

Advocatory Method

The advocatory (or adjudgment) manner of decision-making
has been described by John Bowling in a series of articles
entitled "How We Do Our Thing," as pertaining to policy formulation in the United States by the Department of State. According to this scheme, the decision maker, at whatever level, occupies the role of judge, with those at lesser levels
advocating policy prescriptions for approval or disapproval.
Unitary advocations merely require a "yes" or "no" determination, and many minor matters or details may be decided in

this fashion. Dual and multiple advocations on a given issue
place the decision maker in the role of exercising choice a-
mong them on the basis of the advocations presented.

This system may be conceived as assimilable to the pattern of water drainage in a river valley, a rivulet feeding a
brook, and it together with other small tributaries flowing
into larger streams and ultimately into the main river, culminating at its mouth where it flows into the sea. This patterning may be viewed as applying within the Department of
State, with the Secretary representing the mouth of the river, or it may be regarded as pertaining to the entire executive branch of the government with the decision-making delta
culminating in the President. Structurally, this constitutes
the hierarchical organization for policy-making, with each
level advocating recommendations and decisions upward and,
according to Bowling, results in "mini-advocacies within
macro-advocacies within mega-advocacies." In some respects
this method is employed by the military and many other bureaucratic agencies.

On the other hand, the traditional judicial process, also utilizing the advocatory system, functions differently in
that the judge (or adjudicatory body) balances prepared advocations of adversary contentions and elects among them in arriving at decisions. While the image of decision making in
the Department of State is that it pursues the river basin or
hierarchical system which allows for the emergence of competing options, actually the Department, according to Bowling,
utilizes the judge/advocate method. Thus, he asserts, skilled
experts assemble facts and arguments for particular decisional options, maximizing benefits and advantages accruing to
the specific recommendation advocated. The decision maker (or
judge) realizes that the advocations are made on behalf of
the interests of bureaucratic clients represented by the advocates, and that these are juxtaposed in the adversary proceeding.[87]

The advocatory process is also examined in some depth
and is recommended for foreign relations decision-making by
Alexander George. He analyzes this decisional method as relating to bureaucratic politics, partisan mutual adjustment,
adversary proceedings, devil's advocation, and other ways of
functioning in seeking to arrive at what he calls "a rational
model of decision making." Differing from Bowling, rather
than restricting himself to the operation of the Department
of State, George addresses himself primarily to the top executive level in the United States, and therefore views the
matter of decision-making from the perspective of the President and his principal assistants, including coordinating
mechanisms epitomized by the National Security Council.

He concentrates on such issues as converting the politics of bureaucracies into effective multiple and competitive
advocacy, collegial decision making, past malfunctioning of
the American policy process, the role of a presidential
"caretaker," and the potentiality of improving foreign policy
formulation through the multiple advocation method. He sup-
plements his presentation with analytical commentary on illustrative cases. He concludes by summarizing the practical

limits and costs of multiple advocacy--as he conceives it--
admitting that it is no panacea, that it does not guarantee
"good" foreign policy decisions in every instance, and that
its effective implementation is not easily achieved.[88]

This means of choice determination--in both its hierarchical flow and judge/advocate guises--has merit, is widely
used, and may be effective. As a process, depending on how
it operates, it may enjoy qualities of simplicity, practicability, and expedition. Presumably, if primary or ultimate
decision makers remain uninvolved until the final stages of
consideration, they may be able to maintain an impartial attitude, but they may also lose the opportunity of managing
the process.

Nevertheless this advocatory system possesses serious
weaknesses. Foreign policy formulation is rarely reducible
to a choice between right and wrong or good and bad, requiring a simple yes/no determination. Inasmuch as choice often
is limited to the best among the better, and a complex array
of alternatives is usually conceivable, the advocatory method
may run the risk that non-advocated alternatives are not adequately considered by the decision maker because they are in-
advertently overlooked, ignored, or consciously eliminated
by advocates rather than by those responsible for decisions.
The latter, therefore, may not be assured adequate consideration of all possible, or conceivably even the most meritorious, alternatives. Options may be foreclosed to the decision
maker by the advocates.

Even worse, the latter may be impelled more by their own
interests than by the need to consider all the possible options. The client(s) whose interests are advocated are bound
to be more parochial than those of the body politic or the
country at large, or at least may be shaped by the particularized persuasions or even the predispositions of the advocates.

Furthermore, some decision makers may be induced to determine choice more on the basis of the effectiveness of an
advocation than on the merit of the alternative and others
tend to be influenced by the least costly, the less complex,
or the most recent advocations. President Warren G. Harding
is reported to have told one of his confidants: "I listen to
one side and they seem right, and then I talk to the other
side and they seem just as right, and there I am where I
started . . . . God what a job." At times, advocates may be
impelled to press those propositions that they believe the
decision maker wishes to have presented for approval. Finally, in the hierarchical mechanism alternatives may be compromised as they proceed up the system, resulting in producing
the most widely consensualized and often substantially diluted alternative, rather than the most inherently meritorious possibility.

Options Analysis Method

The options analysis process of decision-making, on the
other hand, poses the primary decision maker at each level in

the role of considering all factors and reasonable alternatives concerned in the foreign affairs equation, and in consciously managing the deliberation rather than passing only upon those considerations that are presented by advisers and advocates. It concentrates upon the identification of the primary and lesser options and the weighing of their desirability/undesirability, advantage/disadvantage, cost/benefit, and feasibility/unfeasibility interrelationships--with the objective of rational prescription of priorities among sets of possible choices and ultimately of selecting the preferred option(s). It induces, or at least permits, consideration of an optimum quantity of alternatives, thereby maximizing discretion. It may be employed empirically, normatively, hypothetically, or historically, and, by its very nature, it encourages systemization of thought. It involves choosing among missions, among measures, among methods, and among persons.

Options analysis enables the user to focus upon the entire spectrum of elements and sequential phases of foreign relations, or to restrict attention to one or a selected group of its ingredients. Table I depicts the principal steps engaged in by decision makers, and those who assist them, in exercising discretion among alternatives. Not all steps are necessarily consciously treated in the decision-making process, nor in the sequence suggested, but they are essential ingredients for systematic treatment.[89]

This method of analyzing options is applicable to the gamut of foreign affairs problems and developments, as well as to all stages in their progression which permit or require decision-making. By way of illustration, so far as substantive policy is concerned, it may be applied to nascent or evolving conditions, situations, or areas of concern. Similarly, it may be employed to analyze the entire range of issues--or any specific matter--in foreign relations planning. Its most obvious pertinence, however, is to the policy-making that concerns the host of contemporary problems and developments--the primary pragmatic sphere of the practitioner. It also readily lends itself to a review of the roles played by the principal participants in decision-making. Consequently, by applying this analysis it is possible to assess how systematic and how sound was the making of actual decisions.

Options analysis is also applicable to matters of diplomatic procedure. Should the determination simply be declared by the United States or should it be negotiated--that is, should it be unilaterally propounded or multilaterally agreed? If the latter, should this be handled by direct diplomacy--in Washington, in the capital of another negotiating power, or in some neutral place? Should it be the subject of an exchange of written communications, or treated orally and personally by diplomatic representatives? Or should it be dealt with at an ad hoc international conference, or under the aegis of an international organization, and if the latter, which one, or should it rather be considered privately in the lounge or corridors of such a forum?

Moreover, how should negotiations be conducted--at the technical level, by professional diplomats, by Foreign Ministers, or at the summit? What should be the end product--a

Table I
Principal Steps in Decision-Making Process

1. Perceiving the decision-making need, as related to the problem, the crisis, the challenge, or the opportunity, respecting the matters on which objectives, policy positions, strategies, and methods of procedure require determination. This initial and sometimes most difficult task is to define the question or issue itself and, when accurately identified and framed, sometimes it evokes automatic response, and the very way in which the problem is posed may help to shape the decision.

2. Designing the assumptions (where essential) and fixing the scope and parameters of the consideration. This is so vital that a major difference in assumptions may conpletely alter the decision determination.

3. Ascertaining, ordering, and evaluating relevant facts and information concerning the problem under consideration. The degree of thoroughness and accuracy of fact-gathering and evaluation may influence or even predetermine certain phases of decision-making. In short, the validity of those decisions that convert observations or perceptions into facts is crucial to the process.

4. Perceiving and analyzing rationally conceived alternative national interests, goals, and primary and secondary, long-range and immediate, objectives to be served by policy formulation.

5. Assessing the desirability and practicality of such objectives, and deciding on the preferred option(s) or establishing priorities among them.

6. Identifying and evaluating rationally conceived alternative substantive policy solutions--both primary and subsidiary.

7. Weighing the desirability, feasibility, practicability, and possible consequences and costs of each substantive policy and sub-policy alternative, assessing the advantages and disadvantages of each, and deciding on the preferred option(s) or ascribing priorities to them.

8. Defining and scrutinizing alternatives respecting foreign relations methods and procedures, agents, and forums which may be employed, and timing relevant to the pursuance of substantive policy.

9. Contemplating the desirability, feasibility, practicality, and likely consequences respecting each alternative diplomatic method, procedure, agent, forum, and time sequence, and deciding on the preferred option(s) or determining priorities among them, paying particular attention to the possible employment, simultaneously or sequentially, of multiple techniques and forums.

10. Analyzing alternatives respecting the form and timing of policy enunciation--both substantive and procedural.

11. Deciding on the manner of policy enunciation and communication--who, how (both forum and format), and when.

12. Allocating organizational and functional responsibility for policy application and implementation.

13. Reviewing and assessing the effectiveness of both the policy and the fashion in which it is instituted and perceived, and determining whether the consequences are acceptable or reconsideration is required or desirable.

formal treaty or executive agreement, an administrative arrangement, or a simple understanding? Should it be embodied in a mutually signed instrument or an exchange of notes, or should it be in the form of a resolution, declaration, decision, or final act of an international conference or organization, or simply a communiqué? These and a great many other possibilities require prudent consideration in order to manage the methodological elements of foreign affairs intelligently and efficaciously.

This mode of analysis may also be useful if not essential for purposes of critical policy review--respecting both that which actually occurred during a given decision-making venture and that which might have been the logical process, and, in the light of historical fact, that which could theoretically have been undertaken by the decision maker. Both of these review perspectives permit evaluating past experience in a programmed way, and consideration of choice possibilities introduces the advantage of assessment resulting from constructive vicarious simulation. By this analytical system the weighing of alternatives and deciding on preferred options may be subjected to careful reexamination or, should normativity be desired, the projection may be extended to define additional potential choices which at the time may not even have been contemplated by those responsible for arriving at decisions.

APPLICATION OF OPTIONS ANALYSIS

It remains to examine how choice determination may function in practice. As indicated earlier, options analysis may be applied in many ways. At times, the projection of options and resolution of choice must be deliberately pursued, sometimes they become virtually automatic, and occasionally they may even be handled subconsciously. Whatever the foreign relations problem and the manner of dealing with it, however, it would appear that the greater the penetration of analysis and the higher the degree of systematization of cerebration-- and, therefore, the more profound the depth of consciousness of decision makers concerning their craftmanship while wrestling with the issues to which they address themselves--the more reliably will their decisions be made.

As an analytical scheme, as well as for operational purposes, the analyst or decision maker may employ either or both of two basic intellectual processes. One technique, which may be called "systematic query options analysis"--or the Socratic method--is theoretically rudimentary but potentially useful and effective for many problems. It encourages the decision maker to raise all the relevant questions pertaining to the matter under consideration and, in responding to the questions, to arrive at decisions respecting them. Alternatively, decision makers may employ "cosmographic options analysis"--or the Baconian dissectional method--by which· in a systematic way (utilizing either an outline or a diagram) they project the spectrum of alternative elements of the complex and, by means of comparison and juxtaposition, arrive at choice determination. Often the components of the

outline or diagram will be framed in an interrogational manner requiring responses that eventually, in the aggregate,
govern the decisional process and resultant determinations.

The following illustrations elucidate varying features
of the application of options analysis to the principal
stages of decision-making in the context of an actual historical experience utilizing the simple systematic query system
--as applied to framing the Monroe Doctrine; a functional
problem awaiting resolution as well as possible contingency
planning, applying the cosmographic outline depiction--as
pertaining to jurisdiction and control over the seas and seabed and their resources; and the overall policy process hypothetically presented but applicable as well in actual practice, in which the diagrammatic representation is employed.

Simple Systematic Query Analysis

While the chronicling of the formulation of the Monroe
Doctrine and its initial enunciation is well recounted and
documented in the annals of American diplomacy, if this historic policy devisement is isolated for purposes of options
reanalysis, illustrating the historical assessment of policy
formulation, at least sixteen major phases of decision-making
are recognizable, in each of which alternatives must (or
should) have been considered and choices made. Assuming preliminary judgments respecting the prescription of issues, national and vital interests, fundamental goals, and concrete
policy objectives, the main options determination points can
readily be adduced from the series of questions raised in
Table II.

In all probability not all of these phases or questions
were considered separately, and most likely not in the sequence indicated. This suggests that analysis pursued with
hindsight often may be more systematic than that which characterizes decision-making in actual practice.   Many of the
questions raised--or the options-determination points--apply
to each major refinement, restatement, and reinterpretation
of the Monroe Doctrine during the century and a half of its
development and application--including its eventual multi-
lateralization by the Rio Pact of 1947.

This query system of analysis provides a general framework or approach which may be applied to analyzing a good
many similar policy problems, as well as to crisis handling
and other matters. In practice, however, this method is most
appropriate for broad and general policy questions or for
precise matters, including procedural details.[90]

Cosmographic Options Analysis--Outline Configuration

Turning to more comprehensive and complex options projection as applied to a major problem with contemporary and
long-range ramifications, the matter of maritime and seabed
jurisdiction and control as of the commencement of the seabed
exploitation era may be viewed as representative of those
compelling issues in need of extensive and intensive policy

Table II
Systematic Query Analysis—
Principal Options Determination Points:
The Monroe Doctrine

1. Should articulative policy be produced or not? If not, the policy will already have been made.
2. If action is to be taken, which primary agent or agency of government (i.e., the executive, the legislative, or both) should be directly concerned? Which should exercise initiative?
3. If the executive should assume decision-making initiative, which administrative official(s) or agency(ies) should play the leading and decisive role?
4. Should the policy be broad, long-range, and general (i.e., primary and strategic), or merely relevant to specific concerns of the moment or in implementation of existing policy (i.e., subsidiary and tactical)?
5. Should policy be regionaly oriented or encompassed within particularized globally applicable policy (i.e., geographic or functional)?
6. Should policy be simple, that is, focused upon a single matter, or should it be multiple-faceted and embrace several matters (i.e., maintenance of independence, self-determination, non-colonization, non-interposition, international political abstentionism, hemispheric security)?
7. Should policy be merely self-applicable, or should it be made a joint bargain with other countries (i.e., a quid pro quo)?
8. Should policy be issued unilaterally by the United States as the formulating country (i.e., merely declaratory), or multilaterally negotiated and agreed (i.e., joint or mutual understanding or more formal commitment embodied in a treaty or agreement, or in some other form)?
9. If policy is to be joint or mutual, how should it be negotiated?
10. What should be the nature of the end product by which the policy is initially proclaimed?
11. How should the policy be enunciated (i.e., forum and format)? By whom? When? Where?
12. What is the intended primary target of the policy (i.e., Latin American, Spanish and Portuguese, Russian, or other European governments and peoples, or some combination of them)?
13. How should the statement of policy be framed for maximum effect upon the specific target(s)?
14. What national capabilities are essential in order to implement the policy in its intended form with respect to the target(s) to which it is addressed?
15. What are the likely costs, benefits, and feasibilities, and what commitments are likely to be needed and made?
16. What are the possible reactions of other countries (i.e., independent Latin American countries, Latin American colonies, the European powers), and of the United States (Congress, the press, and the public)?

consideration. Not only is such an issue of unequivocal importance, but it is also multifaceted and requires decision
makers to scrutinize potentialities that become increasingly
pressing in the course of time. However, to the extent to
which such deliberation takes on the character of contingency
planning, decisions are not likely to be definitive, and they
may need to be reviewed in the light of subsequent developments and the reactions of other nations. Throughout the
process, a host of determinations needs to be made respecting
a variety of desires, precepts, and procedures, as featured
in Table III.[91]

Even casual acquaintance with the subject of maritime
and seabed jurisdiction, management, and exploitation suggests several broad areas of policy concern.   These embrace
the national framing and institution of a program, promotion
of exploitation technology, engagement in resource development, and resolution of jurisdictional and international
control matters.   Except for the possibilities of non-uni-
lateral resource development and exploitation, only the last
of these broad aspects of the resources question has direct
and significant relevance to foreign policy formulation.

Presuming independent resolution of official positions
on such factors as national and vital interests, objectives,
implementation capabilities, the internal governmental mechanism for handling developmental activities and policy-making, and the foreign affairs techniques employable in the
pursuit of policy, there appear to be half a dozen primary
areas of substantive concern: Should jurisdiction and control
over the seabed and its resources be subjected to unilateral
national, to multilateral (i.e., international), or to some
combination of authority and regulation?   Should governing
prescriptions be reduced to principles of parallel national
or of multipartite international law?   What fundamental
type(s) of juridical premises and postulates should prevail?
What should be the principal objects of definable legal
principles--that is, to what kinds of phenomena should jurisdiction and control pertain? Which types of man-made instrumentalities, and what forms of human usage, should be
subjected to jurisdiction and control? Finally, what special
legal issues and international political factors may be involved?

Each of these aspects of the maritime and seabed resources problem, to which options analysis and decision-making may be applied, entails the development of primary and
secondary, and in some cases of subsidiary and even lesser
policy, as illustrated in Table III, which suggests approximately seventy-five options determination points. These
include some thirty primary components, consisting of nearly
one hundred sub-elements, which in turn are composed of a
good many subordinate constituents.

Sets of choices may also be ascribed to diplomatic
method and procedure for implementing national policy, for
achieving negotiated international arrangements and commitments governing jurisdiction and control, and for effectuat-
ing agreed understandings. Other matters requiring decisions
are distinctions in principle and applicability as between

Table III
Cosmographic Options Analysis—Outline
Configuration: Principal Options
Determination Points in Developing Policy
Concerning Jurisdiction and Control Over
the Seas and Seabed and Their Resources

I. BASIC DETERMINATIONS:
- A. Policy Formulation (Nature of Policy Determination):
  1. National?
  2. International?
  3. Combination?
- B. Nature of Policy:
  1. *De novo*?
  2. Extension of Preexisting Policy Regarding:
     a. Seas?
     b. Seabed?
     c. Resources?
- C. Policy Relationship to Law:
  1. Reduce Policy to Rules of Law?
  2. Defer Juridical Application?
- D. International Law (Process of Formulating):
  1. By Preplanning — *De Jure* Precepts Based on Merit?
  2. By Permitting *De Facto* Practice to Determine *De Jure* Postulates?
  3. Combination?

II. JURIDICAL FUNDAMENTALS:
- A. Basic Legal Hypothesis:
  1. *Res Communis*?
  2. *Res Nullius*?
  3. Combination?
- B. Basic Type of Legal System:
  1. International Custom?
  2. International Comity?
  3. Binding Legal Precepts?
  4. Combination?
- C. Legal Precepts:
  1. Continuity / Contiguity?
  2. Prescription?
  3. Discovery and Exploration?
  4. Effective Occupation?
  5. Arbitrary Demarcation?
  6. Combination?
- D. Legal Process:
  1. Asseveration (National) and Acquiescence (International)?
  2. Parallel Municipal (National) Law:
     a. Identical?
     b. Similar?
  3. Treaty Law:
     a. Bilateral?
     b. Multilateral:
        (1) Selective (Limited Number of Powers)?
        (2) General (Concerned Powers)?
        (3) Universal (All Powers)?
     c. Combination?

E. Nature of Juridical Application:
    1. Jurisdiction (Sovereignty)?
    2. Control Without Jurisdiction?
    3. Possession (Property Rights):
      a. Public?
      b. Private?
    4. Combination?

F. Determination by:
    1. International Conference (Ad Hoc)?
    2. International Organization:
      a. United Nations?
      b. Other Organization(s)?
    3. Combination?

III. PRIMARY OBJECTS (OF JURISDICTION AND CONTROL):

A. Seas:
    1. Territorial Waters (Including Seabed):
      a. Width?
      b. Special Water Areas:
        (1) Bays?
        (2) Gulfs?
        (3) Straits?
        (4) Isthmuses?
        (5) Others?
    2. Beyond Territorial Waters (Excluding Seabed):
      a. Contiguous Zone(s) — General?
      b. Specialized Jurisdiction(s):
        (1) Taxation?
        (2) Customs?
        (3) Quarantine?
        (4) Others?

B. Space *Per Se:*
    1. Simple Areal Projection?
    2. Physiographic (Geological and Geophysical) Elements:
      a. Territorial Seaspace — Marginal Waters?
      b. Continental Shelf?[1]
      c. Continental Slope?[2] } .... Continental Margins
      d. Continental Rise?[3]
      e. Deep Seabed (Abyssal Plain or Depth)?[4]
      f. Ocean Ridges (etc.)?

C. Resources of Seas:
    1. Fish:
      a. Finfish?   a. Natural (Uncontrolled)?
      b. Shellfish?   b. Aquaculture (Cultivated)?
    2. Drugs?[5]
    3. Minerals?[6]

D. Resources from Seabed (Surface):
    1. Animal Life?
    2. Vegetable Life?
    3. Minerals, etc.:
      a. Building Materials?[7]
      b. Heavy Minerals?[8]
      c. Phosphorite?[9]
      d. Manganese Nodules?

Table III (continued)

       e. Red Sea Geothermal Deposits? [10]
       f. Others? [11]

  E. Resources of Seabed (Subsurface):
      1. Petroleum and Natural Gas?   ⎫
      2. Sulphur?   ⎬ Extracted From Holes Bored in Sea Floor
      3. Coal?   ⎭
      4. Iron Ore?   ⎫ Mined by Shafts and Drifts
      5. Other Vein Deposits? ⎭

  F. Man-Made Facilities and Intrumentalities:
      1. Location:
         a. Surface (of Water):
           (1) Floating?
           (2) Non-Floating?
         b. Sub-Surface (in Water)?
         c. On Seabed?
         d. Below Seabed Surface?
      2. Type:
         a. Manned?
         b. Unmanned?

  G. Individuals (Persons):
      1. Public?
      2. Private:
         a. Corporate?
         b. Individuals?
      3. Combination?

IV. Usages (Functional):

  A. Transit?

  B. Information Acquisition and Exploration:
      1. Scientific Exploration?
      2. Commercial Exploration?
      3. Salvage Exploration?

  C. Communications:
      1. Cables?
      2. Stations?
      3. Electronic and Other Interception Facilities?

  D. Salvage Operations:
      1. Above Seabed Surface?
      2. On Seabed Surface?
      3. Below Seabed Surface?

  E. Commercial:
      1. Acquisition: Extraction, Farming, Fishing, Mining, Drilling, etc.?
      2. Processing/Fabricating?
      3. Others:
         a. Loading?
         b. Storage?
         c. Shipment?
         d. Transshipment?

  F. Military:
      1. Nature of Instrumentality:
         a. Nuclear Weaponry?
         b. Conventional Weaponry?
         c. Logistical Facilities?

d. Electronic and Other Warning Installations?
2. Nature of Facility:
    a. Mobile:
        (1) Floating?
        (2) Submerged?
    b. Fixed:
        (1) Anchored?
        (2) Attached to Seabed?

V. SPECIAL PROBLEMS AND ISSUES:

A. Administration of Rules:
1. National?
2. International?
3. Joint or Combination?

B. Implementation of Programs — Type of Function:
1. Licensing?
2. Inspection?
3. Policing?
4. Management?

C. Damage and Liability:
1. Ecology — General?
2. Water:
    a. Depletion or Level Changes?
    b. Pollution: Sewage, Dumping, Ocean Waste Disposal, Oil Spills, Thermal, Others?
3. Seabed Surface:
    a. Contamination?
    b. Change of Contour?
4. Resources:
    a. Depletion?
    b. Conservation?
    c. Replenishment?

D. Accidents:
1. To Men?
2. To Facilities?
3. To Equipment?

E. Income and Profits:
1. Licensing Fees?
2. Royalties?
3. Taxes?
4. Others?

F. Resolution of Disputes:
1. Nature of Disputants:
    a. Intergovernmental?
    b. Private Parties?
    c. Mixed?
2. Nature of Judicial Process:
    a. Criminal?
    b. Civil?
    c. Combination?
3. Agency to Resolve:
    a. National?
    b. International?

Table III (continued)

      c. Combination?
    4. Process of Resolution:
      a. Negotiation?
      b. Conciliation?
      c. Arbitration:
        (1) Voluntary?
        (2) Compulsory?
      d. Adjudication:
        (1) Voluntary?
        (2) Compulsory?
      e. Appeals?
      f. Final Jurisdictional Authority?

VI. POLICY MAKING AND IMPLEMENTATION METHOD AND PROCEDURE:

    A. Policy Making:
      1. Initiatory and/or Reactive?
      2. Government Leadership:
        a. Executive:
          (1) Level: Presidential, Cabinet, Professional, Technical, Other?
          (2) Agency(ies)?
        b. Legislature?
        c. Combination?
      3. Private Interests?

    B. Policy Implementation:
      1. Policy Enunciation:
        a. Form?
        b. Forum?
        c. Format?
        d. Timing?
      2. Negotiation:
        a. Parties?
        b. Forum(s):
          (1) Regularized?
          (2) Ad Hoc?
      3. End-Product(s):
        a. Agreement / Treaty / Convention?
        b. Parties: Bipartite / Multipartite?
        c. Integration:
          (1) Package Arrangement?
          (2) Individual Items by Segmented Peeling Off?
        d. Sequence?

---

1. To 200 meters depth or 100 fathoms — varying from 1 to 800 miles distance outward.
2. To 1,400 / 3,200 meters depth.
3. To 4,000 meters depth.
4. Beyond 4,000 meters depth.
5. From organisms in seas.
6. From sea water: salt, magnesium. sulphur, potassium, bromine, boron, etc.
7. Sand, gravel, calcium carbonate shells.
8. Washed to sea but remain near shore.
9. Precipitation of phosphates from sea water.
10. Pools of hot brine on sea floor.
11. Clays, oozes, barite, etc.

jurisdiction, on the one hand, and control, on the other, and the questions whether policy should be fabricated as a comprehensive, coalesced aggregate of precepts, or whether separable aspects should be handled piecemeal.

Even if governments decide to "peel off" individual functional elements of such a convoluted issue for separate policy solution, they must choose among alternative courses of progression. Logically, either they commence with the most basic and significant substantive factors concerned in the policy-making problem, resolve them, and then proceed to the more specific and highly refined. Or, conversely, they begin with the more immediate and precise elements that require urgent resolution and then proceed, step by step, to the more general and comprehensive. Or they may determine policy respecting those matters that become most amenable to international resolution, or on which the greatest vested interest or demand materializes, dealing with each as it emerges into the realm of need or negotiability.

For comparative purposes, Table IV depicts a simplified version of the same kind of outline configuration respecting the development of policy concerning jurisdiction and control over outer space, as of the commencement of the space age. It identifies some forty options determination points, not including basic goals, concrete objectives, benefits, costs, or details of diplomatic procedure. Many of the sub-components consist of additional subsidiary items.

As a matter of actual practice, the major steps taken in the field of space jurisdiction and control appear to evidence resort to the "peeling off" and segmental decision alternative, rather than to the systematized structuring of policy for the entire subject. Consequently, the governments of the leading space powers have proceeded to negotiate separate juridical arrangements for such matters as exploration and use of outer space, registration of objects launched into space, international liability for damage caused by such objects, control of space radio communications, inappropriability of jurisdiction over the moon and other celestial bodies, the rescue and return of astronauts landing in foreign territory as a result of accident or emergency, and various aspects of arms limitation--including the ban on nuclear testing, prohibitions against the establishment of military bases and the testing of weapons in space, the conduct of military maneuvers on celestial bodies, and the placing of nuclear and other weapons of mass destruction in orbit around the earth or in space.

In summary, because of delay in national policy-making and international control negotiation, pragmatic space development has come to circumscribe the international consummation of proclaimed policy respecting space jurisdiction and control. The result has been that by and large de facto practice has tended to predetermine negotiability of de jure policy arrangements--and perhaps even the very national formulation of such policy as well. This should not be too surprising, however, because much the same occurred in developing international law governing aerial jurisdiction.[92]

Table IV
Cosmographic Options Analysis—Outline
Configuration: Principal Options
Determination Points in Developing Policy
Concerning Space Jurisdiction and Control

I. BASIC DETERMINATION:
  - A. National (unilateral) practice?
  - B. International law:
    1. By pre-planning — *de jure* precepts based on merit?
    2. By permitting *de facto* practice to determine *de jure* postulates?

II. TYPE OF FUNDAMENTAL JURIDICAL PRINCIPLES:
  - A. International custom?
  - B. General international law and comity?
  - C. Asseveration and acquiescence (i.e., prescription)?
  - D. Convention: bilateral / multilateral?
  - E. Determination by international organization (i.e., United Nations, other)?
  - F. Combination?

III. PRIMARY OBJECTS:
  - A. Space *per se*: based on atmosphere/gravity / distance from earth/other?
  - B. Man-made physical instrumentalities (see next main   category)?
  - C. Individuals (persons): public / private / both?
  - D. Celestial bodies?
  - E. Several?   F. All?

IV. PHYSICAL INSTRUMENTALITIES:
  - A. Satellites?
  - B. Space vehicles: manned / unmanned; living beings aboard / not aboard?
  - C. Orbiting space platforms?
  - D. Transiting missiles: military/non-military?
  - E. Space refuse?
  - F. Others?

V.   Usage (functional):
A. Information acquisition?
B. Scientific exploration?
C. Communications?
D. Commercial: transit/facilities/resources/others?
E. Electronics?
F. Military and security?
G. Others?

VI. Special legal problems:

A. Acquisition of potential physical assets:
1. Public/private?
2. Administration of: national/joint/international?
B. Liability and damage:
1. In space: instrumentalities/persons?
2. On earth: returning space instrumentalities/persons?
3. Contamination: space *per se*/instrumentalities/celestial bodies?
C. Possessory rights:
1. National/international?
2. Public/private?
3. For profit/non-profit?
D. Resolution of disputes:
1. Intergovernmental/private/both?
2. Civil/criminal?
3. Agency: national/international/both?
4. Process: negotiation/conciliation/arbitration/adjudication/others?
5. Enforcement of determinations: national/international/both?

VII. Special international political problems:
A. National security and defense strategy?
B. National power and prestige?
C. Interplanetary peace and stability?
D. Others?

Cosmographic Options   Analysis--Diagrammatic Configuration

Projecting a comprehensive hypothetical, though nevertheless pragmatically applicable, example of cosmographic
options analysis, using the diagrammatic representation, as
illustrated in Figure 2, it is easily possible to identify
more than three dozen key points at which determinations
among choices are apt to be essential in foreign relations
decision-making of consequence. To recapitulate, the principal phases normally requiring decisions on alternatives
include whether policy is essential or desirable at all, relationship to national interests, basic goals, national capability, and national strategy, the objectives and nature of
the policy to be established, the officials or agencies to
be involved in making decisions, the forums in which and procedures whereby determinations are to be proclaimed and pursued, the nature and format of the end product in which they
are to be embodied, the fashion in which they are to be implemented, and whether reactions in the national or international environment produce such a modification of circumstances or attitudes as to necessitate recommencing deliberation to modify previous decisions.

While Figure 2 depicts the skeletonized elements of the
decision-making process, the configuration of its application
to specific circumstances may vary considerably. So far as
the first phase is concerned, as suggested in Table I, in
some cases it may be most difficult to decide the basic questions whether policy needs to be formulated at all (and this
should be deliberately decided and should not result from in-
advertence or complacency), whether the policy should apply
to the immediate situation or be more general and enduring,
and whether national interests/vital interests are affected.
Often decisions on such fundamental questions govern the extent, intensity, and level of the decision-making experience,
as well as matters related to method, timing, and end product. Moreover, indecision at this initial stage may be tan-
tamount to an overt negative determination.

Throughout the decision venture, but especially during
this initial phase, as already noted, information and intel-
ligence--listed as item three in Table I--are crucial to the
production of sound judgments. Their quality is unlikely to
exceed the capacity of the decisional undertaking and, in
turn, it is generally conceded, the quality of the process
and its end products can scarcely exceed the facts upon which
they are based. To a substantial degree the effectiveness of
formulating aims, policies, and tactics depends on the validity of those preliminary decisions which convert observations
and perceptions into facts. Such decisions, establishing the
verity of the informational base may consequently not only
temper, but even determine the outcome of the entire decision-making venture.

In several phases the decision process consists of four
distinguishable stages, which constitute the central feature
of options analysis and resolution: identifying potential alternatives; analyzing the advantages and disadvantages of
each; weighing the alternatives in relation to interests, ob-

Figure 2
Cosmographic Options Analysis—Diagrammatic Configuration: Principal Options Determination Points in Foreign Relations Decision-Making—Hypothetical Projection for United States

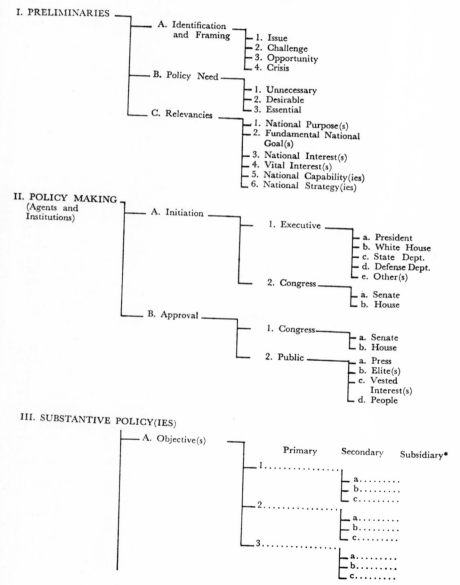

I. PRELIMINARIES

A. Identification and Framing
1. Issue
2. Challenge
3. Opportunity
4. Crisis

B. Policy Need
1. Unnecessary
2. Desirable
3. Essential

C. Relevancies
1. National Purpose(s)
2. Fundamental National Goal(s)
3. National Interest(s)
4. Vital Interest(s)
5. National Capability(ies)
6. National Strategy(ies)

II. POLICY MAKING
(Agents and Institutions)

A. Initiation
1. Executive
   a. President
   b. White House
   c. State Dept.
   d. Defense Dept.
   e. Other(s)
2. Congress
   a. Senate
   b. House

B. Approval
1. Congress
   a. Senate
   b. House
2. Public
   a. Press
   b. Elite(s)
   c. Vested Interest(s)
   d. People

III. SUBSTANTIVE POLICY(IES)

A. Objective(s)

Primary Secondary Subsidiary*

1..................
   a.........
   b.........
   c.........
2..................
   a.........
   b.........
   c.........
3..................
   a.........
   b.........
   c.........

Figure 2 (continued)

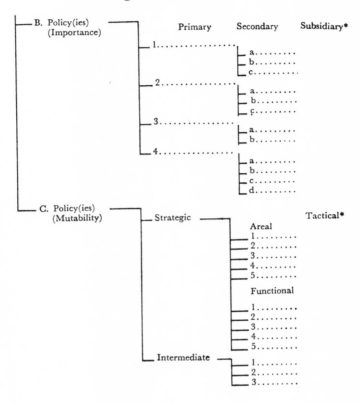

IV. POLICY IMPLEMEN-
TATION
(Procedural Policy)

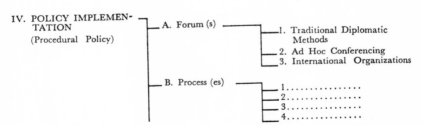

A. Forum (s)

1. Traditional Diplomatic
   Methods
2. Ad Hoc Conferencing
3. International Organizations

B. Process (es)

1. . . . .
2. . . . .
3. . . . .
4. . . . .

* Subsidiary, tactical, and lesser elements are not depicted.

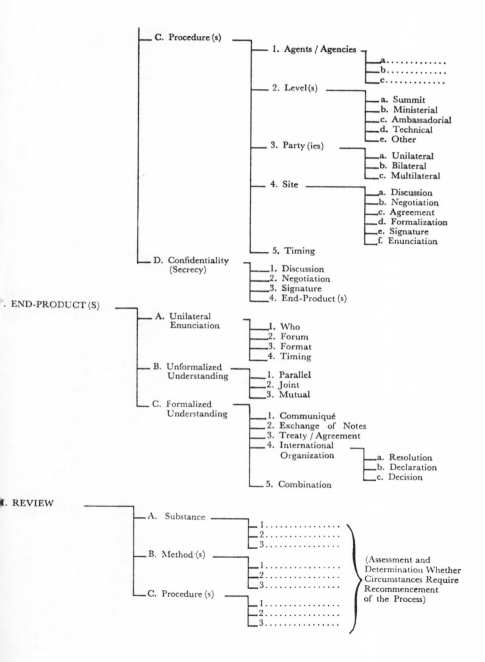

C. Procedure (s)

1. Agents / Agencies
   - a..............
   - b..............
   - c..............

2. Level(s)
   - a. Summit
   - b. Ministerial
   - c. Ambassadorial
   - d. Technical
   - e. Other

3. Party (ies)
   - a. Unilateral
   - b. Bilateral
   - c. Multilateral

4. Site
   - a. Discussion
   - b. Negotiation
   - c. Agreement
   - d. Formalization
   - e. Signature
   - f. Enunciation

5. Timing

D. Confidentiality (Secrecy)
   1. Discussion
   2. Negotiation
   3. Signature
   4. End-Product (s)

. END-PRODUCT (S)

A. Unilateral Enunciation
   1. Who
   2. Forum
   3. Format
   4. Timing

B. Unformalized Understanding
   1. Parallel
   2. Joint
   3. Mutual

C. Formalized Understanding
   1. Communiqué
   2. Exchange of Notes
   3. Treaty / Agreement
   4. International Organization
      - a. Resolution
      - b. Declaration
      - c. Decision
   5. Combination

. REVIEW

A. Substance
   1..............
   2..............
   3..............

B. Method·(s)
   1..............
   2..............
   3..............

C. Procedure (s)
   1..............
   2..............
   3..............

(Assessment and Determination Whether Circumstances Require Recommencement of the Process)

jectives, capabilities, feasibility, and possible consequences; and deciding upon the preferred alternatives or priorities among them. During analysis these stages may be handled
independently, or they may be combined. This process is
graphically illustrated in Figure 3, which depicts the general flow of analysis during decision-making respecting all
major components of the conduct of foreign affairs and exem-
plifies such deliberation at various levels. Figure 4 suggests the hypothetical patterning of the complex of primary,
secondary, and lesser substantive policy components resulting
from the process, illustrating the possibility of overlap and
inconsistency that may occur.

RELATIONSHIP OF OPTIONS DETERMINATION TO CAPABILITY AND FEASIBILITY

Assessments of the advantages and disadvantages of policy alternatives by the decision maker in a practical foreign
relations situation need to reflect both immediate and potential capabilities and overall national strategy. The liber-
ality or restrictiveness of capability interpretation colors
the assessments--and therefore the decisions--that result.
Under the exigencies of actual experience, if too much emphasis is placed on pre-existing capabilities conservatively
construed, the maximum value of options analysis may be un-
achieved. In other words, care needs to be exercised by decision makers that whenever possible all reasonable options
are established and considered on their intrinsic merits, not
only those that may appear most feasible in terms of current
capabilities, so that under potentially achievable conditions
the most meritorious option may be decided upon, if necessary
even at the cost of modifying capabilities to render the preferred option realizable. Often, because of pressures of time
and circumstance, this is not possible and decisions are
based on the greatest apparent benefit--or the least disad-
vantage--or the minimum risk or cost--in view of then existing capabilities.

At the same time, caution needs to be exercised that determinations are founded on the comparative superiority of
foreign affairs choices in relation to consciously determined
objectives, not solely on capabilities, so as to avoid elect-
ing a more extreme option merely because it is regarded as
capable of achievement. There are times when power and influence must be deliberately managed and restrained, thereby
preventing maximum capability from predetermining policy.
Power is accompanied by responsibility and, on balance, the
latter should be overriding. Carl J. Friedrich has found
that "responsibility is a fairly recent term in the vocabulary of political theory," although more than a century ago
Lord Macaulay propounded that "the highest proof of virtue is
to possess boundless power without abusing it."[93] Entirely
aside from moral prescriptions, however, wise decision makers
base their judgments on inherent worthiness as related to ob-
jectives--not merely on the quality or degree of practicability in terms of national capability. As a result, the decision maker needs to gauge capability (potential as well as
actual) of alternative options and then decide upon that (or
those) which should be preferred on the basis of merit and

Figure 3
Substantive Foreign Relations Decision-
Making Options Analysis: Hypothetical
Flow Model

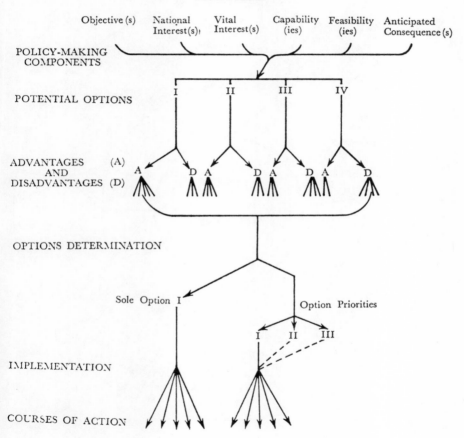

Figure 4
Substantive Foreign Policy Options:
Hypothetical Structure Model

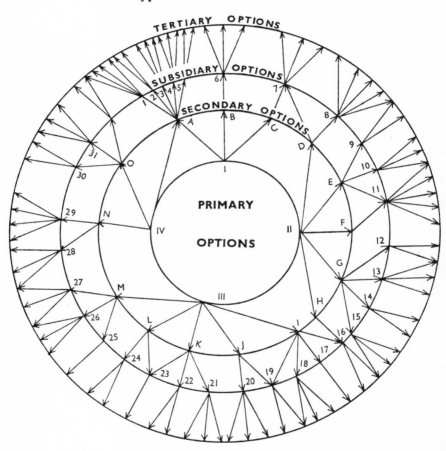

Note: The farther the spectrum of possibilities is extrapolated, the more overlap and inconsistency are likely to occur.

benefit.

Reassessment with hindsight, advance policy-making respecting a new problem, and long-range planning generally need not be pursued under the pressures characteristic of day-to-day or crisis deliberation and afford the advantage of greater lead time. This affects not only the breadth and depth of information and objectivity of analysis that can be brought to bear, but in the case of de novo deliberation and contingency planning also provides an opportunity for determining choices primarily on the basis of mission and value and of tailoring capability to support it. These advantages should induce the managers of the decision-making apparatus to come to grips with problems and issues at as early a stage as possible.

It is equally clear that the options determination process of each country operates in a dichotomous relationship and that this bears an important relevance to options feasibility. Decision among alternatives in foreign relations--as in any competitive or adversary setting--juxtaposes the options of one participant against those of another. Therefore, decision makers need to devote attention to relating possible choices and their ordering to those of each of the other governments that is intimately or seriously concerned. In other words, it is imperative to ascertain, or at least project, what other nations regard as their interests (especially their vital interests) and their objectives and to assess their possible options.[94] In so doing, those making the decisions must consciously, while aggrandizing their own national advantages, also minimize the disadvantages to other governments of accepting their decisions.

As a consequence, it is axiomatic, that in the conduct of foreign affairs merit and capability must be complemented by feasibility, and if decision makers can proffer what may be called "yessable propositions"--if they are able to achieve not only acquiescence to, but also preference for, their choices on the part of other governments--they will have maximized the "effectability" if not the effectiveness of their decisions. In the long run, they are less likely to attain their objectives by coercion than by consent and correlation. In short, the analysis of options cannot be pursued in a vacuum, but, in keeping with Dean Rusk's distinction between "conclusion" and "decision" referred to earlier, must take account of the realizability of choices available in the situational and performance milieu within which the decision maker operates.

THE VERDICT

Finally, calculating the verdict on the nation's conduct of foreign relations is itself complex and perplexing. Are judgments directed primarily at overall national behavior, the foreign affairs process, the functioning of planning, the formulation of policy doctrine or strategies, specific decisions, or particular methods of analysis or theoretical constructs? Do they focus on national ideals, interests, basic goals, concrete objectives, or policies and procedures--or on

some combination of them? Do they reflect the concerns and
expectations of decision makers, or of media commentators,
public opinion, historians and other academic analysts, or
foreign nations and their governments? In other words, who
are those doing the assessing and what are they evaluating?

In addition, do those rendering judgments realize the
significance of such differences as fundamental or initial
and incremental, strategic and tactical (based on durability), primary and secondary (based on importance), static and
dynamic, immediate and long-range, and subtantive and procedural end products? Do appraisals pay attention to what
Lentner calls "units of analysis," including the international system, developing situations, and participating actors?[95]
Do they deal sufficiently--or primarily--with the relation of
means to ends sought, capability and feasibility to desirability, cost to effectiveness, or risk to benefits? For example, is the assessor more concerned with minimum cost or
maximum advantage, and do the benefits outweigh the costs
and risks? If the decision-making process and its results
are less than perfect, are they nevertheless the best among
the possibilities?

Quincy Wright points out that decision-making craftsman-
ship--or statesmanship--requires careful steering between
"the Scylla of rigid national policies and the Charybdis of
unacceptable international policies."[96] Frankel maintains
that only in unusual cases "is it possible to estimate clearly the success or the failure of a decision . . . . Usually,
however, success is partial and inconclusive; the final result is in the direction sought but the objective is not fully achieved, or achieved at a cost higher than anticipated."
He concedes that "it is difficult to agree on a yardstick for
success."[97]

In evaluating the foreign policy made, Kurt London cautions that it is inextricably tied to domestic issues (including economic, social, and psychological as well as political considerations), that it is only as sturdy as the relative defensive and offensive potential it has at its dispos-
al, that it is only as sound as the data on which it is
founded, and that it is only as effective as the degree to
which it can be implemented. "There can be no quick decisions of foreign policy other than tactical and temporary
ones. Basic policies can only hope to become successful if
they can be developed slowly and deliberately."[98]

Commentaries vary on the tests to be applied. De Rivera
appraises such guidelines as consensus, reasonableness (based
on a set of principles), "the structure of the stimulus" that
invokes the making of decisions, "the structure of the situation," the adequacy of information, and realism.[99] Discussing the effectiveness of the foreign relations system within
a nation, Lentner distinguishes between the effectiveness of
overt actions (particularly the application of instruments or
techniques and the mobilization of resources) and effects of
foreign policies. He proposes separate series of eight postulates for each of these considerations. Illustrations include the mobilization of a nation "tends to create new expectations and new norms of behavior in the population," the

creation of foreign affairs bureaucracies "leads to constit-
uency and coordination problems," the expenditure or destruction of resources "diminishes the capacity of a state to act
in the future," and treaties limit the freedom of national
action.[100]

Emphasizing the efficiency of decision-making, John Lovell explores the criteria for examining the ratio of outputs
to inputs and the comparison of actual and ideal performance.
He also recognizes the difficulty of defining and applying
indexes of measurement and reliable empirical and normative
tests, the problem of relating performance to values, and the
differences between democratic and autocratic methods of conducting foreign affairs. He admits that the key task "in
formulating and executing foreign-policy decisions has become
increasingly complex."[101] The problem is most acute, however, for those who develop analysis with a view to prediction
and forecasting.[102]

Commenting on presidential determinations in the United
States, Theodore Sorensen, who served in the White House, observes: "the only way to assure good presidential decisions
is to elect and support good Presidents. For in mixing all
these ingredients, his style and standard, his values and vitality, his insights and outlook will make the crucial difference. A great presidential decision defies the laws of
mathematics and exceeds the sum of all its parts." Crucial
and lasting decisions in human affairs, he says, involve
value judgments that are tempered by challenge and nourished
by responsibility.[103]

Foreign relations decision makers at all levels can
scarcely avoid this responsibility of seeking to produce the
soundest determinations possible in the most thoughtful and
deliberative way. To do this, it would seem that they need
to be as methodical and systematic as they can. The making
of decisions will scarcely achieve an excellence exceeding
the limits of the human intelligence and discretional competence applied to it. To be effective, therefore, decision-
making requires not only the essential qualities of the art
but, as a deliberative process, it must also be managed in
such a manner as to approximate a science.

Intelligently designed and applied foreign relations decision-making has the advantage of enabling the options de-
terminator, the scholarly analyst, and the appraiser to pay
greater attention to normativity--as distinguished from expediency restricted to the circumstances of the moment, of
achieving greater objectivity, and of encouraging greater
systematization respecting both the decision process and the
components of the foreign relations anatomy.

Practitioners of statecraft find merit in having and, if
possible, keeping their options reasonably viable to avert
frozen postures and atrophied methods. History is astatic
and no nation controls its relations with others absolutely.
The conduct of its foreign affairs--except with respect to
fundamentally vital interests--needs to be flexible, and such
resilience is enhanced by assiduous apperception of the entire range of options available, and by the prudent exercise

of discretion in making decisions.

NOTES

1. Harold and Margaret Sprout, *Toward a Politics of the Planet Earth* (New York: Van Nostrand, 1971), pp. 96-98, 191, 193. Because human beings are involved, "psychological factors are crucial in the decision process"; see "Decision Makers," *The International Relations Dictionary*, 3d ed., edited by Jack C. Plano and Ray Olton (Santa Barbara, Calif.: ABC-Clio, 1982), p. 6. For additional comment, see James R. Cobbledick, *Choice in American Foreign Policy: Options for the Future* (New York: Crowell, 1973), pp. 21-23, and Joseph H. de Rivera, *The Psychological Dimension of Foreign Policy* (Columbus, Ohio: Merrill, 1968), Chapter 4, especially pp. 105-6.

2. Quincy Wright, *The Study of International Relations* (New York: Appleton-Century-Crofts, 1955), pp. 572-74. He specifically credits diplomacy, mediation, negotiation, policy-making, and the overall conduct of foreign affairs, as well as decision-making, as being arts. See also his Chapters 15 and 16.

3. See Elmer Plischke, "The Optimum Scope of Instruction in Diplomacy," in *Diplomacy: The Liberal Arts Approach*, edited by Smith Simpson, Monograph 13 of the American Academy of Political and Social Science (Philadelphia: April 1972), pp. 1-3, and Elmer Plischke, "Treatment of 'Diplomacy' in International Relations Textbooks," *World Affairs* 135 (Spring 1973): 332-33. Seé also such volumes as Thomas A. Bailey, *The Art of Diplomacy: The American Experience* (New York: Appleton-Century-Crofts, 1968); Elmer Plischke, *Modern Diplomacy: The Art and the Artisans* (Washington: American Enterprise Institute, 1979); Charles Roetter, *The Diplomatic Art* (Philadelphia: Macrae Smith, 1963); Charles K. Webster, *The Art and Practice of Diplomacy* (London: London School of Economics, 1952). See also commentary in such glossaries as Melquiades J. Gamboa, *Elements of Diplomatic and Consular Practice: A Glossary* (Quezon City, Philippines: Central Lawbook Publishing Co., 1966) and Robert B. Harmon, *The Art and Practice of Diplomacy: A Selected and Annotated Guide* (Metuchen, N.J.: Scarecrow, 1971), pp. 160-74.

4. For illustrations of those who do, see Joseph D. Cooper, *The Art of Decision-Making* (Garden City, N.Y.: Doubleday, 1961); Bertrand de Jouvenal, *The Art of Conjecture*, translated by Nikita Lary (New York: Basic Books, 1967); and Wayne A. R. Leys, *Ethics for Policy Decisions: The Art of Asking Deliberative Questions* (Englewood Cliffs, N.J.: Prentice-Hall, 1952).

5. James N. Rosenau, *The Scientific Study of Foreign Policy* (New York: Free Press, 1971), Chapter 9, especially pp. 251-54. He also deals with the "decision-making approach," its impact on foreign policy analysis, and the need for developing a theory of foreign relations. See also note 73. See also Burton M. Sapin, *The Making of United States Foreign Policy* (New York: Praeger, 1966), Chapter 8 on "Science and Foreign Policy," especially pp. 217-23.

6. For example, see Arnold Kaufman, *The Science of Decision-Making* translated by Rex Audley (New York: McGraw-Hill, 1968), especially pp. 34-35, 244-45, who claims that "a science of action is attainable," p. 244; J. Morgan Jones, *Introduction to Decision Theory* (Homewood, Ill.: Richard D. Irwin, 1977), Chapter 13 entitled "Toward a Practical Science," pp. 300-31, who considers his volume "an introduction to the sci-

ence known as decision theory" (p. 1) and asserts that several aspects of decision theory have even mutated from a science to a useful analytical tool; and J. D. White, *Decision Theory* (Chicago: Aldine, 1969), who discusses "scientific method" which he identifies with the process of prediction, pp. 117-126. See also Russell L. Ackoff, *Scientific Method: Optimizing Applied Research Decisions* (New York: Wiley, 1962), and James Bates, "A Model for the Science of Decisions," *Philosophy of Science* 21 (October 1954): 326-39.

7. See also comments respecting planning in Chapter 8.

8. For examples of general studies on foreign policy-making, see note 44.

9. Joseph Frankel, *The Making of Foreign Policy: An Analysis of Decision Making* (New York: Oxford University Press, 1963), p. 5.

10. See James A. Robinson, "Decision-Making--Political Aspects," *International Encyclopedia of the Social Sciences* (1968) IV: 55.

11. See "Decision Making," *The Public Administration Dictionary*, edited by Ralph C. Chandler and Jack C. Plano (New York: Wiley, 1982), p. 114.

12. Graham T. Allison, *Essence of Decision: Explaining the Cuban Missile Crisis* (Boston: Little, Brown, 1971), p. 10.

13. Howard H. Lentner, *Foreign Policy Analysis: A Comparative and Conceptual Approach* (Columbus, Ohio: Merrill, 1974), pp. 9-10. On choice determination, see also J. W. Burton, *Systems, States, Diplomacy, and Rules* (Cambridge: Cambridge University Press, 1968), pp. 58-63.

14. See Lentner, *Foreign Policy Analysis*, p. 197.

15. See John P. Lovell, *Foreign Policy in Perspective: Strategy, Adaptation, Decision Making* (New York: Holt, Rinehart, and Winston, 1970), p. 220.

16. Charles O. Lerche, Jr., and Abdul A. Said, *Concepts of International Politics in Global Perspective*, 3d ed. (Englewood Cliffs, N.J.: Prentice-Hall, 1979), p. 48.

17. Charles O. Lerche, *Foreign Policy of the American People*, 3d ed. (Englewood Cliffs, N.J.: Prentice-Hall, 1967), p. 339.

18. Frankel, *The Making of Foreign Policy*, p. 1. On the other hand, dealing with mathematical and economic analysis, D. V. Lindley asserts: "It is unnecessary to distinguish between decision and action;" see his *Making Decisions*, 2d ed. (New York: Wiley, 1985), p. 4.

19. Lentner, *Foreign Policy Analysis*, pp. 110-12.

20. de Riviera, *The Psychological Dimension of Foreign Policy*, p. 129.

21. Cobbledick, for example, calls the process "enormously complex and variegated," in *Choice in American Foreign Policy*, Chapter 2, especially p. 20. McGeorge Bundy, discussing the decision possibilities of a mature, powerful nation with responsibilities, contends that the era of "black and white thinking" is no longer possible in the real world; see

"The End of Either/Or," *Foreign Affairs* 45 (January 1967): 189-201. See also Wright, *The Study of International Relations*, pp. 577-82.

22. Lerche, *Foreign Policy of the American People*, p. 338. Lerche asserts that the stance that no choice exists belies reality and reflects a lack of leadership; see pp. 338-39.

23. de Riviera, *The Psychological Dimension of Foreign Policy*, pp. 156-59.

24. For commentary, see Frankel, *The Making of Foreign Policy*, pp. 5-9. The matter of decision-making phases is described in many ways. Kurt London, for example, discusses four of them: recommendation, modification, crystallization, and final decision; see *The Making of Foreign Policy: East and West* (Philadelphia: Lippincott, 1965), pp. 210-12. James Rosenau's three-stage formulation of foreign policy embraces the "initiatory" (which stimulates decision makers to undertake efforts to modify existing circumstances), the "implementive" (which translates stimuli into purposeful actions--or decisions), and the "responsive" phases; see *The Scientific Study of Foreign Policy*, pp. 80-81.

25. Michael Haas, "Fundamental Aspects of Decisionmaking," in William O. Chittick, ed., *The Analysis of Foreign Policy Outputs* (Columbus, Ohio: Merrill, 1975), pp. 147-50. Haas provides a matrix of these two sets of distinctions (see p. 148) with their definitions (pp. 165-71). For comparative purposes, see Harold Lasswell's seven functions in decision-making presented in note 58.

26. Frankel, *The Making of Foreign Policy*, p. 95. He devotes Chapter 7 entirely to analyzing the importance of information in policy-making, as does Kurt London in Chapter 3 of his *How Foreign Policy Is Made* (New York: Van Nostrand, 1949).

27. Bailey, *The Art of Diplomacy*, pp. 97-98.

28. Feliks Gross, *Foreign Policy Analysis* (New York: Philosophical Library, 1954), pp. 10-16. On "securing the facts," Dean Rusk emphasizes acquiring the data and distinguishing "hard facts" from "speculation and estimate"; see "The Anatomy of Foreign Policy Decisions," *Department of State Bulletin* 53 (September 27, 1965): 504, and Theodore C. Sorensen discusses the "limits of available information" in *Decision-Making in the White House* (New York: Columbia University Press, 1963), pp. 36-42. On the other hand, others confess that in actual practice determinations often need to be made by decision makers who are inadequately informed. See Roger Hilsman, *To Move a Nation: The Politics of Foreign Policy in the Administration of John F. Kennedy* (New York: Delta, 1964), pp. 11-12, 565-68; Lerche and Said, *Concepts of International Politics*, pp. 53-54; and Harold and Margaret Sprout, *Toward a Politics of the Planet Earth*, pp. 102-4. For a discussion on the certainty of facts, comparing those in foreign affairs with defense and industrial facts, see Thomas L. Hughes, "Policy Making in a World Turned Upside Down," *Foreign Affairs* 45 (January 1967): 202-14.

29. For additional commentary, see Cobbledick, *Choice in American Foreign Policy*, pp. 23-24; Lovell, *Foreign Policy in Perspective*, pp. 216-20 (on scanning); and Harold and Margaret Sprout, *Foundations of International Politics* (Princeton: Van Nostrand, 1962), pp. 127-30.

30. de Riviera, *The Psychological Dimension of Foreign Policy*, pp. 116-20. For additional commentary on how a person makes a decision, see

Alfred Schuetz, "Choosing Among Projects of Action," *Philosophy and Phenomenological Research* 12 (1951): 161-85. See also note 54.

31. Chittick, *The Analysis of Foreign Policy Outputs*, pp. 112, 118, 183. See also the essays of Glen H. Stassen and Michael Haas in this volume, pp. 123-71.

32. Ralph L. Keeney and Howard Raiffa, *Decisions With Multiple Objectives: Preferences and Value Tradeoffs* (New York: Wiley, 1976), pp. 8, 12, 26, 515. See also R. Duncan Luce and Howard Raiffa, *Games and Decisions: Introduction and Critical Survey* (New York: Wiley, 1957), p. 13, which states that the distinction between individual and group decision-making is functional rather than biological or social. See also note 69.

33. See Keeney and Raiffa, *Decisions with Multiple Obectives*, pp. 6, 142-79, and Luce and Raiffa, *Games and Decisions*, p. 13 and Chapter 13, who discuss the three types, whereas Jerry Felsen, *Decision Making Under Uncertainty* (New York: CDS Publishing Co., 1976), Kaufmann, *The Science of Decision-Making*, Chapter 5, and *Decision Theory*, pp. 71-75, 172-74, emphasize uncertainty. See also Lindley, *Making Decisions*, pp. 7-8, 11, 68. In foreign relations literature, risk and uncertainty are discussed by Jerry B. Jenkins, "Uncertainty and Uncertainty-Reduction in the Global Arena," in Chittick, *The Analysis of Foreign Policy Outputs*, pp. 75-110; de Rivera, *The Psychological Dimension of Foreign Policy*, pp. 138, 175-81; Alan C. Lamborn, "Risk and Foreign Policy Choice," *International Studies Quarterly* 29 (December 1985): 385-410; and Lerche and Said, *Concepts of International Politics*, which links risks with costs, pp. 32, 51-52. See also note 66.

34. See Frankel, *The Making of Foreign Policy*, p. 202. For comment on substantive and procedural foreign policies, see Chapter 6, p. 133.

35. See John H. Esterline and Robert B. Black, *Inside Foreign Policy: The Department of State Political System and Its Subsystems* (Palo Alto, Calif.: Mayfield, 1975), p. 63. The authors relate these five categories to levels of decision makers in the Department of State.

36. See Frankel, *The Making of Foreign Policy*, pp. 202-5, who notes that often initial decisions "introduce a chain of other, sequential decisions" and that "an initial decision in one chain is a sequential decision in others;" and Lentner, *Foreign Policy Analysis*, pp. 173-75, 197, who regards basic or fundamental decisions as those that involve the choice of new objectives and inaugurate new policy, and sequential as those that follow from the basic, and he holds that basic decisions are made at higher, and the sequential at lower levels of responsibility. Robert L. Rothstein, comparing crisis with incremental decisions, distinguishes four types: crisis, fundamental, incremental that are designed to be fundamental, and incremental that are intended to work out details of earlier fundamental decisions; see *Planning, Prediction, and Policymaking in Foreign Affairs* (Boston: Little, Brown, 1972), pp. 22-33, especially p. 32. Incrementalism as an approach to analysis is discussed later.

37. Frankel, *The Making of Foreign Policy*, pp. 202, 206. He adds that those that produce action may lead in various directions--to alter the environment, the value system, the structure of decision-making machinery, or some combination of these purposes.

38. Lentner, *Foreign Policy Analysis*, pp. 175-76. On the distinction between what they call strategic versus repetitive operational decisions, see Keeney and Raiffa, *Decisions With Multiple Objectives*, p. 13.

39. See Frankel, *The Making of Foreign Policy*, pp. 206-10.

40. See Lerche, *Foreign Policy of the American People*, pp. 22-23.

41. For illustrative commentary, see Chittick, *The Analysis of Foreign Policy Outputs*, pp. 31-38, 116-17; de Rivera, *The Psychological Dimension of Foreign Policy*, pp. 125, 278-83, and Chapter 5; Frankel, *The Making of Foreign Policy*, p. 6; Gross, *Foreign Policy Analysis*, pp. 23, 25; Lentner, *Foreign Policy Analysis*, pp. 176-81, 182, 186; Lovell, *Foreign Policy in Perspective*, pp. 21, 208-11, 219-20, 262, 271, 272, 275; Rosenau, *The Scientific Study of Foreign Policy*, pp. 39-42; and Rothstein, *Planning, Prediction, and Policymaking in Foreign Affairs*, p. 139.

42. Such as information sets, stochastic choice, "minimax and maximin" strategies, probability chains, optimization, decision nodes and trees, nonlinear programming, utilitarianism, randomized decision rules, praxeology--the science of action, and many others. See also note 64, and on model building see note 68.

43. See Robinson, "Decision Making--Political Aspects," pp. 55-56.

44. The general study of foreign policy-making, without emphasis on the more systematic analysis of decision-making as a process, and focusing largely on organizational considerations, emerged in the United States in the late 1940s and 1950s in such studies as Andrew Berding, *The Making of Foreign Policy* (Washington: Potomac, 1956); Brookings Institution, *Government Mechanism for the Conduct of United States Foreign Relations* (Washington: Brookings Institution, 1949) and *The Formulation and Administration of United States Foreign Policy*, edited by H. Field Haviland (Washington: Brookings Institution, 1960), second Brookings Institution study; Lawrence H. Chamberlain and Richard C. Snyder, *American Foreign Policy* (New York: Rinehart, 1948), Part 1; Loy W. Henderson, *Foreign Policies: Their Formulation and Enforcement* (Washington: Government Printing Office, 1946); L. Larry Leonard, *Elements of American Foreign Policy* (New York: McGraw-Hill, 1953), Part 3; London, *How Foreign Policy Is Made*, especially Chapter 5; James L. McCamy, *The Administration of American Foreign Affairs* (New York: Knopf, 1950), especially Chapter 2; William Macomber, *The Angels' Game: A Handbook of Modern Diplomacy* (New York: Stein and Day, 1975), especially Chapters 7 and 8; Charles Maechling, Jr., "Foreign Policy Makers: The Weakest Link" *Virginia Quarterly Review* 52 (Winter 1966): 1-23; and Elmer Plischke, *Conduct of American Diplomacy* (New York: Van Nostrand, 1950), Chapter 3. For a comprehensive list, including journal and textual materials, see Elmer Plischke, *U.S. Foreign Relations: A Guide to Information Sources* (Detroit: Gale Research, 1980), pp. 341-47.

For commentary on the President and the Department of State, see Bert A. Rockman, "America's *Departments* of State: Irregular and Regular Syndromes of Policy Making," *American Political Science Review* 75 (December 1981): 911-27; and Laurence H. Silberman, "Toward Presidential Control of the State Department," *Foreign Affairs* 57 (Spring 1979): 872-93, which discusses conflict between political leaders and the Foreign Service bureaucracy in the United States.

45. For commentary, see William Reitzel, Morton A. Kaplan, and Constance G. Coblenz, *United States Foreign Policy, 1945-1955* (Washington: Brookings Institution, 1956), Appendix, pp. 475-79. For the annual study guides, see Brookings Institution, International Studies Group, *Major Problems of United States Foreign Policy....[year]: A Study Guide* (Washington: Brookings Institution, 1947-1954). See also Leo Pasvolsky, "The Brookings Institution Program of International Studies," *World Politics* 2

(January 1950): 295-303; and for a description of the Brookings' problems approach, see Gross, *Foreign Policy Analysis*, pp. 134-48.

46. Richard C. Snyder, H. W. Bruck, and Burton M. Sapin, *Decision-Making as an Approach to the Study of International Politics* (Princeton: Princeton University Press, 1954), and *Foreign Policy Decision Making: An Approach to the Study of International Politics*, edited by Richard C. Snyder, H. W. Bruck, and Burton M. Sapin (New York: Free Press, 1962). See also Richard C. Snyder and James A. Robinson, *National and International Decision-Making* (New York: Institute for International Order, 1961), and James A. Robinson and Richard C. Snyder, "Decision-Making in International Relations," in *International Behavior: A Social-Psychological Analysis*, edited by Herbert C. Kelman (New York: Holt, Rinehart, and Winston, 1965), pp. 435-63. For a broadened version, see Richard C. Snyder, "A Decision-Making Approach to the Study of Political Phenomena," in *Approaches to the Study of Politics*, edited by Roland Young (Evanston, Ill.: Northwestern University Press, 1958), pp. 3-38.

For a brief commentary on Snyder's approach and analysis, see Robinson, "Decision-Making--Political Aspects," pp. 56-57, and Theodore E. Couloumbis and James H. Wolfe, *Introduction to International Relations: Power and Justice* (Englewood Cliffs, N.J.: Prentice-Hall, 1978), pp. 100-1. For more extended critiques, see Rosenau, *The Scientific Study of Foreign Policy*, Chapter 9; Hyam Gold, "Foreign Policy Decision-Making and the Environment: The Claims of Snyder, Brecher, and the Sprouts," *International Studies Quarterly* 22 (December 1978): 569-86; and Meriam Steiner, "Elusive Essence of Decision: A Critical Comparison of Allison's and Snyder's Decision-Making Approaches," *International Studies Quarterly* 21 (June 1977): 389-422.

47. Such as Dwaine Marvick, *Career Perspectives in a Bureaucratic Setting* (Ann Arbor: University of Michigan Press, 1954) and *Political Decision-Makers*, edited by Dwaine Marvick (New York: Free Press, 1961); Donald R. Matthews, *The Social Background of Political Decision-Makers* (Garden City, N.Y.: Doubleday, 1954); Peter A. Toma and Andrew Gyorgy, "The Decision Makers," in their *Basic Issues in International Relations* (New York: Allyn and Bacon, 1967), pp. 305-46; Thomas C. Wiegele, "Decision-Making in an International Crisis: Some Biological Factors," *International Studies Quarterly* 17 (September, 1973): 295-335, on influence of health, fatigue, age, biological rhythms, and drugs; and P. Wright, "Harassed Decision Maker: Time Pressures, Distractions, and the Use of Evidence," *Journal of Applied Psychology* 59 (October 1974): 555-61. See also certain anthologies on political leaders, such as Richard Nixon, *Leaders* (New York: Warner Books, 1982), and the resources contained in memoir literature.

48. On the relation of the "belief system" and decision-making, see Ole R. Holsti, "The Belief System and National Images: A Case Study" (on John Foster Dulles), in *International Politics and Foreign Policy*, 2d ed., edited by James N. Rosenau (New York: Free Press, 1969), pp. 543-50; see also Kenneth E. Boulding, *The Image: Knowledge in Life and Society* (Ann Arbor: University of Michigan Press, 1956), and M. Rokeach, *The Open and Closed Mind: Investigation Into the Nature of Belief Systems and Personality Systems* (New York: Basic Books, 1960). On "operational codes," see Alexander L. George, "The Operational Code: A Neglected Approach to the Study of Political Leaders and Decision-Making," *International Studies Quarterly* 13 (June 1969): 190-222; Ole R. Holsti, "The 'Operational Code' Approach to the Study of Political Leaders: John Foster Dulles' Philosophical and Instrumental Beliefs," *Canadian Journal of Political Science* 3 (March 1970): 123-57; and David S. McLellan, "The 'Operational Code' Approach to the Study of Political Leaders: Dean Acheson's Philo-

sophical and Instrumental Beliefs," *Canadian Journal of Political Science*
4 (March 1971): 52-75. See also Bruce M. Russett and Elizabeth C. Hanson,
Interest and Ideology: The Foreign Policy Beliefs of American Businessmen
(San Francisco: Freeman, 1975) on business elites and economics and their
relation to realpolitik.

49. On biographical-psychological analysis, see such studies as Or-
ville Gilbert Brim, et al., *Personality and Decision Processes: Studies
in the Social Psychology of Thinking* (Stanford: Stanford University
Press, 1962), and Lewis L. Strauss, *Men and Decisions* (New York: Doubleday, 1962).

50. On incrementalism see note 75 and on rationalism see notes 77,
84, 85.

51. On the bureaucratic approach to decision-making, see note 82.

52. See Graham T. Allison, "Conceptual Models and the Cuban Missile
Crisis," *American Political Science Review* 63 (September 1969): 689-718,
and his *Essence of Decision* (see p. 256 for a summary outline of his models). Also see I. M. Destler, "Comment: Multiple Advocacy--Some 'Limits
and Costs'," *American Political Science Review* 66 (September 1972): 786-
90; Alexander L. George, "Making Foreign Policy: Rejoinder to 'Comment by
I. M. Destler'," *American Political Science Review* 66 (September 1972):
791-95; and Robert J. Art, "Bureaucratic Politics and American Foreign
Policy: A Critique," *Policy Sciences* 4 (December 1973): 467-90, which
questions the validity of the bureaucratic paradigm.

53. Examples include: Ralph M. Goldman, "Decision Making by American
Political Organizations," in his *Behavioral Perspectives on American Politics* (Homewood, Ill.: Dorsey, 1973), pp. 200-40; Allan W. Lerner, *The
Politics of Decisionmaking: Strategy, Cooperation, and Conflict* (Beverly
Hills, Calif.: Sage, 1976); *Political Decision-Making Processes: Studies
in National, Comparative, and International Politics*, edited by Dusan
Sidjanski (San Francisco: Jossey-Bass, 1973); Sidney Ulmer, et al., *Political Decision Making* (New York: Van Nostrand, Reinhold, 1970). See
also note 79.

54. In addition to de Rivera, *The Psychological Dimension of Foreign
Policy*, examples include Anthony A. D'Amato, "Psychological Constructs in
Foreign Policy Prediction," *Journal of Conflict Resolution* 11 (September
1967): 294-311; Jacques de Bourbon-Busset, "How Decisions Are Made in
Foreign Policy: Psychology in International Relations," *Review of Poli-
tics* 20 (October 1958): 591-614; Irving L. Janis and Leon Mann, *Decision
Making: A Psychological Analysis of Conflict, Choice, and Commitment* (New
York: Free Press, 1977). See also note 30.

55. For presentations from the perspective of the practitioner rather than the outside analyst, see Dean G. Acheson, "Responsibility for Decision in Foreign Policy," *Yale Review* 44 (Autumn 1954): 1-12; Rusk,
"The Anatomy of Foreign Policy Decisions," pp. 502-9; Sorensen, *Decision-
Making in the White House*. See also the extensive memoir literature of
political leaders.

56. Such as Richard Nixon, *Six Crises* (Garden City, N.Y.: Doubleday,
1962). See also some of the case studies listed in note 62.

57. Herbert A. Simon, *Administrative Behavior: A Study of Decision-
Making Processes in Administrative Organization*, 3d ed. (New York: Macmillan, 1976); "Theories of Decision-Making in Economics and Behavioral

Science," *American Economic Review* 49 (June   1959): 253-83;   and *The New Science of Management Decision* (New York: Harper, 1960). See also James G. March and Herbert A. Simon, *Organizations* (New York: Wiley, 1959), especially Chapter 3.   For Simon's works on rationalism, see note 77.

58. Harold D. Lasswell, *The Decision Process: Seven Categories of Functional Analysis* (College Park, Md.: Bureau of Governmental Research, University of Maryland, 1956).   These functional factors include intelligence and information, recommendation, prescription (decision among alternatives), invocation, application, appraisal, and termination.

59. For   references on incrementalism and rationalism, see notes 75, 77, 84, and 85. For general commentaries on decision-making, see *Decision-Making: Creativity, Judgment, and Systems*, edited by Henry S. Brinkers (Columbus: Ohio University Press, 1972); Donald Davison, et al., *Decision-Making: An Experimental Approach* (Stanford: Stanford University Press, 1957); Allan Easton, *Decision Making: A Short Course in Problem Solving for Professionals* (Somerset, N.J.: Wiley, 1976); Ralph Pettman, "On Method and Against It: The Decisionmaking Process," in his *Human Behavior and World Politics* (London: Macmillan, 1975) pp. 23-64; Sidney Siegel, et al., *Choice, Strategy, and Utility* (New York: McGraw-Hill, 1964).

60. In addition to those cited in note 59 and elsewhere in this chapter (such as Kaufman, Lindblom, Lindley, and Robinson), for additional materials on decision-making in general (not restricted to foreign affairs), see Peter Bachrach and Morton S. Baratz, "Decisions and Nondecisions: An Analytical Framework," *American Political Science Review* 57 (September 1963): 632-42, in which they stress the necessity for a model for both decision-making and non-decision-making based on the concepts of power, force, influence, and authority, and suggest a basis for such a model, p. 632; Irwin Bross, *Design for Decisions* (New York: Macmillan, 1953); Paul Diesing, *Reason in Society: Five Types of Decisions and Their Social Conditions* (Urbana: University of Illinois Press, 1962); Gordon F. Pitz and Jack McKillip, *Decision Analysis for Program Evaluators* (Beverly Hills, Calif.: Sage, 1984); Robert M. Thrall, et al., *Decision Processes* (New York: Wiley, 1954).

61. In addition to those cited elsewhere in this chapter (such as Chittick, Cobbledick, de Rivera, Frankel, Gross, Lentner, Lovell, and Rothstein), on foreign relations decision-making, see Elmer Plischke, *Foreign Relations Decisionmaking: Options Analysis* (Beirut, Lebanon: Catholic Press for Institute of Middle Eastern and North African Affairs, 1973); William D. Coplin and J. Martin Rochester, *Foreign Policy Decision-Making* (Chicago: Markam, 1971). See also citations in note 44.

62. Aside from Allison, examples of case studies include Morton Berkowitz, P. G. Bock, and Vincent J. Fuccillo, *The Politics of American Foreign Policy: The Social Context of Decisions* (Englewood Cliffs, N.J.: Prentice-Hall, 1977); Bernard C. Cohen, *The Political Process and Foreign Policy: The Making of the Japanese Peace Settlement* (Princeton: Princeton University Press, 1957); Robert Ghobad Irani, *American Diplomacy: An Options Analysis of the Azerbaijan Crisis, 1945-1946* (Beirut, Lebanon: Catholic Press for Institute of Middle Eastern and North African Affairs, 1978); Joseph Marion Jones, *The Fifteen Weeks--February 21-June 5, 1947* (New York: Viking, 1955) on putting the Truman Doctrine and the Marshall Plan into effect; Mary M. Lepper, *Foreign Policy Formulation: A Case Study of the Nuclear Test Ban Treaty of 1963* (Columbus, Ohio: Merrill, 1971); Ernest R. May, *The Making of the Monroe Doctrine* (Cambridge, Mass.: Harvard University Press, 1979); Glenn D. Paige, *The Korea Deci-*

sion (June 24-30, 1950), (New York: Free Press, 1968); Elmer Plischke, "Resolving the 'Berlin Question'--An Options Analysis," *World Affairs* 131 (July-September 1968): 91-100, and "Reunifying Germany--An Options Analysis," *World Affairs* 132 (June 1969): 28-38; Jack Richon Pole, *The Decision for American Independence* (Philadelphia: Lippincott, 1975); Richard C. Snyder and Glenn D. Paige, "The United States Decision to Resist Aggression in Korea: The Application of an Analytic Scheme," *Administrative Science Quarterly* 3 (December 1958): 341-78; Ronald J. Terchek, *The Making of the Test Ban Treaty* (The Hague: Nijhoff, 1970); Roberta Wohlstetter, *Pearl Harbor: Warning and Decision* (Stanford: Stanford University Press, 1962). For a detailed listing, see also Plischke, *U.S. Foreign Relations*, pp. 317-23, 335-36, and Arthur D. Larson, *National Security Affairs: A Guide to Information Sources* (Detroit: Gale Research, 1973), especially Part 2.

63. For case studies on the atom bomb, see Michael Amrine, *The Great Decision: The Secret History of the Atomic Bomb* (New York: Putnam, 1959); Robert C. Batchelder, *The Irreversible Decision, 1939-1950* (New York: Macmillan, 1961), pp. 190-210; Edwin Fogelman, *Hiroshima: The Decision to Use the A-Bomb* (New York: Scribner, 1964); Len Giovannitti and Fred Freed, *The Decision to Drop the Bomb* (New York: Coward-McCann, 1965); Walter S. Schoenberger, *Decision of Destiny* (Athens: Ohio University Press, 1970); Henry L. Stimson, "Decision to Use the Atomic Bomb," *Harper's Magazine* (February 1947): 97-107. In addition, see Warner R. Schilling, "The H-Bomb Decision: How to Decide Without Actually Choosing," *Political Science Quarterly* 76 (March 1961): 24-46.

64. See also note 42. For guidance to literature on some of these specialized techniques, see Plischke, *U.S. Foreign Relations*, pp. 336-40, 447-58, 489-93, and Larson, *National Security Affairs*, pp. 252-58.

65. See Michael Haas, "Communication Factors in Decision Making," *Peace Research Society Papers* 12 (1968): 65-86; Roger Hilsman, Jr., *Strategic Intelligence and National Decisions* (Glencoe, Ill.: Free Press, 1956); *Information for Decision Making: Quantitative and Behavioral Dimensions*, edited by Alfred Rappaport (Englewood Cliffs, N.J.: Prentice-Hall, 1970); and Donald A. Sylvan and Steve Chan, eds., *Foreign Policy Decision Making: Perception, Cognition, and Artificial Intelligence* (New York: Praeger, 1984). On information see also notes 26 to 29.

66. See Charles West Churchman, *Prediction and Optimal Decision* (Englewood Cliffs, N.J.: Prentice-Hall, 1961); Clyde Hamilton Coombs and Dean G. Pruitt, *A Study of Decision Making Under Risk* (Ann Arbor: Willow Run Laboratories, University of Michigan, 1960); Joseph P. Martino, *Technological Forecasting for Decisionmaking* (New York: American Elsevier, 1972). Arnold Wolfers, discussing "The Determinants of Foreign Policy," asserts that decisions may be seen "as fully determined by the totality of its antecedents" and that every exercise of choice "is the necessary result of all of its antecedents." See his *Discord and Collaboration: Essays on International Politics* (Baltimore: Johns Hopkins Press, 1962), Chapter 3, especially pp. 37-38. On prediction see also Chapter 8, note 45.

67. See Henry A. Kissinger, "Domestic Structure and Foreign Policy," *Daedalus* 95 (Spring 1966): 503-29; Victor H. Vroom and Philip W. Yetten, *Leadership and Decisionmaking* (Pittsburgh: University of Pittsburgh Press, 1973). On elites see also Lentner, *Foreign Policy Analysis*, pp. 186-92.

68. In addition to Allison and others already cited, see Stuart A.

Bremer, *Simulated Worlds: A Computer Model of National Decision-Making* (Princeton: Princeton University Press, 1977); Carl Kaysen, "Model-Makers and Decision-Makers: Economists and the Policy Process," *Public Interest* 12 (Summer 1968): 80-95; William Thomas Morris, *Management for Action: Psychotechnical Decision Making* (Reston, Va.: Reston Publishing Co., 1972); Richard Rosecrance and J. E. Mueller, "Decision-Making and the Quantitative Analysis of International Relations," *Yearbook of World Affairs* 21 (1967): 1-19.

69. See B. Aubrey Fisher, *Small Group Decision Making: Communication and the Group Process* (New York: McGraw-Hill, 1974); Dennis S. Gouran, *Discussion: The Process of Group Decision-Making* (New York: Harper and Row, 1974); Walter C. Swap, ed., *Group Decision-Making* (Beverly Hills, Calif.: Sage, 1984); Charles W. Taylor, "Organizing for Consensus in Problem Solving," *Management Review* 61 (April 1972): 17-25, and *Panel Consensus Technique: A New Approach to Decision-Making* (Carlisle Barracks, Pa.: U.S. Army War College, 1972).

70. See *Interorganizational Decision Making*, edited by Matthew Tuite, Roger K. Chisholm, and Michael Radnor (Chicago: Aldine, 1972); March and Simon, *Organizations*, Chapter 3 on "Intraorganizational Decisions," pp. 35-82.

71. See Kenneth Boulding, "The Ethics of Rational Decision," *Management Science* 12 (February 1966): B 161-B 169; Bartholomeus Landheer, *Ethical Values in International Decision Making* (The Hague: Nijhoff, 1960); Leys, *Ethics for Policy Decisions*.

72. Supplementing works cited elsewhere in this chapter (see note 6), see list in Plischke, *U.S. Foreign Relations*, pp. 323-24, and selected items in bibliography provided by White, *Decision Theory*, pp. 179-82. For summary commentary, see Robinson, "Decision Making--Political Aspects," pp. 57-58; see also Herman Chernoff, "Decision Theory," *International Encyclopedia of the Social Sciences* (1968) IV: 62-66.

73. Rosenau, *The Scientific Study of Foreign Policy*, pp. 269-73. See also note 5. For a survey of theories of international relations, emphasizing the distinctions between traditionalist and behavioralist schools and their paradigms--regarding decision-making theory as a facet of systems analysis within the behavioralist or scientific school, see Arend Lijphart, "The Structure of the Theoretical Revolution in International Relations," *International Studies Quarterly* 18 (March 1974): 41-74. For the view that the "policy studies" perspective on foreign relations is being reoriented in a postbehavioral revolution to enhance the "science or art of statecraft" by improving "the conceptual apparatus of policymakers," see Stephen J. Cimbala, "Policy Studies and Foreign Policy: Emphasis and Cautions," in *Foreign Policy Analysis*, edited by Richard L. Merritt (Lexington, Mass.: Heath, 1975), pp. 73-77.

74. For a brief comparison of these approaches, see "Decision Making," *The Public Administration Dictionary*, pp. 114-19.

75. See Charles E. Lindblom, "The Science of Muddling Through," *Public Administration Review* 19 (Spring 1959): 79-88; see also his *The Intelligence of Democracy: Decision-Making Through Mutual Adjustment* (New York: Free Press, 1965) and *The Policy-Making Process* (Englewood Cliffs, N.J.: Prentice-Hall, 1968). For an earlier study, see David Braybrook and Charles E. Lindblom, *A Strategy for Decision: Policy Evaluation as a Social Process* (New York: Free Press, 1963). For commentary on sequential decisions, regarded as subordinate to initial decisions, see Frankel, *The*

Making of Foreign Policy, pp. 202-5; for the functioning of incremental-ism in the United States, see Rothstein, *Planning, Prediction, and Pol-icymaking in Foreign Affairs*, pp. 21-33; and for criticism of the Amer-ican tendency to decide as little as possible, see Hilsman, *To Move a Nation*, pp. 548-49.

76. "Valid choices," Lippmann observed, "are limited to the question of where, not whether, the opposing terms of the equation are to be brought into equilibrium." See Walter Lippmann, *Essays in the Public Philosophy* (Boston: Little, Brown, 1955), p. 43.

77. For general commentary on rationalism, see Frankel, *The Making of Foreign Policy*, pp. 166-75. More comprehensive treatment is provided in Allison, *Essence of Decision*, pp. 10-38 (including his "rational-actor" model, pp. 32-36), 71-72, 252-55, 268-69, 273-75; Boulding, "The Ethics of Rational Decision;" *NOMOS II: Rational Decisions*, edited by Carl J. Friedrich (New York: Atherton, 1964); Charles H. Kepner and Ben-jamin R. Tregoe, *The Rational Manager: A Systematic Approach to Problem Solving and Decision Making* (New York: McGraw-Hill, 1965); Felix E. Op-penheim, "Rational Choice," *Journal of Philosophy* 50 (June 1953): 341-50; Elmer Plischke, *Foreign Relations Decisionmaking: Options Analysis* and "Intellectual Dimension of Foreign Relations Decisionmaking," in Merritt, *Foreign Policy Analysis*, pp. 63-71; Sidney Verba, "Assumptions of Rationality and Non-Rationality in Models of the International Sys-tem," in *The International System: Theoretical Essays*, edited by Klaus Knorr and Sidney Verba (Princeton: Princeton University Press, 1961), pp. 93-117. See also Herbert A. Simon, *Models of Bounded Rationality* (Cam-bridge, Mass.: MIT Press, 1982), II, 84-108, 239-58, 287-317, 401-94, and "A Behavioral Model of Rational Choice," *Quarterly Journal of Eco-nomics* 69 (February 1955): 99-118; see also his *Models of Thought* (New Haven, Conn.: Yale University Press, 1979) on memory structures, learning processes, concept formation, perception, and understanding, and see also his works cited in note 57.

78. See Amitai Etzioni, "Mixed Scanning: A 'Third' Approach to Deci-sion-making," *Public Administration Review* 27 (December 1967): 385-92. For summary statement, see also "Decision Making," *The Public Administra-tion Dictionary*, pp. 116-17.

79. In addition to citations given in note 53, see *Conflict and De-cision-Making: An Introduction to Political Analysis*, edited by Paul S. Conn (New York: Harper and Row, 1971); and Hilsman, *To Move a Nation*, Part I on "The Politics of Policy-Making," especially the section "Pol-icy-Making Is Politics," pp. 12-13. For literature on legislative and judicial decision-making, see Plischke, *U.S. Foreign Relations*, pp. 307-8.

80. For examples of case studies, see note 62.

81. Richard E. Neustadt and Ernest R. May, in *Thinking in Time: The Uses of History for Decision Makers* (New York: Free Press, 1986), argue that history can serve as a major tool for policy makers and administra-tors and that historical analysis is critical to making decisions within the "stream of time." From the practitioner's perspective, reflecting on his decision-making, President Harry Truman reports that he trained him-self "to look back into history for precedents," seeking "perspective in the span of history for the decisions I had to make . . . . Most of the problems a President has to face have their roots in the past." See *Memoirs by Harry S. Truman* (Garden City, N.Y.: Doubleday, 1956), II, 1.

82. Allison calls this the "government politics" model in *Essence of Decision*, pp. 144-84; see also citations in note 52. In addition, see Marcus Alexis and Charles Z. Wilson, *Organizational Decision-Making* (Englewood Cliffs, N.J.: Prentice-Hall, 1967); Julian Feldman and Herschel E. Kantor, "Organizational Decision-Making," in *Handbook of Organizations*, edited by James G. March (Chicago: Rand McNally, 1965), pp. 614-49; Paul Y. Hammond, "Foreign Policy Making and Administrative Politics," *World Politics* 17 (July 1965): 656-71 and *Foreign Policymaking: Pluralistic Politics or Unitary Analysis* (Santa Monica, Calif.: Rand, 1965); Charles E. Jacob, *Policy and Bureaucracy* (Princeton: Van Nostrand, 1966); William M. Jones, *On Decision-making in Large Organizations* (Santa Monica, Calif.: Rand, 1964); *Policies, Decisions, and Organization*, edited by Fremont J. Leyden, George A. Shipman, and Morton Kroll (New York: Appleton-Century-Crofts, 1969); Francis E. Rourke, *Bureaucracy, Politics, and Public Policy*, 2d ed. (Boston: Little, Brown, 1976).

On the bureaucratic approach in foreign affairs, see also Graham T. Allison and Morton H. Halperin, "Bureaucratic Politics: A Paradigm and Some Policy Implications," in *Theory and Policy in International Relations*, edited by Raymond Tanter and Richard H. Ullman (Washington: Brookings Institution, 1972), pp. 40-79; David Howard Davis, *How the Bureaucracy Makes Foreign Policy* (Lexington, Mass.: Heath, 1972); I. M. Destler, *Presidents, Bureaucrats, and Foreign Policy: The Politics of Organizational Reform* (Princeton: Princeton University Press, 1972); Morton H. Halperin, *Bureaucratic Politics and Foreign Policy* (Washington: Brookings Institution, 1974) and "Why Bureaucrats Play Games," *Foreign Policy* 5 (May 1971): 70-90; Francis E. Rourke, *Bureaucracy and Foreign Policy* (Baltimore: Johns Hopkins Press, 1972).

For a critique of the bureaucratic approach, including nine criticisms, and substantive considerations, with a table of second and third generation bureaucratic case studies, see Dan Caldwell, "Bureaucratic Foreign Policy-Making," *American Behavioral Scientist* 21 (September-October, 1977): 87-110. See also Robert J. Art, "Bureaucratic Politics and American Foreign Policy: A Critique," *Policy Sciences* 4 (December 1973): 467-90; Lawrence Freedman, "Logic, Politics and Foreign Policy Processes: A Critique of the Bureaucratic Politics Model," (review article) *International Affairs* 52 (July 1976): 434-49; and Charles Maechling, Jr., "Foreign Policy-Makers: The Weakest Link," *Virginia Quarterly Review* 52 (Winter 1976): 1-23.

83. Cecil V. Crabb, Jr., *The American Approach to Foreign Policy: A Pragmatic Perspective* (Lanham, Md.: University Press of America, 1985), especially pp. xiii-xvi, with critique on pp. 57-71. Crabb's line of reasoning is not inherently incompatible with elements of the rational, political, bureaucratic, or the national power, behavioral, systems analysis, and other approaches to the subject. See also John G. Stoessinger, *Crusaders and Pragmatists: Movers of Modern American Foreign Policy* (New York: Norton, 1979), which focuses on eight twentieth-century leaders, and Inis L. Claude, Jr., *American Approaches to World Affairs*, vol. IV of series (Lanham, Md.: University Press of America, 1986), on United States pragmatic approach in critical responses to war, using the United States as a case study.

84. Frankel notes the distinction between "rational" and "rationalist," and between "rationalism" and "rationalization." Rationalists "place reason at the centre of things but being rational does not involve being a rationalist." The term rationalist, he says, denotes referring "everything to abstract principles," and rationalization may be understood to mean explication to justify a preconceived notion or position. The expression rational bears a positive implication, whereas rationalization may also connote self-satisfying but invalid reasoning, which

tends to evoke a negative connotation. See *The Making of Foreign Policy*, Chapter 12 on "Rationality and Its Limitations," especially pp. 166-68.

85. Lovell puts it bluntly when he writes: "in real political systems, not only is perfect rationality impossible, but even as an abstract standard it is inappropriate to many decision-making situations." See *Foreign Policy in Perspective*, p. 221.

86. Much of this and the following two segments, with accompanying tables and figures (outlines, diagrams, and flow charts), are based on Plischke, *Foreign Relations Decisionmaking: Options Analysis*.

87. See John W. Bowling, "How We Do Our Thing: Policy Formulation," *Foreign Service Journal* 47 (January 1970): 19-22, 48. See also his "How We Do Our Thing: Crisis Management," *Foreign Service Journal* 47 (May 1970): 19-21 and "How We Do Our Thing: Innovation," *Foreign Service Journal* 47 (October 1970): 25-27, 55-56. See also the earlier views of Charles Ogburn, Jr., "The Flow of Policy-Making in the Department of State," in *Readings in the Making of American Foreign Policy*, edited by Andrew M. Scott and Raymond H. Dawson (New York: Macmillan, 1965), pp. 284-93.

88. Alexander L. George, "The Case for Multiple Advocacy in Making Foreign Policy," *American Political Science Review* 66 (September 1972): 751-85. He applies his analysis to such case studies as the Bay of Pigs, Cuban missile, and Dominican crises of the 1960s, the Multilateral Nuclear Force (MLF) proposal and relations within the North Atlantic Alliance, and certain aspects of the Vietnam War. See also critique of George's analysis by I. M. Destler, "Comment--Multiple Advocacy: Some 'Limits and Costs'," *American Political Science Review* 66 (September 1972): 786-90, and George's "Rejoinder," pp. 791-95.
Much has been written on the functioning of the National Security Council and the President's Special Adviser on national security and foreign policy. For commentary on the problem of coordinating the Department of State and the National Security Council in foreign relations decision-making, with recommendations, see Bert A. Rockman, "America's Departments of State: Irregular and Regular Syndromes of Policy Making," *American Political Science Review* 75 (December 1981): 911-27.

89. For additional lists of steps in decision-making, see Dean Rusk, "The Anatomy of Foreign Policy Decisions," pp. 503-8. He provides a "checklist" of seven items: identifying the questions; securing the facts; determining United States interests, objectives, and responsibilities; assessing the interests, objectives, and responsibilities of other nations; checking legal implications; gauging American public opinion and the role of Congress; and seeking additional counsel. For an alternative version, see also Dean Rusk, "The Formulation of Foreign Policy," *American Foreign Policy: Current Documents, 1961* (Washington: Government Printing Office, 1965), pp. 24-25. See also Sorensen, *Decision-Making in the White House*, pp. 18-19; he lists eight steps: agreement on facts, agreement on overall policy objectives, precise definitions of the problem, canvassing all possible solutions, list of all possible consequences flowing from each solution, recommendation of a final choice of one alternative, communication of that selection, and provision for its execution. For other commentaries on phases of decision making, see notes 24, 25, 30.

90. Examples of broad policy matters include President Washington's isolationism, the Hay Open Door policy, President Wilson's Fourteen Points, President Roosevelt's Atlantic Charter, the Truman Doctrine, the

Marshall Plan, and the drafting of the United Nations Charter, the North Atlantic Treaty, the Nuclear Test Ban, the SALT treaties, and the Shanghai Communiqué. All of these, however, are also amenable to cosmographic analysis.

91. To illustrate the breadth and complexity of this international issue, the perspective utilized for consideration and in Table III is that which existed before the Law of the Sea Conference was held and the Law of the Sea Treaty was signed in 1983.

92. For additional illustrations, using the outline configuration, see Plischke, *Foreign Relations Decisionmaking*, p. 32 to define primary policy options respecting the Cuban missile crisis and the Berlin question.

93. See Carl J. Friedrich, *Man and His Government: An Empirical Theory of Politics* (New York: McGraw-Hill, 1963), p. 309, note 14; and Lord Macaulay, *Review of Aikin's Life of Addison* (1843).

94. Dean Rusk makes this clear when he raises such questions as "What is the probable attitude of other governments, including those less directly involved?" and "How and at what stage and in what sequence are other governments to be consulted?" See "The Formulation of Foreign Policy," p. 26, with commentary in "The Anatomy of Foreign Policy Decisions," pp. 505-6.

95. Lentner, *Foreign Policy Analysis*, p. 276; see also his Chapters 2-4.

96. Wright, *The Study of International Relations*, p. 178.

97. Frankel, *The Making of Foreign Policy,* pp. 213-14. He lists as prerequisites for success such qualities as perseverence and understanding the environment for which decisions are made. He also notes that success can lead not only to greater efforts but also to complacency and lack of concern with further achievement, whereas failure, instead of deterring, may actually increase determination to improve (see p. 136).

98. London, *How Foreign Policy Is Made*, pp. 256-59.

99. de Riviera, *The Psychological Dimension of Foreign Policy*, pp. 90-98. For the argument in support of consensus, for example, see Roger Hilsman, Jr., "The Foreign Policy Consensus: An Interim Research Report," *Journal of Conflict Resolution* 3 (December, 1959): 361-82.

100. Lentner, *Foreign Policy Analysis*, pp. 272-76.

101. Lovell, *Foreign Policy in Perspective*, pp. 306-9, 351.

102. For commentary on prediction, see Rothstein, *Planning, Prediction, and Policymaking in Foreign Affairs*, pp. 180-86, and on "prediction and academic fashions"--namely, traditionalism, realism, and behavioralism, see pp. 186-90. Burton, who discusses efficiency, expectations, and legitimization in assessing decision-making, also addresses the problem of prediction; see his *Systems, States, Diplomacy, and Rules*, pp. 63-73, 77-79, 191-97. See also note 66.

103. Sorensen, *Decision-Making in the White House*, pp. 87, 89.

SELECTED BIBLIOGRAPHY

This constitutes a sampling of scores of books and monographs about the principal components and their interrelations in the foreign affairs process. These are supplemented by several hundred articles in journals and social science encyclopedias, anthologies of official documents, case studies, and descriptive or analytical essays, theoretical disquisitions, and other materials cited in footnotes. Additional collections of bibliographical references are provided in such compilations as Robert B. Harmon, *The Art and Practice of Diplomacy: A Selected and Annotated Guide* (1971) and Elmer Plischke, *U.S. Foreign Relations: A Guide to Information Sources* (1980).

Acheson, Dean G. *Power and Diplomacy.* Cambridge: Harvard University Press, 1958.

Aron, Raymond. *Peace and War: A Theory of International Relations.* Garden City, N.Y.: Doubleday, 1966.

Bailey, Thomas A. *The Art of Diplomacy: The American Experience.* New York: Appleton-Century-Crofts, 1968.

Baron, Dona. *The National Purpose Reconsidered.* New York: Columbia University Press, 1978.

Bayliss, John. *Contemporary Strategy: Theory and Policies.* New York: Holmes and Meier, 1975.

Beard, Charles A. *A Foreign Policy for America.* New York: Knopf, 1940.

————. *The Idea of National Interest: An Analytical Study in American Foreign Policy.* New York: Macmillan, 1934.

Bell, Coral. *Negotiating from Strength: A Study in the Politics of Power.* New York: Knopf, 1963.

Bell, David V. J. *Power, Influence, and Authority: An Essay in Political Linguistics.* New York: Oxford University Press, 1975.

Benson, Leonard G. *National Purpose: Ideology and Ambivalence in America.* Washington: Public Affairs Press, 1963.

Berle, Adolf A. *Power.* New York: Harcourt, Brace, and World, 1967.

Bodenheimer, Edgar. *Power, Law, and Society: A Study of the Will to Power and the Will to Law.* New York: Crane, Russak, 1972.

Braybrooke, David, and Charles E. Lindblom. *A Strategy for Decision: Policy Evaluation as a Social Process.* New York: Free Press, 1963.

Bross, Irwin. *Design for Decisions.* New York: Macmillan, 1953.

Burns, Arthur Lee. *Of Powers and Their Politics: A Critique of Theoretical Approaches.* Englewood Cliffs, N.J.: Prentice-Hall, 1968.

Burns, Edward M. *The American Idea of Mission: Concepts of National Purpose and Destiny.* New Brunswick, N.J.: Rutgers University Press, 1957.

Burton, J. W. *International Relations: A General Theory.* Cambridge: Cambridge University Press, 1967.

_____. *Systems, States, Diplomacy, and Rules.* Cambridge: Cambridge University Press, 1968.

Carr, Edward H. *The Twenty Years' Crisis, 1919-1939: An Introduction to the Study of International Relations.* London: Macmillan, 1939.

Chittick, William, O., ed. *The Analysis of Foreign Policy Outputs.* Columbus, Ohio: Merrill, 1975.

Churchman, Charles W. *Prediction and Optimal Decision.* Englewood Cliffs, N.J.: Prentice-Hall, 1961.

Claude, Inis L., Jr. *Power and International Relations.* New York: Random House, 1962.

Cline, Ray S. *World Power Trends and U.S. Foreign Policy for the 1980s.* Boulder, Colo.: Westview, 1980.

Cobbledick, James R. *Choice in American Foreign Policy: Options for the Future.* New York: Crowell, 1973.

Cook, Thomas I., and Malcolm Moos. *Power Through Purpose: The Realism of Idealism as a Basis for Foreign Policy.* Baltimore: Johns Hopkins Press, 1954.

Cooper, Joseph D. *The Art of Decision-Making.* Garden City, N.Y.: Doubleday, 1961.

Corbett, Percy E. *Morals, Law and Power in International Relations.* Los Angeles: Haynes Foundation, 1956.

Cousins, Norman. *The Pathology of Power.* New York: Norton, 1987.

Crabb, Cecil V., Jr. *The Doctrines of American Foreign Policy.* Baton Rouge: Louisiana State University Press, 1982.

_____. *Policy-Makers and Critics: Conflicting Theories of American Foreign Policy.* 2d ed. New York: Praeger, 1986.

Davis, David Howard. *How the Bureaucracy Makes Foreign Policy: An Exchange Analysis.* Lexington, Mass.: Heath, 1972.

De Rivera, Joseph H. *The Psychological Dimension of Foreign Policy*. Columbus, Ohio: Merrill, 1968.

Deutsch, Karl W. *The Analysis of International Relations*. Englewood Cliffs, N.J.: Prentice-Hall, 1968.

Ferris, Wayne H. *The Power Capabilities of Nation-States: International Conflict and War*. Lexington, Mass.: Heath, 1973.

Flathman, Richard E. *The Public Interest: An Essay Concerning the Normative Discourse of Politics*. New York: Wiley, 1966.

Frankel, Joseph. *International Relations*. New York: Oxford University Press, 1964.

_____. *The Making of Foreign Policy: An Analysis of Decision-Making*. New York: Oxford University Press, 1963.

_____. *National Interest*. New York: Praeger, 1970.

Friedrich, Carl J. *Foreign Policy in the Making: The Search for a New Balance of Power*. New York: Norton, 1938.

Gibson, Hugh. *The Road to Foreign Policy*. Garden City, N.Y.: Doubleday, Doran, 1944.

Goffman, Erving. *Strategic Interaction*. Philadelphia: University of Pennsylvania Press, 1969.

Graebner, Norman A. *Ideas and Diplomacy: Readings in the Intellectual Tradition of American Foreign Policy*. New York: Oxford University Press, 1964.

Gray, Colin S. *Strategic Studies: A Critical Assessment*. Westport, Conn.: Greenwood, 1982.

_____. *Strategic Studies and Public Policy: The American Experience*. Lexington: University Press of Kentucky, 1982.

Gross, Feliks. *Foreign Policy Analysis*. New York: Philosophical Library, 1954.

Gulick, Edward Vose. *Europe's Classical Balance of Power*. Ithaca: Cornell University Press, 1955.

Halper, Thomas. *Foreign Policy Crisis: Appearance and Reality in Decisionmaking*. Columbus, Ohio: Merrill, 1971.

Hart, B. H. Liddell. *Strategy*. New York: Praeger, 1967.

Herz, John. *Political Realism and Political Idealism*. Chicago: University of Chicago Press, 1951.

Higgins, J. M. *Strategy: Formulation, Implementation, and Control*. Hinsdale, Ill.: Dryden, 1985.

Hilsman, Roger, Jr. *Strategic Intelligence and National Decisions*. Glencoe, Ill.: Free Press, 1956.

Holsti, K. J. *International Politics: A Framework for Analysis*.

Englewood Cliffs, N.J.: Prentice-Hall, 1967.

Janis, Irving L., and Leon Mann. *Decision Making: A Psychological
    Analysis of Conflict, Choice, and Commitment.* New York: Free
    Press, 1977.

Jessup, John K., et al. *The National Purpose.* New York: Holt, Rine-
    hart, and Winston, 1960.

Johansen, Robert C. *The National Interest and the Human Interest: An
    Analysis of U.S. Foreign Policy.* Princeton: Princeton University
    Press, 1980.

Kaplan, Morton A. *System and Process in International Politics.* New
    York: Wiley, 1957.

Kennan, George F. *The Cloud of Danger: Current Realities of American
    Foreign Policy.* Boston: Little, Brown, 1977.

_____. *Realities of American Foreign Policy.* Princeton: Princeton
    University Press, 1954.

Keohane, Robert O., ed. *Neorealism and Its Critics.* New York: Columbia
    University Press, 1986.

Kingston-McCloughry, Edgar J. *Global Strategy.* New York: Praeger,
    1957.

Landheer, Bartholomeus. *Ethical Values in International Decision Making.*
    The Hague, The Netherlands: Nijhoff, 1960.

Larrain, Jorge. *The Concept of Ideology.* Athens: University of Georgia
    Press, 1979.

Lasswell, Harold D. *The Decision Process: Seven Categories of Func-
    tional Analysis.* College Park: Bureau of Governmental Research,
    University of Maryland, 1956.

Lasswell, Harold D., and Abraham Kaplan. *Power and Society: A Framework
    for Political Inquiry.* New Haven, Conn.: Yale University Press,
    1950.

Laszlo, Ervin. *A Strategy for the Future: The Systems Approach to World
    Order.* New York: Braziller, 1974.

Lentner, Howard H. *Foreign Policy Analysis: A Comparative and Concept-
    ual Approach.* Columbus, Ohio: Merrill, 1974.

Lerche, Charles O., Jr., and Abdul A. Said. *Concepts of International
    Politics in Global Perspective.* 3d ed. Englewood Cliffs, N.J.:
    Prentice-Hall, 1979.

Lerner, Allan W. *The Politics of Decisionmaking: Strategy, Cooperation,
    and Conflict.* Beverly Hills, Calif.: Sage, 1976.

Leys, Wayne A. R. *Ethics for Policy Decisions: The Art of Asking Delib-
    erative Questions.* Englewood Cliffs, N.J.: Prentice-Hall, 1952.

_____. *Philosophy and the Public Interest.* Chicago: Committee to Ad-
    vance Original Work in Philosophy, 1959.

Lindblom, Charles E. *The Policy-Making Process*. Englewood Cliffs, N.J.: Prentice-Hall, 1968.

Lindley, Dennis V. *Making Decisions*. New York: Wiley Interscience, 1971.

Lippmann, Walter. *Essays in the Public Philosophy*. Boston: Little, Brown, 1955.

_____. *U.S. Foreign Policy: Shield of the Republic*. Boston: Little, Brown, 1943.

London, Kurt. *How Foreign Policy Is Made*. New York: Van Nostrand, 1949.

_____. *The Making of Foreign Policy: East and West*. Philadelphia: Lippincott, 1965.

Lovell, John P. *Foreign Policy in Perspective: Strategy, Adaptation, Decision Making*. New York: Holt, Rinehart, and Winston, 1970.

Marshall, Charles Burton. *The Exercise of Sovereignty: Papers on Foreign Policy*. Baltimore: Johns Hopkins Press, 1965.

_____. *The "Limits" of Foreign Policy*. New York: Holt, 1954.

McClelland, Charles A. *Theory and the International System*. New York: Macmillan, 1966.

Merriam, Charles E. *Political Power: Its Composition and Incidence*. New York: McGraw-Hill, 1934.

Morgenthau, Hans J. *Dilemmas of Politics*. Chicago: University of Chicago Press, 1958.

_____. *In Defense of the National Interest: A Critical Examination of American Foreign Policy*. New York: Knopf, 1952.

_____. *The Purpose of American Politics*. New York: Knopf, 1960.

_____. *Scientific Man vs. Power Politics*. Chicago: University of Chicago Press, 1946.

Nardin, Terry. *Law, Morality, and the Relations of States*. Princeton: Princeton University Press, 1983.

Niebuhr, Reinhold. *Christianity and Power Politics*. New York: Scribner, 1940.

_____. *Moral Man and Immoral Society: A Study in Ethics and Politics*. New York: Scribner, 1932.

Nuechterlein, Donald E. *America Overcommitted: United States National Interests in the 1980s*. Lexington: University Press of Kentucky, 1985.

_____. *National Interests and Presidential Leadership: The Setting of Priorities*. Boulder, Colo.: Westview, 1978.

_____. *United States National Interests in a Changing World*. Lexington: University Press of Kentucky, 1973.

Osgood, Robert E.   *Ideals and Self-Interest in America's Foreign Relations: The Great Transformation of the Twentieth Century.* Chicago: University of Chicago Press, 1953.

Perkins, Dexter. *The American Approach to Foreign Policy.*   2d ed. Cambridge: Harvard University Press, 1962.

————.   *The American Way.* Ithaca: Cornell University Press, 1957. Especially the last chapter.

————.   *Foreign Policy and the American Spirit.*   Ithaca: Cornell University Press, 1957. Especially Chapters 1 and 8.

Plischke, Elmer.   *Foreign Relations Decisionmaking: Options Analysis.* Beirut, Lebanon: Institute of Middle Eastern and North African Affairs, 1973.

————.   *Modern Diplomacy: The Art and the Artisans.* Washington: American Enterprise Institute, 1979.

Rainey, Gene E.   *Patterns of American Foreign Policy.* Boston: Allyn and Bacon, 1975.

Rapoport, Anatol.   *Strategy and Conscience.* New York: Harper and Row, 1964.

Rosecrance, Richard N.   *Action and Reaction in World Politics: International Systems in Perspective.* Boston: Little, Brown, 1963.

Rosenau, James N.   *The Scientific Study of Foreign Policy.* New York: Free Press, 1971.

Rothstein, Robert L.   *Planning, Prediction, and Policymaking in Foreign Affairs.* Boston: Little, Brown, 1972.

Rummell, Rudolph J.   *The Dimensions of Nations.* Beverly Hills, Calif.: Sage, 1972.

Russell, Bertrand. *Power: A New Social Analysis.*   New York: Norton, 1938.

Ryans, John K. R., and William L. Shanklin. *Strategic Planning: Concepts and Implementation.* New York: Random House, 1985.

Sapin, Burton M.   *The Making of United States Foreign Policy.*   New York: Praeger, 1966.

Schelling, Thomas C.   *The Strategy of Conflict.* Cambridge: Harvard University Press, 1960.

Schubert, Glendon A.   *The Public Interest: A Critique of the Theory of a Political Concept.* Glencoe, Ill.: Free Press, 1960.

Seabury, Paul.   *Power, Freedom, and Diplomacy: The Foreign Policy of the United States of America.* New York: Random House, 1963.

Shirley, Robert C., and Michael H. Peters.   *Strategy and Policy Formulation: A Multifunctional Orientation.* New York: Wiley, 1981.

Snyder, Richard C., et al. *Decision-Making as an Approach to the Study of International Politics.* Princeton: Princeton University Press, 1954.

Snyder, Richard C., and James A. Robinson. *National and International Decision-Making.* New York: Institute for International Order, 1961.

Spykman, Nicholas J. *America's Strategy in World Politics: The United States and the Balance of Power.* New York: Harcourt, Brace, and World, 1942.

Strausz-Hupé, Robert, et al. *A Forward Strategy for America.* New York: Harper, 1961.

Tannenbaum, Frank. *The American Tradition in Foreign Policy.* Norman: University of Oklahoma Press, 1955.

Thompson, Kenneth. *Beliefs and Ideology.* London: Tavistock, 1986.

Thompson, Kenneth W. *Ethics and Foreign Policy.* New Brunswick, N.J.: Transaction, 1985.

Ulmer, Sidney, et al. *Political Decision Making.* New York: Van Nostrand Reinhold, 1970.

Vasquez, John A. *The Power of Power Politics: A Critique.* New Brunswick, N.J.: Rutgers University Press, 1983.

Vocke, William C. *American Foreign Policy: An Analytical Approach.* New York: Free Press, 1976.

Wight, R. J. Martin. *Power Politics.* London: Royal Institute of International Affairs, 1946.

Winter, David G. *The Power Motive.* New York: Free Press, 1973.

Wolfers, Arnold. *Discord and Collaboration: Essays on International Politics.* Baltimore: Johns Hopkins Press, 1962.

Wright, Quincy. *The Study of International Relations.* New York: Appleton-Century-Crofts, 1955.

INDEX

About the Author

ELMER PLISCHKE is Professor Emeritus at the University of Maryland and an Adjunct Scholar at the American Enterprise Institute. He is the author of numerous books and monographs, including *Conduct of American Diplomacy* (reprinted by Greenwood Press, 1974), *Modern Diplomacy: The Art and the Artisans, Diplomat in Chief: The President at the Summit* (Praeger Publishers, 1986), and *Presidential Diplomacy: Chronology of Summit Visits, Trips, and Meetings*. He has published approximately 75 articles, essays, and chapters, including articles on U.S. presidents in *Presidential Studies Quarterly* and *Review of Politics*, and was recognized by *World Affairs* as "the foremost authority in the United States on the practice of modern diplomacy."